Tommy Turnbull: A Miner's Life

This is a most enjoyable book … it would be difficult to find another that expresses so well the texture and feel of a miner's life and this particular north-eastern community. The people, the incidents, the experience of all Tommy's family, his acquaintances, including pit ponies and bosses, the entire fabric of the pit and the community, contain all of coal's sparkle, grit, warmth and corrosive quality; and much, including the language of telling, that is Durham, rather than any other coalfield region. The book is real and raw, not to be read as mere text; yet the expression of the experience is, while remarkable and in many ways as deserving of classic status as Roberts' *Classic Slum* or Hoggart's *Uses of Literacy*, a text.

John L. Halstead, *Labour History Review*

I must have read dozens of books about miners' lives but this one is the best. It's the best not just because it is a tale well told, though it is, and not because it is superbly informative, though it is that as well. It's the best because it is about an ordinary bloke and sticks to that. Moreover, it has the clear ring of truth without which biographies signify nothing. Joe Robinson is an accomplished author … the book offers a wonderfully wide-eyed view of Shields from 1911 … the sketching is quick, the touch sure. All urban historians … ought to read these finely shaded passages.

Robert Colls, *Northern Review*

Joe Robinson has done a magnificent job in giving us a full picture of what life was like at home and in the pit. His account is unsurpassed in recalling the perils the miner found underground. This is a vivid, well written and convincing book.

Philip Bagwell, *Tribune*

Joe Robinson's book is in a class by itself. *Tommy Turnbull* is written in first person, so by the time the story is finished, this shy, obstinate old miner whom everyone liked has become your friend. Here is a book for all young people now coming into struggle, who need to know what life was like for those who went before them in the same struggle half a century ago. It will be read and treasured for decades to come.

Peter Fryer, *Workers Press*

This story, seen through the eyes of one miner and his family, gives a far more vivid account of what this meant than the dry statistics and cold factual accounts that may be found in some of the official histories of the industry, and I greatly hope that it will be widely read for every sort of reason.

Tony Benn MP

Tommy Turnbull: A Miner's Life

JOSEPH ROBINSON

For all miners

First published in 1996 by Tempus publishing
This edition first published in 2007

Reprinted in 2012 by
The History Press
The Mill, Brimscombe Port,
Stroud, Gloucestershire, GL5 2QG
www.thehistorypress.co.uk

British Library Cataloguing in Publication Data.
A catalogue record for this book is available from the British Library.

ISBN 978 0 7524 4213 6

Typesetting and origination by
Tempus Publishing Limited
Printed and bound in Great Britain by
Marston Book Services Limited, Didcot

Contents

Acknowledgements

My grateful thanks are due principally to my uncle Tommy Turnbull who told me his life story with such patience and humour even though he was very ill at the time (I didn't know it but he did), to my aunt, his wife Allie, and his two daughters Anne and Christine.

I am very grateful to my mother Evelyn Robinson for supplying so much family background.

For help with the life of a coalminer at Harton Colliery my thanks are due to the late Paddy Cain of Jarrow and to Freddy Moralees and Les Telford of South Shields. For help with understanding coalmining methodology I am grateful to Dave Temple of TUPS.

I am also indebted to the many miners and their families who have written to me with poems and information over a twenty-year period.

For help with photographs and information I wish to thank Jennifer Gill, County Archivist, Durham County Record Office; Elizabeth Rees, Chief Archivist, Tyne & Wear Archives Service; Barbara Heathcote, Local Studies Librarian, Newcastle Central Library; Miss D. Johnson of Central Library South Shields; Catherine O'Rourke, Celestine Rafferty and Jarlath Glynn of County Library, Wexford, and Trade Union Printing Services, Newcastle upon Tyne.

Thanks to Mark Seddon and Roger Smith for their interest and help.

Thanks to Hannah for help with proof-reading.

Finally, thanks to my wife Judy for her considerable help, skill and encouragement with every stage of the book.

About the Author

Joe Robinson was born in Whitehall Street, South Shields in the house Tommy Turnbull's wife came from, within sound of the Harton buzzer. Although he has always had a close affinity with pitfolk he became a scientist in the field of medical and veterinary microbiology and worked abroad in hospitals, universities and industry.

Also by Joe Robinson:

The life and Times of Francie Nichol of South Shields
Claret & Cross-buttock
Francie
Pineapple Grill-time (a play)
Chips on My Shoulders

Foreword

By Tony Benn MP

The story of the Durham Miners and their families and of the coalfield where they worked is central to the history of the British working class and the Industrial Revolution they made possible.

Coal was discovered there 400 years ago and it was that coal which fuelled Britain's economic development in the nineteenth century, not only in terms of its manufacturing industry but also in supplying power to the coal-fired ships which carried our products around the world.

In 1913, there were 166,000 Durham miners at work in 150 pits and it was their labour which gave Britain its pre-eminence in industry.

But, of course, coal mining in private hands led to mass exploitation and it was through trade union organisation that the campaign for the protection of workers' rights was begun.

The Durham Miners Association was formed in 1869, and in 1908 the Association joined the Miners Federation of Great Britain demanding the Nationalisation of the pits in 1919 which led to public ownership less than thirty years later when the NUM was formed.

For those who worked in the pits it was a story of unending struggle for decent wages, shorter hours, job security, decent conditions and safety underground. Throughout this period there were lock-outs, strikes, police harassment, arrests and imprisonment.

The General Strike in 1926 was the most bitter that there had been and the Durham miners were the ones who stayed out the longest only to find when they returned that there was victimisation, cuts in wages, a lengthening of hours and anti-union legislation.

Now the pits have been privatised again, we should remember the costs of private ownership in lives and injuries in the inter-war years.

Between 1927 and 1934 – the years immediately following the General Strike – no fewer than 7,839 miners were killed and over 1,200,000 were injured at work.

This book is about the enormous courage and determination of the Durham colliers who retained a degree of solidarity and optimism and reflected it in the Annual Gala, or 'big meeting', which is still held after 100 years even though there has not been a pit in the North East since 1993.

At the Gala a succession of trade union and labour leaders – and a few socialists amongst them – have been inspired by the procession of bands and banners and the huge gathering on the racecourse where the lessons of all this struggle were learned again and passed on to new generations of men and women.

This story, seen through the eyes of one miner and his family, gives a far more vivid account of what this meant than the dry statistics and cold factual accounts that may be found in some of the official histories of the industry, and I greatly hope that it will be widely read for every sort of reason.

Britain has 1,000 years of coal reserves under its territory still, and our recovery will require us to re-open pits and sink new shafts to tap the black gold that lies deep beneath the surface of our country.

But more than that, because the political changes we have to bring about as we approach the millennium can only be achieved if the spirit of the miners and their families can inspire us to fight even more vigorously for the rights we need to live in a decent society free from the new and oppressive exploitation that goes under the name of Globalised Capital.

Tony Benn, MP, 1996

Prologue

When my uncle Tommy Turnbull, the subject of this book, was born, a coalminer's wage in Britain had hardly altered in a hundred years and, little though it was, it was never long before the money found its way back to where it came from. The house the miner and his family lived in, the shop they bought their groceries in and the pub he had his gill in, were often owned by his employer, the Coalowner. But really it wasn't a wage at all. It was merely the juggling of payments and fines by the Coal Company. The weighman, who assessed the tubs of coal sent out of the pit by the miner, had the authority to downgrade or reject this 'produce' and the duty to penalise its 'producer' whenever he could.

In Tommy's father's time, a coalminer – a 'pitman' he usually called himself – could be thrown in Durham Jail for refusing to work. Bad or dangerous conditions weren't sufficient excuse for refusing to work. Neither was having to come home with less than he started with because of the weighman's fines. The Master & Servant Act entitled only the employer to give evidence in a court of law, not the employee. Magistrates, being landowners, were invariably employers, and in coal-producing areas many of them were Coalowners. So any upstart pitman could expect pretty short shrift when his summons arrived.

There was no feeling of loyalty between coalminer and Coalowner, never any of the sentimentality that often existed between farm-worker and farmer – however forelock-touching its nature. Nor was there any of the Yorkshire industrialist's occasional bequests of homes, hospital wards or parks for their employees. That wasn't the Coalowner's style. As far as he was concerned, the only language pitmen understood, was the language of the harsh.

Thousands of men, boys, women and girls had been crushed or suffocated down coal mines over the centuries before HM Government felt obliged to insist that all mine owners sink two shafts instead of just one. But after this costly concession, Coalowners resisted any further expenditure on safety. To them, their employee, the miner, was just an underground peasant, a dirty, ignorant labourer with none of the sensibilities that differentiated noble man from lowly beast.

The Miner's Advice to His Son

Divvent gan doon the pit, lad
I' the long run it's just a mug's game
Remember, doon the pit, son,
Ye nivver win wealth or fame.

Yor workin' hard from start till lowse,
At the end, ye see ne gains.
Ye're rivin' an' heavin' an fleein' aboot,
An' it's sair backs an' heids for yor pains.

Aa divven't knaa w'at aa started for,
A must ha' been wrang in' the heid,
'Cos' many a time when aa've had a rough shift,
Aa've wished that aa wis deid.

Ye git up at two in the mornin'
Ye haven't had time for a sleep
The sleep's still fast in't corner yor eyes
Ye can hardly see, ye just peep

A bite te eat, an on wi' yor claes,
An' off ye gan doon the street
Ye waken the neighbours round aboot,
Wi' the clatter o' yor noisy feet.

Ye git te the pit an wait te gan doon
Ready te myek a few bob,
An' reddy for when its time to gan hyem
Where the pots boiling on the hob.

Ye come back hyem, yor hands on yor belt
Ye feel like faalin' to bits
It's only yor belt that haads ye together,
Yor sick o' the sight o' the pits.

Well, aa've dunn me best te warn ye
But A'a divven't suppose it'll dee any gud,
Ye'll not be content till ye git doon the pit
There's ower much coal-dust in yor blud.

John Thomas Rickaby

1

My name is Tommy Turnbull. I've been a coalminer all of my life. And I've only God and the Union to thank for not still being one. Over half a century down a big black hole not only miles away under the ground but sometimes under the sea as well. My father was a miner, so was my grandfather, my uncles, my cousins and my brother. Wherever there's a pit, you can bet there'll be a Turnbull somewhere down there.

I was born in a two-room cottage in Clink Row, in a pit village by the name of Witton Gilbert on the 7th of June, 1905. My father's name was Jack and my mother's name was Annie. My father's people, the Turnbulls, had always lived there. But the Kellys, my mother's family, had come over from Ireland when she was just a girl. My father was a hewer and he worked at nearby Bearpark Colliery.

The village of 'Jilbert', as we called it, was situated in the North Durham Coalfield, two miles from Durham City. It had one pub, one Walter Wilson's and one church, and that was a Protestant one. They used to say it was like the catacombs underneath, and that if a couple more shovelfuls had been taken away, the whole place would have vanished. That's why everything was on a slant.

The cottage we lived in wasn't the kind of thatched cottage affair you might see on a picture postcard. Any house with no upstairs was called a cottage, no matter what it looked like. It was built of bricks up to about knee height, the rest with wood laths. The wooden part of the walls was creosoted on the outside. The roof, which was also made of wood, was tarred. There was no garden, no gate, railings, path, yard, washhouse, coalhouse or drains. The only outside thing we had was a midden, and we shared that with six other families, along with the tap that was right next to it. If you'd wanted to sound clever, you could have called that side the back. Gas and electric were things you only heard tell of. Folks would say, 'Oh aye, gas does this and electric does t'other'. To hear them you'd think that when electrification came nobody was ever going to have to lift a finger again. And that all you'd have to do was switch on and lie back.

As you came into the house, the scullery part was first. This was where Mam did all her washing and cooking. And when you crossed over the clippy mat you were in the part we called the living room. In here my father had his rocky chair nearly planted in the fire. And this was where our John and me played when we couldn't play outside. There was a big fireplace leading up the chimney with an iron heating range at the side. The only light was from an oil lamp that hung down on a chain from the ceiling. You pulled it down to get it going and then shoved it back up out of the way so you wouldn't bash your head on it. There was one heavy wooden table with two long crackets, and a chair with a spokey back that my mother sat on when she was knitting or darning or if she needed to stop and catch her breath for a minute.

The other room was the bedroom, and everybody slept in there unless any of us was poorly, in which case Mam would bring us into the living room. Night and day the living room was always warm. Although the coal we got from the Colliery was rubbish coal, my mother was able to make do, and the only time the fire was out was when the chimney was being cleaned. She would sort the cinders, take out the ash and blacken the grate, all while the fire was still on, and I never knew her to burn a finger. She could do anything with that fire bar making it talk. The fire, and the huge iron oven it heated, cooked the meals, heated the water we got bathed in and boiled the water the clothes were washed in. And when it was freezing wet outside and you came in needing something extra inside you and there wasn't so much as a crust to spare, it would help to keep body and soul together. Mam kept the iron shining like silver and the brass polished like gold, and when you heard the sound of the little door opening your heart would give a little jump. To us that fireplace was as close to God as an altar in a church.

In the way of decoration we had wallpaper with a pattern of brown flowery things that had been up so long you could only see the flowers in the top corners where it wasn't worn or blackened. You wouldn't see anything like them in a gardening book but they passed for flowers in our house. If ever John and me were carrying on and my father shouted 'Watch the flowers!' everybody looked up at the wall, not out the window. Apart from the wallpaper there were a couple of old photos that were so faded you'd have had an easier job identifying the flowers, and a picture of the Sacred Heart in the bedroom. The iron mantelpiece always had vests, underpants and socks hanging from it all the way round, so there wasn't really room for any other kind of ornament other than the clock, a little candlestick holder and a chipped china dog somebody had won at a fair.

The wooden floor, table and crackets, had been scrubbed so hard over so many years, that if you didn't keep still you'd get a spelk in your bum as long as your little finger. In our house unless you were sitting on my father's rocky chair, and you wouldn't be, it paid you to get straight up and sit straight down.

The whole place was really tiny but being pitfolk we were used to small places. It was comfy, and nobody else's was any better.

There weren't many kids of my age in Jilbert, and our John was too small to play with. In any case there was nearly always something the matter with him. So I used to go to my two Grandmas'. There were plenty of uncles at both houses and they were always more than ready to have a bit of carry-on. If they couldn't find something to make a game out of, they'd chase you around the table. Or if the weather was fine they'd give you a game of footer outside. Not like my father. He was no sooner home, than he was off out again. So when I wasn't at school I was more at the Grandmas' than at home. Both Grandmas were very kind to me, and although Grandma Turnbull was very poor compared with us, she'd always find half a slice of bread with a bit of jam or something so you never went away empty-handed.

Granda Turnbull had died a long time ago and all I knew about him was that he'd been a coalminer. Grandma had found it so hard with four children to bring up, that she'd married another miner called Jack Russell who'd lost his wife. Shortly after, Russell had a bad accident down the pit, and though Grandma did everything she could to keep him going, he died and left her with his two to bring up as well as her own. But she was a tough little woman. Her proper name was Isabella but everybody just called her 'Bella'. Every other woman you knew was called Bella in those days. 'John' was the first choice for the lads. Protestant fellers were often called 'Albert' or 'George', after the King. Protestant lasses were called names like 'Doris' and 'Ivy'. Queens didn't seem to matter so much.

Except for her shawl, which was as white as her hair, you'd never see Grandma Turnbull in anything but black from head to foot. She was short and stout and had these eyes that looked right into you. She was kind-hearted but she was no mug and she was very firm with her own family. She had to be, with five out of the six, lads. Every one of them was a miner so there was always somebody going out and somebody coming in, and she was up at half past four every day to see to them. You could never see the fire for all the boiling pots on it and the clotheshorses all around and the whole place was as steamy as a laundry. When one of the lads came back for his dinner, off would come the pot with the washing in and on would go the one with the broth. On and off they went all day long, and the only time she went to her bed was on a Saturday night. The rest of the week she just slept in her chair in the kitchen until the latch on the door went.

She wouldn't use tap water for washing because she reckoned it wasn't good enough. It was fine for making a pot of tea but not for washing the lads' shirts. So she collected the rainwater that ran off the roof into a barrel underneath and used that instead. Everything got washed at least twice. Boil and scrub once, boil and scrub twice, rinse once, rinse twice, and then out on the line. The front street of Jilbert looked like Amsterdam, with all the washing flapping like the clappers. Many's the time somebody's come racing along on his bike and practically hung himself on a clothes line because a sheet had flapped in his face, especially if he'd one too many gills in him.

When Grandma had finished the washing, ironing and darning which she had to do every day because of all the lads, and was sitting in her chair waiting for one or other of them, she'd have her box of bits of old rags out and would be working away on her clippy mats. They'd have lovely coloured patterns and were so well made that she never had any trouble selling them, when she managed to get them finished that is. Sometimes at night you could hardly see across the room it was so dark yet she'd still be at it. All her life she was plagued with a double hernia but she never stopped working. She was even registrar of births, marriages and deaths for the district. That of course brought in a few extra coppers as well. Every Tuesday there'd be a little queue outside her door and you'd be able to tell by their faces what kind of news each one had come to register.

Making quilts with a Prince of Wales Feathers design was my Grandma Turnbull's one and only hobby, if you can call it that, because she gave them all away. You could always tell if you were in a Turnbull house by popping your head around the door and looking on the bed, because they all got one. Good they were too, warm as well as fancy.

Although she was poor and did everything herself, neither that nor her trouble ever stopped her from being full of cheer. For some reason she always seemed to be a really happy little roly-poly.

Grandma Kelly wasn't as tough and hardy a woman as Grandma Turnbull, I never thought, although she was a good bit bigger, but because of her lovely manner and the gentle way she had with her, she was every bit as well liked and every time she put her shawl on and went out for a walk, which she loved to do, people would see her going by and come out of their houses just for the pleasure of having a little chat with her. She wasn't so full of busy as Grandma Turnbull always was and she'd put things down and make time for you.

Coming from Ireland, and with Granda working on a farm in Esh Winning, which was only a few miles from Bearpark where they lived, both Granda and Grandma Kelly loved animals and the place was always full of them. How they managed it in the little back garden they had was a wonder. Grandma kept hens and ducks and Granda kept pigs, and all of them were great things to play with. If you chased them they'd go fleeing about and make such a din. Other times you just needed to put one foot in the garden and they'd come running after you as though they were going to take a chunk out of you. It depended on the mood they were in.

Grandma used to do the poultry in herself, and the poor things always knew when she was coming even though she always hid the knife behind her back. So did everybody else. You couldn't blink an eye in Bearpark or in Jilbert without somebody seeing you and telling everybody else. No matter when Grandma came out of the house and no matter how quietly, they'd all know. 'Oul' Ma Kelly's on the hunt,' they'd say to each other. 'It won't be long afore some poor bugger's head'll be sayin' good-bye to its body.'

But Granda could never bring himself to do the necessary with the pigs, and if he hadn't taken them to market they'd have gone on until they died of old age. If he'd a few ready at the same time, Mr Black, the Co-op butcher from Brancepath, would come. This feller would just walk into the garden and hit them straight over the head where they stood, no messing about. Then he'd cut them up and wrap the pieces in brown paper, load them on to his horse and cart, and away. Mind, quick and handy though he was, they still squealed blue murder and long before he was finished everybody in the street would be patiently standing by with buckets cleaned out and ready in their hands, all hoping for something to make a few sausages or a mince pie with, and maybe something for the cat.

On the occasions when Granda had only one ready and it wouldn't have been worth Mr Black's while coming, Granda would get a bit of strong string and wind it round one of its back legs with the intention of taking it to Brancepath himself. In no time the squealing would have all the neighbours out and they'd know exactly what Granda was planning to do. 'Why divvent ye keep it a bit longer, man? It's too young for a trip like that. Ye could loss it afore ye get there… Hang on till that one over there's ready, then Mr Black'll come and save ye all the bother.'

Just to get this far would have cost Granda a lot of heartache, and no matter how much they pleaded, once he'd made up his mind it was going, it was going.

If I was off school, which I always tried to be, I'd go with them. Brancepath was a real day out. I'd get on the pig's back and hold on to its big lugs and Granda would be walking behind with the string in one hand, a long stick in the other, and a face as long as a fiddle. Every time it stopped, he would stroke it gently on the behind to remind it of what he had in his hand, and it would take no notice. Then he would tap it, and still it would take no notice. Then he would get mad and give it a really hard whack, and away it would go again, off to meet its maker with me hanging on for all I was worth, and Granda running after it and apologising for hitting it so hard.

There's a big difference between a horse with a saddle, and a pig's bare back. A horse's back has a dip in it put there for sitting on but a pig certainly hasn't. Its back is as round as a big greasy palony and there's nothing to hang on to except its lugs which you have to use to try and steer it. When we got to Brancepath and Granda had sold the pig, he'd carry me home on his shoulders. My behind would be sore for days after.

Granda was very soft-spoken and even quieter than Grandma, all the Kellys were the same. They'd come over from Sligo after they were married to make a better life for themselves, and I think they went out of their way to be respectable and well liked. Granda had been a blacksmith before working on the farm, and he was a big, fresh-cheeked, fine figure of a man when he was all dressed up in his swallow-tail coat and his pork-pie hat, his big boots and his walking stick. He was a very strong Catholic and when he went to Mass on a Sunday there was none prouder. He was just a farm labourer but he would never be seen in a muffler and cap with string tied under his knees unless he was at work. 'Poverty's bad enough without paradin' it in front of one and all,' he'd say.

Even though they were very friendly people, and there were twelve of them altogether, there were never any parties or anything in the Kelly house. I think they were too careful of the law. They hadn't been over here more than about three years, when they'd got into trouble with the police and the people at the post office, and they never forgot it. Everybody knew about it. Every Christmas Grandma's sister Anne used to send a turkey and a goose from Ireland and they'd arrive in a brown paper parcel cleaned and drawn and ready for the table. There'd be a lump of butter, a packet of biscuits, and two bottles of poteen. One bottle would be inside the goose, and the other inside the turkey. The reason, it was said, was so that they wouldn't get broken. Everything had been going hunky-dory for a few years until this one time the paper must have got damp and the turkey came out of its parcel in the post office with the head of the bottle of poteen sticking out of its behind. The pollis was called in and there was quite a to-do. They still got their turkey and their goose every Christmas after that, but never with anything more dicey than a bit of bacon and a few sweets inside.

Grandma Kelly was a handywoman and she was the nearest thing most of the poor people in the district ever got to a doctor. She could give first aid, act as midwife or lay you out if necessary. She had old wife's remedies for everything and people would come with all sorts of complaints, often as not just for a bit of comfort.

Yet for all she was so level-headed and well used to death and bad accidents, what with the collieries nearby, every now and then she'd go queer and wander off and leave everything. The first Easter Sunday morning after she and Granda had come over to England, their littlest son John had been playing in the burn with two other lads and fallen into a deep pool. He was only eight years old and they never found his body. They always said Grandma would have accepted it if they'd been able to give him a proper burial and Fr Fortin said he would give him one if they could find even a small part of his body. But they never did, not a trace, not even of the clothes he was wearing. Every now and then all through her life Grandma would get it into her head and disappear and they'd always find her in the same place by the burn, bending down with the water up to her shoulders, feeling around for his body and calling out to him as though she was expecting him to come up after all this time. Whenever she was under one of these spells they just let her alone. Sooner or later she'd always come out of it, and then she'd go back home and get on with things as if she'd never been away.

Although their mother and father came from Ireland and they had a background of working in the open air, every one of the Kelly lads went down the pit as soon as they were old enough. Esh Winning, Bearpark, Ushaw and Sleetside, all had Kellys in them. There was nothing else for them to do.

The school I went to was called St Bede's. It was three miles away in Sacriston and five of us had to walk there and back every day. A pony and trap would have cost threepence a week so we walked even if cats and dogs were coming down. If the nearest Catholic school had been a hundred miles away, we'd still have had to do it. To have gone to a Protestant school and set one foot inside a Protestant church, which you'd have had to do sooner or later, would have meant spending the rest of eternity in Hell with the devils poking you further and further into the flames. At least that's what Fr Beech said. If my father hadn't married a Catholic, which he did when he married a Kelly, things would have been different. Protestant hells were nothing like as bad as Catholic hells, which was just as well, because if you weren't a Catholic that's where you went.

Catholic schools only had lady teachers, so the parish priest would act as headmaster and his main job was to thrash you. Fr Beech was ours. If you did something wrong outside school, a grown-up would usually say something like, 'Get out of it, ye little beggar!' and take a swipe at you which might only get you on the back or miss altogether if you were quick. Not at school though, not with Fr Beech. First you'd be brought out in front of all the lads and little lassies. Then you'd have to stand there while he made a speech that made you feel like the greatest sinner that ever lived. He'd speak slowly with a little smile on his face while pacing from one side of the room to the other, up the aisles and around the back. You'd be standing there on your own during all this and he'd know you were doing your level best not to cry and you knew that when your time came he'd do his damnedest to make you.

Every day without fail he would come galloping up on horseback, the way you see cowboys do on the pictures, fling open the door and stand there looking as though he'd just ridden in from Hell. Then he'd stamp into the classroom in his long coat and long brown leather boots, cracking his whip in the air and whacking it against his leg. You'd sometimes hear kids arguing about whether it's worse to be hit with a leather belt or a stick but I've never heard anybody say there's anything worse than a whip. And he used that whip far more on us than he ever did on his horse. He wouldn't have got away with it if he had.

The schoolmaster and Father in the parish before him – Fr Fortin – had been tough enough, my father said, but he had been a great friend of the pitmen and was known throughout Durham as the 'Pitman's Priest'. Whenever there was any trouble at the Colliery he would always be one of the first to help. Not only when there was a disaster or an accident, but during a strike or a lay-off when you might have expected a churchman to have no sympathy at all – that was certainly the case with the Anglican Bishop of Durham. During the long strike at Ushaw Moor when many had been turned out of their homes, Fr Fortin brought them into the school – no matter what their religion –and gave them a roof over their heads until they could get sorted out. The same man many a time stood up to the Board of Guardians at the local Workhouse on behalf of the inmates and got the regulations changed so they were allowed a smoke and any other little comforts he could get for them. Fr Fortin never handed money out, his way was to give the wives vouchers to buy food and then square up with the shopkeepers himself afterwards.

Although he was a Catholic priest, his generosity never stopped at Catholics, and everybody raised their caps when he trotted by on his horse. The time he came back from the Boer War, Catholic and Protestant had carried him shoulder-high from the railway station, and when he died they put his coffin in the middle of the playground at St Bede's School so all the kids could march around and pay their last respects. He had all his vestments on as though he had just lain down for a sleep after saying Mass. He had been born in the West Indies, come all the way to Ushaw College to be trained as a priest, and then just stayed. So they weren't all the same – not by any means.

2

My father would always be moving from pit to pit to get the best rate he could, and in 1911 when I was six years old we came to live in South Shields. Pits with more water, gas or weak roofs, paid more, and because Harton Colliery was a particularly wet pit the wages were higher than they'd been at Bearpark. My father was a good hewer and knew he could make twelve shillings a week at Harton. He also did part-time insurance work, so he could get more from that as well in a town like Shields with its four big pits. He brought the furniture over on a horse and cart himself, and me and our John came over on the train with Mam because she was expecting our Monica and wasn't able for the cart.

Coming to South Shields, which was nearly twenty miles away, was like emigrating to Australia. The cost of going back and forth to Jilbert and the time it would take meant we'd hardly ever see our relations. Because of that and other things our lives would now be very different. Shields was divided into villages, and where you lived depended on what you did for a living. The likes of doctors, lawyers and businessmen lived in Westoe. Shipping people lived on the Lawe Top, seamen near the market, and dockers and railwaymen near Tyne Dock. Pitmen lived in Boldon Lane and Whiteleas. My father had found us a terrace house next to a few pit families in Lemon Street, just off Stanhope Road, through somebody he knew. This house and the area we'd come to live in was a very big step-up from what we'd been used to.

The house had an upstairs and a downstairs, and we lived in the downstairs part. In the yard was a small washhouse and coalhouse in one, and a toilet. And all of it we only shared with the people upstairs. In Jilbert they used to come round with a horse and cart once a week to take the stuff from the midden and dump it on farmers' fields along with the ashes and whatever other rubbish was in with it. The midden cart, the milk cart and the coal cart used to stand side by side in the street.

Here in Shields the Corporation came and emptied the toilets at night and took it away and dumped it off a barge in the sea. You had to put pink disinfectant down the toilet, and keep the rest of your rubbish separate in a bin which the Corporation took away another time. The toilet, which we called 'the netty', was big enough to play in, and when it rained we'd play in there for hours.

South Shields was a fantastic place after little Jilbert, and much bigger than Brancepath. There was so much to see and do, and places to go, things I'd never dreamed of. There was the River Tyne which was the lifeblood of North and South Shields, Gateshead, and the great city of Newcastle-on-Tyne which was far bigger even than Durham. Every day of the week huge steam ships would come up the river, many of them with foreign names, blowing their horns and whistles and huge bales, crates and barrels would be loaded off and on to the docks in big rope nets. Hundreds of men would be shouting to the fellers operating the slings, telling them where to set them down, and grabbing them with hooks as they came down.

And then there were the shipyards with their great cranes that went right up into the sky with their massive hooks swinging from side to side. Underneath, huge skeletons of ships half-built stretched out, and rang with the clanging of hammers and sparkled with the welding torches of hundreds of tiny men working inside them.

All kinds of bridges crossed the river. One carried the London to Edinburgh express and all the freight trains, another carried local trains from Sunderland and South Shields through Gateshead and across the river to Newcastle. There was a swing bridge that swung away from both banks to let the big ships get up the river. You could sit on one of the great coils of rope on the quayside and wonder how they ever got the different parts of the bridges to stay up while they were building them and about the brave men that must have worked on the very top with huge spanners, sometimes in bitterly cold weather. Every time I was on the Tyne Bridge it was always windy and yet every single part had been properly painted inside and out, on the top and underneath. Nowhere had been skimped, not even the parts that seemed impossible to get at.

On Sunday mornings the quayside was a different place altogether. It was a market for all sorts of things and nothing cost more than a few pence. Quacks and tricksters would be gathered there selling their wares, doing their acts, and up to every kind of trick. You could see and hear it all and it didn't cost you a farthing.

You could never go down to the River Tyne without there was something going on. Sometimes they had rowing races with world champion scullers, and everybody would be shouting and cheering as though they were at a horse race. One boat might go flying ahead at the start, and you'd think the other ones had had it. Then one of them would move up and the other might drop back, just the tiniest bit, and this would give the others the encouragement they needed. Everybody would be yelling like mad as they went neck and neck and you could see the long muscles in their arms and legs, and their faces screwed up as though they were in agony. Then as soon as the winner passed the finishing line, all the foghorns would blast and the ships' whistles would blow, and everybody would be jumping up and down.

Shields even had its own railway stations and trams, so if you had the money you could go anywhere. It had parks with shuggy boats and swings, lawns to play on, trees to climb, and lakes chock full of tadpoles and tiddlers. There were tennis courts where you could watch them batting the ball back and forward, and when you got fed up with that you could chuck gravel at them. They could never catch you because they were trapped inside the wire. On Sundays there were bandstands with iron seats where you could sit and listen to the music and have a bit of a laugh at some of the players.

Down town there was a proper market that was always packed with people and stalls with rough men and women shouting and yelling one on top of the other. There were streets like Fowler Street and Ocean Road with big stores you could go in for a poke around, and variety halls with pictures of famous singers and dancers and magicians and comedians that were coming soon, maybe that very night.

Best of all were the beaches. Sand was great stuff to play on, and the sea was fantastic. There were pools with crabs and queer fish in them, and winkles under rocks. There were cliffs and caves and lovers to spy on in the dunes. There was even an all-year-round fair with swings and stalls where you could win things if you were lucky. And if you looked hard enough you could always find a few coppers or a silver threepenny bit in the grey grass, usually in front of stalls like the coconut shies where people got excited and got their money out in a hurry. As soon as anybody won on a particular machine or stall or anything, everybody would run over thinking they could do the same. They were far more careless there than in the amusement arcades. In the arcades even though farthings and halfpennies were going in non-stop, most of the ones having a go were kids and if they dropped anything they'd practically tear the ground up to get it back.

I never thought there were that many kids in the whole world as there was in Shields. Anywhere you went there was somebody to play with or at least who wanted a fight. There were a lot more pollises as well. I'd only seen two in the whole of my life before I came to Shields and that includes Brancepath. Here they had more to do than come up and start bossing you about for nothing at all. My mother was once taken to court when we lived in Jilbert just because I'd kicked a tin can in the street on a Sunday. Here it didn't seem to matter, there was so much else going on. Even if you broke a window or snapped a branch off a tree, they'd never know who to blame unless you just stood there with a silly look on your face. In Jilbert if a window got bust or some apples got pinched, they always came knocking on our door because I was the only kid of an age that would do that sort of thing, or so they reckoned. If they knocked on the door of every house in Shields with kids in it every time an apple went missing off a tree, they'd never have had time for anything else.

The people themselves weren't much different though and we were still living among our own kind. Many of them had come in from the country for the better wages, and my father would have known a canny few of them already. His own brother Jim was one. Not that it would have mattered if he'd known them or not because pitmen and pitfolk are always the same wherever you go. You could walk into any pit house at ten o'clock at night and you'd find the same thing. A red hot fire, a tired-looking woman, and heavy damp clothes hanging up all over the place.

At Harton they called my father a 'hillbilly' because he came from Jilbert, and he called them 'sand-dancers' because Shields was on the coast. Pitmen had all sorts of daft names for things and for each other, and it would only take them a couple of days to give somebody a nick-name that would stick with them for the rest of their life.

In parts of Durham and down into Yorkshire they used 'thee' and 'thou' a lot, but not because they were particularly religious or any-thing. Ones that would be cursing and swearing all day long would be 'thee'ing' and 'thou'ing' along with everybody else. That was the way they spoke in different districts and not just the pitfolk. But the differ-ence between the speech of ordinary people living on the north side of the Tyne wouldn't be as different from those living on the south side, as it might be between two pits that were only down the road from each other. And any Shields miner could tell which of the four Shields pits, Harton, St Hilda, Boldon or Whitburn, a man came from, as soon as he opened his mouth. My father tried to drop the thee'ing and thou'ing when he came to Shields because the fellers used to take the mickey out of him, but he could never get rid of it entirely. It came out whenever he lost his temper and always with his own people. Sometimes you could hardly understand a word when he and Uncle Jim were going on at each other. He used to say to my mother, 'Ye might put on airs and graces with the rest of the world but ye can never get away with it with your own brother. My God, he'd give ye credit for nowt.'

If my father was coming off shift during the daytime, I'd go to meet him whenever I wasn't at school. I loved to watch him coming across the colliery yard with all the men with their black faces and white eyes and mouths, and hear the clatter of their boots. I'd be waving and shouting 'Dad! Dad!' But he wouldn't pay any attention. If he saw me he might nod if he was in a good mood, but he'd just carry on. I'd follow behind till all the others had gone their own way, and then I'd run up. 'How, Dad!'

He'd never stop or slacken his pace. 'Well, what've you been up to, ye little bugger? The schoolboard man'll be round lookin' for ye, if ye divvent watch theesel'.'

When we got home and went in the door, Mam would always leave what she was doing and go half over to him, which was as close as she'd get, and say the same thing, 'Have a good shift, Jack?' She'd stand there wiping her hands on her apron and looking at him but he wouldn't give her a look. 'It's over now, and that's all that matters,' he would say as he hung up his jacket and cap and went to get washed.

Even if my father wasn't coming off shift, I'd still go up to the Colliery with the other kids if ever I was playing anywhere near and heard the buzzer. It was the greatest sight in the world to see men coming out of a pit. There were no pit 'lads' as far as we were concerned. Anybody who dressed like a man, worked at the pit and got filthy black, was a man. Sometimes one of your pals' big brothers would leave school and get started at the pit. Straightaway he was different and would never be the same again. Sometimes the big lads would play centre-forward or goalie with us kids if there wasn't enough of them to get up a game of their own. But not after they started at the pit. From then on they were men and would never be seen dead playing with 'daft bloody kids'.

As soon as the buzzer went we would climb the railings and sit on top of the wall. The men would teem out of the pit in all shapes and sizes. Some would have their caps set at a jaunty angle to show they were right ones with the lasses, others would have theirs pulled straight down like fighting men, while others would have theirs at the backs of their heads as if they couldn't care less about anything. The young 'uns would be wearing jackets that were too big for them or too small for the buttons to be fastened. Others had pants that were way above their ankles or turn-ups halfway up to their knees.

When they first came into the yard they'd all be mixed up together, but by the time they got to the gates they'd have sorted themselves out according to their own drift. Like a rabble army they'd come marching by, every one as black as the Ace of Spades. The younger ones would always be at the front, shouting and laughing, pushing and shoving, and chasing each other. They thought they were men, but inside they were as daft as we were, and still as full of energy, even after eight hours down the pit. Next would come the middle-aged ones arguing the toss. Then the old fellers, quiet and grim and very tired. Last of all would come the stragglers with bad backs and gammy legs and those who couldn't walk far without stopping to catch their breath.

By the time the first lot had reached the gates, a stream of bicycles would have caught up with them and the young'uns among them would be racing each other out. You could see them trying to knock each other off. Some of the ones without bikes would pitch in and try to drag somebody off. Others would be jeering. Then one would topple over and crash into the middle of the older men coming up behind. 'Get out of it, ye stupid buggers!' a shout would go up. After a few catcalls back and forth and a few threats, and maybe a few chases with somebody running cursing after them for a bit, everything would quieten down and everybody would go their own way.

Everybody told the time by the colliery buzzer. 'Eeeh, it must be half an hour since the buzzer went. If I divvent get me skates on, the cobbler's'll be shut. Wor Bob'll gan mad if I divvent get his boots for him.'

Most of the time it was a very homely and comforting sound. It was the pit calling out to the women at home to tell them their men were coming home, and that they could start setting the table. It meant the pit was in business and the men were in work.

Everybody listened for the buzzer; they planned their lives around it.

3

Every night I'd lie in bed and hear the same pantomime outside the window. First the sound of heavy boots would come clomping up the lane together with raised voices and then they would stop. There'd be a couple of long louping steps, followed by a couple of short quick ones for balance.

'Whoops!'

'Watch theesel', thou stupid bugger!'

Then a double lot of clomping, grinding, sliding and cursing, as if people were pushing each other about.

Two miners full of stout, even little ones like these were, can make a hell of a noise, especially in a cobbled back lane in the middle of the night. I've heard many a horse pulling a wagon, sometimes big ones like Clydesdales with feet like capstans and a driver bawling out to the women in their houses but none that made more noise than my father and my Uncle Jim coming back from the Stanhope Hotel.

'Thou thinks like an imbecile... Thou talks like an imbecile... And thou looks like an imbecile. And nebody... nebody in their right mind, that is... could have a reasonable discussion with anybody... like that.'

'There's an ould sayin'... and I'm ganna give it thou for nowt... "It taks an idiot... to know one". And if we're seriously talkin' about looks... If I looked like thou... thou knows what I'd do? I'd break every bloody mirror in the house... That's the first thing I'd do. The next thing I'd do is drown meself.'

'Listen who's talkin'! Thou's ne oil paintin'. And thou wouldn't need ne expert to tell ye that.'

'Ahht, shut thee gob!'

There'd be a laugh like a foghorn followed by a few more shouts and curses. Then a noise like a donkey braying. Those laughs were like nothing else on earth. The foghorn would be my father, and the donkey would be Uncle Jim. They were always laughing at one another in between arguing, because each of them thought the other was an idiot for not seeing things the way they did. They argued about the Colliery, the Government, the Labour Party, Newcastle United, Sunderland, what it would be like in Heaven and what it would be like in Hell. There was nothing on the earth, above the earth or below the earth that the two of them didn't argue about. My father wasn't so bad with anybody else, drunk or sober. Though that's not to say he was the easiest man in the world to get along with, because he wasn't. But when he was with Uncle Jim, drunk or sober, they were like flint and steel.

After they'd been at it more than long enough my mother would get up and go out.

'Hush, Jack. Ye'll waken folks up.'

'Aye, all right, pet... I've just been tellin' him the same thing.'

'It's not me, thou bloody liar! It's thou!'

'She knows who's makin' all the noise...don't ye, pet?'

'Is that you, Jim?' my mother would say, knowing it couldn't be anybody else. 'Like a cuppa tea before ye go home?' She knew he wouldn't say yes at this time of night, there'd be ructions enough as it was when he got home. Not all pit wives were as soft as my mother, not by a long chalk and certainly not Aunty Ethel.

'No, thanks, lass. I'd best be on me way. Talkin' to this husband of yours is like talkin' to a bloody brick wall. I never realised until tonight just how thick he really was. As a babby we always thought there was somethin' wrong wi –'

'Shut thee gob, will thou! If thou art gannin'... gan... afore they come an' lock thou up.'

Then they would start up again and my mother would know it was no use, so she'd come in and go back to bed and leave them to it. Eventually Uncle Jim would have had enough and decide to head for home. My father would wait till he was halfway up the lane, then just before he shut the back door he would shout something after him. You would hear Uncle Jim's boots come to a stop while he listened. Then he'd realise my father had already gone in, and away he'd go again with every dog in the street barking its head off after him.

The last sound I heard before I went to sleep at night was my father's boots coming in, and the first thing I heard when I woke up the next morning was his boots going out. Mind, the morning-after boots were much different to the night-before's. All the stotting and jigging had gone right out of them now. Now they were deadly serious boots. There was no bragging about how so-and-so was going to be told where to ram his shovel now. No yelling so the whole street would know who was going to put the world to rights and how he was going to go about it. At this hour of the day all that had vanished without a trace. The best that could be managed now was a few grunts in reply to my mother's cheerful chatter. I'd hear her quietly fussing, making sure his water bottle was filled right up and he had his bait in his pocket. It wasn't his idea for her to get up this early, she wasn't all that strong and she didn't come from mining stock. She just seemed to feel it was her duty even though he'd told her umpteen times there was no need. 'I'll have your other shirt ironed in time for you tomorrow. It's still not quite dry, and –'

'All right, all right.'

'Look after yourself.'

'Aye.'

'Ta-ta, Jack.'

'Aye.'

The back door would open and the boots would go out, shuffle for a couple of moments as though finding their bearings, and then begin their steady tramp in a straight line down the lane. Every now and then you'd hear a howk and you could imagine the thick black phlegm flying through the air and splatting on the cobbles like a small fried egg. It would lie there for days and slowly go stiff like a bit of dirty gelatine, just like all the others in the lane, until a shower of rain came along and washed them away. Suddenly the boots would turn the corner, and he'd be gone.

If seeing my father and all his mates coming out of the colliery gates was the greatest sight in the world, better than all the bridges and ships of the Tyne put together, then the sound of their boots – a working man's boots – must be the grandest sound. No two people walk alike, and you can tell how big a man is and how old he is, just by listening to the way he puts his boot down and the way he picks it up again. You can easily tell if he's going to work or coming back, even if he's a total stranger. There could be a dozen pairs of boots in the lane going in different directions at the same time, and I could always pick my father's. I could pick most of the others as well. Lame people make the deepest impression on you, it's so easy to picture them dragging that leg, and it takes ages to get them out of your mind. Hearing the same boots coming and going every day and keeping their own time, I used to lie there and imagine all sorts of things about the different individuals inside them. Hearing their boots was like hearing them talk.

My father was short and thickset and he had a voice that could shatter a crate of milk. His hair was grey and cropped short, though he always left a little tuft sticking straight out at the front like a compass pointer. And when he had his cap on, and it was rarely off, it was always up and back a bit so you could see he had all his hair, and the tuft would be pointing straight at you. If ever my father was out of the house and his hat was off, you could be sure something was wrong.

From his nose down to his bottom lip he had a thick droopy moustache that was permanently stained orangey yellow at the edges from the regular soaking it got in Burton's bass. And when he sat down to his dinner, after doing a 'bit of business' at the Stanhope, the bubbles of froth on the ends of his whiskers would burst as he shoved the pickled onions through them with his fork. I loved to sit and watch him chewing and cracking his onions. The hairs would go in with them and then they would spring out again and waggle about up and down and from side to side. He was very proud of that tash. He would sometimes look at it in the mirror and if he didn't know you were watching he'd be making all kinds of faces with it. Nothing daft, just generals and prime-ministers and people like that.

Eating his dinner was a very serious matter, and every now and again when his face was down near his plate, he'd look up with his black Turnbull eyes and sort of scowl. His jowls and his tash would be working slowly and deliberately as if he had something very important on his mind. Then he might stop and look around the table at each and every one of us, with the onion still stuck in his cheek, and the fork stuck in midair. After a bit, as though he'd decided nobody was able to deal with the kind of things he had on his mind and he was sure nobody was looking at him with anything less than utter respect, he would look down again and get back to chewing his onion. Silently and in slow motion at first, just to make sure, then back to normal. Every time he swallowed, his collar stud would shoot right up and jiggle about and then down again. And whenever the vinegar went into a hole in his tooth, he would suck hard and whistle 'Jeeeeeze!' You couldn't help screwing your own face up just watching. He really enjoyed his grub and loved to make a meal of it. He liked an audience and the more people that were watching, the greater the performance.

I think we were the only ones who ever took my father seriously. He had four younger brothers all down the pit but only he and Uncle Jim had come to Shields. If they all got on with each other as well as he and Uncle Jim did, probably it was just as well.

Uncle Jim was stockier than my father, though smaller, but very strong. He had the same thick short hair, only darker, the same perfect ears for propping a cap up, and the same fierce eyes. Although my father certainly liked his drink, with Uncle Jim it was rather more than that. At one time he'd been a crakeman which is somebody who goes around the pit houses giving news about the colliery and that, a kind of town crier for pitfolk. But he was too much of a drinker to hold the job down, most of the time he couldn't shake the crake without falling over. It was a pity because he certainly had the voice for it. If they'd had him at one end of the Tyne, and my father at the other, the two of them could have been heard across the whole of the north of England.

Many's the time he would come to our house on his way home from the pit, so drunk he could hardly speak. He would stagger over to the fire, flop down on the hearth, and sleep right through to the next shift. No wash, no food, nothing. When the buzzer went he would hear it and up he'd get and away he'd go, straight back to the pit. He was very different to my father in that way. Apart from anything else, my father had too much regard for my mother.

One of the reasons Uncle Jim came to our place so much was because Aunty Ethel was such a tartar. She'd go looking for him and create at all hours of the day and night, and he wouldn't be safe even in the Stanhope which was a man's hang-out. When she came knocking on our door my father would say he hadn't seen him and hadn't the faintest idea where he was. Sometimes if she was really on her high horse, a brick would come flying through the window. 'Quick, dook!' my father would shout. But by then the brick was lying on the mat. 'My godfathers, what a temper that woman's got,' he'd say as my mother bent down to pick the pieces up. Even that wouldn't wake Uncle Jim if he was really flat out, only the buzzer would. When he eventually woke up and saw the hole in the window, still lying there he'd say something like, 'I see thou's had a visitor, Jack?'

The only time Uncle Jim was awake and not arguing with somebody, was when he was reading one of the books he got second-hand from a stall in the market. He would read one and then take it back and swap it for a different one. Love stories and poems to 'satisfy a romantic nature' and tec stories to 'exercise the brain', according to him. All miners have bad eyes because of spending so much time in the dark, but his eyes were so bad he could hardly see the words unless his nose was touching the page. Yet it was the one thing I think he really loved doing in life and the only time you ever saw him with a really contented smile on his face was when he had it stuck in a new book.

Uncle Jim had his ways, some of them funny, some of them not so funny, but whatever else he was or wasn't, like my father, he was a great hewer. And like my father he was an unshakable union man.

As long as my father had his drink and a few coppers for a bet on the horses, he was happy. He never drank in the house and he never needed to because he practically lived at the Stanhope Hotel. When my father was 'carrying a full cargo', which is how he used to describe other people, you could see where he was coming from a mile off. Some men can sit down and drink all night, and then get up and walk out the door as though they've just been drinking water. But my father wasn't one of them. Sometimes I'd have to go and fetch him for one reason or another and when he got up and headed for the door, every time he passed a table it was like rounding the Cape of Good Hope. Although he never touched spirits he made up for it by never drinking anything lighter than bass. That and rough tobacco was 'the only stuff fit for a hewer'. Cigarettes, with their dry brown fluff and paper were for cissies and women with men's voices. Men smoked dark brown baccy twist with the juice still in it, stuff you ripped up and kneaded in the palm of your own hand and then filled into your pipe yourself. Clays cost a halfpenny each and he wouldn't throw one away until it was burning the end of his nose, just as he wouldn't leave his glass until every last bubble had burst or been sucked out.

The Stanhope, or the Stanhope 'Hotel' as they called it when they didn't want somebody to know it was nothing but a big pub, was halfway up on the left-hand side of Stanhope Road, going towards Tyne Dock from Chichester. Everybody in Shields knew somebody who went there. Little bairns that could hardly walk would many a time have been told the Stanhope was where their daddy had gone to 'see a man about a dog', and they would know better than to expect him back with a puppy under his arm.

In the bar at least they moved about up and down and back and forwards to the counter, and the door was always open. But in the saloon where my father had his 'office' on a Friday night, the smell of Shag tobacco smoke and McEwan's bitter or Burton's bass coming off the men's breath, would just about knock you out. In here, where they sat in the same place at the same table drinking, smoking and talking for hours on end, the air would be so thick you wouldn't be able to see from one end of the room to the other. They would breathe it in and cough and splutter it out, then breathe it in again and do the same with that, over and over again. You could nearly smell the lung in it. The cards, the dominoes, the clothes, the seats, the carpet, the wallpaper, even the old fox terriers lying under the table, all stank the same way. And in the corners there'd always be a whiff of vinegar and old man's pee added to it. Yet nobody would ever dream of opening a window. Neither the pitmen nor anybody else was there for the fresh air. This was fresh air compared with where they'd been working all week. 'Hadaway to the beach and have yoursel' a walk along the pier, if it's fresh air ye want,' they would sharp tell anybody who so much as looked at the sneck on a window.

In a corner, under a cloud of his own, my father would be sitting at his little foldy-up card table. On the beige top, which in the middle was worn through to the black backing, would be a battered receipt book and a tin box that was only opened when he was putting money in or taking it out. A thick copying pencil would be taken from behind his ear and licked before he very carefully wrote anything down, pronouncing every letter of every word like an engraver, so there could be no mistake. He was no scholar – as he would admit whenever he was about to put somebody down who thought he was better educated than he was – but he was very good with figures. And as Secretary of the Stanhope Hotel Sick Fund he would be there every payday between six o'clock and eight o'clock, taking in or paying out as the case may be. The scheme wasn't just for pitmen. Anybody could join and everybody gave and got at the same rate.

After he'd been at it for a long while they voted a feller called Jackie Franks in his place, and Jackie Franks took the job without a second thought on the matter. Maybe they thought he could do a better job or would have a better manner or something. But the upshot of it was in no time he chucked it in, and they asked my father back. But he told them where to stick their copying pencil, their receipt book and their cash box, and the whole thing fizzled out. It was a great shame because it had been a good scheme that kept sick men out of the Workhouse for just a few coppers a week, and it had had over three hundred members.

My father wasn't a big gambler but he was regular, and he was quite lucky. The horses were his favourite. Whenever he won, even though it was out of his own pocket money, he never forgot to give something to my mother. And when he got his pay packet she always got her money without ever having to ask. He knew my mother was a good woman and most of the time he treated her like one. I don't think either of them had much to complain about. My father loved his home and all of the comforts of home including his bairns, it was just that he didn't believe in spending any more time in it than he had to. Mam did most of the bringing up of us kids, and she was all that a mother could be. All she had to look forward to was to be able to sit down at the end of the day.

John and me went to St Peter and Paul's School near Tyne Dock and it was no better than the one in Sacriston. The only difference was it was catechism and the cane, instead of catechism and a horsewhip. No Protestant schools seemed to be named after saints, so maybe they didn't have any. The priests seemed to think we should suffer because all ours had had horrible deaths. I don't know whether Protestant schools were any better or worse than Catholic ones but I know they had bibles instead of catechisms, and they didn't have to learn them off by heart. Anything to do with religion, and there were very few lessons that didn't have something to do with it, meant getting a hiding somewhere along the line. If you forgot the difference between Limbo and Heaven or you hadn't brought the card they gave you at Sunday Mass to prove you'd been, you could expect none of the forgiveness they were always saying was such a wonderful thing. They left that to God on Judgement Day, the second Judgement Day that was. For some reason there were two.

Practically every teacher I ever had was a Caulfield, even the head-mistress at Sacriston was one. People used to say the Pope must have been one at one time. One day, after one of them had given me a hiding for something I hadn't done, I went home and told my mother and she told my father when he came in. My father says, 'Divvent depend on me gannin' up, Tommy. 'Cos I'm not. If ye hadn't done nowt wrong, ye wouldn't've got welted. And that's all there is to it. No lady teacher would welt ye just for the sake of it. Any more on the matter, and I'll give ye one mesel'.'

I hated school and I hated everything about it. I hated the lessons, the hidings, and hearing about Hell. And every day I schemed and looked for any excuse to stay off. On washdays I'd even offer to mind our Monica, take her for a walk in the pram even, rather than go. Like all Irish mothers Mam was very keen on sticking in at school but she was dead soft as well. And if I told her that if I went on such and such a day they'd be giving me the lash just because I couldn't pronounce a certain word, she'd nearly always give in.

One day my father fetched home a little canary in a cage that he'd got from the pit. Monica had been poorly for quite a while and he thought it might cheer her up. She was too young to look after it herself so I got the job. Every morning I had to blow the husks out of the seed hopper and top up the seed, change its water, go out and find some groundsel or shepherd's purse and every Saturday I had to clean out the cage and put fresh sand in.

It was a border canary that had gone blind in one eye. My father used to say that of all the creatures that went down a pit, these poor little things that never did anybody any harm had the worst time of it. Yet in spite of that they brightened any place they were put into and would sing their heads off at the slightest excuse. Whenever gas was suspected a deputy would pick one of them up in its tiny cage and take it with him to check. If there was anything in the air that would kill a man, it would flop off its perch and that was it. They never got to do the same job twice. Local bird fanciers would breed canaries for shows, and ones that were the wrong colour or had wings that crossed a little bit usually went to the colliery. That way at least they helped to pay for the other ones' seed.

Every cock would sing no matter what it looked like and the one we got was a real champion. My father had been told it had German Roller in it, which meant it could warble. All you had to do was turn on the tap and his throat would come right out as though it had a burr in it and he'd sing so hard you'd think his head was going to come off. Although he would have been quite able to do the job he was supposed to do down the pit, the bloke in charge of canaries said it was asking too much to expect a bird that was half blind to test for gas.

We must have had it at least six months by which time everybody in the house had become very attached to it, when it suddenly stopped eating and fluffed itself into a ball. If you tapped the cage, its head would come half out and then go straight back in, and the whole body would give a little shudder. One night my father came home with one of his pals who was a canary man. When this feller came in and I saw the size of his hands, I thought to myself, 'Joey's had it here. If that bloke picks him up, he'll squash him before he gets him out of the cage.'

As it was, his hands were too big to get through the cage door so the bloke started strumming his finger along the wires and poking it in to try to get Joey to move from his perch. But Joey's head was buried under his wing and he just kept shuddering. I couldn't take my eyes of this feller's finger it was so huge. It was thicker than my wrist. There were big cracks in it that were blackened with coal and the rest was dark brown with baccy stain. The end was missing and the nails of the fingers on either side were all cockeyed as though they'd been forced sideways into the finger. He had this soggy wet dumper on the end of his tongue that went inside his mouth and then came out again, still alight. When he spoke he flicked it onto his bottom lip. When he finished, it would disappear again. He never once touched it with his fingers.

Suddenly he sat back. 'It's had it. It'll be gone by tomorrow.' He looked at all our faces and then he said to me, 'I'll tell ye what I'll do. If your Ma here'll let ye have another one, ye can come round to my place next Sunday before dinner and I'll see what I can do for ye.'

Mam of course smiled and straightaway said yes, so on the Sunday I took John with me and we went to the feller's house. He wasn't in when we got there but his wife told us where his allotment was and that was where he'd be. It wasn't very far, only at the end of the railway cutting at the bottom of the street.

When we arrived he was sitting inside this tiny hut with three other men. We knocked on the door and they told us to come in, sit down, and be quiet. I'll never forget the sight when that little door opened and we went in, nor the wonderful smell when the door closed behind us. There were rows and rows of neat little box cages from the ceiling to the floor, along two walls and one big flight cage along the other, all with birds in them. The place was full of birds. There were linnets and goldfinches and canaries of all kinds and colours. I never knew you could get white canaries. There were seed husks all over the floor, and bird droppings and sweet-smelling sawdust swept into little piles under the cages ready to be shovelled away.

One of the men was a little old feller with a trilby and a lump on the side of his neck like a bunion. He was sitting on a bairn's cracket with some whopper sticks of rhubarb across his knees and a parcel of mint wrapped in newspaper sticking out of his pocket. Another feller, this one with a big scar down one side of his face, was running his fingers through a sack of seed by the door and saying something about there being too much hemp in it and not enough red rape. The feller with the lump was rubbing baccy in his hand and filling his pipe but not lighting it. He had two fingers and a thumb on one hand, and three stumps and no thumb on the other. 'Best stuff in the world for red mite, this is. Shag... Ye cannot beat it.'

'It'll shag the mites all right,' said the feller with the scar, and his hand in the seed.

'Watch your language. There's bairns here... '

'Hadaway and ask Mrs Charlton for a saucer of sugar, bonny lad, and I'll give yous a bit of rhubarb when ye come back,' said the feller with the lump.

Eddie, the feller with the huge finger, whose hut it was, sat down. He'd been tying a sprig of chickweed to the bars of every cage when we came in and hadn't bothered to turn round. He had a thin stick, like a long pencil, and was leaning forward and tapping the bars of the cages to get the birds to hop from one perch to the other. After a few minutes he would sum up the bird inside, in birdman's talk.

We sat for ages, John and me, sucking the bitter juice out of the rhubarb, smelling the bird-smell and listening to the men talking. The three of them had forgotten us completely and were on about this one being a good sitter and that one always missing a day between laying and the why's and wherefore's of using red pepper to colour a bird up for the show.

At one end of each of the double cages was a chalky white bowl, not much wider than a tea cup and only half as high, which was held up by a wire ring fastened to a tiny hook in the wall and inside every bowl was a beautiful nest finely woven and lined with feathers. Some had a bird in them with its back flat across the top as though that particular nest pan had been specially made for it. Others had birds that were so small they were right down in them and all you could see was a little tuft of hair at one end and the white tip of their tail at the other.

'Flat as a cap, just like always,' said Eddie. 'It'd take a stick o' dynamite to get her off once she settles down. No earthquake'd do it, I'll tell ye that.'

'I had one just like her,' said the feller with the lump. 'Best little sitter ye ever saw. Buff green she was. Not much to look at, I'll grant ye. But a team of wild horses couldn't've dragged her off… Am I right there, Bill? You know. Ye saw her many's the time, didn't ye?'

'Aye, she were all right. Nowt to look at, mind. But not bad when it came to sittin''.'

'I didn't say she was a show bird! What we're talkin' about is sittin' ability.'

'Why, I know we are. There's ne need to get your knickers in a knot… I was just meanin' ne bird can have it all ways, that's all.'

'Why, anybody knows that.'

Eddie gently shooed a bird off a nest with his finger and there was dead silence. All eyes were fixed on that nest. He put his finger to his lips and then curled it towards John and me to take a peek. At the bottom of the nest, deep down in the fur, were the four tiniest eggs I'd ever seen. They were pale blue, speckled, and as cosy as could be. With his huge thick fingers he then lifted the eggs out one by one, weighed them in his hand, looked up at the light through them, and then put them back safe and sound. Not a single one was broken. Next he carefully opened the little wire door of another cage, reached in and brought out a whole nest with three young'uns in it, pink and skinny, all eyeballs and beak, and set it down on his knee. He then tapped the side of it and all three mouths immediately opened wide and the heads started swaying from side to side. While the other two fellers had been arguing, Eddie had been chopping up a bit of boiled egg and mixing it with bread crumbs, and now he was feeding a tiny morsel to each little bird off the end of a flattened and smoothed matchstick. First he'd feed one, then another. Then another, till they'd all had something. Round and round he went again and again, every now and then dribbling a little bit of his saliva into the food and mixing it in, until they were so full they hadn't the strength to raise their heads any more. One by one they settled back down into the nest and all their eye-slits closed. The bald heads with their few long hairs sticking out were bent over double, and their necks bulged so much you could see the yellow of the egg and the bits of green chickweed beneath the skin. I asked him if he did this with all of them. This was the first time John or me had opened our mouths except to say thanks for the rhubarb.

'No. Just these.'

'Why not the others as well?'

'Their mothers aren't dead.'

'How did that one die?'

'It just took it into its head and keeled ower… the way everythin' does.'

The other fellers laughed.

'Aye but why did it die?'

'I divvent know, bonny lad. If ye want to know why one creature gets sick and dies and another one doesn't, ye'll have to ask the Feller who made it all in the first place.'

The other two slapped their thighs and laughed again and the one with the scar had tears running down in it.

We came away with a young cock canary in a little cardboard box, and hurried back home as fast as we could without shaking it up too much. As soon as we got home we burst in and plonked the box on the table. Mam was making pastry, Dad was sitting in his chair smoking his pipe and reading his paper. We were full of it all. The birds, the birdmen, the rhubarb, everything.

'Aye, well see yous look after it properly,' Dad said with a wave of the hand, not even bothering to look over. But Mam wanted to hear everything. So while she was going backwards and forwards to the sink or the cupboard, John and me were following her and telling her everything that had happened and everything we could remember that had been said. She took it all in and laughed and laughed and thought it all ever so good.

My mother was very soft-hearted and would do anything for anybody. She would bend over backwards to avoid a row, no matter who it was with or whatever the reason was. She wasn't quite as short as my father but she always managed to make herself look as though she was. She had lovely dark hair and a pink complexion like Granda, only it lacked his hardy look. She was never very strong and the hardship of being a pitman's wife was something I don't think she was made for, particularly if he worked in a wet pit. Every night she had to dadd my father's heavy pit clothes against the wall in the back lane to get the thick off and then clean them up. And every night she had to clean the muck off his boots and get what she could out of the insides. I don't know how she'd have managed if she'd had as many to do for as Grandma Turnbull had.

The only time she went out was when she went once a year to the Miners' Gala in Durham or to family do's like weddings and funerals. But you never heard her complain. And she never interfered with pit or union business or tried to tell my father what to do or what not to do. She never said a word about his gambling or his drinking and the only thing that ever upset her was if he stayed at the pub so long his dinner got spoilt or if he had so much beer in him he couldn't eat it. Making meals to feed her family was the most important thing in life to her. We only had one real dinner in the week and that was on a Sunday and it was always special.

My mother would go without altogether rather than see my father short of anything on his plate. He was the man, the breadwinner, the boss. And if he was entitled to nothing else, he was entitled to a dinner once a week that nobody would be ashamed to sit down to. She would walk two miles to get a bit of cress growing wild at a place she kept to herself. Marigolds in a little vase, salt in the cellar, pepper in the pot, vinegar in a decanter, and everything arranged just the way he liked it. His was the only china plate in the house and his was the only knife and fork with bone handles. She would put the dinner on before she went to Mass on Sunday morning and then hurry back without stopping to gossip so she could get back to it.

If he came home so late it was ruined, that was the only time she would ever tell him off. Even then she'd always go over to him afterwards and apologise and he would just grunt. And on the times when he was drunk and lost his temper with her for standing up to him, her anger would soon go and she'd cry bitter tears. 'I'm sorry, Jack. You've a perfect right to a drink after the work you do. Try and forgive me. Please, Jack... Things just get me down at times. I won't say anything again. I promise.'

One Sunday he came back so late it was practically tea-time and straightaway he started demanding his dinner and saying he was starving. She had done everything she could to keep it nice because she was never so spiteful that she'd deliberately let it spoil, the way some would, like Aunty Ethel for instance. But when she put it out, it was very sorry-looking. My father took one look at it, picked it up, flung it straight through the window and walked out. There were pieces of china and dinner mixed up with bits of glass and stones and dirt, all over the backyard. Potatoes with the sprinkle of mint still sticking to them, the week's one slice of mutton, and the plate with a scene of old Killarney that had been a wedding present from Ireland, all wrecked. She picked up the brush and shovel, ran the floorcloth under the tap, went out, picked up the pieces and cleaned up the mess, and there wasn't a word out of her.

4

When war broke out in 1914 my father was dead against it. I was nine years old at the time and I remember he was always going to meetings. Not only at the Stanhope or the lodge but at church halls, picture halls, the market square, the park, anywhere. And if it was an open-air meeting and it was a fine day, I'd tag along for the fun.

My father always managed to get himself into trouble. Not only with the speakers that came from other parts of the country but with his own mates and relations as well. Some, like Keir Hardie and Arthur Henderson wanted to join the international workers' movement and refuse to support the War which they said was a war between royal families that had nothing at all to do with the likes of us. Others said the Coalowners were behind it because they needed a war to push the price of coal up, and to get the Government to bring in martial law to put the miners down. There were those who thought war was a glorious thing, whatever the reason and whatever the cost, and there were just as many women among them as men – most of them with posh loud voices. And then there were the odds and sods who were fanatics or maniacs who just wanted to rant at the whole world.

When a woman got up, no matter who she was, things would usually quieten down for a while. She'd start off politely enough and maybe with a few airs about her but it wouldn't be long before she got herself worked up and started screeching at certain ones that had already been up and said their piece, and the crowd would get fed up with her and tell her to shut up and get down. Maybe in their colleges or big houses wherever they came from, they weren't used to this kind of treatment but tempers could run pretty high and if the crowd was already stirred up it wouldn't much matter who you were. On a good day there'd be a fight and the pollises would come pouring in. Somebody would come by with a broken nose and their face smeared with blood, followed by women wailing and cursing at the same time. 'They've killed him!' one of them would be screaming. 'Oh, my God! My poor man! They've gone and killed him!' But usually there was more scuffling and big talk than anything else. Nobody got killed that I ever saw, though when we got back my father used to tell my mother there were ructions on. 'Terrible it was, Annie... Terrible. Ye should've been there.'

She must have taken him with a pinch of salt though, otherwise she'd never have let me go.

Before we left the house she'd always beg him to watch himself.

'And look after that bairn, Jack. Stay beside your father all the time mind, Tommy. Keep tight a hold of your father's hand and don't let go... d'ye hear?'

John would never come, he was too young and always wanted to keep himself to himself. You could hardly get him out of the house even when the sun was blazing down. So there'd nearly always be just Dad and me.

We would hardly have been at the meeting five minutes before Dad would be getting himself areated. And once that happened he wouldn't be able to keep quiet to save his life. A couple of sentences was all he needed to hear to make his mind up about any speaker. He didn't need to see them, which was just as well with him being so short. Whether it was somebody he had praised all week or somebody he absolutely detested, he bestowed no favours. At first he'd be muttering away to himself but loud enough so anybody near could hear. Then he'd pick on the feller standing directly next to him and start moaning to him. He seemed to think that just because they were standing where he was, they'd have the same views as he did. He was always the same. And when he found they didn't, he'd start an argument with them even though they hadn't been saying a word before he started. 'Ye haven't a bloody clue,' he'd say, and turn back again to listen to bigger fry. His hand would then go up and he'd be shouting his head off at the speaker, yelling so loud nobody around would be able to hear a word the bloke was saying.

'Wrap up, will ye! Give the bloke a chance.'

'Put a sock in it, big mouth!'

'Shut up, Jack... We all know what you think. We've come here to hear what he thinks.'

'Aye. Hadaway back to the Stanhope and gi' we some peace!'

'Peace? Peace?? What the hell d'ye think I'm on about, ye stupid bugger? Listen to these sods and ye'll end up with a bayonet in your hand! Or one in your belly.'

'Somebody wants to shove one up that bugger's behind.'

'It's about the only thing that'd shut him up.'

All the same my father kept going. He didn't like to see people standing like sheep and being ranted at. There was enough of that in the Catholic Church, he thought.

'If what they say stands up to fair criticism, I'll be the first to give them credit,' would be his answer to anybody who wanted to be allowed to listen to a speaker. But he never would of course, and the kind of things he'd been shouting would hardly have amounted to 'fair criticism'. The thing was that outside his own house nobody ever listened to what he had to say. Down the pit they just laughed, so did his own brother.

If you were a little man, even a little man with a very loud voice, you couldn't change the course of history if nobody could see you. So after everybody who was anybody had got back in their cars and driven off and most of the crowd were so tired and fed up they'd gone home, my father would get up and have a go himself. The few stragglers that were left would have had got so sick of him yammering on, they'd have said 'Gan on, then! You get up if ye think ye can do any better! All you're doin' down here is givin' everybody a headache.'

'It's a pain in the arse he gives me.'

Once he was up there, suddenly trying to sound like such a reasonable chap, he looked tiny and with the loudhailers gone even his voice was no more than a drop in the ocean. He'd keep going till he'd said his piece about the Government only wanting to send pitmen to the Front so they could kill them off, about his own far better proposal to send Coalowners instead, and had got it in about the Tynemouth battery shooting its own lighthouse. He never missed a chance to remind the whole world that down at Tynemouth the local defence battery had hit their own lighthouse during target practice, as though that was one of the greatest arguments against the War. 'There won't be a man, woman or child left on Tyneside… And that's before the Germans have fired a shot!'

After his speech he would step down very pompously and shake hands with one or two in the front who'd given him a bit of a clap and thank them and he'd be really pleased with himself. When we got back and he was telling Mam how he'd been 'invited to take the platform', to hear him you'd think the crowd was bigger than the total population of Tyneside.

By the time the War had really got going and thousands of our soldiers were being killed, it was treason to speak out against it. My father realised there was no way of stopping it and no point in opposing it, not when so many of his own friends and relations had long gone from pit to trench. If he'd kept it up it would have been like saying they were all giving their lives for nothing.

The different Labour movements of Europe which had mostly been for uniting with each other in the first place were now following the lead taken by their own governments and supporting the War, no matter what side that meant being on. Patriotic feeling was now so high that women were walking up to any man they thought should be away fighting and either handing him a white feather or sticking it in his jacket pocket, right there in the main street with everybody looking. In South Shields people were breaking the windows of shops owned by people with German names or names that sounded as though they might be German. They weren't giving them the benefit of the doubt and it got so that it didn't matter if they'd been born in the next street. After a while they realised it wasn't right and it fizzled out.

My father was going on for forty, which was just as well because he didn't have the kind of personality that would have been appreciated in the Army. So he stayed in the pit. Coal had become as essential to the war effort as food and guns, and nothing could be produced without it. Also it was easier to give a man a rifle and get him to jump in a trench, than to shove a pick in his hand and get him to go down a pit. Pitmen from every coalfield in the country had joined up as soon as war had been declared and mines were now so desperately short that as many as possible were being brought back. But that wasn't easy. Right from the start, soldiers were no sooner kitted out than they were shipped over to France and once they were over there, even if they were still in one piece the chances of finding them and getting them back were very slim.

To try to produce more coal and faster, the Government started putting in machines to cut and carry coal. But the new methods and the operation of dangerous machinery, particularly in dark and cramped conditions, needed skills British miners didn't have. Most of the machinery was of German type, so there were no company experts coming to supervise installation. As a consequence more miners were being seriously injured than ever before. But safety wasn't a priority and the pressure to increase production meant miners were having to work longer hours and take more and more risks with machines and methods they knew little or nothing about. Men who had always worked with pick and pony and relied on their ears to tell them how safe the roof was, had to learn how to use dangerous and noisy machines in the dark and on the job.

To make matters worse, 'conscientious objectors' and other people who were out of favour with the Government were being made to go down the pit, supposedly to provide extra labour. Nobody could seriously have believed that people like these who had never been down a mine in their entire lives would increase coal production. Quite the opposite, they were a danger to themselves and to everybody else. At best they were just a nuisance. But in the eyes of many people, if they got killed down a coal mine they'd have got no more than they deserved and if they managed to shovel up a couple of bucketfuls of coal in the meantime, fine and dandy. As far as pitmen were concerned, if the Government wanted to kill these people, they should have taken them out into a field and shot them and they should have got the Army to do it. Not treat pits as though they were the gallows and make pitmen suffer for it as well.

The 'war effort' had become an excuse for anything and everything and if anybody complained no matter whether it was about poor pay, bad conditions or anything else, they were made to feel as though they were traitors. The same went for any criticism of the Government and anybody who worked for it or was connected with it in any way. Eleven-year-old kids might not go down pits any more but they knew what went on. My father wasn't allowed to shout outside now but at home he never stopped talking about it.

During the War many things became scarce, though not that we noticed. 'Ye never miss what ye never had,' my mother would say. And for those who worked in the pit and their families life was pretty much the same as it always was. The Durham Miners Gala, which was the annual meeting of pitfolk, had been suspended 'for the duration', along with other things like that but I was a young lad and didn't need a gala to keep me occupied. There were plenty more interesting things to see and do now there was a war on. Every Sunday there were soldiers in their different uniforms and hats, with all their medals, marching behind the bands, carrying flags and rifles and banging drums. There were sailors in their navy blue suits and white hats whistling at all the lasses. There were cannon guns, armoured cars and tanks. And on the Tyne and out at sea there were huge battleships with massive guns pointing everywhere.

We hadn't been at war very long before the Government took over the running of the mines completely. Coal was one of the greatest necessities and there wasn't enough of it being produced. They realised now, if they hadn't done before, that the Coalowners were useless. They hadn't organised the industry properly, they were too mean and too stuck in their ways to modernise and they couldn't get the best out of their own employees.

Those now in charge soon found out that pitmen worked better for carrots than sticks, and as a consequence pit wages rose so much that our family was better off than it had ever been. By 1918 when the end of the War was in sight and there was talk of slum clearance and massive building schemes, demand for coal both at home and abroad looked like it was going to be greater than ever. There was serious talk about the Government hanging on to the mines and passing them over to the state after the War. The prospects for pitfolk looked good for the first time ever.

My father had got himself an allotment so he could grow vegetables and keep a few hens and I was allowed to keep a few pigeons in an old shed I was making into a loft at the bottom end. Apart from the canary, which had really been Monica's, these were the first pets I ever had. It was fantastic to let them out for a fly around in the sky and watch them come right back down to their own little loft in our own allotment. My pals often came round to watch and then afterwards when I'd seen to the birds and locked them up, we'd have a wander to see if there were any pitch-and-toss schools on the go. When you had a few coppers in your pocket, like I had now, you'd have no difficulty getting a game. It was always better if you could get into one with the older fellers. You nearly always lost but the way they played was the best way, not messing about like we did. When we were playing on our own, the slightest excuse and somebody would be yelling 'Ye dirty cheater!' and diving in to get their money back and you'd all be rolling over on the ground yelling and fighting. If you'd carried on like that with the older fellers, they'd have thumped you and told you to bugger off and not come back. When they played, they left their dosh on the deck where everybody could see it.

But when they picked your money up and it went into their pocket, that was the last you saw of it. You didn't mind so much then, it made you feel like a man, even though sometimes you were close to tears when they'd won the whole lot.

When we had no money there was always 'footer', that was a game you never tired of. We would play till long after dark and by the time we were finished the can would be pulverised. Every back lane in Shields rang at some time every day with the bang and clatter of a tin can being kicked. They made one hell of a noise when you booted them hard. Anybody on night shift must have cursed the day Heinz invented them. Of course if you could get hold of a rubber ball that was far better. With a tin can you just played on the run, scrambling and fighting to get a kick of it and it didn't matter where it went. You could start at the cut at the bottom of Lemon Street and before you realised, be at the top of Stanhope Road. But with a ball you could have a proper game with headers and everything.

The trouble with the balls was they were so bouncy and you could get such a good kick of them, that sooner or later they'd go over old Mr McKie's wall. And once they landed in his yard, that was it, you could kiss them goodbye. It wouldn't have mattered if the cans had gone over but they never did. The thing was his gable end was the best place for miles for a goalmouth. Kids from all over would race to get there first and there'd be fights as soon as somebody started chalking up. Poor old McKie would have to put up with all the shouting and yelling even before the game began as we argued and fought over who was going to be on whose team and who had to go in goal. The sound of that ball hitting his wall every couple of minutes from dawn to dusk every day, unless it rained nonstop, must have just about driven him nuts. He must have cursed when he saw the sun coming out.

If anybody kicked the ball miles away along the road, there'd always be a row about who would go for it. But whenever the ball went over into McKie's, there'd be a mad dash to get over the wall before he came running out and everybody would be piling over. He might have had half a leg missing but the old bugger could move like lightning when he wanted to. Any balls he got – and he got most of them – he'd take straight into the house, store them up until he had a decent number and then flog them to a bloke in the market. He never showed any mercy, never once gave a ball back that I ever heard about, and every kid around hated him. We'd do things like wrap a lump of dog's business in a bit of newspaper or the tail of a cat that had been run over, and shove it through his letterbox. A couple of minutes later he'd come fleeing out crazy as hell and we'd scatter for our lives. He always ran after the littlest first, then gave up and tried for another and then another until he ended up hanging on to the wall, gasping with one hand over his heart and not enough breath left even to swear. We were the enemy as far as old McKie was concerned, not the Germans, and he was permanently at war with every one of us, and us with him.

The War ended in 1918 and although by no means everybody was demobbed straightaway, the number of lives now known to have definitely been lost and not just gone missing for a while or maybe in a prison camp, could be counted. But the amount of limbs that had been blown off, cut off or made useless, were beyond reckoning, as were the faces that were permanently blinded or badly disfigured. Practically every one of them was a young feller, some of them scarcely out of short pants. All of them would have been breadwinners and now many of them would just be burdens. Because we were pitfolk we could probably accept our losses easier than other people. All our lives we had to deal with sudden and violent deaths of fathers, uncles, husbands, brothers, sons and friends. Not only men in their prime, like the young soldiers, seamen and airmen in the War, but also men past their prime and boys that had never reached it. One in every fifty Durham miners were expected to be killed in the pit and ten times that number would have a serious accident at some time. Every miner expected to lose fingers or bits of them but they were just counted as minor injuries. The colliery would have laughed at them if they'd tried to say that sort of thing should be counted as 'maiming'.

And we were used to looking after men who were permanently disabled and felt they had nothing to live for any more. We knew very well what terrible injuries can be caused by iron and steel, explosives and gas – we didn't need a war to show us. The difference in war though is that it's the ones you least expect that cop it, and the ones you wouldn't give a ha'penny for their chances that come through. Though that wasn't the case with Uncle Geordie and the way he went would shock anybody. Geordie had been a big strapping feller and was well respected down the pit. One night about four months before the War started he had been drinking with his best pal, a feller called Sandy Gallagher, and the two of them had drunk too much and started arguing. It turned into a fight and Geordie got knocked to the floor. Barely was he down before Gallagher, who completely lost his rag, started kicking him as though he was trying to kick him to death. Again and again he kicked him in the head and body, and wouldn't let up. By the time they managed to drag him off, he had damaged Geordie's brain, and when Geordie finally managed to get up, he had no feeling in his hands or feet. The feeling never came back but what was worse, he was left with a terrible pain in his head that never went away. It was so bad at times that he used to wander about like an idiot holding his head in his hands and bumping into things, he just didn't know what to do with himself. He was classified as being completely useless for pit work and finished without a penny. Because he was incapable, all he and his family had to live on was what Aunty Betty could earn from taking in washing and she had to scrub her fingers to the bone to get through enough to keep six bairns as well as themselves.

After the War had been on for a while and things weren't looking too good, and more and more men were being called up, a woman walked up to Geordie one afternoon when he was standing looking in a shop window and says 'What's a big strappin' feller like you doin' lazin' about, lookin' in shop windows, Geordie? You should be away fightin' with the rest of them. The fresh air and exercise'd do ye good. It might even put ye right so ye can gan back to the pit after the War and be a proper father to your bairns instead of what ye are now.'

Everybody who knew Geordie knew what had happened to him, and you could tell just by looking at him that he wasn't all there. That afternoon without saying a word to anybody he walked to Durham City, enlisted, got sent to France and was blown to smithereens in less than a week. The only good thing that came out of it was his wife and kids got a bit of a pension which is more than they got from the coal company after Geordie had worked nearly twenty years in their pit.

His sister Lila's luck wasn't any better. She was accidentally hit in the mouth with the buckle of her husband's belt and it caused a disease that closed her mouth up so tight it was agony for her to try to get so much as a pea into it. At first they tried to keep it open with a spoon handle but that kept falling out. Then she went round with a lucifer taped to her chin with a bit of sticking plaster. That was no use either. In the end, the mouth closed up completely and she frittered away to nothing. She was only forty-three when she died.

Uncle Bill and Uncle Dick Turnbull had left the pit and joined up in 1914 as soon as war had been declared. Miners could do that then. They signed up for the Royal Artillery on the same day, trained at the same barracks, came home on leave on the same train and went back on the same train. And when they got sent to France they got the same boat over and ended up at the same camp. One night after they'd been there a while, the sergeant, who knew about Bill and Dick being brothers and always trying to stick together, told Bill that Dick was going to be sent on a mission first thing the next morning and because it was very dangerous he wasn't able to let them both go. A dozen men were needed for the job and none of them was expected to come back. As soon as Uncle Bill heard this he asked if he could see the officer in charge and the sergeant agreed. 'Yes, what do you want?' says this officer. 'I want to go instead of Dick Turnbull. Whatever he's supposed to do, I can do. I've got no bairns. He has.' 'Righto,' says the officer. 'If that's the way you want it, that's the way it'll be.'

Nobody told Uncle Dick anything about it until it was too late and Uncle Bill had gone. Some of the fellers did get back but Uncle Bill wasn't among them. Dick stayed on till the end of the War and did everything he was called on to do but he could never get over the way Bill had gone. Shortly after the War he went to work in Deanside Drift. This was a very safe mine, you could even use candles in it. There were no shafts to get blocked, no cages to fall out of. You just walked in, did your work, and then walked out again. One night after the shift finished, the deputy was counting the blokes coming out, and he says 'Has anybody seen Dick Turnbull?'

'I seen 'im a while back,' says this feller.

'What was he doin'?'

'Doin' his work like anybody else.'

'Well I wish he'd hurry his bloody sel' up. I want to gan home.'

They hung around for a while longer but there was still no sign of Dick, so the deputy went in to look for him. He found him in-bye, stretched out on the ground as though he was fast asleep, a long skinny feller with thick fair hair, and his watch still ticking. He was as dead as the stone lying beside him and nobody ever knew how. He was the first and only man ever to be killed in Deanside Drift. Shortly after he was buried Aunty Evvie had their last baby.

Uncle Basil was another one who left the pit to join the Army and he was hit in the stomach by a mortar shell on his very first day in France. A pitman like him couldn't have had time to get his bearings, let alone anything else. What use he was to them after that I can't imagine but they kept him on all the same, right to the end. He used to open his shirt and say to the new blokes, 'Get a gander at that, son. That's how they take your appendix out in the army.' They wouldn't take him back in the pit after the War because the wound wouldn't heal and he had to keep a bandage on all the time. He couldn't get a proper job anywhere. The only thing he could get, was part-time doorman at a working men's club. At that time things were so desperate, in particular for men who'd been badly injured, that there were umpteen going around the doors with one arm or leg, selling bobbins of thread and bootlaces. Blind ones walked up and down queues playing battered old fiddles and ones with their faces covered up, or no legs, sat on the pavement drawing crucified Christs with chalk. Ones who couldn't do anything at all just stood all day with their hands out. No employer wanted them, not with thousands of fit men to choose from, so Basil was better off than some. Either way he hadn't been in the job more than a few weeks when he dropped down dead on the front steps. It was only then that they found out what a mess his stomach had been in, septic and stinking and with a huge hole in it. It had given a him a lot of pain, people knew that, and there were very few things he could eat, so maybe it was for the best.

By now both my Grandmas and Granda Kelly were dead as well.

5

On the Friday I was a schoolboy, on the Saturday I was fourteen and on the Monday I was a coalminer. A pitman at last! It was 1919.

All my life, practically from the time I opened my eyes, I wanted to go down 'The Pit' and be a miner like my Dad, like my uncles, and like their marras. The day could never come soon enough. The pit was in my blood, it was all that real men ever talked about. All the good people I knew in the world were pitfolk. I knew all about 'The Face' and the money a good hewer could make. I knew what you could say to a deputy and what you couldn't to a manager. I knew how you handed one token in and always kept the other so they'd know if you were missing. I knew that 'snap' was the break you took when you ate your bait and that you had to be damned quick about it because you wouldn't get paid for it. I knew you never had to knock your lamp out or a long shift in the dark would be the least of your problems. I knew how you always looked after your marra and how he always looked after you. I knew how it would look when you marched across the colliery yard with all the men, chattering, joking and arguing, with the sound of the buzzer, your buzzer, in your ears. I knew what to do when a couple of idiots bumped into you as they went past on their bikes trying to knock each other off. And I knew how it would feel to have people in their beds listening for the sound of your boots, and recognising something so special that of all the pairs of boots that had ever clomped down a back lane at dead of night or before dawn on any morning since time began, none had ever sounded quite like yours.

There was nothing else I could do except go down the pit. Thousands of men were still coming back from the War looking for jobs and jobs were very hard to get anywhere. If you were a lad you might get taken on as an apprentice in a small firm or in a factory doing labouring for next to nowt. But the minute you were twenty-one and had served your time and become entitled to a man's pay, they'd sharp tell you, 'On your way, mister,' and get another young lad to take your place. It wouldn't have mattered whether you were a plumber, a fitter, a joiner or anything else. They were all the same.

My mother said I was silly for wanting to go down the pit, that it was very dangerous, that it wasn't a proper job and that it was a life of constant strife. My father said he knew I was an idiot from the start, pig-headed as well. 'Takes after his Uncle Jim.'

'You young'uns think it'll be like a bed o' roses down there and that the money'll just come pourin' down the chute. Ye'll soon find out how wrong you are… Divvent get taken in by what that Welch git, Lloyd-bloody-George, says. It's coal he's talkin' about nationalisin', not the bloody mines. They'll still belong to the Vane-Tempests, the Londonderrys, the bloody Bishop of Durham, and all the rest of them just like they've always done.'

'Ordinary people ne better than theesel' will look down on ye 'cos you're always mucky. And you're mucky because ye spend your life scrattin' around down a filthy black hole.

'And it's not pigeons you're ganna be seein' fleein' about down there. It's blacklocks! And I'm not talkin' about the little black beetles ye see around here. I'm talkin' about monster bloody cockroaches that'll nearly knock ye over when they bump into ye. Have one of them buggers smack ye in the gob and ye'll think you've been hit by a bloody brick. They're too big and nasty ever to come up out of the ground. That's why people divvent know about them.

'When they get ye on shifts, ye'll be lucky if ye see the sun from one month to the next. The dust'll blind ye. It'll get in your hair. It'll block your ears up. It'll choke ye. It'll get up your behind. Aye, and it'll even find its way up your little bit tassel.

'Divvent smirk at me, lad! I'm tellin' ye these things for your own good, not for the sake of hearin' me own voice.

'If ye divvent get hacked up afore you're old enough to drop dead, ye'll be able to count theesel' lucky. Very, very lucky. Barely ten years ago a hundred and sixty-eight men and lads were killed at Stanley.' He snapped his fingers under my nose. 'Just like that!'

Maybe he was right but grown-ups have a habit of telling you not to do the things they're always doing themselves. Anyway when you're fourteen you think nothing can kill you.

'I know all that, Dad. But I'm ne scholar. What else can I do?'

'Ne scholar? You're not tellin' me owt I divvent know already. You're as thick as two short planks, and twice as bloody awkward... Now, there's a thing... What about servin' your time to be a joiner? Ye mightn't be much good but at least it's a safe job.'

'A joiner? Knockin' nails in bits o' wood all day long? Ppphh!'

'There's a lot more to it than that! Look at Sandy McGregor. He seems to do all right out of it and he doesn't have to gan home mucky every night of his life.'

I stood there with my hands stuck right down in my pockets, staring at the ground. He knew I was going to go down no matter what. He just had to say his piece that's all. So I just waited on.

'But,' he says after a couple of minutes, 'I suppose you're old enough to make up your own mind. So if ye still want to gan, I'll be seein' Billy Oliver later on. I'll ask 'im to have a word with Billy Cowell and see if he can get ye started on Monday'.

And he did. And that was that. It was Harton Colliery, here I come! Make way for Tommy Turnbull, lads! Who wants a good marra? Yipeeeee!! A pitman at last! A coalminer! A collier! Just like I always wanted to be and knew I would be. I hated school. Bar learning to read and write a bit, I'd learned nowt. Most of the time was spent learning the catechism. What use is the catechism to anybody? I don't even think the Caulfields knew what half of it meant.

From now on I'd be wearing long pants and a pitman's cap and smoking real cigarettes. No more puffing away at bits of rolled-up newspaper that just about choked you. I'd be bringing in my own wage packet and handing it straight to my mother, unopened just like my father always did. 'There you are, Mother,' I'd be saying. 'How about that then? Pretty good, eh?'

Straightaway I'd start saving up for my own muffler and when I got that, a waistcoat next.

'How!' I'd greet the old-timers when I passed them down the pit. 'Alreet, Tommy,' they'd say as they came by. And when I came home late at night, clomping along on the cobbles in my big boots, steel on stone, sparks flying, my hands and face would be jet black. And under my shirt, 'blue buttons', the mark of a true miner, right down my back. Everybody was going to know I was a working man. I'd have my new mates and I'd walk with the gang. There'd be no kicking a can around with kids any more. People would say 'Eeeh, look at that! There goes Tommy Turnbull! He's a miner just like his father.'

Already I had a few whiskers on my chin. They were pretty soft and fair yet and I had to get right up to the mirror to see them but give them a week or two down the pit and they'd soon be thick and black. Then when I rubbed the back of my hand across my face it would crackle like sandpaper just like my father's. I might even grow myself a tash. Not drooping all over the place like his but neat and flashy. And all the while the coal dust would be hardening my voice and making it sound like a man's. It would get into the creases of my skin and harden that as well. In a few weeks nobody would be able to recognise me, I'd have changed that much.

Of all these things there was nothing I wanted more than to be carrying my own lamp, the miner's lamp. I couldn't wait to get my hands on one. If there was one thing that stood a pitman out from anybody else, it was his lamp. Other men got dirty at work, and they might get a few bruises or scars. Many could handle a shovel or an axe, drive an engine or load a wagon. But none of them ever carried a lamp, none of them went deep under the ground into a world that nobody but the pitman knows, and none of them could know what it meant to have your own 'marra', something all the money in the world couldn't buy. They had mates, yes. Good pals, no doubt, oppo's, probably. But not marras... A marra wasn't somebody you could point a finger at and say 'That's one,' or 'There goes one'. The word comes from 'marrow' and just like the other kind of marrow, it's begun underground and cultivated over a long period of time. A marra's work fitted into yours like a piece into a jigsaw. He knew you inside out and you knew him the same way. You might curse him from time to time and he might quite happily cheat you out of a few bob if he thought he could get away with it. But your life was as precious to him as his own was and when something really mattered he would stick beside you to the bitter end. I'd never heard of a feller working in an office who'd risk his neck any day of the week for the feller who sat next to him... Or a joiner.

I loved the look of coal and I loved the smell of it. There were all kinds of it, as with rocks. There was hard stuff and soft stuff, black, blue and grey stuff. Some was dull, some shiny. Some sharp as shale, some smooth as glass. Some came off the seam big as a boulder, other stuff was more like gravel or muck. But a good piece of coal is a beautiful sight.

Pitfolk say you should always treat a lump of coal with respect because it might contain a miner's soul. I'd save a small chunk off my first piece and keep it forever. I'd tuck it away in my bait poke and fetch it home and put in a drawer and keep it to show my grandchildren. One day I'd say to them, 'Look at that! Where d'ye think that came from, eh? That was the first piece of coal your Granda ever hewed over fifty years ago… on his very first day down the pit.'

Oh, was I going to have a great time when I got there! I could hardly wait for the weekend to get over. I went round everybody I knew to tell them. I don't know whether I expected them to put the flags out or what. Most of them just said 'Oh, are ye? Be careful then, son.'

On the Monday morning my father was on a different shift to the one I was on but he got up with me and made my breakfast. It was jam and bread and a cup of tea, the same as he had himself. While I was eating it he was putting my bait up which was two jam and bread sandwiches and a bottle of cold tea. It was four o'clock.

'I'm ganna do this for ye for three days, Tommy,' he says very quietly. 'After that, you're on your own. I've never made your mother do it for me and I'm not havin' her doin' it for you either. There's the clock. If ye divvent get theesel' up, ye'll be late for work. If you're late for work, ye'll get your pay docked. And if ye loss any pay, for any reason, ye'll get ne money out of this house… And if ye loss your job because you're ne damned good, ye'll be a bloody joiner whether ye like it or not… Understand?'

'Aye.'

'Are ye sure ye do?'

'Aye, I'm sure.'

'Now, ye won't need to get shaved yet, no matter how much ye might like to kid theesel', so –'

'I've already had one.'

'Aye… well… we won't argue about that. But see ye always get theesel' washed afore ye gan out of this house and always get theesel' washed as soon as ye get back. I don't ever want to come in or get up and find ye sittin' around in mucky clothes. Ye cannot help gettin' mucky at the pit but that's ne excuse for keepin' it on the way some do. There's a big difference between a workin' man covered in honest muck and an out-and-out dirty bugger.'

I had on my father's old clothes that my mother had laid out ready. He had finished with them and Mam had neatly patched and pressed them, and they looked and felt really champion. I was nearly the same size as my father so neither his jacket or his pants needed to be taken up very much, just a fraction at the cuffs and a bit at the turn-ups. When I could afford to buy some new Sunday clothes, I'd use my old Sunday clothes for work.

You could walk to Harton Colliery in fifteen minutes from our place but I was up there in less than ten. When I got to the gate I shouted my number through the time-office window in this gruff voice I'd been practising on the way up. 'One-five-three!' I shouted. That was the number I'd been given on the Saturday when I'd gone up to see Mr Cowell.

'All right, then. Steady on,' says the old feller inside. He looked a bit like a weasel. 'This is Harton Colliery not the barracks of the Durham Light Infantry. Round here we like to hear a pin drop... What's your name?'

'Tommy Turnbull.'

'Wait till I see now... Oh, yes... T-h-o-m-a-s T-u-r-n-b-i-l-l.'

'Turn-bull.'

'Oh, ye can spell as well, eh? I can see you're ganna be very useful around here.' He winked at the fellers standing behind me and handed me a little wooden board a few inches by a couple of inches. 'Write your name on that and then go over to Number Two Screen and give it to Mr Quick.'

I wrote my name on it with the bit of chalk I had in my pocket that my father had given me. You had to bring your own.

'And try not to bust his eardrums,' he shouted after me and got a bit of a laugh from some of the other fellers.

Jimmy Quick was Head Keeker. He was oldish and plump with a stern face. Most of the buttons had come off his waistcoat and you could see that one of his braces was tied with string. He pointed to a huge slow-moving conveyor belt with coal and stones spread all over and along it. There was a line of young lads and a few old men at each side picking stuff out and chucking it onto two other belts.

'Get yourself down on the end. They'll show ye what to do.'

I stood there looking at him.

'Well, what are ye waitin' for, lad?'

'I'm supposed to be gannin' down the pit.'

'Who told ye that?'

'Nebody. I just thought...'

'Ye divvent get paid for thinkin', lad. Not round here anyway. If ye want a job at this colliery, get yourself down there and quick about it.'

The conveyor belts were called 'screens' and the three of them moved along together. There was a splint screen on one side for splintered coal, a stone screen on the other, and the main coal screen in the middle. At the top end tipplers emptied out the tubs that came up from the pit shaft, into the jigging machines. The jiggers shook it up and sieved out most of the dust. Everything that was left came along on the screens. We stood at the sides picking out the stones and chucking them on their screen, and picking out the splint coal and chucking that on its screen. Apart from the old ones there were a number of fellers who were either crippled or had done their backs in down the pit. All of them were dead slow compared to the lads. Their hands reminded me of crabs' claws shooting out, so many of their fingers were missing.

'Howay, man!' Jimmy Quick would shout down at them from his platform up above, when they missed a stone or threw it on the wrong screen. All day long he stood there, hands on the iron rail, watching the screens coming on and on with their never-ending loads scattered all over the rattling steel plates. We were kept going all the time but it wasn't hard work and it certainly didn't require any brains. As everybody said, 'Even Baldwin could do it.'

We were allowed a break at eleven o'clock but we had to take it in turns because the screens had to be kept going all of the time. One lad was 'bottle warmer' and it was his job to heat your tea up five minutes before you were due off. He was supposed to know who was coming off when but he kept getting the times and fellers mixed up, so if it wasn't clay cold by the time you got it, it was stewed to hell. The only ones he didn't get wrong were the hardcases'. I think he was concentrating all his brainpower on getting theirs right and that's why the rest of us suffered.

Jimmy Quick was strict enough but to give him his due he tried to be fair. He had a little tattered old bible which he kept in his pocket and every spare minute he got he would have it out. He must have been long-sighted because he had a pair of wire spectacles that he would put on to read and then take off to look at the screens. Off and on they'd go all day and if he was carried away with what he was reading in the bible and there was suddenly a shout from the screens, he'd whip them off and they'd be hanging off his ear as he looked to see what was up.

Although he'd been at the pit a very long time, he wasn't keen on old-fashioned pit language at all. He wouldn't use any on you, not even if he was vexed and you wouldn't use any when you were talking to him. And he left it at that. He knew Matthew, Mark, Luke and John all pulling together couldn't have stopped swearing in that place. He didn't care for violence either but he was more inclined to give way on that than the other.

Some of the keekers – and Jim Grey was one of them – would walk around chucking their weight about all day. Jim Grey would think nothing of stotting a lump of coal off your nut just because you looked the wrong way. The others would usually only do it if you were cheeky. But they'd all had so much practice they hardly ever missed, so you had to watch yourself. You might be having a bit of a joke with the lad next to you and let a couple of stones go by and all of a sudden a stone would hit you on the back of the neck and your cap would go flying onto the screen and into the muck. It was better to let them hit you first time and get it off their chest because if you ducked and made them miss, they'd hit you next time for sure and it wouldn't be just with a piece the size of a tennis ball. It wasn't like a snowball fight. These stones went only one way. If you as much as looked as though you were going to throw one back, you'd have had one right between the eyes.

On the afternoon of my first day, when Jimmy had gone for a jimmy-riddle or something, somebody had put a banana skin at the bottom of his ladder, the one leading up to his 'spy tower' as we called it, for him to slip on. And no sooner was he back than he obliged. Down he went with such a clatter, spectacles, bible and all, that I thought he must have done himself an injury. But I was beginning to realise that these pit blokes were even tougher than I'd imagined because up he got without a word. He'd already made up his own mind who'd done it, because the minute he got to his feet he went straight for Joe Cullen. For a non-violent man he fetched him such a skelp around the lughole it's a wonder the lad's head didn't come off. Joe Cullen wasn't the guilty one as it happened but it was no use telling Jimmy Quick that. Jimmy had been put on his behind, somebody had got thumped for it, and that was the end of it.

It seemed to me that in this world 'justice' meant that somebody got punished. Whether they were guilty or not was another matter. It saved any further messing about and it served as a lesson to everybody else. That was definitely the way it had been at school and my father said it happened all the time in court. So I suppose there was no reason things were going to be any different here.

At the end of my first day I came home proud and black, probably blacker than anybody at Harton Colliery if not the whole of the Durham Coalfield. After eight hours of picking out sharp coals, rough stones and shale, of having muck jumping up at me every time somebody flung something that landed in front of me, I was covered in dust. Even so I still rubbed a bit more on my face just to make sure. I couldn't have anybody thinking I'd got myself a job at the Post Office or something. My hands and fingers were cut in a hundred places and they were a bit on the sore side but the dust had filled them in and there was no blood or anything. And I certainly wasn't going home complaining, not about anything.

My father had gone to work himself when I came in but my mother was waiting by the door.

'Well, son?' she says.

'Aye, it was all right, Mam,' I says. 'Grand. I'll be back there tomorrow.'

She just gave a sigh and went to put my dinner out. There was never any more said.

6

By the time I'd done nine months on the screens I'd seen and handled coal in every shape, size and form imaginable. I'd seen ugly stuff and beautiful stuff and all kinds in between because everything that came out of the pit came along the screens. Big coals were what they always wanted, big black lumps without any muck in it. And whether it was being sold for the fireplace or the furnace it had to be clean. Nobody wanted stuff that wouldn't burn properly or that would give off fumes or explode, especially not in the home.

Anything that wasn't wanted was called 'muck', whether it was big stones or tiny coals. But there was no machine that could sort it. A machine could riddle it and get rid of the dust but it couldn't recognise a strand of shale in a lump of coal, hit it with a hammer, dump the bit in the middle and pass on the two halves. It was tedious work. The novelty of picking out bits of coal and throwing them in one place, picking out bits of stone and muck and throwing them in another, wears off pretty quickly. It has nothing to do with picks and lamps and marras.

It looked as though Billy Oliver and the rest of them down the pit had forgotten me and that I'd be picking bits of splintered coal and muck off never-ending conveyor belts for the rest of my life. Then one day I was told to come out of it and get myself over to the Heapstead, which were the buildings at the pithead, 'the heap' everybody called it.

The work I was given to do at the heap wasn't what you would call labouring, not heavy work anyway. It was mainly just tidying up, sorting out boxes of screws and nails, sweeping the floor, cleaning shelves, and polishing the handles and knobs of the various gear, that sort of thing. Sometimes I got to oil and grease things, though more often it was taking filthy old oil and grease off. And sometimes I got to paint things, if they were hard to paint – like grids and bars and plates with lots of lettering and places you needed to be an acrobat to get at, places the painters had missed. Even then I had to take a lot more old paint off than I ever got to put new paint on.

It was much lonelier than being on the screens and sometimes after days of wire-brushing on my own with only the sandpapering to bring any variety, the screens seemed a great place. I'd forgotten the worst things about that job as I sat in a corner near the top of the shed in a freezing cold draught with a bit of sandpaper that I had to use until every last grain had been rubbed off. Now I could only remember the good things about it, like the jokes with the lads, the old fellers' tales about what it used to be like working in the pits in the last century and how they'd lost their different fingers, each had its own story. And of course the laughs when the keeker had stotted somebody and they had yelled out something funny.

I'd been at the heap about three months when the moment I'd been waiting for all my life came, though at first I didn't realise it. One of the gaffers at the heap got hold of six of us on the Friday afternoon. 'The boss's office for you lads. Five o'clock. On the dot.'

We finished at four so we just hung about waiting and wondering if we were going to be given the sack or a really big bollocking or what. Five o'clock was the time all the action happened at The Office and even if you'd been on shift and had finished hours ago, you'd either have to wait around or go home and come back. No business but coal business was done in Colliery time. Pitman business was done in 'pitman's time', his own time. Complaints about ill-treatment, underpayment, faulty equipment or bad conditions, all came into the category of pitman business.

We knew that the Government was intending to hand the mines back to the Coalowners now that the War was finished, the older fellers never stopped talking about it. And we knew that because they were making the Germans pay for the War in coal as well as in iron and steel and other things, the price of coal was bound to drop. That would mean less work and lower rates for us, and anybody who didn't like it would be told to pick up and get. There was talk of cutting the pay of every working man in the country, farm labourers' wages had already been chopped in half.

We also knew the Colliery always got rid of what they called 'trouble-makers' whenever they got the chance but we were just lads and hadn't been there any time at all. I hadn't said anything or done anything wrong and the other lads said the same thing. Anyway they wouldn't be wasting their time bringing the likes of us up here to give us a bollocking. The gaffer at the heap could manage that, no bother at all.

Suddenly there was a loud voice. It was the undermanager, the second most important man at the whole Colliery. 'Names! Call out your names! Quick! Biggest first… That's you, lad!'

'Watts, sir.'

'Billy Thompson, sir.'

'Albert Scott.'

'Douglas Lewis, sir.'

'Kiely, sir. Pat Kiely.'

'Tommy Turnbull, sir.'

'Right, the lot of you are going down the pit on Monday… Turnbull, you report to Mr Carter. Watson, you're with Mr Summers. Thompson, Mr Roche...'

We weren't getting the boot at all! We were going down!! We were going to be getting our own lamps and going down the Pit!!! I could hardly believe it! I thought I was going to be spending the rest of my life at bank sorting the coal and stuff that real miners hoyed up, or fiddling about at the heap. Instead I was going to be getting nearly fifteen shillings a week as a miner, a pitman. I could become a 'financial member' of the Durham Miners' Association if I wanted to. For half-a-crown entrance fee and sixpence a week, I could even get death benefit if I wanted. Seven pounds for me, the miner, five pounds for my wife if I had one, three pounds for a child between the ages of ten and fourteen, and a pound for any child under ten. All that, if I was over eighteen. If something happened to me before then my family would get four pounds. It was grand to know but I'd let it be for the time being. I hadn't even got started, I certainly wasn't planning on getting nobbled or anything yet. First I wanted to feel the money jingling in my pocket. I wasn't going to have it disappearing into a battered old baccy tin, the lid coming down and then taken away to God knows where. I wanted to spend it!

I couldn't wait to get home and tell Dad, I thought he'd be so proud.

'Well, I suppose you're happy now you've got what you've always wanted… ye stupid bugger.'

'Aye, I am. I think I've been there long enough now to start hewin' me own coals. I got fed up sortin' other people's long since.'

'Aye, and it won't be long afore ye'll be wishin' ye were back sortin' somebody else's. Because once ye gan down there... That's it… Ye'll stay down till you're finished… But it'll be a while yet afore you're hewin' coals, I'll tell ye that.'

'I'm fifteen next week, ye know.'

'Oh aye, I know. You're practically an ould man.'

Poor Mam never said a word, she just had this look on her face.

First thing on Monday morning I went to the lamp cabin and drew my lamp. It was a huge place and there were thousands of lamps in it and hundreds of fellers getting them. There were hewers, fillers, putters, the very best of men. And there I was, right amongst them. The lamp had already been tested and was already lit when I got it. It felt great in my hand! I also got my two tokens with the lamp number on. The lamp man was a feller called Ernie Woodcock. He hung one token up in the cabin and I shoved the other in my pants pocket. 'See ye divvent loss it, lad,' he says. 'Cos if ye do, ye'll have the whole pit lookin' for ye. And if they find ye alive, they'll murder ye.'

You kept the same lamp all the time and if you lost it you were fined one pound and a good bollocking. Ernie told me they once had a bloke called John Nelson who lost two in a week. He hadn't bothered to report the second one, he just walked out the pit and buggered off and joined the Army. Ernie said if he'd lost rifles at the same rate he lost lamps, they'd have shot him.

In the lift, which everybody called the 'cage' because that's all it was, there was supposed to be twenty fellers in the top half, and twenty in the bottom. But there was a good few more than that when I got in, up and down. And the roof was so low the bigger fellers had to turn their heads on their sides. There was a feller called a 'banksman' who looked after the cage at the top of the shaft and one called an 'onsetter' at the bottom. They looked after the cage and it was their job to lock you in and send you up or down, the same way they sent ponies, tools, equipment and everything else. The entrance to the shaft was just fastened with a hook even though there'd been many complaints about the number of men who'd gone down without the benefit of the cage. My father had told me the shaft was a deep one and to be very careful of it. 'Anybody who doesn't want to end up lookin' like a dog's dinner treats that thing with the greatest respect.'

As soon as everybody was in, the gate was slammed shut. The other fellers shuffled into place and then stood there quietly. I didn't want anybody to think I was scared so I stood in the middle, whistling, without holding on. All of a sudden, whoosh, ye bugger! It took off with such a clash my stomach felt as if it had been left on the roof. I grabbed out and held on tight. 'Whew!' I looked around. Although there were a few smiling faces, nobody said a word. Then I realised I was hanging on to this feller's jacket. Not that anybody could have fallen over, because we were packed in like sardines. He just grinned and I let go.

The cage was now getting up such a speed I thought the ropes must have snapped. It seemed to have gone out of control and kept tearing down and down, faster and faster. I didn't know whether the other fellers were just putting a brave face on it for my sake or whether this was normal. Suddenly it changed speed again and a few seconds later it had clanged to a stop. A great big sigh of relief came out of me like wind out of a bag, I couldn't help it. I could feel a stupid grin on my face and I couldn't get rid of it. I felt a bit light-headed and it was all I could do to not start giggling like a lunatic. I looked at the other fellers. They were still just standing smiling. One of them winked towards the bar. I pretended I wasn't in a hurry to get out and nodded to him to go first. Then the gate suddenly clashed open with such a bang I almost filled my pants, and everybody stepped out. Then I stepped out. I was now, at last, down the pit. A hundred and seventeen fathoms beneath the surface of the earth, according to my father. It wasn't as dark as I'd expected – quite well lit in fact – and big. It was a very big place, far bigger than I imagined it would be – and freezing. I thought it was supposed to be warm.

I asked somebody where I could find Mr Carter.

There were two seams being worked at Harton. One was the 'Hutton' and the other was the 'Bensham', and I'd been told on the Friday that I'd be working in Boldon Way on the Bensham. I was on foreshift which was from six o'clock in the morning till two o'clock in the afternoon, for the first week. And on backshift which was from two o'clock in the afternoon till nine o'clock at night, the next. And every Saturday morning I was on from four o'clock to eleven o'clock, the last hour to be worked in the timber yard.

Jack Carter was foreoverman in Boldon District and he was sitting in his cabin, writing in a big book. There was a little light hanging, just enough to see by.

'Are you Mr Carter?'

He was little and stout and had a very serious expression on his face.

'And who wants to know that?'

'Me.'

'And who might you be, if that's not an impertinent question?'

'Tommy Turnbull.'

'Tommy Turnbull, eh? Any relation to Jack Turnbull?'

'He's my father.'

'Ganna be a hewer like him one day, are ye?'

'Aye.'

'Well, well. I'll bet ye'll be a good 'un an' all… I'll tell ye what I'm ganna do with ye, Tommy. I'm ganna put ye with Jack Ditchburn. Jack'll show ye what to do and he'll see ne harm comes to ye. He'll be by any minute…There you are, what did I tell ye. Here he comes.'

A pair of white eyes came out of the dark of a low tunnel.

'New lad for ye, Jack. Jack Turnbull's lad.'

'Oh aye.'

He came right up to me.

'Are you a singer an' all?'

'Me? No.'

'Thank God for that. One singin' Turnbull's enough for any pit. Your father has a voice like a bloody battleship.'

'He never sings at home.'

'Ne wonder! The neighbours'd gan out of their minds, just like we do down here. Isn't that right, Jack?'

'He's some singer all right, Jack Turnbull.'

'We're away then.'

'Rightio. Keep an eye on the lad.'

'Right, Tommy,' Jack Ditchburn says to me. 'You just folly behind me and be careful ye divvent knock your lamp out. 'Cos if ye do, it's out till the end of your shift. And a shift's a long time in the dark.'

As I walked behind him the road got narrower and narrower and the roof got lower and lower, until we were both doubled up. It was getting darker and darker as well, and I had a real job keeping up with him. His light kept getting swallowed up and every now and again I'd lose him. If I looked at his lamp, I couldn't look at my own and I wouldn't see the bumps in the ceiling and the holes in the bottom. And if I looked at mine to see where I was going, I lost sight of his. When that happened I'd scramble along as fast as I could, banging my head and my back on the roof, and my shoulders, hands and elbows against the sides, in an effort to catch him up. Then when I did, I'd nearly knock him over.

'Keen to get there, are ye?' he'd say, not stopping but keeping on going in this funny stride he had with his head bent down and slightly on its side.

Where we were now it wasn't just dark, it was pitch black, the kind of black where you cannot see anything no matter how long your eyes take to get used to it. No back lane I'd ever been in or any place I'd ever seen had primed me for this, not even on the darkest night. To think my father had been coming down to this every day of his life... I wasn't scared but I was going to stick as close to Jack Ditchburn as the wart on the back of his neck, even if it meant nearly knocking myself senseless. He was a canny age and a fair bit bigger than I was yet he was going along like a mole. He didn't hang back one bit for me, at least it didn't seem to me that he did, and no time was being wasted getting to wherever it was we were going. Nobody at the pit ever got paid for travelling time, even if they had to crawl for five miles from the bottom of the shaft to where they were working. That was miner's time, I knew that. You only got paid from the time you got to your place of work and got started.

The tunnel we were going along which he called the 'roadway' obviously wasn't made for the convenience of any man. It was two tubs wide and not an inch higher, and it took us half an hour to get the mile and a half to the top of the stapple. This was a shaft that began down the mine and went further down still. It was as warm here as it had been cold before.

The 'chummins' were empty tubs that came in-bye from the main shaft, six at a time. They were hauled along the rails by a steel rope called an 'endless', and it was my job to 'lowse' them off, which meant uncoupling them and sending them down this other shaft, in twos. When they were filled with coal down below, another feller was coupling them up in sixes again and sending them out-bye to the main shaft. From there they were sent up and out to bank. Jack Ditchburn didn't hang around once he'd set me on.

'Can ye manage that all right then, Tommy? Cos' I have to be gannin'.'

Jack was the waggonwayman and it was his job to make sure all of the tubs went in and out of his district without any hold-up. And I was now one of his 'off-take lads'. Back and forward along the rollawayboard Jack went all day long. If any tubs got jammed or came off, he had to get them freed, back on and moving again as quickly as possible. He was paid by the number of full tubs that went to the shaft. If he didn't do his job properly, nobody else could do theirs. That's the way it is in the pit.

The roadways were for the men to get to the face, and for the tubs to bring out the coal. They got longer and longer as the face was worked farther and farther in. And the longer they got, the more important it was that they were kept open. The Harton Coal Company didn't want them blocked because it would slow the flow of their coal. And the men didn't want it either. Not only because the longer the tubs were blocked, the smaller their pay-packet would be but because every minute they were blocked put them in danger. The roadways, narrow and dark and winding though they were, were the only way out for everybody. Because it only took one man at any point on the line from the top of the shaft at bank, all the way to the face and back out at bank again, to slow things down or put a stop to everything, everybody would be on his back the minute there was any delay. So if you didn't keep your mind on your job, it wasn't only the overman or deputy you'd have to worry about. Although I was a dataller, which meant I only got paid by the day, I was now part of the system and pieceworkers at the face relied on me to do my job properly. At bank, on the screens or at the heap it wouldn't have mattered if I'd dropped down dead or thrown a fit, everything would have just carried on. Down here I could bring the whole pit to a halt. Well...just about.

Where I was now, there was no dinner break like there was at bank. I just had to grab a bit bait when I could on the job. The blokes at the face, stripped to their underpants, some with nothing on at all, would stop for neither nowt nor nobody. Get in their way and they'd run over you like a steamroller. They'd be hewing, filling and putting with a jam sandwich stuck in their mouths like a dog carrying a bone and dust, sweat, muck and jam would all go in together. It wasn't much better here. I'd already found that when you work at a pit, no matter how well your bait is wrapped or wherever you put it, it's full of dust even before you get it out of the paper. You had to eat it as it was and wash the grit and muck down with your water. I hadn't brought tea down here because there was no way to heat it up. Some blokes prefer cold tea to cold water but I don't. I'd rather wait till I got home and have a decent cup of hot.

When I got back to the shaft at the end of the shift after that first day down the pit, my back was like a butcher's shop. I'd jagged the back of my head, my shoulders and my spine so many times on the roof getting there, that I'd practically crawled all the way back. Nine months on the screens had made the skin on my hands like emery cloth, but not my knees. I must have left half a mile of skin behind.

Jack Carter came out of his little hut.

'All right, Tommy? Did ye enjoy yourself?'

'Aye.'

'Good lad. Now get yourself straight home and let your mother see you're still in one piece. Take my tip and have a good wash, eat your dinner up, and then gan straight to bed. Ye'll be stiff tomorrow but it'll wear off in a couple of days. Ye'll soon get used to it.'

'Right. Ta-ta, then.'

I'd been given no rules or regulations to read because there weren't any. Like everybody else I was going to have to rely on my own instincts, and most of all on the men I'd come to work amongst. And as I shuffled into the cage with them, black and dusty and tired and sore, I'd no fear on either account.

I'd been down the pit for just over a month and was entirely on my own in a place I'd never been before, when I knocked my lamp over and it went out. I was standing in for somebody that had injured himself and I'd only just come on. In the short time I'd had it I must admit I'd given my lamp rougher and rougher treatment every day and had never managed to put it out. I'd come to think you could do almost anything with them. Now I knew I'd just been lucky. I'd been sent to this place, which hadn't been used for a while because of an old roof fall, to clear the roadway. That's what the other feller had been doing when he happened the accident.

It couldn't be darker if you'd been born blind. All the years I'd dreamt about being down the pit and imagining what it would be like, I'd never for a second thought it would be this dark. It was one thing to sit with a few blokes and joke about the roof collapsing when you had light enough to see it was still up there. But it was a different matter altogether when you were on your own and it was pitch dark, when it was so quiet you could feel the slightest waft the air makes when a ventilating door moves somewhere, when you could hear the mice rustling your bait paper and the rats squealing and fighting like little mad dogs, when little bits of things were dropping down your neck and there was a splash somewhere as something fell into a puddle of muck, when something hit against your cheek and something tiny ran across your hand.

I wasn't scared of rats and mice, at least not when I could see where they were. It was the blacklocks I hated. Ugly, shiny black-backed buggers they were that never died. You could stamp on them, jump on them, squash their guts out, and still they'd crawl away. Their feelers would be reaching out even when their head was off and their body was squashed flat as a penny. I didn't want any of them buggers dropping down my neck. They're clumsy things at the best of times and they never seem to be able to find their way about properly. That's why they have feelers as long as boot laces. Even on the ground they'll start going one way, and then stop and go in another. It seems to me they should never have been given wings to fly with if they cannot make their minds up which way to go. There's another thing: one minute there doesn't seem to be a one, and the next they're all over the place. That's because they send scouts out and if you look hard enough you'll always see them. Creepy ones they are, with extra long feelers or whiskers. They know their business and don't mess about eating or anything. After that one's been out looking around, he'll usually disappear for a bit. Then before you know it they're coming out of every nook and cranny and swarming all over the place.

A lad of fifteen isn't as brave as a man of forty, not down a pit. He might think he is but he's not. And I knew that now... By, was I glad when the end of that shift came. Seven long dark hours I'd had to myself in total darkness trying to keep things off me, some of them alive, most of them probably just bits of muck, though I couldn't tell the difference. And all that time I'd been doing my work to the best of my ability, feeling for everything with my hands and feet. I knew when the gaffer came by with his lamp he'd sharp see what had been done and what hadn't, and putting my lamp out would be no excuse.

When I heard the heavenly sound of men's boots and the talking and laughing and I saw the little lights come swinging along, the relief was something I'd never be able to boast about.

'Put your light out, have ye, bonny lad?'

'I bet the lazy little bugger's been asleep.'

'If ye ask me, he's been playin with his little feller.'

'Is that right, ye dirty little beast?'

They must have seen the silly look on my face. I couldn't say anything.

'Howay, lad... That'll learn ye to be more careful next time.'

One thing I'd been dead right about was the men. And now I was one of them. I loved it when I was sent to work with a bunch of them. I didn't speak unless I was spoken to, because they still regarded me as a lad. In any case they would never give a straight answer. Apart from saying 'Hand's that' or 'Watch yoursel'!' they'd always be taking the mickey. But they were every bit as friendly a bunch of blokes as I always knew they would be, and from the time they started till the time they lowsed, they joked and cursed about everything and everybody nonstop. Every shift was the same, anywhere you went.

Long before I was fourteen and started the pit, I thought I knew every swearword there was. And then I came down here... Some of them used the most foul words for everything even for the most ordinary things, things they had no cause to get annoyed at. I think they'd reached the point where they couldn't help themselves. Unless they were really witty and some of them were that all right, they knew they couldn't rely on the rude words themselves to get a laugh, so what they would do was use so many they could hardly get the words out.

'Winston fuckin' Church-fuckin'-hill? That bastard should fuckin'-well have one of his own fuckin' cigars fuckin'-well shoved right up his fuckin' arse, hot fuckin' end out, so he fuckin'-well burns his fuckin' fingers when he tries to fuckin'-well pull the fucker out.' That would get a laugh, especially if the feller had buck teeth. 'Christ! Keep back! We should get fuckin' wet money for workin' with you, ye fuckin' slaverin' git!'

'The greatest fuckin' man who ever lived? I'll tell ye who the greatest fuckin' man who ever fuckin' lived was... Keir fuckin' Hardy, that's fuckin' who.'

You'd hear an Irish feller say 'He wasn't only a fuckin' saint, he was a fuckin' gentleman,' and somehow it seemed to carry more weight.

I don't know what these fellers were like at home with their families but I could imagine some of them who'd 'Fuck him!', 'Shite on it!' and 'Cunt!' all day long, would go back home at night and never say tweet in front of their own wives. Some fellers would only swear when they were angry, others had worked sixty years down a pit and never sworn at all.

Cursers or not, what they liked most of all was taking the piss out of each other, and nobody was spared, especially if they didn't like it. And anybody who was a bit thick got no mercy at all. Poor Sammy Ellis had a hell of a time. If a bunch of them had run out of cracks to make about each other and had been through all the politicians and lodge officials, and then they saw Sammy standing by, they'd immediately start on him. Or maybe there'd been an argument and you could have cut the air with a knife and nobody was speaking to anybody. After a bit you might hear 'Hey, Sammy. I hear your father sawed the legs off the couch to stop the dog gettin' underneath?'

One of the others would be listening and wouldn't be able to stop laughing. 'Clever idea, that,' this one would say. 'Hey, man. Why divvent ye do the same thing to the table afore he gets home from work one night? When he comes back and sees it he'll say "Nice work, son. The bloody dog'll never get under that."'

It was a good job Sammy was so good-natured because he was a very big bloke.

Some people seem to think miners are specially bred to go down holes as though they were Jack Russells or something, but pitmen are all shapes and sizes like anybody else, and there were some hacking big blokes at Harton. The Turnbulls were all like my father – short and thick-set – and I'm the same. But the Kellys were tall lads. Low seams – the kind my father was used to working in – where you crawled in, lay on your side with a pick and chipped away like a woodpecker all day, would have been hard for a really big feller. Not that it made any difference to the Colliery. Big fellers weren't put into high seams and little ones into low. If they didn't like where they were sent, they could do what they could always do, they could pick up and get.

The overman was the feller who did the 'ettling', telling the men what they had to do and how much they'd get paid for it. Some overmen had more say than others depending on how long they'd been there for, and he and the deputy might argue, especially if the deputy was a bit above himself. Sometimes one of them or both of them would argue with the waggonwayman or the weighman. But above them all was the under-manager, and then the manager, and nobody would argue with these fellers. They let their wishes be known and then it went right down the line. So although you might get on quite well with the deputy, if the overman had it in for you there was nothing the deputy could do about it. And if the manager had it in for you, more than likely you were out, no matter if the deputy and the overman sang your praises, which they'd never do. If you did something wrong or something the manager didn't like and somebody tried to stand up for you, that somebody had better watch out no matter who he was. Keekers, waggonwaymen, onsetters and the likes, no matter how long they'd been there, could get sacked like anybody else. A word or just a wave of the manager's hand was all it took. And if the manager told the Coal Company he wanted an overman or a deputy out, that man was out. The manager had absolute charge of the pit. And collieries and managers, like pits and pitmen, have very long memories.

If you wanted to make money in a pit, and everybody did, you went to the face if you could stick it. That's where the toughest and best men were, and that's where I wanted to be. Anywhere else you were just a labourer. My father was working at the face and he tried to get me there, but they wouldn't have it. They said they couldn't have a father and son working in the same place because of the danger. My father laughed at that. They didn't like situations that might be a bit too cosy, more like it, he said.

Pneumatic picks – what we called 'windy poms' – were coming in to replace hand hewing with picks. 'Divvent be in so much of a hurry,' my father would say. 'All the cutting will be done with machines afore long and they're ganna be needin' younger fellers like you to do it. These new German contraptions are ganna change everythin'. Durham collieries are ganna have to bring themselves up to scratch like the ones in Yorkshire and Nottingham...else they'll be out of business.'

Wait, wait, wait, was all I ever seemed to hear. There were plenty other jobs to be done at the face apart from coal-cutting. Filling and putting, for instance. No matter how the coal was cut it still had to be loaded into tubs and taken to bank. They still needed timbermen and drawers, gummers and stonemen. The last two might just be labourers but at least they worked at the face and were in the money. I think the reason was they thought I was too young, even though plenty men had hewed, filled and put when they were my age, and the collieries had been glad to have them. I was fit and I was strong and I was sure I could do any job on the face if they'd only give me the chance. But I'm not sure my father wanted me there yet and maybe he wasn't pushing as hard as he tried to make me think.

After a while I did manage to get a job at the kist which was farther in-bye, so at least I was going in the right direction. The 'kist' was the name given to the place where the deputy kept a big chest which had tools and first aid and things like that in it. The chest was called a 'kist' as well, and I suppose this is what gave the place its name. The various gaffers would meet here at the beginning of the shift to discuss how the work was going and anything that cropped up.

This particular place was like a railway junction and my job was to clip chummins coming from the shaft, off or on the main-and-tail, and send them whichever way they were wanted. The 'main-and-tail' was a pair of steel ropes used for drawing tubs instead of having a man push them or a pony pull them.

To send messages about how many tubs were wanted down this road or that, we used the 'rapper', which some fellers called a 'telephone' but it was more like Morse code. 'Moses' Cord' according to Farty Smith the feller who had the job before me. We rapped out signals that went up the line such as, one for 'stop', two for 'haul in-bye', five for 'tub off', eleven for 'ropes not to move'. Different places had different codes and woe betide you if you made a mistake and sent something the wrong way. But once you'd learnt it and knew what you were doing, it was dead easy. So easy in fact that it was boring especially on days when you wouldn't see a soul from one shift to the next. If the gaffers had had a meeting they'd have done whatever business they had to, and gone. Nobody got paid for doing nowt, they told you that all the time. I had to stay there though, even if in between sending three tubs here or four tubs there, there were long gaps when I had nothing to do.

At such times I'd get out a Sexton Blake or maybe a western that I'd borrowed off Uncle Jim and have a bit read. The light from my miner's lamp was very dim, the pages would usually be worn, and I was a slow reader in any case, so one book would last me a very long time.

Sometimes I'd just sit and polish my lamp with a bit of paper I'd picked up off the floor and watch the rats. If you kept dead still they'd sit up like a dog begging and wash their faces with their paws. Then maybe I'd chuck a stone and watch them scarper. A couple of minutes later they'd be back again, bold as brass. Even the mice were as cheeky as hell. You sometimes hear people say that wherever you see mice you'll never see a rat because the smell of a mouse keeps a rat away. All I have to say is, they should go down a pit. What's a rat if it isn't just a big mouse? They eat the same things, they both like the dark, and they both live in filth. And if one or the other of them dies, their pals will be at them in no time. They'll knock back fur, tail, the lot. All they'll leave is the two front teeth. You might never see a mouse eating a rat but that doesn't mean they don't. They certainly eat each other no bother. And rats will eat anything the minute it stops moving, sometimes before. I'd been warned about blackdamp, the gas that lies along the ground and can put your lamp out, you as well if you're not quick about it. But it wasn't the gas that put me off lying down. There was no fear of any overman finding me having a kip on the floor.

What attracted vermin down the pit in the first place nobody seemed to know. It couldn't have been the men's bait because they left damned little, and the tiny bits of bread and crumbs that fell to the ground couldn't have been any more than a little treat. It was only the odd silly fool that liked them and would give the different ones names, that would deliberately feed them. Most people, if they were off their grub for any reason and couldn't finish their bait, would either give it to somebody else or give it to a pony if one was nearby. Failing that, it went back to bank and got hoyed down for the starlings.

The thing that attracted them down, in my opinion, was the shit. They probably got something out of the pee as well. It had to be. It was certainly the shit that attracted the flies and beetles.

There were no toilets of any kind down the pit and there was no particular place for you to go except 'around the corner'. There was the goaf, there was plenty space in there and you could be pretty sure you wouldn't be interrupted. But that was because the goaf was one of the most dangerous places in the pit. The goaf was the place that was left behind when the coal and stones had been taken away and the face had moved further in, and all the props had then been taken out to use somewhere else. So what roof the goaf had was entirely unsupported. It fell when and where it felt like it, without any warning, into piles shaped like huge bells. It was a hell of a place to be, with or without a light, and if you were so shy you had to get away from everybody and went in, you took your life in with you. The sides of the goaf were packed with the waste that came from the face, and from the caunch when the roadway had been heightened. It was a place for muck, not for man nor beast.

Most blokes just went a bit away from where they were working, and because of it the smell could be pretty bad in some places, especially inbye where it was so warm. Sometimes you could get something on your foot and carry it around with you all day, no matter how much dust and grit you stamped on. And if you were really unlucky you could carry it all the way home. With thousands of men down there twenty-four hours a day there must have been tons of it.

After I'd been working at the kist for a while I was sent to the bottom of the stapple to work for Billy Winter, doing the same job of coupling and uncoupling tubs. And I'd only been there three days when a runaway tub ran over my foot. The first wheel went clean over but the next one stopped right on the top. Could I hell get the damned thing off! No matter what I tried, it wouldn't budge. My foot was acting like a chock and the tub seemed perfectly happy to stay where it was. The blood was seeping out between the lace-holes of my boot, and the more I shoved the more it squelched. The wheels were made of solid iron and they never moved easily anyway, not when you wanted them to. Even along the track you always had to heave and shove before they'd take it into their heads to get going. Then you'd have a hell of a job stopping the buggers, especially if there was any kind of slope. Everybody said pit ponies had a mind of their own, and maybe they should, I couldn't see anything wrong with that. But tubs are a different matter altogether. Yet anybody who has worked with them day in day out, pleading with them and cursing at them, will tell you they can be as contrary as any pony.

Pushing and pulling the tub was just making things worse for my foot, and I realised I was going to need somebody to give me a hand. There wasn't any signal that I knew for 'tub-on-me-flamin'-foot', and in any case I couldn't reach the rapper, so either somebody was going to come along to see what the hold-up was if they were waiting on tubs, or I was going to have to hang on till the end of the shift when the men would be by. In the meantime I was going to be praying that no more tubs would be coming down the line. Even though they might knock this bugger off, before I'd be able to get my foot away the others would likely be over it. The thought of half a dozen more going over nearly made me sick. There was nothing else I could do except pray. I couldn't even sit down, I was having to hang onto the tub to keep myself up even though I knew my own weight was making it press down harder on my foot.

Whether it was the prayers or just good luck I don't know but I'd been like that for about half an hour when I heard footsteps. Out of the dark comes this tall lanky feller I'd never seen before, chewing a bit of string. He took one look and said 'If God had wanted ye to have flat feet, he'd've made ye a penguin, not a silly bugger... Move yoursel' round a bit so I can get under it. We'll sharp have the bugger off.'

For quarter of an hour he heaved and pulled the tub until his nose bled from the effort. All the time he was cursing and swearing.

'Come up, ye bastard! Come fuckin' up!!!'

At last he made it, and I'd have to say it was a bloody sight more painful coming off than going on. A little yelp like a puppy dog came out of me, I couldn't help it.

'I'm sorry I took so long about it, son,' he said, wiping his face with his arm. 'Can ye walk, d'ye think?'

'Aye, I think so.'

'Hadaway and get it seen to, then. I've got to look for my cap.'

'What about the tubs? I'm supposed to –'

'Divvent worry about them. I'll get hold of one of the gaffers as soon I find my cap.'

Both his hands were streaming with blood, and the skin was off one side of his face where he'd been pressing himself against the side of the tub to try to take the weight off my foot.

As long as you could get out of the pit by yourself it was counted a minor accident. 'Ye can get down to Dr Marks's without the barrow, can ye?' the feller in the first-aid hut had said. If they took you in the wheelbarrow it meant another man's time, and it made it look more serious for the record. If there was any way you could get down to Marks's on your own, that's the way you went.

Dr Marks was the Colliery doctor and he knew which side his bread was buttered on. He didn't clean my foot or anything, he didn't even give me a hand to get the boot off. All he did was hand me a knife. But I wasn't going to use that, there was too much wear in them yet. 'Come on, hurry up,' he kept saying. 'I haven't got all day.'

When I got the boot off, and it was no treat, all he did was poke it with his finger. 'It's not as bad as it looks,' he says. 'Go home and put a clooty bag on it, and see me in a week's time.'

A clooty bag was a flour bag filled with hot bran that you clagged on and tied with strips of rag, it was a kind of poultice that was used for all sorts of things.

The first thing I did when I got home was give my foot a good wash under the tap.

'Let me do it, Tommy,' Mam said. 'Sit yourself down, pet. Give it a rest a bit while I fill the bowl.'

But being the stubborn feller I am, I wouldn't let her, and I hopped down the yard to the tap with her hanging on to me pleading 'Please, Tommy. Let me do it. I'm your mother'.

If getting the boot off and on at Marks's, and back off again here had been painful, cold water gushing on it was no better at all. And it wasn't until I'd sat down and Mam had begun to dress it with her warm gentle hands, that I could see an end to it. She was tut-tutting about the pit and about Marks and whistling through her teeth all the time. Whenever she looked up there were tears in her eyes, and I knew she was feeling the pain every bit as much as I was. It was impossible to tell if there were any bones broken but there didn't seem to be any really deep cuts, and there wasn't a doctor or a nurse in the whole world who could have done more to get it on the road to healing. Even when my mother fussed she never irritated you, she was always so tender.

It wasn't until I got to bed that night that I knew what pain really was, when even the bedclothes felt like a ton weight. From the time it first happened I'd had other things on my mind, like how to get the flaming tub off, what a miserable bugger he was in First-Aid and what a sod Marks was. Now I was in bed I had nothing else to think about except how bloody sore it was.

Next morning my foot was up like a big black pudding and I couldn't get my sock on. When I put my boot beside it, it was impossible to see how that foot would ever again go inside that boot. It would need a kit-bag. And because I wasn't used to having a foot this size I kept knocking it against anything and everything. What with chair legs, table legs, the side of the door and my other foot, there didn't seem to more than six inches of space anywhere. Each one brought tears to my eyes and every time I cursed myself more and more for being so damned clumsy and for being so stupid as to ever have let it happen in the first place..

A penny a week was kept off your pay for the Colliery doctor and another penny a week for the lodge doctor. Dr McHaffie was the lodge doctor and it was a toss-up between him and Marks who was the worst. Because Marks was the Coalowners' man and McHaffie supposedly ours, it was up to the two of them to fight it out how much compensation you got. That is if it was a question of getting anything at all. But nobody expected any blood to be shed and in any case everybody knew Marks had the final word. If Marks had said you were fit for work and you hadn't gone back, you'd have been sacked even if McHaffie had given you a certificate saying you were dying on your feet. We all knew it was just a game with them and that they couldn't have cared less one way or another as long as each of them got his salary. Marks took a dim view of any injury caused by what he called 'criminal carelessness', even though everybody knows that all accidents are due to carelessness on somebody's part, maybe several people's.

I knew I wouldn't get a bean out of the Colliery, and I couldn't draw anything from the lodge sick pay fund because I hadn't joined it yet, so it was a good job my father was bringing in a hewer's wage. Not that he was happy about it at all. 'Maybe ye cannot help havin' an accident. Nebody can. But at least ye can pay the few coppers it costs to cover yourself like anybody else. I'll keep ye till you're able to gan back. But when ye do, see ye join the sick fund straightaway... And divvent be such a little tight-arse!'

If ever you were off work you could always find somebody to knock about with. Some lads would be out of work because they'd been laid off, others could never get a proper job because there was something wrong with them. If it was wet we'd play nap or brag in somebody's washhouse, a halfpenny a game and owe each other. I was a working man now so I wouldn't waste my time playing anything for nowt any more. I didn't care what game we played as long as somebody coughed up, even if you had to wait months for it.

One day after I'd been off work for four or five days we were playing football in the back lane and I was in goal, when who should come by but Marks.

'I'll see you in my office first thing tomorrow morning, Turnbull,' he says. There was no 'How do you do, is your foot getting better?' or anything like it.

Next day I went to see him.

'I think I can guess what you're thinkin', I says as he's examining my foot, 'but the truth is I was just tryin' it out. And I'm sorry to have to report that it's not quite right yet. I was only playin' in goal. I wasn't doin' any of the kickin'.' It was the truth as well. I was fed up being off. I wanted my foot right so I could get back to the pit and earn some money. I was getting more in debt than ever playing cards with the kind of cheating buggers I played with.

'Is that so?' he says. 'Well you can just get yourself back to the Colliery and "try it out", as you put it, there.'

'It's still sore when I put any weight on it.'

'That's because there are a few small bones broken. But you're young and strong, they'll mend in no time.' He had his hand between my shoulder blades and was pushing me out the room.

'Will they mend all right down the pit, then?'

'They'll mend as well down there as anywhere. You're not a ballet dancer, you're a coalminer. Now be off and don't waste any more of my time... Or your employer's.'

That was the end of that little holiday. I reported for work on the Monday like he told me to.

That week away from the pit was the longest I'd been away since I started. The lads were all right for a day or two but after that you soon got fed up with them. They were quite happy to lark about down the beach and mess about around the market and tell corny jokes, but I was used to something else now. I missed the sound of real men's voices, of pitmen arguing the toss about politics and pigeons, football and philosophy, women and whippets, religion and racing, ferrets and beer. And they didn't only talk. There were those who could recite things like 'Ned Haak's Men' which was about the battle of Waterloo and there were those who could recite poetry. One feller was called 'Two Williams' because he was always reciting William Blake or William Wordsworth. Or was it William Shakespeare? At times maybe something had happened and the machines had stopped running, or you were somewhere away from the main part of the pit and somebody had said something that had made everybody go quiet. Then all of a sudden you'd hear this big deep voice of Two Williams:

> Ti-ger, ti-ger, bur-ning bri-ght
> In the for-ests of the ni-ght.
> What im-mortal hand or eye,
> Could weave thy fear-ful sym-me-try.

Nobody would say a word because it was so powerful and some fellers were pretty superstitious. Then somebody would laugh and break the spell and in no time everybody would be laughing. There were those who specialised in the rude stuff and they would take something that was popular in the music halls and change a word or two to fit somebody we all knew, nearly always one of the gaffers at the Colliery or somebody in Parliament. Some of the things they said would be pretty bad but damned funny, sometimes so funny you'd nearly choke yourself laughing. I never knew whether it was a sin for a Catholic to laugh at things like that, particularly if they were said by a Protestant, though

I never raised the matter at Confession. In any case there was no way I could ever have stopped it or helped hearing it. But if I was to be damned for laughing, at least I'd be in good company.

Two fellers had a little act where one would pretend he was playing the trombone with all the arm movements and everything, and the other would pretend he was staggering around with one of those great big tuba things and both of them would be farting their heads off the whole time. Farty Smith was one of them, and the smell after the two of them had done one of their numbers would have everybody getting up and waving their hands to waft it away.

'Poaaarrgh! Bugger off, ye stinkin' bloody skunks! Talk about deadly gases! Does your lass not know how to cook owt but fried dogshit and boiled turnip?'

'Why aye, man,' another voice would come. 'She's great with beans as well.'

'Aye, and peas and cabbage.'

'Fu-ckin' he-ll…! Je-sus! Get out of it, ye fuckin' pigs!'

But they weren't all like these. There were fellers like Holy Jos as well. His real name was 'Josiah' but I never heard him called anything other than 'Holy Jos', even the overmen called him it. Jos would never stand up and start preaching when Farty and his pal were having one of their sessions or when the fellers were effing and blinding about something. He knew that wasn't the time and that they'd have quick as a flash turned on him if he'd tried to spoil the fun. At those times he just turned away and got on with his job and I suppose prayed for their souls. You could tell he was listening because he'd be shaking his head in disgust. How he could manage not to laugh was beyond me. You didn't need a sense of humour to see how funny they could be, even though they were absolutely bloody filthy at times. Jos usually spouted when something bad had happened to somebody. He'd then get his little bible out of his pocket and start reading chapter and verse and making a moral out of it. Some fellers would be mollified by it, others would say 'For God's sake, shut ya face, will ye!' A lot of the men went around with no clothes on at all when it was warm but not Holy Jos. He was a stoneman and he was a hard worker but he was always what you'd call 'properly dressed'. He said it was enough we had to work like horses without going around looking like them as well.

It might seem a funny thing but there were some lovely whistlers as well, fellers who could hold their own with any flute. They could whistle church music, carols for you to sing along to if it was Christmas, Irish songs, songs from the War, anything. Certain ones competed with each other to do bird songs and one or two could warble better than any canary I ever heard. I wasn't an expert on different kinds of birds and their songs but I fancy they made some of them up, especially the ones they said were 'tropical' ones. Any bird I ever knew sang exactly the same way day in, day out. Every time you heard these fellers' birds, in particular their 'rare' ones or ones that were now supposed to be 'extinct', they'd added a bit more to it, maybe an extra long trill that sounded more like a train whistle. I don't know what they took the rest of us for, they must have thought we were bloody daft.

Best of all were the singers, they were everybody's favourites. The other stuff could be entertaining for a while and there was no denying you got a good laugh out of it. After a while you got tired of it though and sometimes when the language had got as bad as it was possible to get, and there'd been so much of it you felt you couldn't take any more, everybody had to shut up for a while until the air cleared.

But nobody got tired of listening to somebody who could really sing. Because of Dad's and Uncle Jim's terrible voices, I'd always thought the pit must do something to your voice. When I went down I found this wasn't the case at all and I've never heard anybody on the wireless or anywhere sing better or sweeter than some of the fellers I worked with in the pit. Sometimes I've walked two or three miles underground in the dark and dirty bowels of the earth; I've been on my own, not a soul to be seen, and the only sound has been my own footsteps; it's been pitch black, deadly quiet and still. And then I've turned a corner, seen a tiny little light in the distance and heard a voice like John McCormack singing 'I'll take you home again, Kathleen', and a lump has come into my throat. Like as not the same feller hadn't seen a soul for hours, he'd just been singing to himself. Even fellers that had been arguing fit to kill each other would stop and listen when somebody with a voice like that started singing.

Good though these things were and they certainly made life down the pit much better than it would otherwise have been, the most important thing to me was the men themselves. Many of them like me had no gift for amusing people or for getting into a chalk ring with another man and trading blow for blow. You could be the greatest singer or sportsman that ever lived but it was only what you were like as a marra that was of any real consequence. Not how big or small you were, how long you'd been down the pit or what your religion was if you had one. The fact that you were a pitman and they were pitmen, was all that mattered. And I'm not just talking about your best pal or the fellers you worked with, I mean everybody. If ever you were in a spot of bother and a bunch of fellers came by, they'd always stop and help you even though they'd finished their shift and were on their way out. They might be tired and grumpy or not feeling the best but that would never stop them helping you out. None of them would ever pass by anybody who was in trouble even if they didn't like the bloke. They'd just do what they had to do and no more than that and then be on their way, and they wouldn't want any thanks for it. This isn't saying a miner is a saint – you'd need your head examined for saying that. They can be unforgiving especially about things like blacklegging or going back on your word. They're very slow to give praise wherever it's due, and most of them are as awkward as hell. I suppose these things would apply to me just the same.

Fighting wasn't allowed down the pit, so everybody knew they could afford to let their tongues rip and the worst they'd get would be a mouthful back. But sometimes two of them would get really het up and wouldn't be able to settle the matter with words, in which case they'd arrange to fight it out after lowse. There'd never be any shortage of seconds, referees, trainers or timekeepers and in no time the whole pit would know about it as word went from district to district faster than fire.

The whole place would be looking forward to the scrap and there couldn't have been more excitement if it had been a contest for the championship of the world. Bets would be laid and odds changing right through the shift as different bits of information about one or the other came to light. This one beat so-and-so but he had a bit of a gammy knee. The other one was a really dirty fighter but he was slow off the mark. So when the time came even if the two of them had cooled off a bit, they'd have no choice but to go through with it. To have backed down at this stage would have cost them a lot more than a good hiding. The last thing anybody wanted was some do-gooder spoilsport trying to patch things up, somebody saying 'Come on, lads, why don't you just shake hands? Nobody's perfect in this world.' There was plenty of time for that stuff when the fight was over.

When the shift ended and the crowd poured out of the Colliery gates nearly going crazy with excitement, everybody would pile down the nearest back lane and there'd be a hell of a lot of shouting and yelling and pushing and shoving.

'Here, man! This'll do! What do they want to gan up there for?'

'I'm buggered if I know. Have we got a fight or haven't we, is what I want to know.'

'I'll bet ye owt ye like they call it off.'

'They'd better bloody not or I'll get in there meself and kick the shit out o' the two of them!'

There'd be a lot of messing around, drawing of lines and rules made, before the two of them stripped down. Then a few more, as self-appointed ones started laying the law down to try and make themselves look big.

'Get on with it, ye bloody whoors!' an Irish voice would shout.

By this time ordinary people would be out of their houses and kids would be running up from all over. 'The pitmen are at it! They're havin' a fight at the back of Lemon Street! Howay, man! Hurry up or ye'll miss it!'

All of a sudden there'd be a crack of bone against bone and a groan would go up from the crowd as they imagined how that must have felt. Even if you couldn't see, you could tell from the sounds the crowd made, how bad somebody had been hit and where. There'd then be a deadly pause as the feller who'd just got whacked, got over the shock that he'd actually been hit that hard, especially if he wasn't a fighting man by nature.

'You bastard! You bloody bastard!!'

Right! Now it was for reals. Too late to make a full apology now. Now the breathing would be heavy as the one who'd been hit narrowed his eyes and tried to look the other one to death. But that wouldn't work, certainly not on the crowd. It was going to take more than a pair of red eyes ringed with coal dust and a bad stare. 'Gan on, hit him!' the crowd would yell. Neither would know who the crowd were shouting at and they'd both throw a punch at the same time. Then there'd be the most sickening sound as the worst of all possible things happened and two fists clashed head on, knuckle to knuckle. Some of the crowd would turn their heads away with the imagined pain of it. Nobody could see or hear something like that without wincing. But they'd soon turn back again.

After that sickener the two would decide to wrestle for a while, probably until the feeling came back into their fists and you'd hear a lot of scuffling and sparks as the boots hit the cobbles, followed by a thud as the two of them hit the ground locked together. Everybody would be shouting for them to get up and fight properly so they could see what was going on. But it would be a lot more comfortable being hugged and sat on than having another whack on the fist like the last one. It must have been like punching a tree trunk and wouldn't have been forgotten in a hurry. They'd now be rolling over and over and the crowd would be making way for them. All of a sudden the two faces covered with more snot than blood would be right at your feet and they'd now be looking more determined than angry.

'All right! Break it up… Come on… On your feet, the two of ye.' A couple of older blokes who were always at the centre of these things had now taken over. 'Now, look... If yous've had enough and ye just want to shake hands and gan home, do it. If ye haven't, then for Christ's sake get on with it! Any more rolling around like a couple o' kids and it's null and void... a draw. This is gettin' to be like a pantomime.'

That would do the trick and the two of them would set to smartly, sparring and getting in a few good blows to the ear, the chest and the guts. This was more like it! Strings of blood and slaver were being sent flying and there was very little coal dust left on their faces now except for a bit inside the ears and around the nose. The rest of us would be cheering on whoever we wanted to win, and yelling and shouting at the other to try and put him off, calling him a dirty fouler and a pansy at the same time. Now it had really got going there'd be some pretty rough all-in stuff and they'd go at it hammer and tong. Neither would be the one to pack in but you knew it couldn't last much longer. Eventually one of the older fellers would have to step in between them and say 'That's enough, lads. Ye've both put up a good fight… Now shake hands, the two of ye... Come on, you an' all… That's right. Now get yourselves home and get cleaned up.'

Nobody could quibble with that and the crowd would give them a cheer, even though there was always a few that would have been satisfied with nothing less than murder.

They never used anything but their hands and feet in fights like these and nobody ever got badly hurt, although noses would sometimes be broken, teeth knocked out, thumbs dislocated, thick ears given, and there'd be some very black eyes. By the next day both of them would have thought they'd won and they'd usually have got over the quarrel whatever it was. It could easily have been their own marra they were fighting with, maybe over something one or the other had said in joke about the other's wife that hadn't been well taken. Arguments with a marra had to be sorted out one way or the other. You couldn't let bad feeling go on for long.

7

At midnight on the 31st of March, 1921 the gates of Harton Colliery and every other colliery in the country were closed and padlocked by the Coalowners. We, the coalminers, the employees, had been locked out. The reason the gates were locked wasn't because it was a holiday. There was no such thing in the life of a coalminer. It wasn't because the Colliery was being modernised or fitted with anything to make it a safer place to work in. Coalowners didn't believe in spending money on things like that. And it wasn't because we'd refused to work or threatened the owners or their property. Nobody even pretended it was any of these things.

The sole reason for locking us out was because this was the way the Coalowners like the Duke of Northumberland, Lord Londonderry and the Bishop of Durham, always did business with their employees, at least those that worked in their pits. This was the way they negotiated. When the last shift before midnight had finished, all the men had been hustled out of the pit, off the Colliery property and out of the gates. And no more shifts started. The gates had then been locked by the manager, a notice of the new rates of pay and conditions put up and the whole place surrounded by police.

The act of locking the gates meant that every miner who worked there, no matter for how long, no matter how desperate his financial or domestic circumstances might be, was sacked as from that minute. There was no point in locking everybody out and sacking them if all you wanted to say was that their wages were going to be increased or that their working conditions were going to be improved. Nobody was going to need a couple of months to think that over.

This notice was to say that wages were being reduced, that working conditions were going to be harder and that the working day was going to be longer. If we agreed to work under such a contract, we could apply to the management and our applications would be considered. Troublemakers of course would not be taken back. A 'troublemaker' was somebody who complained a lot, somebody who stirred things up, somebody who got 'involved in politics'. There was a black list with these fellers' names on it that covered every pit in the country, which the Coalowners passed on to their managers. So if you went up to the office at your Colliery and said you wanted to come back and that you'd agree to all the new terms and they told you to beat it, you could bet your life your name was on the list. If this was the case you might as well pack up and go to Australia because you were never going to get a job in this country as long as you lived, certainly not in the coal mines. If you hadn't the money or you couldn't go because one of your kids were sick or something, there was always the Workhouse.

During the War when the Government had taken over the pits, it had suited the miners because they wanted the pits nationalised. This way wages and working conditions could be state controlled. But as soon as the War was over the Coalowners wanted them back again, and the Government wanted rid of them. Instead of demand for coal shooting up because of all the rebuilding that was supposed to be done, it had dropped drastically. One of the reasons was the Germans were being made to pay for the War with coal as well as iron and steel. So the price had dropped. To make matters worse, cheap imports of it were coming from America, Japan and other places.

The way Coalowners and every other big British manufacturer dealt with the problem of competition was by decreasing the wages of their workers and increasing their working hours. Anything else seemed beyond them. My father said Britain had learnt nothing from the War and that it couldn't learn anything from anybody because the ones in charge were too bloody vain. The minute it was over they'd gone straight back to their old ways: out-of-date methods, little regard for the safety of those who worked for them, no responsibility for the injuries and disabilities they suffered, and wages that would guarantee their poverty and ignorance, was what miners came back from the trenches to. All Lloyd George's promises about rebuilding and everything else turned out to be a load of Welsh blarney. The new jobs that had been promised amounted to no more than going around selling bootlaces and drawing pictures on the pavement – that's if they could scrape up enough to buy their own laces and chalk – because the Government gave them nowt.

Before the War was even over the Coalowners had let it be known what they intended to do. They were going to have nothing to do with unions and they alone would decide what the wages and conditions would be in their industry. And they invited heads of the other big industries to follow their lead and join them in their fight against 'slump and socialism'. When the miners heard about it, they voted to strike. The Government were terrified of revolution because of what had happened in Russia – British pitmen had already protested about British troops being used there. So they appointed a Royal Commission to look into the state of the coal industry and the Durham Miners Association leader Peter Lee persuaded pitmen everywhere to hang fire and see what came of it. Chief Justice Sankey headed the Commission and he very quickly recommended shorter hours for all underground workers, increased wages, improvements in safety and Government regulation of the pits.

Although the Government had pretty much accepted Sankey's recommendations, as we did, the Coalowners weren't having any of it. They had demanded their pits back and the Government had given in without any fuss. A date had been set for the hand-over and all parties told to prepare for it. Then without giving any notice whatsoever to us or our unions, Lloyd George handed them back to the Coalowners, lock stock and barrel, three months ahead of the date he himself had set. Knowing there'd be trouble, he called out 'Butcher' McCready the man who started the 'Black and Tans'. Regular troops, reservists and troops not yet demobbed because of the supposed threat of revolution were camped in coalfields all over the country. A bunch of Cabinet Ministers led by Winston Churchill and including Neville Chamberlain and several senior civil servants drew up an 'Emergency' plan that included volunteers and police 'specials' besides the normal police and the Army.

That's how we came to be locked out.

The notice told us that at Harton our wages were being just about halved and that 'all rights and privileges' – whatever those things were – were being 'suspended indefinitely'. My father, who had been averaging £3 18s 10¾d a week before the lockout, was now going to be on £2 1s 2¼d. Now that I was sixteen, mine was going to be 10s 3½d. The Coalowners, who belonged to a very powerful national federation of their own, refused to recognize ours. They refused to make any national agreements with us and they insisted that every coal company draw up its own contract with its own miners. This way they would remain united and strong and we would be left bickering amongst ourselves, pit against pit. At least that was the idea.

In the year previous the Communist Party of Great Britain had been formed. It had nothing at all to do with us but to hear Lloyd George and the Coalowners you'd think it was a pitman's club. Very few miners were communists, we were too reserved in our outlook and too fixed in our ways. We regarded ourselves as English as anybody and we cared about our country as much as anybody else. But that didn't stop Lloyd George jailing our leaders for what he called 'treason', and bringing in the Emergency Powers Act. This was a law that was supposed to 'safeguard the means of life', and it covered the 'supply of food, water, fuel, light and locomotion', which of course meant everything. Churchill and Birkenhead had been pushing for this for a long time, they thought an Emergency Powers Act should always be in force.

Before the War the railway and transport workers' unions had joined up with the miners' federation and formed what was called the 'Triple Alliance' and their members said they were now ready to come out on strike to support us. By now every working man in the country knew his employers were just waiting for the chance to reduce his wages and that if the Coalowners helped by the Government managed to beat down a million miners, it would only be a matter of time before they beat down everybody else. The leaders of the Triple Alliance decided it was time to show the employers and the Government that they had clout of their own and that they weren't simply going to lie down and take anything and everything that was handed out to them.

The strike was planned for Friday, the 15th of April and we were all sure it would force the Government to make the Coalowners end the lockout and treat their miners like human beings. But at the last minute J. H. Thomas, the leader of the railway unions and head of the Alliance, backed down. We were shattered. All the workers were. The first time the Alliance had been asked to help, their first chance to do something that would have benefited all working men – be they miners, railwaymen or anybody else – and it had given in. Thomas was always more a politician than a trade unionist, more for himself than for those he was supposed to represent, and he was acting in nobody's interests but his own when he called the strike off. He thought the Alliance would mean he'd have more power, that he could interfere in the miners' and other unions as well as his own. He thought of himself as a kind of king of all the unions.

But that wasn't the way the Alliance was supposed to work. Coalminers, dockers, railwaymen and the rest had enough of a battle as it was, getting their own members to agree on things, without having somebody who knew absolutely nothing about their problems poking his nose in. When Thomas had started interfering in the affairs of the coalminers' unions, he'd been told to mind his own bloody business. And he hadn't liked it. Thomas was also an MP and in politics a man's vanity is reason enough for causing thousands of people to suffer, never mind his greed.

Even though it was a lockout and not a strike we were denied any kind of relief and all we had to live on was what we could get from our own lodges. In our case it was ten shillings a week.

We'd done nothing, yet in Parliament and in the daily papers we were called 'communists', 'anarchists', 'traitors' and 'robbers'. We were described as being 'ignorant', 'filthy' and 'greedy'. The Daily Herald was the only national paper that supported us. The Newcastle Journal, with its letters from Coalowners like Barrass and Pease saying we should be made to work longer hours because we had nothing better to do with our time, and that pubs and picture houses should be closed because that's the only way we'd spend it if we got the chance, was typical.

For thirteen long weeks we stuck it out. Labour councils opened soup kitchens, local shops gave food and other necessities on tick – especially the CWS – and lodges organised sporting matches, raffles, concerts and other things to raise money. But it couldn't last. There was a limit to how much charity you could expect from ordinary working people buying tickets they couldn't really afford for entertainment they didn't really want. And little corner shops nigh on their own beam ends couldn't go on giving out credit when they couldn't get it themselves.

By July it was all over. My father and me were able to go back but many good men weren't. 'Ringleaders and agitators' was what the papers called them. Before the List they could have moved to another pit in the Midlands or even Scotland or Wales. But not any more. During the War and up to 1920 my father had been getting one and tuppence short of four pounds a week. From now on it would scarcely be one and tuppence more than two pounds. His hens had become nothing but skin and bone and he couldn't make up his mind whether to do in the few that were left and get one good meal out of them before they starved to death or hang on to them a bit longer and see if things changed. Good scraps had been hard to get for a long time and that was the way things looked as though they were going to stay. Women were making stews out of almost anything. It was a case of 'Shut your eyes, hold your nose, and gulp it down. Divvent even think about it'.

This was the first time I'd ever been involved in anything like this. Before, I'd never really bothered about what went on, I thought my father had always moaned because that's what pitmen always did.

For a while now Mam had been getting one cold after another and other things as well. No sooner did she seem to get shot of one thing than she went down with something else. Sore throats, ulcers, anaemia, she never had enough time to get her strength back. Her hair had lost its sheen, her teeth all seemed to be going crooked and even her lovely sweet breath had gone sour. Her eyes were dull and glassy and her face sometimes had an awful look about it. Her skin was slack and stringy and whenever she changed her expression the skin seemed to take half an hour to alter. She never seemed to have any energy.

Mam had never been what you might call a robust woman but she'd always been light on her feet and graceful for her build, which was sort of dumpyish. At one time she used to flow through the house. Now she just trailed about, dragging her feet and sighing. It was an effort even for her to smile. Sometimes her mouth would go up a bit at the side as though she was going to, then it would stay there as if she was wincing instead. She had this scab at the corner of her mouth like a cold sore and I think it bothered her more than anything: not because it was painful – which it must have been because sometimes it opened up and bled – but because she was ashamed of it and would do anything she could to hide it. By always touching it and putting different things on it, either to make it better or try to cover it up, all she managed to do was draw more attention to it.

'Can ye see it from where you are, Tommy? D'ye think your Dad'd notice it? He never says anything but... Would ye say it was a bit better than it was yesterday. Or...? Be honest now, Tommy. I want you to tell me the truth.'

Although she never complained about herself or anything and wasn't complaining now, I think she thought the sore was a bit of a last straw. Every day it was becoming more and more of a battle for her to get through the day's work. Scrubbing two sets of pit-clothes was hard physical work for any woman, even one from a farming background. And my mother thought they had to be clean on nearly every day. Where she came from in the country at least the food and fresh air would have been good and although the hours might have been long they wouldn't have been so harsh. And when you lived on a farm and your husband or your son went out in the morning to cut his corn or mind his animals or whatever, you'd have every reason to expect he'd be coming back and with all his fingers and toes.

At the end of the day she'd just flop down, none of her lilting singing, none of her gentle chatter. She'd just sit with her darning on her lap and hardly enough strength to lift the needle, eyes a hundred miles away. If Dad was in a stroppy mood she wouldn't say anything, she'd just let things slide and let him have his own way. She couldn't stand any commotion, not even when John and me were having a bit carry-on.

Then she got much worse and Dad got Dr Rattle the family doctor to come to the house. To this day I don't know what was wrong with her and I don't know if she really knew herself or even if my father did. Nobody told me anything and I didn't see I had leave to ask. One night he went out and sold his allotment. Hens, spade, rake, the whole lot went except for a single head of lettuce. When he came back he was pushing a bathchair with the lettuce in it. From then on, every spare minute he had was spent wheeling my mother round the West Park. He wouldn't let anybody take her but himself.

Mam died on the 11th of July, 1922. According to the death certificate it was pneumonia and heart failure. According to death certificates practically everybody who died of natural causes died of the same thing. I think there was more to it than that. Some time afterwards I heard my father and Aunty Winnie talking in the parlour and 'galloping consumption' was mentioned, the dread disease nobody spoke about except in a whisper. There was shame as well as fear attached to it for some reason, something similar to having somebody in a lunatic asylum. I think there'd probably been a lot of it in Ireland when she was young.

Lots of people came to Mam's funeral. All the relatives and neighbours were there, many pitfolk and quite a few I'd never seen before. You always get some people that will go to any funeral. The Irish are like that. Maybe they think a good acquaintance with the cemetery will make it easier when their own time comes, maybe they're just being nosy. But most of the people that came to Mam's would have come for no other reason than they liked her, of that I'm sure. There were people came up to me afterwards to say what a fine woman she'd been in her younger days and how kind and obliging she always was, and things like that. I never knew she'd been such a comfort to so many people till then and it made me realise that you can leave a mark on this world just by being pleasant. It's funny how you can live with people all your life and then maybe just a couple of days after they've gone you learn things you never knew about them and probably never would have got to know. There again, I suppose people are more inclined to praise you after you're dead. That's the way it was with Christ.

She was only thirty-seven years old.

Soon after, John left school but he couldn't get a job at Harton Colliery so he started at Boldon which was still within walking distance of the house. John was a bit taller than me and a bit thinner, and not really cut out for the pit, I don't think. He'd never been all that strong and because he'd been born with rickets he had some bone lumps in the wrong places. We never knew he'd had rickets, until he was twelve. Mam had had him to the doctor because there was something wrong with his spine and it turned out that his skull, as well as the top of his spine and his neck, were all slightly deformed. The doctor told her they'd get worse as he got older and that he'd always have to watch himself, not too much strain or heavy loads, that sort of thing. Part of the reason he was so quiet and kept himself so much to himself was probably because of this. He hardly ever went out. I wasn't very close to him not because we didn't like each other, because we did, we were brothers. It was mainly because I liked going out with the lads and a bit of rough stuff, and he didn't.

It was John's own decision to go down the pit and I don't know if my father gave him the talking to he gave me. Maybe he thought I'd do it. I didn't though. As far as I was concerned if a feller made up his mind to go down the pit, nothing would stop him. And the more pitmen there were in his family the more likely it was that he'd go down. The fact that they'd gone down and were still down made a strong argument. If he went down the pit and found the work too hard he'd soon know he'd overstepped his own mark. And if he didn't, others would. If he was any good they might give him the choice of working at bank. Otherwise they'd just kick him out. In my opinion though, if a lad's bones were too weak to let him work down a pit, they wouldn't be much use anywhere else either. He could probably get a job as a clerk in an office somewhere if he brushed up his reading and writing, or maybe he could drive a bus. But there wouldn't be much else in the way of light work, not around Tyneside, not for a feller.

Apart from the time the tub went over my foot I'd been pretty lucky in the two years I'd been down the pit. There was always somebody getting killed or injured, usually from machines of one kind or another, and the odd one you'd hear about who'd gone a bit funny in the head. But I never ailed anything and although the work might be boring if you were working on your own, I couldn't say it was particularly heavy. They never kept you in one place very long, so by this time I'd been in most places in the pit, even if it was only a matter of helping out for a couple of days because somebody was sick. But one day I had an experience that really shook me up. In itself it was nothing and I never reacted the same way to anything like it again. I never told my father or John or anybody about it because they'd probably have laughed. The reason I think it affected me so much was that I let my imagination run away with me. Never again though. It was a mistake you can't afford to make if you work in a dangerous place.

I was on the foreshift and hadn't been long on when I went into the goaf to have a 'number two'. I knew I shouldn't have been there, especially not when they were firing but I'd had diarrhoea for the past few days and even though I'd never go in the pit if I could help it, this time I had to. So when I heard the deputy shouting to everybody to get clear, something I'd heard many a time, I decided to ignore him and just carry on.

Why, I don't know – maybe he'd used too much powder – but all of a sudden there was the most bloody awful noise and my eardrums felt like they'd exploded. And it didn't stop, it kept coming on and on till the whole place shook as if there was an earthquake.

I'd thought I was far enough away to be safe. Maybe it was the position I was in, maybe it always sounded like that when you were too close. I didn't know. All I knew was I was still sitting on my honkers and I couldn't see a thing. I could feel clouds of dust hitting my face and my mouth was full of it. But that was all. Then I realised the noise had stopped. All noise had stopped. I couldn't hear a damned thing… I was deaf. My eardrums seemed as though they were shattered. I was too stunned to move. I just sat there looking and seeing nothing and listening and hearing nothing except the ringing in my own head. I didn't know how long I'd been here. I didn't know if I'd been knocked unconscious and just woken up. I didn't know if I was still unconscious... What I did know was that it was blacker than pitch and so quiet I began to wonder if I could be dead. Because if I was, I couldn't have been in Heaven.

I reached down and felt my pants and pulled them up. So I was alive all right... I felt for my lamp and remembered I'd left it around the corner in case anybody had come by and seen me. Then I tried to stand up. I hit my head on the roof and fell over. I stood up again, crouched this time, the proper way, and held on to the wall. I was as dizzy as hell. And now there was a roar in my ears like a giant waterfall. I thought maybe there'd been an explosion followed by a roof-fall and the reason I couldn't hear was because I was blocked off from the rest of the pit.

I began to feel my way along to get out, to get to the place where they'd start jowling when they realised I was missing. I stopped and listened for any sound, the distant shout of men's voices and my father calling 'Tommmeeee... Are thou there, lad? Hang on, we'll soon have thou out.'

They'd be here sooner or later, I knew that for certain. Then I remembered I was deaf. I shouted out but heard nothing, not an echo, not even the sound of my own voice. I shouted again, harder... Total silence. Could it be I was trapped in one of those places that are supposed to soak up all sound I wondered, where rescuers move to another place because they cannot hear you even though you're yelling your head off barely a couple of feet away?

I came up against something... A solid wall... Hell! If it was this close the air would last no time. I turned around and started going in the opposite direction. I hadn't gone far when I felt something sticky on my hand. I put my hand in front of my face. 'Pooarghh! Shit!' Damn it if I didn't put my other hand in some! It was warm so at least it was probably mine. Deaf, maybe blind, and with my hands covered in it, and probably my legs as well, I was crawling along a roadway that couldn't have been more than waist high. The reek from the blast was all over the place and I couldn't tell which direction I was going in. I stopped for a minute. I really didn't know which way to go or what to do for the best.

'Shit, shit, shit! F-u-c-k!!' That's what a hewer would have said. Cussing's what he'd have been doing from the start. I'd try it again. 'Shit! Shit! Shit! Shit!! Shit!! F--u--c--k!!!' I imagined if my father was on the other side, putting his hand up. 'Hold it, lads. That sounds like wor Tommy...' 'Are ye sure, Jack? Sounds more like some fuckin' madman to me.'

I don't usually use bad language myself because Mam brought us up to try and get by in life without it. Maybe I should try something else.

I had finished a run of about fifteen Hail Mary's without once swearing whenever my head hit the roof and the roof was gradually getting higher, when I saw a tiny light in the distance. Then another one... then a couple more. The roof was now about four feet high and I was running along in a crouched position. They were human figures. It was for sure they weren't angels, not with the sounds they were making. Miners aren't too fussy about where they let off when they're down a pit: that's always been one of their best source of jokes and these lot were having a competition by the sound of it.

Whether they were rescuers or not I didn't know. But I knew I was safe now and I knew beyond any doubt that I was still in Harton and not in Heaven. I didn't want to look daft so I slowed down. I thought I'd wait till I got right up to them before I told them I was all right and that they could call off the search. I was working out what I'd say so as not to make myself out to be a hero or anything, and not some silly bugger caught with his pants down either. They were talking seriously among themselves when they passed and one just winked. It was all I could do to stop running after them and shaking them by the hand. But I said nothing, I just kept on walking and in a couple of minutes I found myself back at the spot I'd been working at before the blast. There was my lamp still standing there alight. I could now hear men shouting over the clash of shovels, the way they do when they're hard at it, so I just picked up with what I'd been doing before anything happened. My ears still kept going deaf and I kept losing my balance but otherwise I was fine. After one long deaf spell I heard a sound behind me and looked around. Three fellers were packing the wall of the goaf. They were laughing and looking over towards me. I'd never seen them before so they didn't know me. They probably thought I was one of those useless buggers that get sent from one place to another because nobody knows what to do with them.

Right to the end of the shift I kept going deaf and I couldn't help thinking what I'd do if my hearing turned out to be damaged permanently. What other jobs could I do supposing I was lucky enough to get one? Navvying? Builder's labourer? Docker? There didn't seem to be a whole lot of jobs where it wouldn't matter if you were half deaf. You might never hear the shout, 'Watch yourselves below, there's a load o' bricks comin' down!' And when the foreman was giving you your work for the day, you could be standing there gawking at him with a silly grin all over your face. 'What d'ye say, mister? Can ye say it again for the tenth time, only much louder?'

There'd be no compensation from the Harton Coal Company, that's for sure. They'd say it was my own stupid fault. I could just imagine Marks. 'You don't hew coals with your ears, do you, Turnbull? Get yourself back to the Colliery and don't be such a blackguard.'

Every now and then I'd stick my fingers in my ears and give them a damned good poke and rattle around. I half expected to see bits of eardrum, like bits of burst balloon, on the end of my finger. All that came out was coal dust and muck, the same stuff that was always there. You often hear people say that when one of your senses is damaged the others work that much better to make up for it, especially if the accident happens to you while you're still young. Maybe I'd develop some inner sense that might stand me in good stead, like being able to tell what people were thinking. Who knows, I could even have a stage act like one of those Professor Marvo fellers. 'Professor Marvo Turnbull'? Not really... I don't think I'm the type.

At the end of the shift when I got in the cage there was an almighty bang in my ears as soon as it started going up. The noise of the winding gear and all the clattering and rattling and men talking, was unbelievable. Surely it was never this loud before? It was as though a great big plug had been yanked out of my ears. Being deaf was one way to get a bit of peace, there's no doubt about that. By the time the cage stopped and I had stepped out, everything inside my ears was normal again. I was so relieved, it was like coming back into the world again.

You didn't have to be at a pit like Harton very long before you realised that if there was going to be an accident where more than one man was going to be killed, ten to one it was going to be because the roof fell. Nearly all the big pit disasters when so many men and boys have been killed have been caused by gas explosions. All mines have some gas and sometimes it takes no more than a hewer's pick to release a pocket. In bad weather when the atmospheric pressure is low there's likely to be more of it about, especially firedamp. And if it is firedamp and there's enough of it, a few lungfuls can kill you. On the other hand, when there's only a small amount of it and it's mixed with air, you can breathe it but it'll be highly explosive. It's lighter than air, so the lower you stoop the better the chance you have of getting past it. Too low of course and you could find yourself in blackdamp, the stuff the older fellers call 'stythe'.

Harton was so big and old, and so much coal has been taken out of it and so many long roadways driven, that there'd been trouble with subsidence for a long time.

Roof-falls mainly happen because the stuff the roof is made of is too weak, such as shale or clay. But even sandstone, which is one of the best, is weakened by continually dripping water, by extensive undercutting and by constant firing. Whatever the state of the roof, the only thing between it and the floor is the prop. So how many you have, what they're made of, where they're put, how well they're placed and what kind of a state they're in, decides how long the roof is going to stay up.

But putting up props isn't just a matter of seeing where the roof has dropped a bit, sticking a pole or two in and leaving it at that. Whenever you relieve pressure from one place it automatically goes somewhere else. So you always have to be on the lookout, always have to have an ear half cocked, that is, for what the roof is doing. Sometimes you can hear the 'bowking' noise that different layers make when they crack. Or you might hear a 'fissling' noise which means the floor is beginning to creep. This usually happens because the pillars of coal that are supporting the roof are too narrow and being forced into the ground. If the floor then begins to heave up, it'll 'rattle', and that's the time to get if you aren't on your way already. But nobody scatters just because you hear the roof 'settling': that just means it's adjusting itself, it has to do that.

The deputy is the main one responsible for making sure his district is properly timbered, but the pit's a big place and he cannot be everywhere at once. Sometimes for the sake of quarter of an hour, every minute of it meaning money, blokes will stick up a prop that should have been chucked out, or they won't spend sufficient time putting it up properly. Or maybe the wastemen, the old and clapped-out fellers whose job it is to clear away all the loose stones and muck, might have built a pillar that was no more than a joke. Even steel props will buckle and strong oak props bend like bows if the roof pressure is great enough. And the biggest of props, so heavy it might take two men to lift it, can splinter and snap like a matchstick. When that happens, everything's likely to collapse.

And if you're in there when it does, you're either going to be crushed or suffocated.

When roofs collapse down a pit, it isn't the same as being in a house or a building that has collapsed or been bombed. If you're in a building, in a few minutes the air will usually clear and you'll be able to see where you are, what to avoid, and where other people are. And they'll be able to see you. Even on the darkest night you can still see and other folk can get to you quickly, bring more light with them and give whatever help or first aid you might need.

But not down a pit. Even when the dust settles you still cannot see, not if you haven't got a light. Nobody can. And no matter how long you're down there, it's the same. You could be down there for a hundred years and it wouldn't get any lighter, not by a single jot. Down the pit you have to rely on injured people to tell you where they are and how bad they are. And it can takes ages for help to come, sometimes days. Even then only people who are used to going down a pit can help. Good-hearted neighbours cannot start lifting things off you and bringing you something, the way they would if you'd been anywhere else. And no women and children can help.

All the time you're waiting, nobody has any food or drink, no bandages or clean clothes, no lavatory or any of the comforts that even wounded soldiers get as soon as the battle is over. To add to that, with the disturbance to the structure, gas might very well have been released to foul the air you have to breathe or to make it highly inflammable. And down a pit whatever else is happening or not happening, all of the time the oxygen is running out. And as long as anybody else is alive they're using up what little there is for you to breathe and replacing it with carbon dioxide from their own lungs. You are doing exactly the same to them and neither of you can help it.

You sometimes hear people use the word 'pitfall' when they're talking about the little problems or nuisances of life. If you do you'll know they're not pitfolk. A man who makes his living down a pit will never use the word so lightly, neither will any of his family.

A hundred men might be buried or trapped down a pit and if they're released in time, hardly any of them might be hurt. It's not likely but it's possible. Accidents are something else. All the machines down a pit can cause terrible injuries. Pneumatic drills, saws, cutters, steel ropes and such like are obviously dangerous. But things like electric cables and hand tools can be dangerous in a badly lit place where there's hardly room to get by. Even big machines tend to maim more than they kill and there's usually only one feller hurt. But they're no respecters of persons and they give no warning. I've seen deputies, fellers who are supposed to know everything in the pit, conscientious fellers whose job it was to see to safety, happen the most terrible accidents. One minute they're there, chatting away, whole men. And the next, they're like nothing else on earth. Soldiers tell you that's one of the worst things about war.

After a terrible accident, if the feller's still alive people will say 'Well, at least he's still alive, he's got that much to be thankful for.' There's maybe not much else you can say if you don't want to feel too bad about being in one piece yourself. They'll also say things like, 'I can't get the image of that poor man out of my mind.' They will though, soon enough. That's how in a very short time that miner or that soldier will become very poor and so will his family...and they'll lose every scrap of dignity.

8

With three of us at the pit our Monica was left to do as much of the housework, the cooking and the washing, as she could, as well as see herself off to school. And she was only ten. The wife next door would always be popping in and out and she would show Monica what to do as far as she could. But she had a growth and wasn't very strong. Every once in a while she'd put her hands to her head and cry 'Oh my God! Oh my God!' And then she'd sit down. 'It's all right, hinny. It's passed now. Just leave me be for a minute,' she'd say. Then she'd get up and carry on, she wouldn't let you make any fuss. As well as her there was an old woman up the street who'd been very attached to my mother and she came in twice a week to bake the bread and do a bit darning. She'd lost a husband and two sons in an accident at the pit and the third son was paralysed and mad as a kite. She kept having to go hobbling back every twenty minutes to make sure he was all right, because he'd wail fit to wake the dead if he woke up and found she wasn't there.

And there were other ones who'd come in now and again to give what help they could, never mind that some of them had a lot worse troubles than we had. Yet even though they were all poor people none of them would ever take a penny. 'What's this for? Divvent be so daft! Now ye'll offend me, Jack, if ye gan on like that... Put it away, this minute!'

We couldn't go putting on them for ever. And what would happen if any of us had an accident down the pit? One day my father said the only thing to do was get somebody to come in as a housekeeper and that he was going to start asking around. It soon turned out that practically everybody had some cousin or niece to recommend, they knew there'd be a few shillings in it and wanted to help their own. With three men in the house working at the pit I imagine we must have seemed a good prospect. The work might be hard and the money wouldn't be great but at least it would be regular.

Unfortunately anybody who was any good, any bright young lass, had already gone into service in London. Seemingly they liked our north country girls down there. The ones that were left tended to be girls who were a bit simple or had something else wrong with them. There were plenty of widows, but if they didn't look absolutely worn out my father would have it they were too crafty. 'She knows a good thing when she sees one,' he would say when they'd gone. We weren't exactly sure what he meant by a 'good thing', whether he meant himself or the job. I do know that John and me would sigh when yet another one was turned away and we knew we'd still be scrubbing our own shirts, making our own beds and falling out with each other over the cooking for a while yet.

Before they came to the house for the interview my father would insist we hid all the washing to make it look as though looking after us wasn't going to be that bad a job. Three sets of dirty pitmen's clothes hanging up or piled in the corner would have sobered any woman up. Then on the morning they came to start for their trial period he'd make us bring out every dirty hanky and every holey sock in the place. 'Howay man, Dad,' we'd say to him... '"Howay" what? We've got to see what she's made of, haven't we?'

Ones we liked, he didn't. Ones he liked, we didn't. I think he was really looking for somebody like my mother, somebody who looked like her and had the same nature as her. Somebody who from the moment she started would care more about us than anything or anybody on earth. Mam had had her little faults, like sometimes not letting his tea mast long enough, or being what he thought was too soft on John and me. And he'd been patient with her because she was his wife and he loved her. But if he was starting again he wanted somebody perfect. After all, he would be paying this one for what many would have seen as a privilege. So when the odd one flounced in as though she was coming in to run the house and save the liver of everybody in it, he'd leave her in no doubt about who was doing who the favour. A few of them looked as though they might have been really good workers but were rough as guts and obviously used to anything. None of us wanted anybody like that. 'To hell with it. We'll manage by ourselves if that's the best we can get,' my father would say.

I think it was only now that we realised how much Mam had done for us for all those years and what a lovely job she had always made of it. And that although there must be other good women around, none of them would be the same as her. We couldn't think that any way different to Mam's, whether it was the way the table was set or the beds were made, was the right way.

After six months of it my father got tired of looking and we all got fed up of making do. Neither my father, me or our John were any good in the house. We were going to work in damp or dirty clothes, the house was a mess and nobody ever knew where anything had been put. On top of that Monica wasn't being looked after properly.

Then one day he came out of the blue and said he'd found what we were all looking for. He'd stopped asking us what we thought a while back and had said that from then on he'd be relying entirely on his own judgement. So we pretty much guessed what was coming. She was a widow called Isabella Tanner. I think he probably wanted a woman for other things apart from cooking and cleaning and that he'd come to the conclusion that the only way he was going to get one, was if he married one. He knew if he waited too long Isabella Tanner would go somewhere else and they might marry her and then he'd be left with nothing. Also I think he knew the longer the trial, the greater the likelihood she'd fail it. It was obvious what was on her mind because she'd had her feet right under the table from the start. I knew that when I caught her washing his back one night. She had a little lad she always fetched with her called Wilfred but he never spoke a word and wasn't any bother. He'd just sit by the fireplace all day until my father came home and then he'd clear out of it.

I dare say by now my father had realised he wasn't perfect himself and that as time went on he wasn't becoming any more that way. So in spite of the advice he got, a lot of it from his own people, he married her. She wasn't a bad housekeeper compared with us. But when you'd said that, you'd covered all her good points. She wasn't provident but she was mean. She'd buy the dearest brand of tea you could get and then stew the life out of it. Yet if somebody down the street had a bit of luck and there was little enough of that, she nearly went mad with jealousy and couldn't stop moaning about it. Next thing you'd see her flapping about wearing something she'd just bought to make up for the other body's luck. She looked after Monica all right and saw that her hair was combed before she went to bed and things like that but she never tried to treat her like a daughter, the way many would. Not that she was any better to her own lad.

She wasn't a patch on Mam, not even to look at. Mam had gentle rounded features and a lovely soft Irish voice. Isabella Tanner's features were thin and hard and her voice would set your teeth on edge. I'd never call her 'stepmother' or anything else with the word 'mother' in it. Nobody could ever take my Mam's place.

Wages were now a little better than they'd been after the Lockout, and because we had three people working in the house, one of them a hewer getting the pit's top wage, we were better off than many. Pneumatic drills and cutters were being used more and more but there was still ample work for good hewers in the low seams. We were all pretty fit and healthy and John seemed to be managing all right on the screens at Boldon. He was still very quiet but he was definitely getting stronger. And now that we had our own permanent housekeeper we didn't have to worry about looking after ourselves. It was 1923, I was eighteen, and I wanted to get out and enjoy myself a bit now.

Since my father had got rid of the allotment his only hobby was the Stanhope and whatever he kept out of his pay-packet for himself was invested in baccy and bass. I was now smoking Woodbine cigarettes like the rest of my mates but I didn't drink. I'd seen what people were like when they were drunk. They'd think they were so damned funny and clever and tough, when everybody else knew they were just a pain in the arse. It seemed to me there were better things to spend your money on.

If there was one thing I'd always wanted since I was a little kid, it was a bike. You could go anywhere if you had a bike. Out in the country, up to Newcastle, even down to London if you wanted to. A feller from Newcastle was the cycle-racing champion of the world. Everybody was getting one. If I had a bike I'd be able to get to Roker to watch Sunderland without having to bother about catching trams or trains. Walking there and back was hopeless. By the time you got there, the match was half over. And by the time you got back it was the same with the night. You could get to see South Shields all right but who'd want to watch South Shields? Fine and dandy if all you wanted was a laugh. But if you wanted to see a really good game of football you had to be willing and able to travel.

Just being on a bike gave you a great feeling. It gave you a feeling of power being up there on the saddle and part of the traffic on the road. Trams, buses, cars, they always treated you with respect when you were on a bike. If you were just walking on the road they treated you as though you were trespassing on their property. Sometimes my father would get me the lend of one off one of his pals, and away I'd go. After being cramped up in a dark dirty pit all day or all night, it was marvellous to be out in the sunshine and fresh air, breathing in the salt and seaweed if you went along the cliffs at Marsden or breathing in the new-mown hay and wild flowers if you went beyond Cleadon. I was rarely able to borrow it for more than a few hours at a time because the feller needed it himself. But whenever I got the chance I'd take it, even though it was belting down with rain and I just spent the time cleaning it. In twenty minutes I could be down at the beach. Five was all it took to get to the docks or up to one of my mates'. It was an upright, black and heavy, and although I'd have been over the moon with it if it was mine, what I really wanted was a racer. I wanted to buy my own racer so that I could join a cycling club and go off with them wherever they went. My pal Billy Durkin had made his own out of spare parts because he had an uncle in the business. He belonged to a cycling club and said they had a smashing time in it.

I began putting away a shilling a week in the post office. Some weeks I wouldn't be able to afford that much but whenever I could I'd make up for it.

Round where we lived there were a lot of Irish families and a good many of their men worked down the pit. Half the ones who worked at Harton were Irish, or like me their mothers or fathers were. They were mostly labourers that had been forced off the land or couldn't make any kind of a living in their own country. Thousands of them came to Tyneside. Their farm skills were no use so they went down the mines and every pit in the Durham Coalfield had Irish names in it. There weren't so many in the south because they weren't so welcome down there but we liked them and they were part of us now. The Irish are good people to have around when the country's at war because hard times seem to bring out the best in them and some of them are great fighters. There were those who had stayed down the pit for the duration but quite a few joined up to fight alongside their English marras. And nearly all those that managed to return went straight back down the pit. They loved to play fiddles and whistles and dance and sing and no songs were more popular than Irish ones.

Every pit had its own boxing champion, even the different religions had them. Nearly all the Catholic champions were Irish but so were umpteen of the others as well. Wesleyans, Baptists, Church of England and ones nobody had ever heard of, were very often Irish. I don't know what Fr Beech would have made of it but I doubt whether many of these blokes would have cared one way or the other. All kinds of money would be bet and down the pit we talked about nothing else in the days leading up to a contest and nothing else for days afterwards.

These fights were nothing like the scraps in the street after lowse to settle an argument. These were real sporting contests with fellers that had put themselves up as proper fighters. And because they were representing the honour of your pit or your religion, everybody was expected to give their support and the fellers themselves had to put on a damned good show. They would train for it, members of the public would be invited and paid for tickets and the purse would be a golden guinea. We all chipped in towards the prize-money but more than a few would have laid every penny of their wages on their man. Those with nothing at stake except the honour of their pit would be encouraging their man and shouting at the other one to put him off. But those with a big stake on him would be going daft every time he hit the other. And they'd be calling the other bloke worse than muck and shouting to the referee to disqualify him for fouling every time he hit their man.

Although it was called boxing, it would sometimes be a lot closer to set-to's in the old style, particularly if they were older fellers. On those occasions they wouldn't even wear gloves but would just slug it out with each other until one of them went to the ground and failed to get up again. Now and then you'd get two heavyweights that would think it was a hugging match rather than a boxing match and fellers would be yelling and jeering from both their corners and from all sides.

'It's supposed to be a fight, not the last bloody waltz! Gan on, ye big useless lump! Give it to 'im! I could do better with one hand tied behind me back!'

Lightweights were the best. They were quick with their hands and fast on their feet. In-out, in-out, and whap, ye bugger!

Once in a while there'd be a real cracker of a contest. Maybe the two of them didn't like each other or had fought before and there'd been an unsatisfactory verdict. Skin and hair would then fly all over the place.

The overall champion at Harton for many years used to be a big ginger Irishman by the name of Pat Hannon. 'Grecian Pat' he was called, though why 'Grecian' I've no idea. It would be for some daft reason, of that you could be sure. The Irish always gave each other daft nicknames and I wouldn't be surprised if that's where the pit habit originated from. When Pat passed his seventieth birthday he thought it was time he officially resigned as Harton's champion, and a feller called Big Bob Hooley took over. Hooley was broader than Pat but not as tall and I'd say there was a fair amount of fat on him, though he wasn't the kind of feller you'd poke to find out. He had little eyes and if he caught you staring at him he'd screw them up and slowly point a big thick finger at you. That meant 'Look somewhere else, Blossom. Better still, beat it!'

Pat and my father had always been good friends even though my father was only half his size. Maybe it was because both of them were full of the gab and both of them liked their drink. One night a few months after Pat had retired my father and him were having a drink in the Tyne Dock Arms, when in came Big Bob. Unlike most boxers I ever met, Bob was a bully. Straightaway he started picking on my father.

'What d'ye think you're doin' in here, Turnbull?' he says.

'Havin' a drink,' my father says. 'What does it look like?'

'It looks to me like you're sittin' in my seat and drinkin' my beer.'

'Well I can tell ye he's not,' says Pat. ''Cos I gave 'im the seat. And I bought 'im the beer.'

'Nobody's talkin' to you, Patrick. So mind your own bloody business.'

'Away out of it,' said Pat. 'I didn't come in here to have to listen to a gobshite like you.'

'Will ye listen to that?' Bob says to his mates standing behind him. 'The oulder they get, the lippier they get.' He then leans right over to Pat. 'Just be thankful you're an old man or I'd put ya lights out, ye geet heap o' bogshit.'

'Outside!' says Pat, getting up.

They were scarcely out the door when Pat got hold of Big Bob by the collar and gave him a hell of belt on the side of his head. Then he pulled him up and stood him up against the wall and gave him another. By the time he'd given him a few more, Bob's face was unrecognisable and he hadn't managed to hit Pat once. Pat had just let him go and was wiping his hands when he caught sight of Bob's son standing by. Without a word he walked straight over and knocked the lad clean out with one blow. The poor bugger went to the ground without knowing what hit him.

When they came back into the bar my father says to Pat, 'What d'ye do that for? I didn't think the lad meant any harm.'

'Two heads are better than one,' says Pat. 'So I thought I might as well do the two o' them while I was at it.'

Ganty McGuire was another Irishman but he was a flyweight and a different feller altogether to Pat. He used to go round selling what they called 'French letters', though they had very little to do with France. I don't know what he said when he went to Confession if he went, but he'd have had a bit of explaining to do unless he was only selling them to Protestants. He and his mates once got into a spot of bother with the police during a strike and the lot of them were marched into court. As soon as they got him in the door Ganty went completely crackers as though he'd gone clean off his head. He was screaming and yelling, flinging his arms about in the air, and rolling all over the floor. They couldn't do a thing with him so they put him in a lunatic asylum. He was back out in a fortnight laughing his head off. The rest of them did six months' hard labour.

Mick Moran was another one, mad as they come, but it didn't stop him becoming chairman of the lodge. Although he never had a penny to his name people used to say he'd have given anybody anything. 'Oh, aye,' my father would say. 'Anybody can afford to be generous when they've got nowt. He probably started the rumour himself.' My father never cared much for Mick, he thought he wasn't genuine at all. 'He'd say owt but his prayers, the smart-arsed little prick!'

Maybe he was, but he usually got what he wanted. He was a lousy dresser even for a pitman and he'd walk round Shields as though he'd just come off the tip. One day the Lodge were going to meet the Coalowners and Mick strolls up to join the rest of the committee, lookin' like a rag man. Matty Jackson the secretary says to him, 'We cannot gan in with you lookin' like that, man. They'll think we're a bunch of bloody tinkers.'

'D'ye think it matters that much?' Mick says.

'Course it does or I wouldn't be sayin' it. You're not in Tipperary now. There's a right way of gannin' about things and there's a wrong way. And gannin' in dressed like a bag o' shite is definitely the wrong way.'

'Hang on, then,' says Mick. 'I'll not be five minutes.' And runs off.

Quarter of an hour later he comes back all spruced up, rubbing his hands.

'Right! Let's go and sort the buggers out!'

'Hang on! Hang on!' says Matty. Where d'ye get that shirt from?'

'My missus borrowed it off your missus's line,' says Mick. 'I knew ye wouldn't mind, bein' as it's such an important meetin' an' all.'

'How the hell we picked a chairman like you is beyond me. You're a bloody twat, d'ye know that?'

'Well, think of it this way, Matty... Jesus Christ picked a committee of twelve. Out of that, one doubted him, one deceived him, and another betrayed him... If he couldn't make a job of it, fat chance you buggers.'

My father wasn't a fighting man in the sense of using his fists. He fought with his tongue. It wasn't because he wasn't strong enough, he was now nearly fifty and had spent the last thirty-five years doing harder labour than any prison sentence. It was because for all his talk he wasn't a violent man. He preferred to argue, I'd go so far as to say he loved it.

Seeing him sitting in his tin bath in front of the fire with his little clay pipe in his mouth and his eyes closed in utter pleasure was a sight I'd seen nearly every day of my life. It was one of the reasons I'd never wanted to be anything but a miner myself. His chest and back were as deep as his shoulders were wide, and all over his back and shoulders as well as on his arms and hands, he had the 'buttons' that were the mark of a true coalminer. Old healed-over wounds with coal dust in them that he would take with him to the grave. They were quite blue against the lily-white skin and he was as proud of them as any soldier of his medals. At one time my mother always washed his back. Then John or me did it when we were in. Now Isabella Tanner mostly did it. But now and again, if there'd been words between them, he'd ask me or John. And if she came over then, he'd wave his hand and say 'Ehhhhht!' which meant 'To hell', and the drips would go all over her.

The hair on his chest was grey and wiry and stuck straight out like a brush. The hair on his head was still a mop but going greyer and his pointer tuft wasn't what it used to be. His arms were short and thick like his legs and he never had what you'd call wrists or ankles. The arms grew straight out of his hands and the legs straight out of his feet. His hands were almost an exact square and half as thick as they were wide and his fingers so short and thick he could never close either hand to make a fist.

Rubbing him down was like rubbing a cloth over a boulder, his whole body was a pack of hard tight muscle. He didn't have a shapely body with different muscles standing out on his arms and legs like an athlete or a bodybuilder and he had no waist at all. From a distance seeing him come down the street you couldn't have been blamed for thinking 'Here comes a fat little feller.' But as soon as he took his jacket off you'd have soon seen he hadn't an ounce on him. What wasn't muscle, was bone, and there wasn't too much of that either. He wasn't a boxer but he'd have been a hard man to put down if he had no drink in him.

Before I started at the pit I had no interest in politics. For years I'd had to listen to Dad and Uncle Jim going on about the Union, the Coalowners and the Government and I was sick to death of hearing the name 'Lloyd George'. It had always seemed to me that these people so far away had very little to do with us or how we lived our lives. The school teacher and the parish priest had more to do with mine than any member of parliament. And when I started at the pit it was the keeker or the overman who could send me home happy or give me a hard time. As a result, a lot of what my father had said when he'd been talking politics had gone in one ear and straight out the other. But since the 1921 lockout and because our wages had gone down again I was beginning to think differently.

The men I worked with went on about the same things as my father, sometimes all day long. Young fellers only a few years older than me, fellers I admired and wanted to be like, talked about it. These were the same fellers who talked about all the other things I was interested in, like lasses, football, bikes and dance bands. So if something interested them, it was nearly sure to interest me. If it was important to them, it was important to me. Some of them, Paddy Cain for instance, were good talkers and clever with it as well. They knew the history of coalmining, about the struggles of the working class and about the Labour movement. They knew about other unions and how they went on. They knew about coalminers in other countries and other kinds of miners. They could tell you that John Lambton the Earl of Durham owned 12,500 acres and got £40,522 every year from royalties just because somebody happened to mine coal under his land. And that not only did he never get his own hands dirty, he never lifted a finger.

Everybody who worked down a pit should know things like that. And they needed to know there was over a million of us in Britain and that we had the strongest trade union. We were a staple industry, we were the ones that had made Britain wealthy. There couldn't have been an Industrial Age without coal. No transport system, no steel industry, no shipbuilding, engineering or anything else. Every one of them needed power and that meant coal. It was no wonder we were the best organised and hardest fighters of any union. We'd been battling Coalowners for centuries, long before there were any such things as factories, power stations or railways. We'd been battling since before the word 'union' was invented.

Yet for all that, we'd taken such a hiding in 1921 that even now four years later everybody still talked about it. The politicians and Coalowners still boasted about it, as did the other industry bosses, the newspapers, and the BBC... And the Union still complained about it.

The papers said the Government and the Coalowners had put down a 'revolution', when what they had really done was show that the British middle class was Liberal enough and Tory enough to stomach their police force and their Army being used against a large part of its own people. Not only in the colonies but here on its own home ground. Before the Lockout working people used to say that for all their education the middle classes were really just gullible and as soon as they realised what the Coalowners were really like there'd be an uproar... Not a bit of it... They queued up to sign on as special constables. All they needed was to be fed sufficient tripe about 'communism', and not to have to think for themselves. Sing a song about the British Empire and you could guarantee to bring tears to their eyes, even if it was absolute drivel. They believed that if God wasn't actually in the Cabinet of the British Government, he certainly voted for it. At least we argued our case and fought our battles without claiming God was a fully paid-up member of the Durham Miners Association, even though he was supposed to be everywhere.

The Lockout had also proved that people with no food in their bellies only fight harder, not better. And factory owners, shipbuilders, landowning farmers and all the rest of them had got so much encouragement from this that they were all closing their fists. It was the same story everywhere. Lower wages, longer hours and no wasting of resources on 'modernisation for modernisation's sake' or on 'being ridiculous' about safety.

When I came back to the house at half-past ten my father was just in from the Stanhope. It was Christmas Eve. He hung his cap up, picked up his paper, glanced at it, and then flung it back on the chair. He then sat down to his supper and started eating without a word except for a snort every now and then. I opened the tin of polish, put it on the hearth and started polishing my boots. Outside some kids were singing carols and knocking on the door every couple of minutes. My father was clicking his tongue and spitting bits off his lip. One minute he was dead quiet, chewing and chewing. The next he just about stuck his fork through the bottom of the plate and the sound went right through you. Still nobody said a word. John was doing something in the back, Wilf was helping Monica to make some paper decorations, and Isabella Tanner was flitting about trying to make herself look busy. Everybody was waiting for my father to blow up.

'Tommy, hadaway and chase the buggers! They should be abed this time of night.'

I got up and went to the door. They were just tiny, one of them couldn't have been more than four or five.

I came back in. 'We'll have to give them somethin'. It's startin' to snow.'

'I'll give them somethin' all right,' my father says. 'I'll give them a clip around the lughole. That'll get them on their way!'

Isabella Tanner then went but they must have done the same to her they did to me, sticking their scruffy faces up and trying to look like little angels, and then when you tried to stop them, singing louder than ever.

'Ye'll catch your deaths, the lot of ye. Have yous not got mothers and fathers, and homes to go to?'

They drowned her out with 'Good King Wenceslas' and then without stopping started on a very fast version of 'We Three Kings of Orient-ah'.

She came back in for her purse. 'There's one little'un out there'd hardly be any older than our Wilfed… He looks half frozen.' She went out, gave them something, and they immediately started on 'God Rest Ye Merry Gentlemen'.

'Shoo now! Go on! Away ye get, back to your homes.'

She then shut the door, came back in and sat down. All the time she was watching my father out of the corner of her eye.

All of a sudden he flung his fork aside and it hit the mantelpiece. The old china dog fell on to the hearth and smashed. Uncle Dick had won him at the fair before I was born. He'd been glued back together at least a dozen times, each time with a tiny bit more missing. But Isabella

Tanner hadn't the patience Mam had. There'd be no carefully folded newspaper this time, no gentle fingers picking every last piece up and carefully examining it to see where it went.

There were more carol singers at the front door and 'Good King Wencelas' was back again.

'For God's sake, go and chase them while I see to this, will ye?' Isabella Tanner said to me as she began sweeping up the dog with the brush and shovel.

'Leave it where it is!' my father shouted.

'But Jack, I was only –'

'Leave it, I said! I've got somethin' to say and I cannot say it with all that clickin' and clackin' gannin' on.'

As he was talking he was looking straight at me, I could tell. I kept on brushing my boots. To get the attention he wanted, he shoved the plate away so hard he knocked the knife on the floor and the plate went straight after it. He was really niggled that nobody had stopped what they were doing to listen to what he had to say. He'd been out all night and he'd obviously had a hard time getting anybody to listen to him. Back in the Stanhope he'd very likely been told on more than one occasion, 'For Christ's sake, dry up will ye, Jack? It's Christmas. Forget about the soddin' Coalowners! And the bloody Government! We want to have a bit of fun for a change.' So he'd come back here to lay down his burden. He knew nobody here would dare tell him to shut up or get lost. But that wasn't sufficient. What he wanted was an audience who were interested in what he had to say, one who wouldn't remember that they'd heard it all before and were sick to death of hearing it. He wanted somebody who even though they mightn't clap would at least have the decency to say 'You're right, ye know, Jack. You're dead blo-ody right! I never thought about it like that… Christ knows what this industry would do without you'.

My father thought half the catastrophes in the world could have been avoided if they had only listened to him.

'And where the hell have you been the night?'

'Nowhere. I just had a game of footer with the lads.'

'Footer? Christmas Eve and you've nowt better to do with your time than play football, ye useless nowt? You're ganna have to wake your bloody ideas up, lad! That's what you're ganna have to do. Your mother and me always told ye never to gan down the pit in the first place. But clevershite that ye are, you decided "To hell wi' that".

'And now whether ye like it or not, you're one of us. And you're ganna have to do your bit just like everybody else. You're ganna find out it's not a bloody game we're playin'. You young'uns are all alike, you've had things far too bloody easy. Ye should've been at the meetin' the other night. Better men than you gave their time up to be there.

'We worked for years and sweated blood to get a Labour government in. And what did we get? We got bloody Ramsay MacDonald! We got a damned crawler who ignores a man like George Lansbury, a man who might have stopped the War, just because the bloody King doesn't happen to like him! And who does he pick instead? He picks Lord-bloody-Haldane! The same Lord-bloody-Haldane that wanted to bring the troops in to put down a dock strike... No wonder the bloody Tories are back!'

I knew he was right. But if a Labour government couldn't or wouldn't change things, and men like A.J. Cook, one of the best miners' leaders ever, coupled with a tough old prize-fighter like Arthur Henderson, couldn't make or persuade them, what could I do?

For a long time he sat there. Then very quietly he said 'I'm not kiddin', Tom. This next year comin' up's ganna see strife the likes of which this country's never seen afore. When that coal subsidy ends in May, all hell's ganna be let loose.'

He then went out into the yard and as the clock struck twelve I head him vomiting down the drain.

Because the Coalowners had told the Government they were going to increase our working hours and decrease our wages, the Government had been paying them a subsidy rather than telling them they weren't allowed to do that. This subsidy was due to end on the 1st of May and neither the Coalowners or the Tories wanted it extended. The Government, especially Churchill and his gang, together with the Coalowners and the owners of every other industry in the country, wanted a contest of strength with the miners. They wanted to destroy unions once and for all, ours and the others. And they reckoned that if they flattened us that would be it for the rest of them.

We all thought my father's temper would gradually die down over the Christmas what with the drink and the celebrations and all that. Usually he would blow up, get it off his chest and then simmer down. But it didn't, not this time. Maybe nobody ever took him seriously enough. Being short and having that big voice of his always threatening to come over there with his thick waggling tash and belt somebody around the lughole and never taking more than a step towards them, it wasn't easy. And although I loved him and respected him, I suppose I tended to see him more and more the way everybody else did. It's hard not to when you work in the same place especially a place like the pit where they never miss a trick as far as taking the piss out of anybody is concerned. He was tough, nobody could have doubted that. He could hew with the best, fill and put with the best, get injured and never complain. But he was too short to be a leader. A big feller with his voice saying what he said – and some of the biggest have voices on them like thirteen-year-old girls – and maybe people would have paid attention. As it was they didn't and it only made him roar all the louder.

When Mam was alive, no matter how hard up we were she'd always find something from somewhere to make a little bit of this or a little bit of that. And even when she couldn't, she still brightened the place up with her smile. If any of us had a birthday or it was Easter Sunday or whatever it was treated like an occasion and my mother would never fail to change her pinny, press her shawl and comb her hair a different way. There was always something nice or extra to eat that she'd been saving up and even the usual would be served up to look like something special.

With Isabella Tanner there was nothing like that. One day was the same as the next as far as she was concerned. Even when my father and me managed to fetch in a few extra shillings between us, there was never anything to show for it. Whether she was burying it or drinking it on the sly, which is what my father thought, we never found out. 'You men have no idea where the money goes,' she'd say when my father asked her about it. And she'd get herself in a right kerfuffle and flounce out like she was deeply offended.

'That's for bloody sure!' he'd say after her. 'But I'll tell ye, one thing. If it doesn't do any good around here, we'll put it somewhere where it will... From now on, anythin' over and above the usual, put it towards your bike, lad,' he said to me.

That certainly suited me because I wanted a bike more than ever now. Every week the newspapers had advertisements of young couples in blazers and frocks cycling along the country lanes with their hair neatly combed and smiles on their faces. Cycle shops were full of bikes of every kind and colour. You could hardly walk down the street without seeing somebody you knew on a bike. There were cycling clubs that anybody could join, no matter who you were, be you Catholic or Protestant, bank clerk or docker. And they had some great-looking lasses in them. You'd see the different clubs every Sunday, whole streams of them going by, two by two, lads and lasses, calling out to each other and laughing and having a bit carry-on. They went right out into the country. Billy Durkin was now in the Belle Vue Tyne Dock Cycling Club and he'd got them to let me go for a run with them once when I was able to borrow my Dad's mate's bike for the day. It was wet and windy and we had to come back early but it was smashing and I'll never forget it.

Every Monday Billy told me where they'd been on the Sunday. They might have been down south to Durham City one week, and then as far west as Hexham the next. Then maybe as far north as Alnwick the week after. If there was any nice place anybody had heard of that they hadn't been to, you could bet it would be on their list to go there very shortly. Anybody in the club could put a suggestion forward and then everybody would vote on it. Billy said if ever I could get a lend of a bike, he'd fix it so I could go with them.

As soon as the new year started it was obvious that the Coalowners and the big employers in every industry had made up their minds to crack down on the working man and on the pitman in particular. Britain was now having to deal with something it had never had to bother about before. And that was competition for mass produced goods... And it was coming from America, Japan, even from Germany. These countries and others besides were producing cheaper and better goods than we were. They were even producing the lorries, trains and ships used to transport them.

The British manufacturers' way of dealing with the situation wasn't to produce something better or different from what the others were producing. The British way was to continue manufacturing the same things in exactly the same way and deal with competition by lowering prices. The only way to do this without touching their own profits was to reduce the wages of their workers, increase their workers' working hours, and cut expenses by saving on safety, which they regarded as a luxury.

In the weeks leading up to May one of our leaders thought up the phrase, 'Not a penny off the pay, not a minute on the day', and it was a catchy one. But for every slogan we dreamed up, the far better educated Coalowners and particularly their friends in Parliament and the press, came out with more. We were the 'New Red Threat', we were 'worse than the Hun'. We were this and we were that but we were never anything good. And always we were 'ignorant'. Ignorance was an unforgivable sin as far as they were concerned, not a matter of being born on the other side of the fence. Yet those who did try to educate themselves, such as through the Workers Education Association or in the various workers' institutes or at colleges and in their own time, were always put down. Grown men going to college to learn how to write their own name was something to scoff at as far as they were concerned, not something to give credit for. And if they'd been able to pass a law banning working people from getting educated 'above their level' as they called it, they'd have gladly done it.

It was becoming obvious to me now that politics controlled everything and that they had more to do with whether people anywhere in the world had a good life or a bad one, than anything. Age, climate, health, talent, religion and geography all put together were nothing compared with the power of a handful of politicians. British governments had set up any number of Royal Commissions from Sankey to Samuel to look into organisation, wages, working conditions and safety in the coal industry. But they wouldn't be bound by any of them. They only set them up to shut us up and they only referred to anything in them that suited their own purposes.

9

On the 30th of April, 1926 the Coalowners closed every pit in the country and we were locked out again. Their terms to us amounted to pre-war wages and an extra hour on the working day. Their terms to the Government amounted to no state interference in the running of the coal mines, all strikes to be banned by law and the state to take over control of all funds belonging to trade unions.

This time the TUC said they'd back us to the last man. They realised that all workers' jobs, wages and conditions were under grave threat and their members were determined there would never be a repeat of 1921.

Three days later the General Strike was on and workers in almost every industry laid down their tools and walked out. Buses and trains stopped, factories were silent, docks deserted and offices empty.

The Government went straight into action to show they were more than ready for what Winston Churchill was already calling 'War'. Stanley Baldwin was more concerned with keeping his job as Prime Minister and leader of the Tory Party than anything else and apart from doing his bit by calling pitmen 'ruthless', he left everything to Churchill. Baldwin always wanted everybody to think he was such a reasonable man, thoroughly decent, a perfect Christian and that butter wouldn't melt in his mouth. If everything went well he'd be happy to take the credit and if things went wrong he'd still be a gentleman and above it all. Pictures he put out of himself showed this smartly dressed fatherly man with a beautiful pipe, sitting at his desk with a concerned but calm look on his face. 'Pontius Pilate with a Pipe' was what we called him.

Churchill on the other hand wanted everybody to be terrified of him. He saw himself more like Napoleon Bonaparte than Chancellor of the English Exchequer and his pictures showed him with a bulldog expression and a cigar the size of a bazooka sticking out of his face. Both he and Sir William Joynson-Hicks, the Home Secretary, who had a face like a mouse, wore toppers to give them an extra six inches. But for all their fine words, Churchill never looked more than a bag of shit in a silk hat, and Hicks like somebody out of a music hall act.

Joynson-Hicks regarded the police as a civilian army and he wanted them to do the job of crushing the striking workers and the locked-out pitmen. Churchill, an old army man, wanted to use real soldiers and navy marines. Churchill's chief assistant was Sir John Anderson. Anderson was a typical senior civil servant who hadn't the faintest idea what life was like for the common man and didn't give a damn either. Lord Birkenhead, 'Galloper Smith' as he was known, of the bookshop business, was a snob like Joynson-Hicks and another hater of the working class. Birkenhead was as cunning as he was smarmy, but for all his brains he couldn't come up with any better way of dealing with the situation than brute force. His contribution was to bring back General McCready.

Churchill, Hicks, Birkenhead and Anderson had been setting up the O.M.S., the 'Organisation for the Maintenance of Supplies', for a long time. Since the 1921 lockout in fact. So they were very well organized and dying to go into action. The O.M.S. brought in the Army, the Navy, the Police and a large civilian volunteer force that included police specials.

One thing Britain has never been short of is 'decent law-abiding citizens' only too ready to 'do their bit' for King and Country, and the sillier they look doing it, the better they seem to like it. They teemed out of their law offices, banks, cathedrals, universities, clubs and associations, to play bus-driver and policeman. The upper-class women mainly drove the vans and cars because they liked to be seen in charge of something. Others who maybe weren't so photographable did the paperwork. The rugby-playing students and others who liked a bit of rough stuff joined the police specials. The rest, ones who didn't want to come into contact with the striking workers, did loading and unloading while being guarded by soldiers with rifles. Although these people all had a good income and many came from wealthy families, the Government paid them £1 15s a week to do strike-breaking work, plus £1 14s 6d a week for food, and 5s a week for clothing. And they accepted it. A total of £3 14s 6d for work that working people could do far better and were fighting for the right to do, for much less.

The TUC had given a guarantee to the Government that no matter how long the strike went on, their members would continue to supply food, hospital supplies and other essentials, and would allow their members in the building industry to carry on doing slum clearance and building hospitals. But Churchill and his gang would have none of it. They'd accept nothing that looked like a favour from strikers or that showed them in a good light. Everything had to be done Churchill's way and only by his people. Baldwin and a number of others in the Government, including the Labour MPs, weren't so sure this was the best way to deal with things. They thought it would be better to have the minimum of strife rather than the maximum. But Churchill wanted his war with us and the rest of the working class. He wanted to show us and the whole world who was boss.

The Navy moored its submarines and destroyers along the docks of all the major rivers, the Tyne included. Marines were marched with fixed bayonets into towns to escort trams. The Army drove through the streets in armoured cars and marched its troops through them. Tanks rolled up. The police mounted their horsemen like cavalry and lined up their bruisers on the ground. And if it hadn't been for some of them in the Cabinet warning Churchill that the whole country would object, he'd have had a machine gun on the corner of every street.

Even though the printers and paper handlers were on strike, a tiny version of The Times and a normal-sized Daily Mail which was being printed in Paris, came out to give the news from the Government's point of view. But that wasn't enough for Churchill. He wanted them to print the news exactly how he dictated it, not how they saw it. And because they wouldn't go that far he brought out his own paper, the British Gazette. In it he printed nothing which showed the Government in a bad light, and nothing which showed miners and strikers in a good one. According to the British Gazette, as soon as the strike started everything was immediately in short supply. There was no mention of the fact that the Government had been stockpiling for months. No mention of the fact that it had known there was a strike coming. No mention of the fact that it had allowed it to happen and welcomed it when it did.

Churchill said whatever he could get away with. When the fire brigade unions offered to join the strike, the TUC told them not to. When Churchill heard about it, his gazette said the fire brigade unions had refused to support the strike. He said volunteers had more trains and buses running than they really had and that they were shifting more goods than they were. He exaggerated the number of strikers that were going back to work. And if ever there was a report of violence, the violence always came from striking dockers or factory workers and never from the police or the 'specials'.

Everything was written in such a way as to on the one hand get people worked up about the terrible coalminers and horrible strikers, and on the other to let them know that their wonderful Government had everything under control and was winning the battle. The 'nation' was 'winning the battle' against the 'organised menace'. We pitmen who were the nation's coalminers, and the strikers who were the nation's bus drivers, factory workers, tradesmen and the likes, were called 'wicked and treacherous'. The world was being told we were threatening the British state and all things bright and beautiful that went with it.

What Churchill was writing in his paper were the same things he'd been saying in Parliament for years. He said it whenever he was making a speech about a group of workers that were protesting because of poor living standards or awful working conditions. The same refusal to regard working people as human beings came out all of the time. The same hatred, the same determination to humble anybody who wasn't lucky enough to belong to the same class as him and to keep them on their knees forever.

The TUC brought out the British Worker to try to tell the strikers and anybody else who was interested what was really happening. The Daily Worker, the communist paper which had supported us even more than the Daily Herald, had been snuffed out by the Government. The British Worker was the only means we had of spreading information, there were no other papers being printed that supported us. And it was the only paper we were allowed to publish. Local bulletins were banned under the Sedition Act and people were jailed for writing them, printing them, selling them or buying them. The Daily Mail told people that the British Worker was full of communist lies and not to believe anything they didn't read in the British Gazette.

Getting our paper to people outside London was very difficult. The Government had planes, the buses and trains that were driven by volunteers and many private cars to distribute theirs. All we had were bicycles, a few motor-bikes and Shanks' pony.

A judge called Astbury tried to split the strikers off from us by saying that only we were in 'lawful dispute'. This meant it was illegal for anybody to go on strike in support of us and illegal for their trade unions to give them anything out of their own funds. Sir John Simon, the Attorney General, said striking workers were criminals and should be sued 'to the uttermost farthing of their personal possessions'. Neville Chamberlain, the Minister of Health, ordered the Workhouse Guardians to refuse relief to all strikers. Lord Balfour said they were an 'evil power'. Lord Asquith said the strike was the 'cruellest form of warfare in this the freest of all nations'. Rudyard Kipling said 'The German's shirt must be nearer to us than the miner's coat'. Lord Raglan, as if he hadn't made sufficient of an ass of himself in the Crimea to last a lifetime, had pictures taken of himself on the back of a train playing at being a railway guard.

Students and the well-off who would never have stooped to dirty their hands doing lowly jobs like driving buses and loading lorries for a career thought it 'great fun' to be doing it now. The MCC said it was 'the public duty of all counties to field their best elevens', whatever that meant.

The lockout, the strike, the whole thing, was just a game to them. They got paid, they got their photos taken and they kidded themselves the working class had it easy. They got to wreck equipment through lack of skill and not get charged for it and they got to split people's skulls and not get taken to court for it. And they knew that in a few days they'd all be back at their colleges and clubs having a laugh about it over their cocktails or whatever it was they sniffed, sucked and gargled before swallowing.

It was a big surprise when the Archbishop of Canterbury suddenly came out and spoke on our behalf, or at least pleaded for a peaceful settlement. The British Gazette wouldn't have anything to do with it, the BBC cancelled his broadcast, and Baldwin was very put out about it. It wasn't very long before the Archbishop regretted it and did his best to explain it away but at least while it lasted it was something from a quarter that had always sided with the Government, right or wrong. At the end of the War something called the 'Fifth Report' had been written by a committee of churches looking into the working conditions of the working class. Not a great deal of attention had been paid to it and I'd never heard of it until now. It was published in one our local bulletins before they'd been banned. In my opinion the needs of the pitman or any other working man couldn't be better put.

> By 'a living wage' we mean not merely a wage which is sufficient for physical existence but a wage adequate to maintain the worker, his wife and his family, in health and honour, and to enable him to dispense with the subsidiary earnings of his children up to the age of sixteen years. By 'reasonable hours' we mean hours sufficiently short not merely to leave him unexhausted but to

> allow him sufficient leisure and energy for home life, for recreation, for the development through study of his mind and spirit, and for participation in the affairs of the community. We hold that the payment of such a wage in return for such hours of work ought to be the first charge upon every industry.

Cardinal Bourne couldn't have read it. Or if he had, he obviously hadn't agreed with it because he said the strike was a 'sin'. That upset a tremendous number of people including a lot of strikers because many of the working class were Catholics. Some said it was the finish as far as they and the Catholic Church were concerned but the great majority were put in a right quandary over it.

Baldwin made a statement from 10 Downing Street telling the strikers that the Government would protect them from any loss of trade union benefits if they returned to work, that the courts would take action against any trade union that expelled a member for returning to work, and that anybody caught jeering or insulting such a person, a blackleg in other words, would be liable to a fine of forty shillings. Shortly after, miners, strikers, sympathisers and even a few old Labour MPs, were arrested, quickly convicted and sentenced to hard labour. Some were given up to two years, others between six and ten. Anybody found picketing on main roads could now be jailed for 'interfering with the King's Highway'. Trade union offices were ransacked, private papers, printers and typewriters removed, anybody in the building arrested, and all funds frozen.

Hundreds of noses, fingers, wrists, arms and collarbones were broken by truncheons and many decent men and women suffered very bad head injuries. University students, members of sporting clubs and the Fascist Movement were particularly vicious. A. J. Cook, who was only a little man with one leg, was kicked so badly in the head by Oxford students that he was given a wound he'd eventually die of. The Government insisted these people be referred to as 'peace-keepers' rather than 'strike-breakers', even though that was what they liked to call themselves.

On the 12th of May, 1926 J. H. Thomas welched again and the General Strike was over. Thomas, Citrine and Pugh, dressed like stockbrokers had gone to Baldwin to offer an unconditional surrender even though neither of our representatives, Cook, who wasn't well, or Herbert Smith would have anything to do with it. The whole thing had only lasted nine days, hardly more than a week. Anybody could have survived that.

When it was first announced we thought we'd won and there was cheering everywhere. Then the truth came out and everybody was disgusted, most of all with Thomas. Dockers, railwaymen and factory workers were all shouting that things were just getting going and that many more workers were getting ready to come out. The intention of the strike had been to make Coalowners treat their employees fairly and make other manufacturers do the same with theirs. Not to show them the working class were just a lot of useless whingers who'd give in at the first chance they got. The campaign hadn't just been against pitmen, it had been against all working folk. When Lord Londonderry, the Durham Coalowner, said he wanted 'them smashed from top to bottom', he meant everybody.

But it was too late now. When their trade union leaders had completely surrendered without gaining a farthing either for us or for them, there was nothing the strikers could do. It was all over for them, they'd have been better off not showing their weakness. The kind of inconvenience suffered by the average person in Britain had been no more than having a fly on the end of their nose. For some of them it had been an exciting holiday. Many told newspapers, newsreels, and the BBC, they'd really enjoyed themselves.

Our greatest mistake was that neither the workers who went on strike for us or we ourselves had been properly organised. Nothing like what the Government had been. One of the reasons was nobody had dreamt the British people would have supported the Coalowners the way they did. We thought that if it came to a general strike it would all be over in a couple of days. We thought that as soon as the British people who were always writing to the papers saying how decent and fair-minded they were, knew that the Coalowners had locked us out, and why, they'd have protested as strongly as we did. We thought they'd have acted the same way as if their own bosses had told them their wages were going to be cut and that they were going to have to work till six o'clock every night instead of five. If they had, neither Churchill, the Government or any of the rest of them, could have done what they did.

But a number of things had helped swing opinions against us. The first was the Government had the advantage of reaching far more people through their newspapers than we were able to do. Not only did they have more of them, their distribution was much better. Plus they had the BBC. Very few pitfolk or ordinary working people had wireless sets, whereas most of the middle classes did.

The second thing was the Government kept on saying the strike was against law and order and against King and Country, and British people and that included us, were very patriotic. It was barely eight years since the War and everybody in the country had been hurt by it one way or another. So an 'enemy of the state' was something hateful.

The other thing was Cardinal Bourne. Because he was a Roman Catholic cardinal he was normally never listened to except by the working class, certainly never by middle-class Protestants. Yet here he was telling the whole nation the strike was an offence against Almighty God and they were paying attention. His speech hardened the attitudes of the middle classes because whether you were a Catholic or not, a sin was still a sin. And of course it put the wind up many Catholic workers whether they were on strike or still waiting for the call.

The arselicker, Ramsay MacDonald, the gutless Walter Citrine and the big-headed traitor Jimmy Thomas had only been concerned about their own careers in Parliament. None of them had been prepared to put his neck on the line for us. Thomas might have come out of a meeting with Baldwin crying like a baby for the whole world to see. But the very next day the same one was back in there, slapping the back of a man like Birkenhead, with a grin on his face a mile wide.

Many had thought that together Cook and Smith would have made a great combination but as it turned out their natures were too different. Cook had been an open-air evangelist at one time and was a highly emotional man. Any mention of miners accepting a cut in wages before talks with the Government or the Coalowners had opened, and Cook blew his top. Smith was just the opposite. Smith would sit like there like a barrel of haddock waiting until everybody had exhausted themselves standing up and arguing their case and then getting down on their knees and practically begging. He would take out his false teeth and put them on the table, turn a huge fish eye on everybody and say 'Nowt doin'.' There was 'nowt doin'' all right.

As soon as the strikers went back they were punished. Those who'd been most involved with the strike were put on the list of 'professional agitators' and not taken back. Some employers said all previous employment contracts were now null and void, and pensions, long-service bonuses and promotion prospects could no longer be honoured. Anybody wanting to get back would have to sign a form saying they would never strike again. Railway companies, the ones Thomas had been elected to deal with, were the hardest of the lot. Whatever steps Baldwin took to make sure no trade union punished its members for going back, he took none against any employer.

We were now on our own. The railwaymen and dockers might have been shocked that the strike was called off but we'd half expected it all along. None of us believed McDonald, Thomas, Citrine or any of them would have sufficient backbone to stand up to even Churchill, let alone Birkenhead, Hicks, Anderson, Simon and Chamberlain as well. We knew the Government and the Coalowners would now be thinking they had us right where they wanted us, and that it would be only a matter of time before we gave in.

Our greatest weakness now was the same as it always was, lack of financial resources. It wasn't long shifts, filth or danger that we'd been griping about all these years. It was lousy wages. That's why we hadn't gone down on our hands and knees to the Coalowners and crawled back in when they offered us less than we'd been getting for the last ten years. When the workers had gone on strike the Government hadn't allowed them any relief, not even from their own union funds, because it said the strike was 'unlawful'. We now weren't allowed any because we were 'failing to accept' our 'employers' reasonable terms'. Without money for rent, sooner or later we'd be evicted from our homes. Nobody owned their own and those in colliery houses would very soon be put out. Without money for medicine we wouldn't be able to take our wives or bairns to the doctor when they needed it. Without money for food we would starve. Never mind heating, lighting, clothing and shoes. And we could forget completely about luxuries like tobacco, beer, the paper, a bet or anything like that. Already the Ministry of Health had told Workhouse Guardians throughout the country that giving outdoor relief was no longer a question of guidelines. From now on it was a matter of law that no able-bodied man was to be given any money or vouchers of any kind. A Board of Guardians in West Ham refused to obey and the whole lot of them were sent to prison.

The Co-op had always been good to us in times like these and they had huge assets. But they hadn't been paid back from the 1921 lockout yet and their headquarters told all branches they were to give no credit out this time. A million miners and their families could make a big dent in anybody's assets. Little corner-end shops always gave tick or they couldn't have done business but they could only do it for so long. There's a big difference between giving out on the Monday and getting back on the Friday, and not getting it back for six months. Every landlord and grocer in areas where pitfolk lived knew what they were like. They knew we'd be fighting long and hard so they knew what they themselves were in for. At least where our family lived, near Stanhope Road, there were many other people that weren't pitfolk who could keep landlords and other shopkeepers going. But in pit villages like Jilbert where the Coalowners owned the houses, the streets, the shops, the churches and the cemeteries and controlled even the emptying of the middens, it would be a different matter. People there were as dependent on pitfolk as pitfolk were on Coalowners.

It was up to the lodges in every district of every coalfield to look after their own people, whether it be to argue for them or to protect them. Whether it be landlords, grocery stores, the law or the cemetery keeper, they'd have to do everything they possibly could. Sometimes they would be successful and sometimes they wouldn't. Sometimes they'd be successful for a time, then all patience, credit and charity would run out. There were plenty ordinary decent people about but most of them weren't much better off than we were. There were plenty willing hands but willing hands don't fill bellies. They can make rag bandages and dig graves if it comes to it but they cannot take an appendix out. And they can no more keep the bailiff away than they can the cold. But they can pray and they can comfort and that helped.

The best way to keep bodies and souls together was to raise money and that was the lodges' most important job. After that it was to keep us informed, keep our spirits up and help keep people amused. With the funds the lodges already had and the food they could beg, they immediately organised 'fellowship dinners'. These were between midday and one o'clock and everybody went – man, woman and child. After the dinner was finished we'd sing a few hymns and then somebody from the Union would get up and tell us how things were going regarding negotiations. That never took long because there wasn't any. Nobody would meet any of our leaders.

Somebody else would then give us a pep talk and tell us we were good people being wronged and that because we belonged to a great nation that believed in justice, sooner or later all decent people would realise it. And in any case their bloody coal stocks wouldn't last for ever. All we had to do was hang on, keep our chins up and keep smiling. A big cheer would go up and there'd be more than a few eyes with tears in them. Then somebody else would get up and crack a few jokes and sing a couple of songs and we'd all have a laugh. He would ask if there were any birthdays or wedding anniversaries or anything and get people to shout them out. Then they'd be called to the front and a little speech would be made for them.

One day my father put his hand up. 'It's not your anniversary or anythin'. What ye got your hand up for?' I says to him. 'Mind your own business,' he says and starts shouting out because they couldn't see his short curly arm. Eventually he got their attention.

'Yes! It's Jack Turnbull... What've you got for us, Jack?'

'It's my lad, Tommy here!' my father shouts.

'What!' I says. 'Quit it, man!'

'He's twenty-one today!'

'No I'm not!'

'Yes ye are, ye silly little bugger... I'm your father... D'ye think I divvent know when me own lad's turned a man?'

'Bring him up, Jack! Come on... Up here, Tommy lad... Everybody, let's have a big hand for Tommy... Key of the door for Tommy. Never been twenty-one before...never been kissed either.'

Everybody was singing and laughing. But I wouldn't go. I wouldn't have gone up there for a thousand pounds. So they all just sang happy birthday and I stayed where I was.

'Ye shouldn't have done it,' I said to him when everybody had turned back round again.

'Divvent be so daft! What's the matter with ye.'

Apart from that, the dinners were a great thing because they got us all together and we were able to enjoy ourselves for an hour or two.

To raise money, brass band concerts, dances, raffles, lottoes, talent competitions, athletic contests, boxing matches, coconut shies, skittles, darts, 'guess-your-weight', pony rides and practically everything you would get at a fairground aside from the big roundabouts, were got under way. The weather was good and this made everything a whole lot easier than it might otherwise have been. Quite a few took it as a sign that God was on our side.

The men fished the rivers and the sea and the women and children picked winkles, crabs, seaweed and sea coal. And they fetched sand from the beach, washed it in buckets and sold it to builders and anybody else that wanted it for a few pence. Everything was shared out. Anything we got that wasn't eaten was sold from stalls or carried in pans and sold from door to door. We went to farms and picked spuds and turnips and got paid in swedes and kale and other vegetables that were cheaper. We scratted around coal tips and rubbish dumps for stuff we could use, repair or make something with and sell. There were always rags to be found on the rubbish dumps, and now that the women weren't having to spend time scrubbing pit clothes, they were able to make things. Some of the church and lodge halls were like clippy-mat factories, knitting factories or sock-darning factories. Old woollens were found or scrounged and unwound. And scarves, socks, Fair-Isle pullovers, bathers and gloves made out of them. Things like tea cosies and rugs were made out of almost anything.

Many of the men were quite handy and could make crackets, cots, little tables and things – nothing high class but things that would come in useful. Those that weren't so nifty could always get hold of a bit of sandpaper and make knobs, rolling pins and doorstops. Anybody could give a gate or a set of railings a lick of paint and anybody could scrape a door down. Some could do tinkers' work and repair kettles and pans and do soldering jobs. Some went knocking on people's doors to see if they wanted anything fixed or sharpened or cleaned or if they wanted to buy something cheap that we'd made. Others cut hair, dug gardens, mowed lawns, fixed roofs, cleared away rubbish, cleaned chimneys, groomed dogs or ponies. And yet others collected fish and vegetable scraps from the market and from people's bins and sold them to people who kept hens or pigs. Kids went out with shovels and buckets following cart-horses and picking up their manure. Some of them collected dogshit and sorted it into black piles and white piles and put it into little bags for those that wanted different types for their garden.

In Durham the Co-ops were good to us, no matter what their bosses in London had told them. So were Hunters of Gateshead who gave a thousand loaves of bread and Fry's Chocolate who gave 7,500 packets of cocoa. Bookies lent money and so did many other people. Ordinary householders, some of them complete strangers, gave all kinds of things to help out. Sometimes it was food, sometimes clothing, sometimes little bits and pieces they didn't want any more that they thought we might be able to do up and sell for a few coppers.

But the strike dragged on and after it was going into months rather than just a few weeks, people began to get a bit fed up with donating and lending and helping. The same ones tended to get bombarded all the time.

The papers seemed to think we had it cushy, they thought we weren't being treated firmly enough. Neville Chamberlain who should have been the one to know as he was the Minister of Health, said starvation still wasn't in sight, 'only signs of under-nutrition'.

Everybody including us was calling it a 'strike'… It wasn't of course, it was still a lockout. At the very worst, it was a 'stayout'. If the Coalowners had taken down their notices and opened the gates we'd have all been fighting to get on the first shift. But they hadn't and they didn't look as though they were going to. I think we called it a strike because 'strike' sounded more as though we were in charge, as if it was us that were taking the action, instead of them.

Sometimes you'd hear that somebody in the paper had said the Government should see if the Germans had any of the gas they used against our soldiers in the War left and see if they could buy some of it off them. Or that we should be put up against a wall and shot. They joked about it and they could afford to. The weather was great... Who needed coal? And if they did, it could be bought from the Americans or the Germans. Better they got the benefit than British coalminers. We were just a nuisance as far as they were concerned but more a spelk in the finger than a thorn in the side. They seemed to think of us as hundreds of dirty little men blocking up the entrances to every coal mine in the country, stopping the coal from bubbling up like some kind of oil geyser. Very few seemed to realise coal was very firmly stuck to the walls and that it was a long way down and along, and that it was buried in layers of stone. That it wasn't just lying there in neat piles waiting to be shovelled up, the way they shovelled it out of their coalhouses and into their scuttles by their fancy firesides.

All the time one of the biggest problems was finding out what was really happening at other collieries throughout the country. The printers were back to normal and so was the transport system but we still weren't allowed to publish our own bulletins. We had to rely on rumour and suspicion and tales from people we had no way of checking up on. The news in the newspapers was no news at all and you couldn't believe those buggers any more now than you could before.

By now many pitmen were in Durham Gaol doing hard labour and the number was increasing all the time. During the general strike a group of fellers had pulled up some of the railway track near Cramlington and four of them had gone to warn the volunteer who was driving the train. He ignored them and drove on and the train had been derailed. Nobody was killed but the four who had given the volunteer driver notice were given sentences of up to ten years' hard labour. If it had been an ordinary train it mightn't have mattered quite so much seeing as nobody was hurt but the Flying Scotsman was like a symbol of Empire. A dozen miners who sang the 'Red Flag' outside the court were jailed for treason. In some places you only had to blink an eye or open your mouth and they had you. Look to the left and it was sedition, look to the right and it was treason. The minimum sentence was usually £50 or two months in jail. That kind of money couldn't have been raised in the whole of the Durham Coalfield and there wouldn't have been so much as a sosser from the Church that owned so much of it.

The Bishop of Durham wasn't bound by the head of his Church the way the Catholic bishops were bound by the Pope, and he certainly hadn't supported his Archbishop when the Archbishop had spoken on our behalf during the general strike. This feller had a tradition of letting his stables be used when Durham Gaol was full, the only accommodation he ever made available to any pitman. No wonder they once tried to drown him at a Durham gala. A group of pitmen went for him, so they thought, and chucked him in the River Wear. It wasn't until afterwards they found they'd got the wrong one and that one of his lackeys had been ducked instead. It goes to show how familiar the Bishop of Durham's face was in times of trouble.

Apart from all the other hurts we had to put up with – and we'd had to put up with it for years – was the lie that we were 'traitors'. Calling us 'filthy and ignorant' was bad enough. They'd see us in the street going home dirty because our work was dirty and because we had to go home to get ourselves clean. But our houses were just as clean as anybody else's and we didn't need to hire anybody else to clean them. Most were as clean and tidy and as cosy and homely as it was possible to make them, even though they were often so cramped people were practically sitting on top of each other. Washing was always hanging up because in bad weather it might take a week just to get everything properly dry and there was so much of it. A few mightn't have been but some of those might have had a man lying in the corner with his back broken or a ten-year-old bairn with froth coming out of its mouth. In more than a few, a woman would have worked herself to death before she was out of her thirties. Sickness and poverty was part of the furniture. Though clean and tidy or not so clean and tidy, none of them would turn you away from their door. As for ignorance, what do you expect?

But calling us 'traitors' was going too far. Loyalty is our creed, we need it to be able to go down a pit every day of our lives. And we are as patriotic as anybody else. We lay down our lives in the pit and on the battlefield when we are called. I cannot recall the name of any of those who sent this country to war, being killed or wounded himself in the War. But I could name many a good miner who was.

If anybody had stood up anywhere in Britain and called Winston Churchill a traitor, he'd have sued them for slander and Law Lord John Simon would have jumped to take his case.

10

In Durham over two hundred pits were closed, more than 150,000 men were out of work, and the lodges couldn't cope any more. It was August and we'd been out for over three months. The fellowship dinners had turned into bowls of soup and the bowls of soup into little more than bowls of dirty water. We were tired people, anxious people, hungry people, people who'd run out of energy and ideas. At first the Lodge had paid us ten shillings a week and they did that twice. Then it was five shillings a week and they did that three times. Then four shillings a week and that was only for one week. Then three shillings a week for three weeks. And that was it… For the past five weeks there'd been nowt. It was up to each individual to do what he could and for each family to manage the best way they could. If somebody decided they had to go to the Workhouse, that was entirely up to them. Nobody would blame them. Better a pauper than a blackleg.

People who had hung on to their prams since their last bairns were babbies were now counting their lucky stars and any that had bairns still in them would be doing double duty. If you had a choice of a cart, a wheelbarrow or a pram, the pram was by far the best for transporting stuff. Carts were hard to pull and even harder to push and they were buggers on banks. Wheelbarrows were better, if you had a good back. But anybody could handle a pram. Coal, rags, scrap metal, old wirelesses, anything and everything went in them on one trip or another and it was a rare sight to see a bairn in a pram on any day but a Sunday. We had a bogey with three odd wheels and it was nigh on impossible to steer. It had a bit of string tied to the front which you put over your shoulder and pulled. But no matter which way you pulled, it kept going off the pavement into the gutter. We swapped the wheels around umpteen times but it made no difference, it was doomed to go skewwhiff. Second-hand wheels were as scarce as hen's teeth and the bogey could only carry so much, so in the finish we sold it. A few days later we saw the feller who'd bought it, picking up sea coal from the gutter, with the bogey on its side. 'I told ye it was ne good,' my father says to him as we walked past.

Neville Chamberlain was still refusing to let the Workhouse Guardians give coalminers a penny. If they wanted any relief, if they were that desperate, they could go into the Workhouse to get it. That was his attitude. And they could take their families with them.

My father had sworn he would never go to the Guardians. Not to beg, not to borrow, not even to try and trick the buggers. 'Nobody, and I mean nobody from this house, is gannin' to those sods, not while I'm still alive.' At first practically every day Isabella Tanner had complained she couldn't manage any more. Now she didn't say anything, she just sat around and moped. Somebody said she was suffering from melancholia. 'What's that but no spirit?' was my father's answer. 'She's got no bloody go in her, that's her trouble.' She was very skinny though, nobody could deny that. By this time none of us were what you might call fat. But because the women always gave the men the best of whatever the house had in case they suddenly got the call to go back to work and then gave the children the best of what was left, there was never much more than would dirty a plate when it came to themselves.

Nobody who knew her could say Isabella Tanner was a ray of sunshine and I can't honestly say I ever liked her. That's not to say I didn't feel sorry for her. A miner's life is hard enough but a miner's wife's is no better. All day long she's scrubbing, washing, ironing, cleaning, polishing and baking, in a place that's always steamy with clothes drying and pans boiling and always smelling of sweaty boots. And this is when she's lucky, this is when the men are in work. When they are and there's a few of them, no sooner has she finished one lot of washing or cooking than she has to start on another. And then she has to look after the kids. And sooner or later she's going to have to nurse somebody, maybe many times, maybe several at the same time, maybe for the rest of her life. All in the same damp tiny little room.

One day my father and me came back from a march and we were really fed up. Every time you tried to get people's attention, no matter how peacefully, the pollises always arrested somebody either for 'conduct likely to cause a riot', 'thinking about causing a riot' or some other bloody thing. You could hardly raise your hand in the air without breaking some law. But it was the leaders and their families that they were always after. The police knew who they were and they'd hound the life out of them till they got them for something or other. So many good men were now in jail that we could only hope they were in good company because very few got to visit them. One week a hundred of us younger blokes walked to Durham to make a protest about the pitmen and other fellers who'd been jailed during or after the general strike. It beats me how they expected a wife who lived in Shields to get to see her husband stuck all the way down there. It was nigh on twenty miles and then she'd have to get back. So we thought we'd go down, see how they were, and maybe cheer them up a bit. We had a few letters and little mementoes for them from their families and quite a few messages. At six o'clock in the morning we set off from Shields.

Twenty miles is a long way on an empty belly when it's been empty for months and by the time we got to Durham we were nearly all in. As soon as we got to the boundary of the city, a gang of well-fed, hale and hearty pollises on big strong horses, were waiting for us. The one in charge said we were 'causing disaffection'. That was a new one on me. They'd obviously thought there was going to be more of us than there was, because there were many more of them than there were of us. We were so weary we hardly had the strength to defend ourselves and when they rushed at us with their batons they just about flattened us. I ended up with a bruise on my back the size of a cricket bat but some of the others got much worse. At least half a dozen were knocked unconscious. They wouldn't give us first aid or let us get a drink of water or even rest a few minutes to get our breath. We had to turn around and go back the best way we could. Two of the fellers had to be carried, until somebody came out of a house and gave us some help.

We'd done nothing except walk the public roads. We hadn't been yelling and shouting or breaching any peace. Did they think a raggy bunch of tired pit lads who'd come all the way from South Shields was going to pull down their jail for them… I've never been inside Durham Gaol but I've seen it. You couldn't get in with a tank.

No wonder tempers were getting worse. People were so hungry and frustrated they'd either become apathetic or so angry, the slightest thing would spark them off. My father was no exception.

'Bella, where did ye put that Colman's mustard tin I had on the mantelpiece?' he says one day.

'I haven't put it anywhere. Is it not still there?'

'I'd hardly be askin' where it was, if it was still here, would I?'

'It was there before.'

'Well it's not bloody-well here now, so where the hell is it?'

Isabella Tanner came in and she looked awful. Her pinny was dirty, her hair was a mess. She looked as though she hadn't been to bed for a month.

'Look at the bloody state of ye! Can ye not keep yoursel' lookin' better than that? We're not in the bloody Workhouse yet!'

'I don't know where I am these days, Jack.'

'Aye. Well ye'd better find out quick and look for that bloody tin. I had half a crown in there and everybody in this house knows it.'

'You're not blamin' me for losin' it, are ye?'

My father nearly went crackers, I thought he was going to murder her. He grabbed hold of her, flung her backwards and she tottered from side to side and fell on a heap on the floor. Then he went into every drawer and cupboard, emptying things out and flinging everything out all over the place. Two old Coronation mugs he and Isabella Tanner had been given for a wedding present were smashed to smithereens on the hearth. Pans were flung against the wall clashing and banging. One fell to the ground dented and bent, another went along the floor like a cockeyed wheel with its handle hanging off. The only vase we had in the house fell on the mat and the thick sour water spilled out all over the floor. Isabella Tanner went into hysterics and started banging her fists on the floor.

'Where's my bloody half-crown? Where's my bloody half-crown!' my father was shouting as he was kicking the chairs over and getting closer and closer to where she was lying. I could see he was going to kick her next so I grabbed hold of him. His face was purple and he was close to tears.

'Howay, Dad… Divvent upset yoursel'… If it's here we're bound to come across it sooner or later. An' if it's gone, there's nowt we can do about it. Anybody could've come in and took it.'

'I need a drink, lad. Just one gill is all I need.'

'Howay and sit down. I'll go and see if I can get ye a paper.'

'He's mad, he is! He should be locked up! He would've killed me if you hadn't been here!'

'Shut up, will ye! Ye'll only make matters worse.'

'Divvent leave him with me! Take him away with ye!'

'He wouldn't do no such thing. And you know it!'

My father just sat there with such a look on his face, not saying a word. I thought maybe something had snapped. But he got up after a while and went out.

Neither the mustard tin or the halfcrown ever turned up but I cannot believe Isabella Tanner would have dared take it. And little Wilf would have been too scared to go anywhere near it.

Monica had been getting free school dinners but that had stopped over a month ago and she was as pale and washed-out looking as the rest of us. She'd had ringworm and impetigo for ages and no matter what we tried we couldn't seem to get rid of them. No sooner would it go from one place than it would start up in another. Wilf had mouth ulcers and could hardly open his mouth without making a face. John had gone into himself more and more and hardly spoke a word. Dad was becoming more and more breathless and had patience for neither nothing nor nobody. Isabella Tanner wouldn't get up in the morning. 'What's the point?' she would shriek. 'There's nowt to cook and there's ne workers in the house to do for.' My father would lose his temper and shout at her. Then he'd start going on about the strike, the Government, the Coalowners, the Union, the Labour Party and just about every bloody thing else.

The Miners' Hall had given out second-hand clothing from the very beginning but my father would neither ask for anything nor take anything that had been offered to him. He wouldn't let any of us either but I'd have bet anything Isabella Tanner had been up a time or two and got a few odds and ends for herself and Wilf. Sometimes you'd see him in a pullover you'd never seen before but always when my father was out. Yet Monica was running around in bare feet because she'd grown out of her shoes. I know my father hadn't sat down and decided that his pride was more important than his little daughter's feet. If he had, he wouldn't have. He just wouldn't allow himself to be forced into that position. It wasn't a question of pride, no more than it was a question of Monica's feet. It didn't do to think too much about some things.

Although Durham miners had always had a reputation for being stroppy, right though the general strike and afterwards there'd been very little trouble anywhere in the Durham Coalfield, either in the way of colliery damage or clashes with the police. But when St Hilda's gave in it was a different matter altogether.

Hilda used to belong to what we called the 'joint four' – the other three being Boldon, Whitburn and Harton. The reason for getting together was because the Harton Coal Company, like all the other Coalowners in the country, would never agree to national agreements and as long as we stuck together and negotiated under the joint board, we had some clout. Certainly more than we would have had on our own. But for about a year before the general strike the Hilda lot had been in dispute with their own management and had broken away from the Four. They weren't satisfied with the joint board and had decided they wanted to sort the matter out themselves. The joint four board had been a bit of a joke, nobody could deny that. They were forever getting people to march up to the Company offices or the town hall or some other place, having a barney with whoever it was, and then marching them back again. They used to call the chairman the 'Grand Old Duke of York' because of it. But you had to put up with that sort of thing, it was part of being in the group, and it was no reason for breaking away. All that did was weaken themselves and weaken everybody else.

They had got nowhere with their own private negotiations and as a result they'd been out on strike for eight months before the lockout and general strike had even begun. Their local MP had managed to get them some unemployment relief until then but as soon as the lockout happened, it stopped. From the 30th of April they'd been in it with the rest of us, part of the whole thing and just as deep, whether they liked it or not. They were now fighting the same battle we were. The enemy was the same, the terms were the same, and we felt they should have acted the same way we did. After nearly fourteen months they probably felt they'd had enough but that was their fault not ours. It was no excuse for going back and they shouldn't ever have even thought about it.

In Nottingham an MP by the name of George Spencer had told the men in his constituency that the general strike and everything else had been a complete waste of time and that he was forming his own union, the 'Spencer Union'. In his union each man's contract would be on a day-to-day basis. Nottingham coal was good coal and the pits were more modern than most, so if the man kept his mouth shut and did as he was told by the union, he might do all right. If he didn't, he was out and the union wouldn't be responsible for him. Between the Spencer Union and the Workhouse, the Nottingham miners had chosen the Spencer Union. Hilda's management had found out about the Spencer Union and was now offering to take back anybody who joined it. Some of the men had already given in.

At first only a few went back, mainly deputies and the likes to check the state of the pit. Then we heard that more were going, less than a hundred but more than enough to leave any doubt in anybody's mind. These blokes were blacklegs. They knew it, we knew it, and the police certainly knew it and that's why hundreds of them were now being drafted in from other counties. Whether the blacklegs were all Hilda men or whether some of them were scabs from somewhere else, didn't really matter. They were still blacklegs. If they were Hilda men it just made them that much worse.

As soon as we in the other three Shields pits found out how many were going back, we made up our minds to do something. If there'd only been one or two blacklegs, as there'd been in the first place, it wouldn't have mattered because their own mates would have taken care of them. In any case no pit can go into production with just a couple of blacklegs.

We divided ourselves up into gangs, one for every shift, so that no matter when they were trying to get in or out, somebody would be waiting for them. There was supposed to be at least one man from each family on picket duty and I was picked from our house for the first one. I'd never been involved in anything like this before. In the past I'd been too young and had just skived off and left it to the older fellers. I'd done my duties during the general strike, whatever I was asked to do. But that had mainly been delivering messages and that sort of thing. The picket duty I'd done had hardly been any duty at all, nobody in their right mind would have tried to get into Harton.

Although the lodge secretary had told us to stay calm and conduct ourselves in an orderly fashion, according to some of the lads there was very likely going to be some serious trouble. I'd never had a scrap with anybody since I was a kid, I'd be what you might call a quiet sober sort of a feller. That's what I thought anyway. I didn't hold with violence, I never had. My father never had. Pitmen were our friends, often enough our only friends. It seemed terrible to me that our quarrel now had to be with some of them. But fellers who knew more about these kind of things than I did, blokes who were a lot older than me and knew their politics – some had been soldiers in the Great War – said we'd all have to do as we were told. It was the only way if we were ever to win the battle and get our jobs back. And I put all my faith in these fellers.

They told me to bring a pick handle or poss-stick, something heavy and hard. I wasn't too happy about it but my father said it was only to scare them. So the following day when I joined on to the gang that were waiting outside Harton, I had my baton if you could call it that. It was only a bit of a leg off an old basket chair and I had it tucked well away inside my jacket. You could just about have flattened a scone with it provided the scone had been fresh. I wasn't out to kill or maim anybody.

Bill Mack, who was a really big feller and loved nothing better than a good scrap, saw me and came up grinning.

'Got your weapon, Tommy?'

'My what? I thought I only –'

'Your Ma's choppin' axe, man? Your Da's hammer? Somethin' to split their bloody skulls with?'

'Oh aye! You bet!' I says, patting my jacket and trying to sound like I was raring to go. 'Right here!'

'Get it out and gis a look at it, then.'

'This is just the handle,' I says, pulling the end out so he could see a bit of it.

'Champion! Good man! Divvent be afraid to use it when the time comes.'

'Don't worry,' I said, squinting my eyes to look vicious.

'That's the way, Tommy! That'll put the shits up them.'

There must have been three or four hundred there at least. Some of them, like Billy, were shouting and organising and pushing everybody around. Others were laughing and carrying on. Some of them were even fighting amongst themselves with their sticks, sword fencing like The Three Musketeers. A group of them were standing over somebody groaning on the ground with a busted lip and blood all over his face. A little old feller who was standing back a bit like me, says to me, 'If this is what they're like now, God help us when we get there.'

'I was thinkin' the same thing. Have ye ever been on owt like this afore?'

'Aye, I have. Many a time.'

'What's it like?'

'Ye never can tell... It might gan all quiet and peaceful or it might be bloody chaos. There's never more than a hair's breath between the two.

One minute they're kiddin' on and laughin', the next they're yellin' and screamin' like bloody madmen. In situations like these, people are like powder kegs. The least bit thing can spark them off.'

'D'ye think anythin' like that's likely to happen today, with all these pollises around?'

There were dozens and dozens of pollises standing in lines eyeing us up.

'That makes it even more likely. Them's not olive branches they've got stuck in their belts.

"Lingumvity" they're made of and that stuff's as hard as bloody hell. Get one of those across the back of your neck from somebody up on a bloody horse and ye'll gan doon like a ton o' bricks.' He made a swinging action with his arm and then pulled a face as though he'd been hit.

'Is the neck a worse place than the back?'

'Ne comparison! Get hit on the back and ye mightn't even know it, not if you're a pitman. The neck's far worse than the head in my opinion and I've been hit in both places. But not any more… Not if I can help it.'

'That sort of thing shouldn't be allowed.'

'Ha! Just you look at the faces on some of them... Tak him over there for instance, the big bugger wi' the ginger hair. Nebody can tell me he's not burstin' to have a go at somebody... Now look at that one in front... Aye, him with the tiny lugs. He'd happily scatter your brains on the pavement. Before this day's out somebody's ganna be mighty sorry they met up with him.'

I pulled out my little basket-chair leg.

'D'ye think this'll be any good?'

'Put it away, lad… Whatever ye do, divvent make the mistake of thinkin' they'll tak the size of it into consideration when they're bearin' doon on ye like the Bengal bloody Lancers.'

I put it away and straightened my jacket so it didn't look as though anything was there. Though if I was going to have to go around all day, pulling it out to show the fellers and then shoving it away before the big pollises saw it, sooner or later I was going to make a mistake.

'Tak my tip, son. Gan along wi' them, because you have to do that much. But keep well out o' the road. Everybody expects ye to do your bit and that's fair enough, but ye divvent have to get your bones broke or land yoursel' in jail. That won't do nebody any good. And it'll break your poor mother's heart.'

One of my mates saw me and shouted for me to go over and join their little gang.

'Hang on, I'll be there in a sec! Thanks, mister,' I says. 'I'll be seein' ye.'

'Aye, all right, son. Take care of yoursel'. Divvent forget what I told ye.'

'Howay man, Tommy! We're gannin' up front!' It was Geordie Wilkins and Freddy Blair and a few of the others.

'What d'ye think of all this then, Freddy?' I said, hoping he might say things were looking pretty steady from where we were.

'I divvent know. But the way those big-gobbed buggers over there with Chas Fenwick are carryin' on, it won't be long afore there's some action.'

One group was singing 'Land of Hope and Glory', and another, 'The Red Flag', while the paddies were trying to drown them both out with 'Kevin Barry'. There was a lot of pushing and shoving going on even over that. Freddy had a Woodbine dumper and he offered me a drag.

'Fowler Street's the place for these, outside any of the pictures or places like that. I got five on Sunday night all in the same spot. One of them couldn't have had more than one or two puffs out of it. You want to come with us, man.'

I wasn't too keen on picking up dumpers, you never knew whose mouths they'd been in. But sometimes you just wouldn't think about it, you just lit up and enjoyed it when you got the chance.

There was quite a commotion going on somewhere but I couldn't see what it was in aid of. I looked around. Not everybody was going on like mad. There were a few looking very nervous and hanging back, saying nothing but nearly jumping out of their skins every time a shout went up. Older fellers were muttering among themselves, smiling and sucking pipes with nothing in them except a bit of paper or a bit of dried dandelion.

Four big fellers came by swinging their sticks. One of them had a lump of lead piping that would have dropped an ox. 'If the bastards try to get past me, I'll lay them oot, one by one.'

'Be careful somebody doesn't take it off ye and shove it up your arse,' says one of the older fellers.

'It might just shut 'im up for a bit,' said another.

'I'd like to see them try! I'd wrap it round their bloody neck! Why, would you like to give it a try, Granda?'

'Me? God, no! I'm just quietly offerin' up a little prayer of thanks that you're on our side and not theirs.'

Everybody laughed.

Suddenly there was a loud command. 'Right, lads! Away we go!'

There was a lot of cheering as we moved off in the direction of Hilda's, more like a rabble than a regiment, and some of them were singing 'It's a Long Way to Tipperary'. As we were going under the railway bridge a couple of well dressed blokes shouted something down at us that didn't altogether sound like 'Good luck'.

'Hadaway an' shite!' a young voice yelled back.

'Now, here! We'll have less of that!' said one of the leaders. 'Just you behave yoursel' if ye want to come with us.'

'You tell 'im, Isaac. That's ne way to gan on, they're not down the pit now.'

We passed a field with lots of tents and soldiers in it. They weren't in any order, they were just standing around looking. Some of our lot started booing at them and a few of them shouted something back. Then an officer feller rode amongst them on horseback and must have told them to shut up because they turned back to whatever they'd been doing. At the same time somebody at the front of our lot shouted to leave them alone. Just as well, I thought. We'd enough trouble as it was without those buggers coming after us. We'd been told to keep our sticks away, but as usual a few daft sods were waving theirs about and shaking them at anybody who didn't smile as we went past. Somebody was banging a tin drum to the tune of the 'Dead March'.

When we got to the Hilda Colliery there were many more pollises lined up waiting for us, but not a word was said by either side. Our procession just broke up into little gangs muttering and whispering. The pollises looked very big and hard to beat. They were standing up very straight in rows the way soldiers do. I'd never seen so many policemen in my whole life. Every pollis in the country must be here, I thought.

All of a sudden somebody shouted 'Here they come!' and the whole mob of us rushed to the colliery gates. For days we'd all been trying to guess who they'd be, some fellers had been ready to stake their lives on it. Everybody knew somebody at Hilda, and one would be saying it'd be this one and another would be saying no, it could never be, it'd have to be somebody else. Everybody was trying to get to the front so they could see for themselves who the blacklegs were. We were booing and swearing and calling them scabs and yellabellies and God knows what else before we'd even clapped eyes on them.

When I eventually managed to get close enough to the front to see them, there wasn't all that many, about forty or fifty as far as I could tell. They didn't look like devils or anything, they just looked like all pitmen do, with their pit clothes and their bait in their pockets and their bottles of water. I really don't know what I was expecting but it was a surprise to see them like that, so ordinary looking. I think we expected them to turn around and go back home when they saw all of us there. And we were so shocked to see them, heads down, quietly going through the lines of pollises, that we didn't know quite what to do about it. They were into the colliery yard before we realised it. A few did turn back and were given a big cheer but most of them had got by. I think we thought they were going to try to come through us and that they'd have to fight every inch of the way, like running the gauntlet. But it hadn't happened that way at all. They'd got in and there they were, safe and sound inside.

Suddenly the gates were slammed shut and locked and it was then we realised we'd failed. We'd failed completely. Some of them began to go crazy and chuck bricks over the railings. That did a fat lot of good. They were in and we were out, and that was all that mattered. We were left standing there like idiots with capstans for legs and the pollises had grins all over their faces. There was no point hanging about to listen to a whole lot of moaning about how we should have done this or done that, so I just came away.

'Don't forget, Tommy!' a voice called after me. 'Back at eight o'clock sharp!'

'Aye, I know.'

11

When I got back home, the front door was wide open and the place was full of pollises. Isabella Tanner was standing in the passage waving her arms about and shrieking. As soon as she saw me she came running up.

'Go and fetch your father, Tommy! Quick!'

'What's gannin' on?' I says. 'Where's me father and wor John?'

Several pollises looked up when I came in but carried on pulling out drawers and chucking things all over the place.

'And who might you be?' one of them says without even looking up.

'I live here.'

'I didn't ask ye where ye lived, ye cheeky bugger! I asked ye what your name was.'

'Thomas Turnbull's my name, and this is my father's house. And I'd like to know what yous are all doin' in it. What d'ye think you're lookin' for?'

My father had been doing a bit bookie-running to try and make ends meet and I didn't know whether they were after him for that or because of his political shenanigans. Having any kind of papers connected with politics, even a Tory Party pamphlet, could get you a jail sentence. They knew my father was a very strong union man and they knew he was a runner. But so far he'd been too clever for them and they didn't like it one bit.

'We'll ask the questions round here. And you'll keep a civil tongue in your head, sonny boy. Or ye'll be in big trouble.'

'Go and fetch your father!' Isabella Tanner kept shouting. 'Tell 'im there's ructions gannin' on here.' Then she dropped her voice. 'I expect he's at church.' She gave a wink big enough for everybody to see.

I raced up to the Stanhope. Even though he hadn't a penny to spend on beer my father still conducted most of his business there. He knew if he stayed long enough and was obliging enough or if the worst came to the worst and he just sat there with his tongue hanging out, sooner or later somebody was bound to buy him a gill. They wouldn't all be able to walk past and pretend they hadn't seen him.

'What!' he says when I burst in. 'Hang on, I'll be right with ye.' He stood up and drained his glass and then wiped his moustache with the back of his hand. 'By, that was good.' He just couldn't help himself even at a time like this.

'Right! What are we waitin' for? Away we go.'

We ran most of the way back to the house, stopping only to let him catch his breath a couple of times. When we got there the house was empty.

'Bella! Where are ye? Where the hell is she? Bellaaaahhh! He was gasping for breath.

In she rushed with half the neighbours in the street behind her.

'What a time I've had wi' those swines, Jack. Nobody could imagine what I've been through this day.' She flopped herself down in a chair. 'They've got me in a right tizzy.'

'Howay then, woman! Out with it! What the hell's been happenin' here? What were they after?'

He was going around picking things up and looking in drawers and under the bed.

'They turned the whole place inside out as ye can see. Drawers, cupboards, everythin'. They even broke the door on the wardrobe just because it was jammed shut… I told ye, ye should've fixed it.'

'Did they get owt? Did they take anythin' away wi' them?'

'They took a few of your papers, I didn't get a chance to see what exactly. They wouldn't tell me nowt. They just barged in and started ransackin' the place... I'm so upset I'm ganna have to lie down for a bit.'

'Never mind that. Ye look all right to me.'

'No man should ever be allowed to speak to a married woman the way I've been spoken to today. One of them was no older than Tommy, the cheeky little sod!'

'What sort of questions did they ask?'

'I don't know… All kinds of things… I cannot remember everythin'. Me head's still spinnin' from it all. But they took somethin', I know that. 'Cos one of them said "Hey, looka here", and they all had a look at whatever it was.'

'The bloody swines! I'm gannin' up to the station to see what the hell's gannin' on. I'm not puttin' up with this sort of thing. If folks have a right to vote for politicians, they've a right to talk politics. Your mind's not your bloody own these days.'

'Divvent, Jack... Divvent gan up there. What they've got, ye'll not get back. And if ye gan up there and loss your temper, which ye will do, they'll lock ye up for sure. Then where'll we be?'

'She's right, Dad,' I said. 'These days they can get ye for anythin' they want.'

He was probably having second thoughts already, because he agreed which was most unusual for him.

'Maybe you're right, the bloody sods!'

A couple of hours later, after we'd tidied the place up, we were all sitting down to a cup of tea when Isabella Tanner comes out with 'D'ye know what your lot did to Maisie Sutton? They smashed every window in the house.'

'Aye, well... They weren't her windows, they were his. And he's a bloody blackleg and he deserves everything he's got comin'.'

'Ye know her face was cut to ribbons by the flyin' glass, I suppose?'

'No, I didn't. And I don't want to hear about it either.'

'They say she'll be scarred for the rest of her life.'

'Who says?'

'The Infirmary.'

'The Infirmary! That useless dump! Anyway it serves her right for marryin' a lump o' shite like Bill Sutton. She wants her head examined.'

'Jack! There's no need for language like that at the table!'

'Aye, well.'

'One of their bairns isn't expected to see the year out.'

'Give it a rest, will ye!'

'And the other's been practically blind since the day she was born.'

My father jumped up. 'Shut your bloody naggin', will ye! I didn't smash their bloody windows! Or make their babby blind! I'm only tryin' to do the best I can for my own family!' He then turned to me. 'Isn't it time ye were gettin' yoursel' back up to Hilda's?'

'There's plenty time yet.'

'There's not! Away ye go! Now!'

Back at Hilda's there were many more stewing about than there was in the morning, maybe three or four times as many. And more police. There were also quite a few women. And the mood was much different.

Last time the men had been more light-hearted, treating it as though it was a kind of sport. Now they were quieter and more serious and everybody seemed to be grinding their teeth. Instead of being in lots of little groups looking in all directions like they were before, they were gathered into one big mass facing the gates. Now and then you could hear the voices of women trying to calm the men down. Though some of them were just the opposite.

Suddenly the shout we'd been waiting for went up. 'Here they come!'

Immediately a barrage of stones went up in the air towards the colliery yard. At the same time four or five fellers coming up the road to join us, were pelted.

'Sod off home, ye bastards!'

Somebody recognised them and tried to stop it but with all the commotion it was impossible.

'Lay off, ye stupid buggers! They're wor lads!'

But nobody was in a listening mood and the new blokes did the only thing they could, which was to run like hell back the way they'd come. When the crowd saw them running they thought they were blacklegs and began pelting them all the harder. One had blood streaming down his face and they were shouting back at us. God only knows what it was they were saying and maybe it was just as well but they kept on running until they were out of sight. When people realised what had happened, all they did was get madder than ever.

The head of the police, Chief Inspector Scott I think he said his name was, tried to read the Riot Act from on top of his horse. As soon as it was realised what he was on about, everybody booed like hell. He didn't stop, he didn't even pause, he just went on with it till he'd finished. It didn't matter to him whether we listened or not. Once he'd done his duty and read it, that was it, his boys in blue could do whatever they liked. And my, were those buggers ready to get stuck in! They'd been standing listening in a long line, all the while patting the palms of their hands with their batons. Behind them were rows of reinforcements, all of them aching for the signal. These fellers weren't here to keep the peace, anybody could see that. Once they were let loose there was going to be hell on.

The blacklegs were still in the colliery yard yon side of the gates and they were staying put for the time being. And right outside was our crowd, a ragbag mixture of all sizes and shapes packed together. Some of our blokes recognised some of the blacklegs and started shouting at them and calling them by name. They didn't say one word back, they just looked. Opposite us were the well-drilled ranks of big tall men, all the same size, all in uniform. Only a few yards separated us, the pollises and about forty terrified blacklegs. Everything had gone so quiet you could have heard a pin drop.

Scott then shouted something and this big red-faced sergeant stepped out of the ranks and came across the empty space between us and them, with his handcuffs in one hand and his baton in the other. I couldn't see who he went up to but I was told afterwards it was Dick Molloy, one of our leaders. Apparently he put his huge face right up to Dick's so that their noses were just about touching and then he shouted so loud we could all hear, that he was making an arrest under the Unlawful Assembly Act, or something. Then he'd tried to slap the cuffs on Dick Molloy's wrists.

That did it! One of the two big lads that were standing on either side of Dick Molloy smashed his fist smack into the middle of the sergeant's face. Immediately his helmet shot off and his spikey ginger hair stuck straight up. He stepped right back so we could all see him. There was blood and snot all over his face. God, he was an ugly-looking swine! I was glad I wasn't up at the front. Next he pulled out his truncheon, raised it above his head and ran at Dick screaming like a bloody animal and the whole lot of them came pouring over after him. The battle had finally begun and no amount of reason was going to stop it now.

The pollises on horseback galloped into us and lashed out with their truncheons left and right, not caring who they were hitting or where. We were so tightly jammed together that every time they brought their truncheons down they caught somebody. Their horses trampled on our feet and barged right into us. One feller tried to bite one and got his head split. These horses were a different animal altogether from the ones we were used to down the pit. Their eyes were wild and bulging, their teeth were huge, and they snorted hot air like dragons. And when they were right beside you and you were looking up at them, they were massive. Added to that they didn't seem to know what was happening and they were prancing about with their great big hooves and huge muscly thighs.

I was hemmed in the middle and by the time they got to where I was, I couldn't even turn around. I just had to stand there and wait for them to get to me. They were twisting around in their saddles and belting people on their left and then twisting around and belting people on their right. They let nobody alone. Not women, not old men, not those that had something wrong with them. They left no head or shoulders unhit and smashed through any arms held up in protection. They were leaning so far out of their saddles to make sure they got everybody, they sometimes nearly fell out of them. People were yelling and screaming and covered in blood and falling down as if they were dead. A woman in front of me with a basket over her head was shrieking in terror and it attracted the attention of this particular one who couldn't have been more than nineteen years old. He had gone past, heard her, and turned his horse round. I know, I saw it with my own eyes. With one hand he rived the basket up so hard the handle came under her nose and practically ripped it off her face. Her whole head was pulled up, with the blood pouring out of where her nose had come loose. The swine stretched right up in his saddle, baton high in the air, and smashed it straight down into her forehead. Her left eye shot straight out of its socket like a pea out of a pod and the scream that came out of her was the worst sound I've ever heard. She just crumpled up and fell to the ground. I grabbed the bastard's saddle and tried to drag him off but the saddle was tightly strapped with huge buckles and wouldn't budge. He turned around, saw what I was doing, and smashed at my knuckles three times until I let go. After the last blow I spewed up on the side of his horse, I couldn't help it. I don't know whether it was the pain in my hand or the sight of that poor woman's eye dangling on her face. The horse now turned to go somewhere else and as it did, its tail flicked in my eyes and it shat.

Half an hour and it was all over. Umpteen were arrested and taken away and everybody who could get to their feet had scattered, chased by running and mounted pollises. In the distance I saw somebody go down with about a dozen pollises around them, whacking and kicking. Only the injured lying on the ground were left alone. Some of them were moaning, clothes ripped to shreds and soaked with blood. There was blood, horse shit and piss everywhere. All you could hear was blaspheming and cursing and sobbing. When the police finally went away the rest of the men came back. The colliery yard was empty, the blacklegs had all gone. 'It'll be a different matter tomorra,' said this Irish feller. 'We'll bring choppers and saws and cut their fuckin' legs off.'

I don't know whether we were doing the right thing or not. I couldn't say I'd seen any good coming out of it so far. I saw a lot of people hurt, some very badly, and I'd seen people taken away to jail. And I knew some of them would be there long after all this was over. We hadn't managed to stop the blacklegs. Maybe tomorrow or the next day or the one after we would, even if it meant wearing their families down. And if and when it did come, what then? When all was said and done they were only fighting for their rights, like we were. Nearly fourteen months they'd been on strike. It was a hell of a long time. We were desperate, that's why we did what we did. And I'm sure they were, and that's why they did what they did. The shocking thing is that these people were our kin. We had far more in common with them than we had with the police, the colliery managers, the Coalowners, the Government, just about anybody. But they were still blacklegs and to any miner, to all pitfolk, a blackleg is the lowest thing on earth.

By the time I got home my fingers had swollen to twice their normal size and I could feel the broken ends of the bones. I thought the little finger and thumb were just bruised but the other three seemed to be broken in a few places. My father was really concerned and was running around fussing and ordering Isabella Tanner to fetch this and fetch that. 'Sit down and make theesel' comfortable, lad. Because I'm ganna have to line these bones up so they set right. If ye feel the need to, yell out. If ye divvent, divvent do it just for the sake of it. I'll be as careful as I can.'

With Isabella Tanner standing by to pass him whatever he needed, he very gently spread my hand palmwards on the table. Starting with the third finger, he pulled each finger out as far as he could, then he matched the ends of the bones by feeling through the skin with his own fingers. After each one he looked up, black eyes shining and the sweat running down his face.

'All right, so far?'

'Champion.'

He then bandaged each one separately and then bandaged my whole hand to the flat piece of wood we used as a teapot mat. The whole thing had taken about an hour. When he finished he got up and said 'Well, that wasn't as bad as I thought it was ganna be,' and we both had a good laugh.

After a couple of days the bandage must have loosened because the board started slipping all over the place. When my father saw it he said it was no good and we'd have to do something else instead. He then went out for about an hour and when he came back he took off his jacket and rolled up his sleeves.

'This time we're ganna do a professional job. Pull your chair right up to the table and stick your arm out.'

He unwrapped the bandage sufficient to get the wood out, divided it up, and then wound it round and round each finger.

'Right! Get your coat on. We're gannin' out.'

While we were walking along he was kidding on about this and that and I got the impression he wasn't completely happy about what he was going to do, but I said nothing. In a while we came to the Ingham Infirmary. 'Don't worry. We're not gannin' in there,' he says. 'We're gannin' round the back.'

I followed him round to a small building which looked like a mortuary.

'In here,' he says. 'This is the best plaster ye can get, this is what they use in the hospital.'

A tall thin feller with his hair, his eyebrows and his eyelashes covered in plaster, looked down from where he was working on the ceiling.

'You're back then, Jack?'

'Aye... What the hell happened to you?' my father said, going up to him and laughing.

'Divvent talk about it, Jack. I knocked the flamin' ladder with me foot and the whole bloody lot came down.'

'You're in a bit of a mess, all right... Have ye seen yoursel' in the mirror?'

'No, and I divvent need to. I can well imagine... Is this Tommy, then?'

'This is him. This's my lad, Tommy. An awkward little bugger, if ever there was one. But he's not so bad when ye get to know him.'

'Hello, Tommy. Pollis clout your hand, eh? Bad buggers, some of them.'

'Can we use this?' my father asked, pointing to a bucket of wet plaster.

'Aye. Just dig in and help yourself, Jack. Take as much as ye like. I'll just be gettin' on, afore this dries.'

'Right, Geordie. Divvent let us hold ye back. We can manage... Right, Tommy. This is what I want ye to do. Dip your hand in as far as ye can and hold it there. Then bring it out slowly. When the air's had a chance to get at it, put it back in. And we'll keep doin' that till we get a good thick coat on it. This'll do us grand, this will.'

It worked very well and we were finished in half an hour.

'Ta muchly, Geordie,' my father says. 'We'll not keep ye. We're on wor way.'

'Rightio, Jack. I cannot come down 'cos I'm right in the middle of this. But cheerio, and good luck to Tommy.'

By the time we got home it was rock hard and much more comfortable than the wood had been.

'Now we can have our teapot-stand back,' my father said. 'Gis a look at that hand.'

I put my plastered hand out. 'It looks like a geet big clooty bag.'

'Bloody hard clooty bag! That's a good job, that is, lad. Ye know, I might just get meself a job at that infirmary one of these days... Think I'd make a good surgeon?'

'Bloody marvellous.'

A week later he came in and said somebody had told him I should be able to get Relief seeing as I wasn't an able-bodied man any more, not at the moment anyhow. All I'd need was a note from the doctor. This was a lot different to going begging for it, this was an entitlement. Besides, we were practically starving. So I went to see Marks.

'Who in God's name put this mess on? Get it off so I can examine that hand.'

'I cannot, it's set hard. If I take it off I'll have to have another one put straight back on. And I haven't anythin' to pay with.'

'This isn't the result of any conflict with the law, I suppose?'

'I wasn't breaking any law... But a pollis did it right enough. If that's what ye mean.'

'Does this have anything to do with the strike?'

'It isn't a strike, it's a lockout. And everything in our life for the past six months has to do with that. You cannot get away from it if you're a miner.

'Don't you bandy words with me, you impudent...'

'Are ye ganna give me a note to say my hand is injured or are ye not?'

'I am most certainly not! Now get out of here this instant!'

The next day I went to the Guardians and showed them my plastered hand. They said if they paid relief 'to every good-for-nothing who put his arm or leg in plaster', the country would be bankrupt. It was a doctor's note or nothing. And in my case it was nothing. They told me they'd already been warned I might be trying something like this and warned me of the consequences.

By October everybody's credit had run out and not a few other things as well. The band still played and people got up on the platform and sang or did their party piece but there was very little heart in it. Nobody had any money left. All the houses round about who had anybody in work had been pestered to the hilt. Every grandfather and grandmother clock in miles had been cleaned and oiled almost to the point where they'd never need another service, and Swiss cuckoos nearly took off when they came out. Privet hedges had been cut so many times they'd be lucky if they ever recovered. Scissors and knives were almost worn away with sharpening and garden shears and lawnmowers were lethal weapons nearly. The same ones had more tea cosies and doorstops than they knew what to do with and enough clippy mats to give away for wedding presents for generations.

In towns like Sheffield, Glasgow and Cardiff, where there were big engineering or shipbuilding works, as soon as the general strike ended the unions had starting levying their members five per cent of their wages. This went to support their local miners and was given willingly. Maybe it happened on Tyneside with some of the Northumberland pitmen because there was plenty of engineering and shipbuilding and a lot of support in Newcastle. But there was nothing like that in Shields.

My father had invested what little spare money he ever had where he said he would and his only dividend was a permanently stained moustache. I'd put mine in the post office to try and make a dream come true and it had long since come back out and gone on bread, potatoes and tea.

Those with things like consumption or pernicious anaemia before the strike were worse now and some of the weaker ones had died. Everybody was skinnier and raggier and their homes shabbier. Dogs had strayed, pigeons had been let go, hens had stopped laying and been eaten and pet rabbits had gone the same way despite the tears.

Meanwhile the rest of the world was just going along in its own sweet way, business as usual. Nobody was interested in coalminers' disputes any more, the general strike was almost forgotten. People were only concerned about such things when they were being inconvenienced by them in some way. When the inconvenience passed, so did all interest. Their coal was coming from abroad, if they really wanted to know. But for them, coal was just coal. Who cared whether it came from our old enemy the Germans or anybody else? It all went the same way, up the chimney.

By November things were really bad. Every last speck of coal had long been gathered from every tip, it was freezing cold and there was nothing to make a fire with. No heat to warm the house, no hot water for cooking or washing, not even to make a cup of tea with. There wasn't a decent dandelion leaf in miles. All our clothes except the ones on our backs were hanging in the pawnshop. And if they were sold because we hadn't the money to get them back, they were sold and there was nothing we could do about it. Clothes were nothing. We were weak from eating food that should have gone to pigs and we were something we'd never been before. Freezing cold. We'd never bothered much about blankets because we'd always had plenty of coal. Now we were making blankets out of old newspapers like everybody else.

In the end, all that misery, all that suffering and all that hatred had been for nowt. A working man is only as strong as his union and the union is only as strong as its members. The Miners Federation of Great Britain knew the state its members and their families were in and couldn't advise us to stay out any longer.

What a 'splendid victory' for the Coalowners, the Government and the nation. The newspapers were full of it. People were interested again for a couple of days. And Churchill and the rest of them were crowing like turkeys.

But in Durham we still stayed out. It was another month before we went back and many voted not to go back even then.

Lists of names went up on the notice board at Harton Colliery beside the disgraceful terms that had been up there for seven long months. If your name was up, you were to report to such and such a one. If it wasn't you were out and it didn't matter if you'd worked there a lifetime. My name was on the list, my father's wasn't. Those of us that were allowed back, went. There was no negotiating, no shaking of hands, nothing.

12

We didn't kid ourselves we were going back like martyrs or heroes or anything. Dogs with their tails between their legs, more like it – dogs that had had their backsides well and truly kicked. The whole world knew we'd been beaten and as far they were concerned it was a victory. A new coalmining act came in and it didn't come in for our benefit. From now on you could be sacked for having a grin on your face.

I went back as a dataller doing the same kind of labouring work I'd been doing before, every day going to a different place wherever they needed an extra man. The only difference was that the day was longer and the wage packet was smaller. I fetched and I carried, I passed stuff to the skilled men, I held things up for them and I tidied up after them. I cleaned things, shovelled pony shit, oiled and greased. I lifted, pulled, shoved, loaded and unloaded. In other words I did everything I was told to do and did whatever job I was given to the best of my ability. What I wanted and needed more than anything now, was to be sent to the face. It wouldn't need to be hewing or cutting, any kind of face-work would do. In any case once you were there you stayed there and sooner or later you'd get your chance to cut coal.

The reason I wanted to do face-work was because that was where the money was. It mightn't have been all that much but it was a damned sight more than you could get anywhere else down a pit. As it was, no matter how hard I worked I was still getting the same seventeen shillings and threepence halfpenny. And that had to keep my father, Monica, Isabella Tanner, Wilfred and myself. John had gone south to try his luck at something different altogether. What with his rickets and the hardship of the long stayout, he'd had enough of the coalmining life. There was no fuss or anything, he just packed up and went.

My father had been a puffler for the last five years at Harton, which meant that if any of the men's wages had been docked unfairly or if they felt they should have been paid for wet work or gassy work or whatever, he was the one who would go and have it out on their behalf. He would argue with the weighman, the deputy, and the overman as well if needs be. They'd argue about whether the wet had been six inches deep or four inches deep. Whether it had been like that for three days or four days. Whether the gas was bad enough to affect the men's breathing and how many lamps it had put out. Whether there had been muck in the tubs of coal and if they'd been properly full or not. He had been elected by them to do whatever he could to get the fines reduced and the payments up to what they should be. If you were a puffler it meant you were arguing with somebody practically nonstop.

My father knew he got under their skins. But if he hadn't he wouldn't have got anywhere. The lockout and what happened afterwards was the chance they'd been waiting for. They couldn't have got him on his work because he was still one of the best hewers in the pit. So they got him for being a 'troublemaker and an agitator'.

There were a lot of men like my father who'd been good workers and never done anything against the Coal Company, that hadn't been let back just because of their political beliefs. Among them were some of the best representatives we ever had, ones who were clever and ones who would never have let you down.

'Nobody has been sacked at any colliery in the country,' the Coalowners told everybody. Aye, that's right. And the reason for it was that everybody had already been sacked the minute they put their lockout notices up way back in May. It was now a question of taking people on, not laying them off.

If I couldn't get face-work my father was going to have to go to the Guardians because my wage wasn't enough to support the family. And he was dreading that. But no matter how many times I asked they wouldn't put me there. Old men of seventy were hanging on till they practically dropped dead and their marras were carrying them. It was plain that if you wanted face-work and you didn't want to lick somebody's arse to get it, you'd just have to bide your time and keep your gob shut. I was now coming down the pit for one reason and that was to make as much money as I could, and I'd never lose a single hour if I could help it.

I'd been back about two weeks when there was a message waiting for me at the gate when I went in one morning. I was to go and see the undermanager. I thought this is it. They're either putting me at the face or they're putting me out.

When I got to the bottom of the shaft he was standing there with his little notebook and pencil, checking every man that came down to make sure none of the wrong ones had got back. He says to me, 'Are you any good with animals, Turnbull?'

'Yes, sir,' I says, 'I am. What kind of animals are ye talkin' about?' It could have been cleaning out the canaries or catching rats for all I knew.

'I want you to go over to the stables and see the horsekeepers. There's two new ponies I want broken in.'

I don't know whether he thought I looked like a bloody cowboy or whether somebody had said so-and-so was good with horses and he'd mixed them up with me. But I wasn't going to say anything, I was only too relieved I hadn't been given the push.

'Get them out one at a time and yoke them up. I want them used to pulling tubs. You can do it on Dandy Bank, it's not being used at the moment.'

I knew Dandy Bank. It was long and it was steep and it was damned dark if nobody was working in it.

When I got to the stables I shouted in and these two fellers came out. One had a bad limp and a harelip, and the other had all his fingers missing on one hand and eyes that were so cockeyed they were nearly staring at each other.

'Are you the horsekeepers?'

'Why? Do we look like lion-tamers?'

'I've come for the two ponies that need breakin' in.'

'Oh ye have, have ye? And who might you be, if ye divvent mind we askin'?

'Tommy Turnbull... The manager said I had to train them to work in the new district.'

'Know much about ponies, do ye, Tommy?'

'Not much.'

'Not much? Well, at least ye know somethin', and that's a start. Some of the useless buggers who come in here know nowt at all!' They both laughed.

'Gan an fetch ye-know-who, will ye, Sam,' says the one with the harelip. 'I think he and Tommy'll get along very well.'

'Right ye are, Charley,' says the one with the cock-eyes, and off he goes into the back.

'What breed of animal d'ye prefer then, Tommy?'

'Well, I don't know much about different varieties or anything. What I meant was I've gone up to one the odd time and it's eaten a crust out of my hand. And I've given it a bit stroke and that.'

'Have ye now? Hear that, Sammy?' he shouts into the back. 'This lad's once gave a pony a crust of bread and a pat on the head.'

'Has he?' says Sammy, coming back. 'Then he'll have no trouble at all... Come and gis a hand a minute, will ye, Charley. It's in the thingy again.'

'Right you are... Hang on, Tom. Divvent gan away. We'll be back in a jiffy.'

The two of them went off laughing.

I don't know why it is but you often find people who know something about animals that you don't, think they're so bloody clever.

There was a lot of banging and thumping in the back and the sound of buckets being knocked over. Then a loud yell followed by a lot of bad language. A few minutes later the pair of them came back. They were leading this dark hairy thing, one of them at either side of its head, and they were keeping a very tight rein on it. Sammy looked vexed and they were both limping now. Sammy's greasy black hair was all over the place and Charley's nose was bleeding. You didn't need to be a jockey to tell it was a right one they were bringing out.

'He's a good pony, son,' says Charley, wiping his nose on his sleeve. 'Only he's inclined to be a bit frolicky at times. The secret is to be patient with 'im and take things nice and slow. That way he'll do anythin' for ye.'

'He's been out a couple times so he knows the ropes, so to speak,' said Charley, as I held it by the head while the two of them shoved it into the limbers.

I thought to myself, 'Aye, I bet he does, ye couple o' sods.'

'What's his name?'

'Name? He hasn't got a proper one yet,' said Sammy as he was fastening the straps.

'Ye can call him owt ye like, it won't make the slightest difference to him,' says Charley laughing.

'Ye could try "Buggerlugs".'

The two of them laughed so much they nearly coughed their lungs up.

'Right. Thanks,' I said. 'I'll be seein' ye.'

As I went off with it I looked back over my shoulder. The two of them were hanging on to each other, coughing and laughing

'Good luck, son!' Charley shouted. 'Divvent forget. Patience is the secret of success!'

On the way to Dandy Bank there were six ventilating doors left hand over and six ventilating doors right hand over and I had to go through the lot with this pony. I hadn't the faintest idea whether it was used to this sort of thing or not. If those two fatheads back at the stable knew, they certainly hadn't bothered to tell me.

'There's only one way to find out,' I thought to myself.

I went to the first door, opened it, got the pony through, and shut it. No bother at all. Came to the next one, same thing. And again. And again. Everything was going just dandy and I was beginning to think those two back at the stable weren't so bad after all, when I got to the very last door. When I got to this one, the pony raised itself right up like a bucking bronco and copped its nut on the roof. But instead of falling to its knees or getting knocked out the way you might expect, it went stark raving mad. Away it shot like a bat out of hell, leaving the tub and half the straps behind. I raced after it yelling 'Come back, ye stupid bugger! Come back!' and copping my own nut on the roof, bashing my shoulders against the sides, and tripping over the stones and holes in the floor.

In no time it was way up and over Dandy Bank.

Now, what was I to do? Go back and tell those two idiots I'd lost their pony for them and ask for another one? And let the undermanager find out I didn't know the first thing about ponies?

I was trotting along faster than I'd ever done before, half stooped and calling out 'Poaannneeey! Come to Tommmeeey! Poaannneeey! Come to Tommmeeey!' And I'd gone quite a way when I turned this bend and saw two fellers coming along carrying some tools. Straightaway I slowed down and started humming to myself, head down as though I was deep in thought.

'Are ye all right, lad?' one of them says when they came up to me.

'Aye. I'm just lookin' for a pony. Ye haven't seen one up there by any chance, have ye?'

'No, we haven't. But if we do we'll know who to send it to. We'll say "Poaannneeeey, gan to Tommmeeey!"' And off they went, killing themselves laughing.

After a while I came to a wall telephone that was used for emergencies and decided to see if this counted as one. Geoff Middleton the overman answered. 'Hello.'

'I think there might be a pony comin' by there,' I says. 'It was a bit wild when I last seen it. D'ye think ye could get somebody to grab a hold of it till I get there?'

'What are ye doin' with a pony down there?' he says.

'I'm supposed to be trainin' it and it escaped.'

'You're too bloody late, lad. It's away past long since. Get yourself up here and we'll ring down the line and see if anybody's seen it.'

When I got to his cabin he was speaking to Willy Rossiter on the telephone.

'I haven't seen a pony all day,' says Willy Rossiter. 'But a bloody race-horse came by about ten minutes ago. I only wish I'd had a bet on it. Wait on! Here it comes now! It's gannin' your way!'

'Right! Quick!' Geoff Middleton says. 'Roll these chummins off and put them on their side to make a barrier. We'll trap it and grab it afore it can gan somewhere else.'

We'd just got the first one in place when we heard such a clatter coming down the way.

'Get out the road!' shouts Geoff Middleton. 'It's not ganna stop!'

With its eyes nearly coming out of its head it came charging through, leaped over the tubs as if it was a seagull and away back out-bye.

We went back to the cabin and Geoff Middleton got straight on the phone to the stables.

'Is that you, Charley? I'm ringin' to let ye know we've just sent a pony up to ye... That's right, a dark'un... No, by itsel'. Just chase it into the stables when it comes up. It shouldn't give ye any bother now. It's just about worn out.'

Charley told him it was too late, that it had already gone haring past towards the shaft.

And there it stayed for the rest of the day. Nobody could get near it, it was so mad it would have killed somebody. In the finish the only way the horsekeepers could get it back to the stables, was to couple it to a tub that was being pulled by the 'endless' and have it hauled back. A couple of days later it was taken to bank and got rid of. A while after, I heard it had never been a proper pit pony at all. It was half donkey, half something else...probably greyhound. It had come from another pit where they couldn't do a thing with it.

I don't know why, whether they thought I had a way with horses or what, but they kept me on pony driving for nearly two years.

Harton Coal Company owned over a thousand ponies and all of them were down the pit. Any you saw grazing in the field were new ones waiting to go down. Shetlands were used in the low seams and bigger breeds like the Galloways in the big pit. At one time putters pushed and pulled the tubs by hand and in some places they still did. But it was mostly done by ponies now and the fellers who drove them were called 'pony putters'. Even with steel rope haulage and conveyor belts ponies were still needed; not only in low seams and places that weren't mechanised, but for hauling in gear and equipment when they were opening up new districts.

The ponies were trained at Lizard Lane Bank by making them walk backwards and forwards attached to tubs, sometimes empty, sometimes full. Then down they went and down they stayed till they either got killed or came up to die. The only time they got a holiday was if there was a strike and even then they stayed down. The papers would criticise us for leaving the ponies down the pit but it wasn't for us to say. I only know that if you brought them up to bank after they'd been down for a while, you'd spoil them. They were intelligent animals most of them and they wouldn't want to go down a pit again, not after they'd had a taste of green grass and fresh air. At least when there was a strike they were always properly fed and their choppy was better than what we had to live on. A pony was worth a lot more than a miner.

All working horses wore blinkers so I suppose it wasn't that much different for pit ponies and a week was usually all it took to get them used to the dark. Some wouldn't be as well trained as others but that wasn't necessarily the pony's fault because some of the buggers at Lizard Lane were as thick as two short planks. If a pony stepped back into its limbers when you said 'Bah! Bah!' and stayed there long enough for you to plonker it in, and came to you when you said 'Howay, boy!', that was really all it needed to know. There were some that could do much more than that, ones that knew exactly what you wanted them to do. And before you said whatever it was, they'd either do it or do the exact opposite. But when you 'flung them off' at the end of their shift every one of them knew how to step out of their limbers as neatly as any man out of his boots.

Usually each driver had his own special pony, this way they'd get to know each other and work well together. That pony was then supposed to be put back in the stables at the end of the shift and allowed to stay there until the same bloke came back to do his next shift. But it didn't always happen like that. Far too often a good pony would be brought out by different drivers, shift after shift, until eventually it dropped dead from overwork. If the drivers were putters, which meant their ponies pulled tubs of coal, they'd be getting paid according to how much coal they brought out. So they depended entirely on the pony. The harder it worked, the more money they got. So the better the pony, the harder its life. Frequently one would be made to pull two full tubs at the same time and that was a hell of a load for a little horse. Sometimes fellers would be so exhausted themselves after a double shift of maybe sixteen hours, that they hadn't the strength to walk out. In which case they'd ride the limbers and the pony would have to carry them as well as its own load. Putters were the hardest on the ponies, as they were on themselves, and they expected the ponies to go like locomotives. Although they wouldn't punish one for accidentally squashing their bait, they'd curse it for pulling a tub over and sometimes they'd flog them damned hard to get them going. But there were limits. I once saw a bloke lay into a putter with a shovel because he was braying his pony with a sleeper.

Heavy loads and hard drivers were by no means all that some ponies had to deal with. Places like Boldon Way were very tough going for them. Boldon was always wet and it was uphill for the full tubs, though coming down the steep bank on the other side was scarcely any better. Their sides always got chafed by the weight of the tubs on the limbers, whether the tubs were pulling back down or pushing forward down, and huge sores were a common thing. Sometimes they'd just conk out and drop dead in their tracks. And sometimes you'd hear of one that nobody had been able to do anything with, happening a 'fatal accident' somewhere. Somebody would then come from the stables, cut them up because they were too heavy to pick up, chuck the bits into a tub and get another pony to draw them away to bank. From there they went for dog food and fertiliser.

To control the movement of tubs we used dregs. These were hard tarred wooden sticks about three inches thick that we used to shove into the spokes of the wheels either to slow them down or to stop and lock them. Somebody once shoved one right up a pony's back end. You could take seeing a man or a pony badly injured if it was an accident but when it was done on purpose it was an entirely different matter. Nobody owned up but everybody was sure it was the bloke who drove the pony. Maybe the deputy had been on to him to get a move on and shift the tubs faster than he was doing, and the pony had refused. He denied he had anything to do with it but somebody put it there, it couldn't have got there by itself. The poor pony was in such a state that if the men had found out who'd done it they'd have wrecked him. Whoever did it couldn't have been all there in my opinion.

Right: 1 'A moment's peace' – Grandma Turnbull.

Middle: 2 'Fresh air and hard but healthy labour' – Granda and Grandma Kelly (on the right) on the farm where Granda worked.

Below: 3 'Bliss' – Jack Turnbull and Isabella Tanner's wedding. From left to right, front row: -?-, Monica, Wilf, Tommy. Back row: Isabella's sister, Isabella, Jack, John.

Top: 4 'The Wild Ones' – Tyne Dock 'Belle Vue' Cycling Club, *c.*1927. Rear left: Charlie Jordison. Second and third from front right: Alice and Evelyn Smithwhite.

Middle: 5 Roadside café stop for the cycling club. Right: Alice Smithwhite. Fifth from right, standing: Charlie Jordison.

Left: 6 A member of the cycling club at last! – Tommy.

Above left: 7 'The hewer in his Sunday best' – Jack Turnbull.

Above right: 8 'No more pit and no more miner' – Tommy at seventy. (Photographed by the author)

9 The Chichester Crossings, South Shields, 1939. (South Tyneside Libraries)

10 Typical miners' houses in the D'Arcy Street area, 1935. (South Tyneside Libraries)

11 Boldon Lane, 1938. Through arch on left: back of Straker Terrace. On right: back of D'Arcy Street. (South Tyneside Libraries)

12 Double Row, 1938. These were the pit cottages built by the Harton Coal Company. (South Tynesidet Libraries)

Top: 13 Housing in the D'Arcy Street area, 1938. (South Tyneside Libraries)

Middle: 14 Harton Colliery, Old Pit, *c.*1900. (James T. Tuck)

Right: 15 Miner's back yard with the essential poss-tub and mangle, D'Arcy Street, 1938. (South Tyneside Libraries)

16 St Hilda Colliery Coal Depot, *c.*1930. (NBC)

17 Harton Colliery before the turn of the century. (James T. Tuck)

'Pay day' – Miners collecting their pay at the colliery office. (NCB)

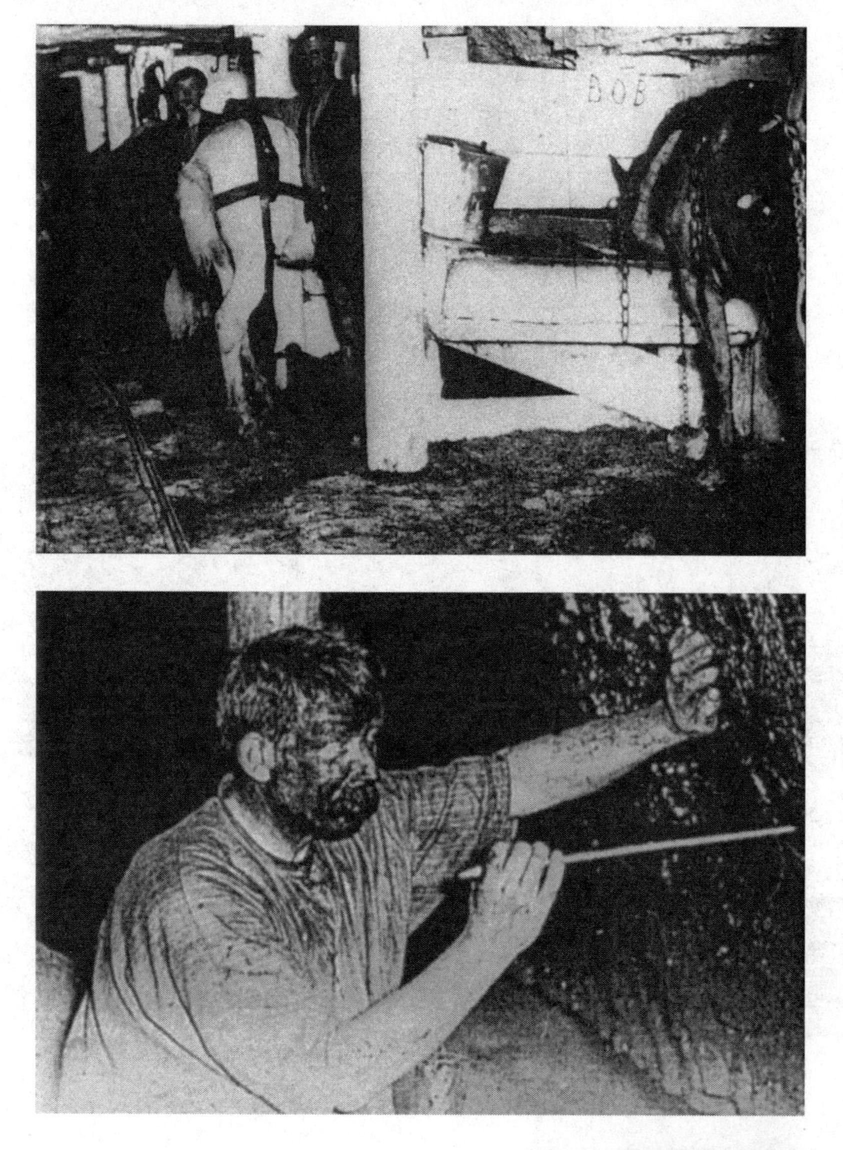

Top: 19 An underground stable. (NCB)

Middle: 20 Stemming a drill hole. (NCB)

Right: 21 Setting a prop. (NCB)

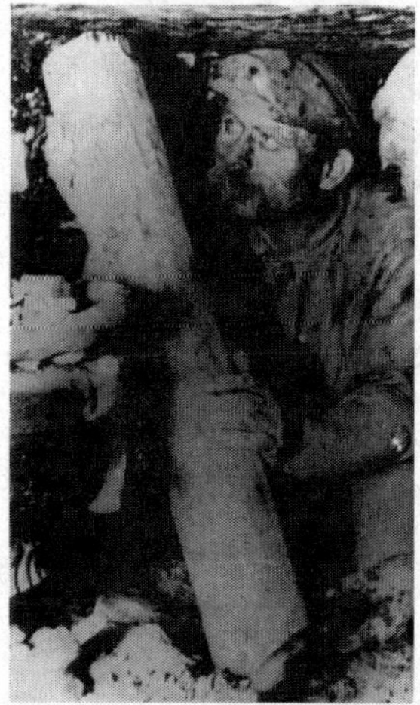

22
Hand hewing
in thin seam.
(James T. Tuck)

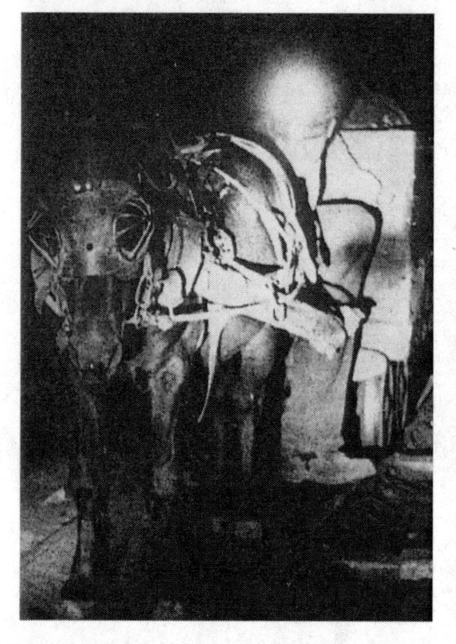

Above left: 23 Pony putter riding the limbers. (James T. Tuck)

Above right: 24 South Shields miners peeling potatoes during the 1926 strike. (South Tyneside Libraries)

25 'Bait Time' at last.
(NCB)

But things like that were rare. Fellers were far more likely to bring a sugar lump to the pit to give their pony a treat, never mind they were half starved themselves. And many would share their bait with one if it was standing by and they saw it looking, even though they weren't working with it. I once had a lovely little pony called Dublin and I'd always give it a bit of my jam sandwich. But then if it saw somebody else eating something different, maybe a bit of corned beef, it would wander over there and greed a bit of that. I wouldn't care, they're supposed to be vegetarians.

No matter what safety measures you use, accidents still occur, to animals as well as men. Faulty or worn equipment, tired minds, weary limbs, poor visibility, misunderstandings, noise, carelessness and stupidity, all play their part. Just as we got little protection from the clothes we wore, so it was with the ponies. And when a runaway tub with half a ton of coal hit them, their little leather caps were no more use to them than our cloth ones were to us. All the same they were tough little buggers. One was once standing limbered to a tub near to where I was working and it must have put its leg in the wrong place. In a fraction of a second the steel rope of the endless sawed its leg clean off above the fetlock. It was so quick I hadn't a chance to do anything. The pony never budged and there wasn't so much as a peep out of it.

In the high seams we had Russian Galloways. These were big shaggy horses with less brains than a chocolate mouse. They were dumb, they were stubborn and they were dead slow. Not even the putters could make them go. They would start when they felt like it and they would stop when they felt like it. One once stood on my bad foot and I pleaded with it, cursed it, slapped it, reached over its back and yanked its tail. And would it budge? Would it hell. I just had to wait till it got fed up with standing on my foot and decided to go and stand somewhere else.

There was one called McKenzie who never saw a lamp that he didn't scatter, he went out of his way to do it. If a number of us were working end to end and we'd put our lamps down in a zigzag line along the bottom, McKenzie would zigzag himself to get every single one. His great big head would come down and then up it would go and send the lamp flying through the air. When you were flinging him off at the end of your shift you had to keep tight hold of his head, because as soon as he saw the new shift coming along, he'd shoot off to knock their lamps out of their hands. And if the fellers weren't quick enough he'd head them in all directions. He wasn't one for kicking, the way some were, which was his one and only good point. But if he caught you bending down he'd think nothing of giving your behind a snip with his big yellow teeth. If you can imagine somebody taking a pair of garden shears to the cheeks of your backside, that's what McKenzie felt like. 'Cut his bloody big head off and he'd make a canny little horse,' fellers who worked with him used to say. In the finish they got shot of every Galloway in the pit. Blokes who worked with them day in, day out for years would tell you eating, shitting and pissing were the only things they did without making a fuss.

The horsekeepers were full-time and did nothing else down the pit except look after the ponies. It was their job to clean them, feed them, make sure they weren't overworked, and then shoot them when their time came. Most of the horsekeepers were either old miners past their best or younger ones who'd been badly disabled in an accident down the pit. Some of them were interested in horses and knew a lot about them. Others knew no more than they needed to and that's as far as their interest went. Whichever way they were, all the ones I ever knew were kind to their ponies. I don't think they could have spent so much of their life looking after them, feeding them, cleaning up after them and nursing them when they were sick, if they hadn't been fond of them. They were all pretty good at first aid and treating common injuries like sores, cuts and bruises, but every now and then the vet would come to check all the stock and look the stables over. Anything he had to do, he would do down the pit. If they had something more serious wrong with them, like a bad case of worms or some disease, he usually had them sent to bank. Once there they had no future. The Harton Coal Company wasn't a charity for useless ponies any more than it was a charity for useless miners.

Part of the horsekeeper's job was to see no pony ever went out with a shoe missing, because it could be very rough underfoot what with iron rails, uneven ground and sharp stones. Shoeing was done by a blacksmith who came down the pit with a variety of shoes of all shapes and sizes and hammered them on cold. A big heavy type they were, not the kind you see on ordinary horses.

You couldn't say the duties of a horsekeeper were all that hard and ones like Johnny Byrnes got by even though he couldn't read the writing on his own notice board. Johnny relied entirely on the various drivers to chalk up the names and times themselves. Jack Telford once went in to the stables and said to Johnny, 'I need a new pony. The other one ye gave us is so old it can hardly walk. Ye should shoot the poor bugger.'

'What's wrong with it?'

'I've told ye. It's too old. It's practically fallin' to bits.'

'Where is it?'

'It's comin'. Bob McPherson's fetchin' it.'

'Oh, right. Now, let's see...'

Johnny looks up at the board and stares at it for a long time. Then he says 'Right you are, Jack. Ye can take Nugget. He's a very reliable animal. Ye'll have no trouble with that feller.'

All the while Jack's staring at the board and looking very puzzled.

'Are we lookin' at the same board? I cannot see any "Nugget". Not up there, any road.'

'That one there, man,' says Johnny, pointing at the board. 'What's the matter with ye? Are ye blind or daft or what?'

'"Nugget"?' says Jack Telford. 'That doesn't say "Nugget"! It says "Not to go out", ye stupid bugger!'

Like all horsekeepers Johnny would always be able to make a few bob out of the manure. Strictly speaking it belonged to the Coalowners but there were no weighmen writing down how much of that came up or whether it was big or small or had any dust in it. When it went to bank the bosses took whatever they wanted for their gardens and the horse-keepers could do what they liked with the rest as long as they got rid of it. It was good stuff with all the straw and strong pee that was mixed in with it and the perfect tonic for any garden. They'd get a horse and cart and go round the streets with it and a full load would fetch a canny bit. Whatever the ponies dropped when they were working down the pit stayed put and just got trampled in. There'd be plenty of it in some places, particularly where the ponies used to stand for any time, but it never bothered anybody. It might have been a different matter if we'd had dogs the size of ponies pulling tubs.

13

After the lockout of 1926 and the long strike that followed, many pits had fallen into a bad state and because Harton was such a big place it had suffered many roof falls. Timber had rotted, water had gathered and a lot of gas had been released. As a result the ventilation was in a shocking state and after months and months of men being made ill and complaining about it, a ventilation inspector was sent down. He very quickly reported that many districts were very dangerous. The consequence of this was over 900 men were laid off. That was one way of dealing with a ventilation problem.

By 1928 there was so much unemployment in the country, the Coalowners were sure they could reduce our wages by at least a third and we wouldn't be able to do a thing about it. Especially now they and the heads of the other big industries had got the Government to pass the Trade Unions Dispute Act which made all strikes illegal. So they locked us out.

In the past whenever they had wanted to reduce our wages or worsen our conditions, they had always locked us out and put up their notices. The notices gave details of new contracts of employment and all previous contracts were ended as of then. Only the gaffers' remained the same. From the moment the notices were put up, anybody not knocking on the gate and asking to be taken back was considered to be on strike and therefore not entitled to unemployment benefit or any kind of relief.

The way the law was now, if we didn't agree to go back and work under whatever conditions the Coalowners decided, they could sue us.

All the same we refused. We knew we might never get our jobs back but we couldn't just carry on 'Yes sir, no sir, three bags full sir' until we were working for nothing. The same Act that made it a crime for us to lay down our tools, also made it a crime for us to use our trade union funds for 'political purposes'. If the Coalowners and their pals that owned the other big industries used the wealth they made from their coal mines and factories to buy their way into Parliament or to get their friends in, that was fine and dandy and the way things had always been done. But if we wanted to save a few pence out of our miserable wages to help get one of our men in, we were breaking the law. How else were we supposed to bring our grievances to anybody's attention apart from going on strike. The only way the Coalowners would pay us a decent wage or make the pits any safer, was if the Government made them. And the only way the Government would do that was if the voters made them. But before the voters would do anything they'd have to know what our working conditions were like, and it would have to bother them.

These voters, these ordinary people who worked in offices and didn't have to earn a living from manual work, didn't know how or why strikes happened. They got their information and opinions from their newspapers and wirelesses. None of them had the faintest idea about what working in a factory or a pit was like. They would see pictures of mill girls at their machines smiling or humming a tune together, and of coalminers coming out at the end of their shift grinning and cheerful, and they'd think everything was grand. They wouldn't stop to think that smiling and acting cheerful is what people do when they see a camera, even defeated soldiers do it. The same workers weren't filmed when a needle had just gone in their eye or if their arm was hanging off because a machine had sheared right through it. They wouldn't be shown cursing the owners of the same factory or colliery or sitting at a table with no food on it in a house that was practically falling down. They'd show the unemployed marching together like an army, but they never got close enough to see into their faces, and they never showed the ones who had to stay at home. People didn't want bad news, so Hampshire's batting averages would be served up to them as more important than the deaths of twenty-four men and boys in some filthy hole somewhere up in Durham.

We'd been going down to the docks to watch coal from America, Germany, and other places, being unloaded. And for any miner who'd worked all his life at a pit only a couple of miles away – some for as long as sixty years – and was desperate to get back, it was a sickening sight.

But we hadn't the stamina to go through another 1926. Our numbers were half what they had been, the laws were much tougher, the

Government had so many forces it could call on, and we were more undernourished and weary now than we'd been when we were locked out in 1926. We'd broken away completely from the TUC after being let down by Thomas and Citrine, not that that made much difference. Whatever poke they might have had was long gone.

In the end, as always, we went back and accepted their conditions and paid their fines for taking so long about it. I was now on £1 14s 6½d a week and 12s 6d was docked from my first pay packet. And Isabella Tanner had a babby, Bernard they decided to call him.

By 1929 things had got so bad that Labour won the General Election and Ramsay MacDonald was made Prime Minister. The first thing he tried to do was cancel the Trade Union Act but there was too much opposition from the Tories. There was too much opposition from the Tories and the Liberals for anything anybody ever tried to do for the working class and in no time he was doing as he was told and cutting assistance benefits. The trouble with MacDonald was that underneath the Labour polish was a Tory boot and in all that really mattered he was no different from them. The way he dressed, the way he lived, the way he bowed and scraped to kings and queens was typical of a nobody trying to be a somebody. He was wishy-washy, he was weak, but he was still vain. And he was a bitter disappointment to the millions of ordinary people who had put so much faith and hope in him. Arthur Henderson who was now Foreign Secretary was the only good thing about the whole Government. It's too bad that Foreign Secretaries are no use whatsoever to ordinary people in their own country.

Up until 1930 Harton had used the bord-and-pillar method of mining which used narrow roadways and left columns of coal to support the roof. Now the management had decided it was too wasteful so they were going to bring in the long-wall system and open up the Yard Seam. This would mean a longer face and wider roadways. The coal would be cut by machines and much bigger tubs and conveyor belts would be used to take larger amounts of coal out – and out faster. It also meant hewers, putters and ponies could be done away with, at least in mechanised districts. Machines, the Coalowners had been assured, were a lot less trouble than that lot.

Most pits in the country had already been mechanised and many had pithead baths for their miners. But Harton didn't intend to go quite that far. The changes here were to get more coal out, not to pander to the comfort of every Tom, Dick and Harry in the pit. And the way they went about it was to shut the Colliery gates and lock us out. That was step number one. Number two was to put up a notice on the board saying that the gates would stay shut until all the necessary machinery had been installed in the pit. We were surprised by this because we knew they'd be needing a lot of men to bring the gear in and set it up and we naturally thought we'd be the ones who'd be doing it. But no. While we were out of work yet again, getting no pay at all, blokes from somewhere else were being brought in.

Apart from the loss of our wage, it was a real put down. We thought of ourselves as skilled men who had created this pit and who every day made it bigger and greater, who knew it inside out and better than anybody on earth. The Colliery belonged to the Coalowners but the Pit was ours. With all its faults it was still a second home to us. We'd been like a big family with fathers, grandfathers, uncles and brothers working there, the same names going back to the time the pit was first sunk. Now it had total strangers working in it, strangers who got paid while we stood by idle and without a wage, and outside. The hewers, the kings of the pit, were told there was no point hanging about because they wouldn't be needed any more, not in the new scheme of things. Hewers had always been thorns in the Coalowners' sides, that's why everybody used to call the Durham union, the 'Hewers' Union'. They were tough blokes who'd never give an inch, not if seven eighths would do. Everything in a pit had always depended on them and they had stuck together through thick and thin.

The miners' Federation was recognised by neither the Government or the Coalowners 'except as an advisory body' and the Durham Union could do nothing because it was up to each district lodge to negotiate its own terms. Negotiating with Harton Coal Company meant only one thing, 'Do as you are told or get out!' Those of us who weren't hewers or putters, were warned that when the time came things were going to be tougher than ever for anybody lucky enough to be taken back. The blokes that had been brought in and were already trained on the new machinery were going to be kept on to run it. Nobody from Harton was going to be trained to use it. And from now on, when any man was kicked out for whatever reason, he was out for good. There were going to be no more punishments of six months or a year without work and then maybe getting back after you'd done your penance. If you were heard whingeing about conditions or whining about off-takes, or got yourself 'involved in politics', you were going to be put out and you were never going to get back, not in any pit in the British Empire, if they could help it.

The hewers and putters began to leave Shields, not now for pits in Scotland, the Midlands or Wales – which had plenty troubles of their own – but to look for other kinds of work. And they were joined by those who had guessed they were also on the List or knew it would only be a matter of time before they were. Some emigrated to South Africa, some to Canada, America or Australia to start a new life somewhere else. For fellers like these who were older men, men very set in their ways, it was a very hard thing to do.

When we heard that everything was just about installed, we started going up to the Colliery every day to see if we could be taken back. Jimmy Green would be standing at the gates selling the Daily Worker, there was no way you could avoid him. He was a member of the British Communist Party which miners were against as much as anybody else, and he'd been sacked for it. As far as the Communist Party was concerned, even we believed what we read in the papers. But Jimmy Green was a clever bloke and you couldn't easily argue with him.

'Yous are all doomed, lads,' he'd say. 'Do yourselves a favour and join The Party before it's too late. The Russians aren't wor enemies, they're wor friends. Take from the rich and give to the poor, that's what they do. It's the only right way. Even Jesus said it.'

'What would you know about Jesus?' somebody would say. 'Yous buggers are all heathens.'

'Not so, comrade. That's what Churchill wants ye to think. Who's a greater threat to ye? Me or Churchill?'

'You.'

'Since when did Churchill ever care a ha'penny toss about pitmen, whatever his race or religion? Or Lloyd George? Or any of them? D'ye think King George has ever lost an hour's sleep in the whole of his life, worrying about saps like yous?'

'Leave the King out of it! That's gannin' too far.'

'Comrade, he's already out of it. He's so far out of it that if he took one step further out, he'd fall off the edge of the world.'

'Divvent take the King's name in vain! And divvent call me "comrade" either, 'cos I divvent like it!'

'Why, is that the same thing as blasphemy? That's what they want ye to believe, man. Gannin' on strike for a decent wage is blasphemy as far as they're concerned.'

'Hadaway, Jimmy. Your name might be Green but you're redder than a bloody beetroot.'

'One day, bonny lad...one day...You'll see.'

Jimmy was a canny feller and everybody knew he wouldn't harm a fly yet there was no hope for him. The Colliery didn't want him and the miners wouldn't listen to him.

There was another feller outside the gates, one who never looked up or spoke to anybody and everybody just went by and pretended they hadn't seen him. His name was Jake McKay and he'd once been prominent in the lodge. Like Jimmy he'd been a strong union man forever agitating on the men's behalf. The Colliery put him out after the 1926 strike and told him never to apply again. Nobody would employ him and he and his family were now in the Workhouse. To help earn his and his family's keep he had to do any work the Guardians gave him.

Workhouse policy was to give inmates humbling work like digging holes and filling them in again and always in places where friends and enemies alike could see them. Jake, who was one of the best self-educated men in the pit, was made to dig sewer trenches right outside the Colliery gates. And to rub it in, he was the only English bloke doing it, all the rest of the gang were coloured fellers. Unlike Jimmy, who was fair game and loved nothing better than a bit repartee, you had to make on Jake wasn't there. You might catch him standing up and stretching his back when you turned a corner but as soon as he saw you coming his head went down and stayed down. The coloured fellers would stand up from time to time and lean on their spades and jabber on among themselves, they'd smile at you or nod, it didn't seem to matter much to them.

All these things were happening while Ramsay MacDonald, still calling himself the representative of the poor and working classes, was sitting in the big chair at the top desk. If he couldn't change anything, what chance was there of us doing it? No wonder the Durham miners eventually paid him the greatest insult ever. Our banner used to have a picture of his head and shoulders with his neatly parted grey hair and carefully combed tash, looking like he might have been Neville Chamberlain's eldest brother, and this used to be carried in every procession at every gala. As a reward for letting us down so many times we cut his head out and sewed Arthur Cook's in. After that the banner was carried around with Cook's head on MacDonald's shoulders.

Things were really tight with both my father and me out of work, especially now that we had a babby in the house as well, and my father had no other alternative but to go to the Guardians. We hated these people who did what Neville Chamberlain told them to do, just as much as we hated the Workhouse itself. In a few parts of the country they used to have working men on their committees and sufficient in number to influence their decisions. But not since 1926. Everything changed after 1926. And in Shields they were as mean as sin. The relief they gave must have been calculated to be the absolute minimum for a human being to stay this side of the grave on, it was even less than a pitman's pay. Yet to get anything you just about had to go down on your hands and knees and beg for it. And then it wasn't money they gave but vouchers. And always loans, not gifts. So you were neither asking for charity or getting it, you were just made to feel as though you were.

The Government had started calling the Workhouses 'Poor Law Institutions', and the Guardians 'Public Assistance Committees' – or 'PAC's'. But they still called bairns born out of wedlock 'bastards', and Workhouse chaplains still wouldn't waste any Communion wine on paupers no matter how good Christians they seemed to be. Mental defectives still did the cooking in the 'institutions' when the cook was away and the inmates were still hired out as cheap labour. They didn't really want to change the system so they just changed the name.

Every morning and afternoon without fail I went up to see if I could get my job back but Harton Coal Company were in no hurry to take us on again. The longer we were laid off and the more desperate we were to get back, the easier we'd be to deal with if and when they finally decided. At any time of day there'd be hundreds of men standing outside the Colliery and all kinds of rumours flying about. 'They're havin' too many problems gettin' the machines to work because of all the water and the Colliery's packin' in altogether.' Or 'In a year's time nobody'll be needed any more. There won't be a man left in the pit. The machines'll be doing every mortal thing'. There were never any good rumours like, 'Everybody's gettin' their jobs back! Wages to be doubled! Shifts to be halved!'

If you were going up to the Colliery and you passed a group coming back they'd say 'There's nowt yet, lads. Yous are wastin' your time gannin' up.' And you'd say 'Right. Thanks, lads,' and pretend you weren't going to bother going. But as soon as they were out of sight you'd get on up there just the same, just to make sure. You'd think 'They mightn't be wanted but that's not sayin' I won't' or 'Maybe a list went up just after they left'. You couldn't leave anything to chance. If your name was up and you hadn't bothered to go and check, nobody was going to come looking for you and somebody else would get it damned quick.

A lad by the name of Arthur Proud who started the same time I did, got married when he was only twenty and had three kids by the time he was twenty-four, was one of the ones who just couldn't cope. He'd always had only the same wage as me and I couldn't see how they managed even when we were in work, let alone at times like these. He used to go around begging old newspapers and everybody thought he was selling them to the fish and chip shops but he wasn't. In their house they used them for practically anything; they used them for table cloths, carpets, blankets, handkerchiefs and kids' nappies. It depended what paper it was, where it went. Ones with plenty of pictures like the Picture Post went over the beds. Ones like the Daily Worker went on the table so Arthur could read it while he was having whatever they had to eat. The Times went on the floor so they could walk all over Churchill and his pals and The Daily Telegraph and the Daily Mail got cut up and shoved on a nail in the netty. All of the kids were as skinny as rakes and their teeth were too big for their mouths. His wife looked the worst of the lot, even though just a few years before she'd been one of the bonniest lasses in the street. She'd started doing daft things and talking daft and folks round about said she was gradually losing her marbles.

One day Arthur said goodbye to his family, the way he always did when he was setting out to go up to the Colliery to see if they were taking anybody on. But he didn't come back and three days later they found his body on the rocks at Marsden. The parish priest wouldn't give him a proper burial because they found a message he'd apparently scratched on a brick wall at the back of the house which they said proved the drowning wasn't an accident. He got a pauper's funeral which seemed to be more of a punishment for his family than for Arthur. I suppose they thought they were doing the right thing but all I can say is, if Arthur Proud went to Hell they'll need a different place again to put some of the other buggers.

Different people act in different ways in times like these. Some seem as though nothing could ever get them down, some can always manage a smile and others fly off the deep end at the least bit thing. Even though we were all pitfolk and all of us were out of work together, everybody's circumstances were different. And every man, woman and child is different. The same one that can step in and take charge during a roof-fall down the pit, mightn't have what it takes to keep an even keel during a lockout. Even those who are very strong and always put a brave face on things have a breaking point if they're pushed far enough. All flesh and blood does, just as do steel props and ships that are supposed to be unsinkable. You might think you have a fair idea what another person's worries might be but there could be things you never imagined.

In our house instead of just making the best of it like the rest of us, Isabella Tanner nagged my father, nagged me and nagged young Monica as well. My father and me gave back as good as we got but it used to upset Monica. In the finish she told my father she wanted to be allowed to go into service in Southend and he let her go. John hadn't been able to get a job anywhere else in England so he emigrated to Australia. We heard from him just the once to let us know he'd got a job in a margarine factory in New South Wales.

At last my name went up and I got started back at the pit. Many others didn't and my father was among them.

Coalowners themselves never came near the pit, the only time you ever saw them was if their picture was in the paper. Their managers did their bidding and they did it to the letter. No matter which side they came from originally, there was never the slightest doubt which side they were on now and from these fellers you always knew what to expect. It was the buggers in between, gaffers like the overmen and checkweighmen, and especially the deputies, that you never quite knew how you were on with. They wanted to be bosses and men at the same time, they wanted to be liked and respected. But you can't have both. They wanted to get on and give their families as good a life as they could and the only way they could do that was by never forgetting which side their bread was buttered on. They knew that and we knew that and that's why we never really trusted them. They weren't all a bunch of lackeys, as some said they were but what they'd say to you on your own might be very different to what they'd say when one of the managers was around. They'd give you a wink as much as to say 'Shsh, here's one of the sods comin' now.' Then when whoever it was came by they'd say 'Mornin', Mr Beamish' or whatever his name was. 'That spot of rain we had last night was just what the roses needed. I'll bet your good lady's happy about it, is she, sir?' Whoever it was would scarcely nod and just pass by. Then they'd wink knowingly at you. 'Got to keep them sweet, Tommy lad. That's the secret.' Then off they'd go whistling and thinking they were dead cute.

Billy Cowell was one and he could never make his mind up whether to be Arthur or Martha. To emphasise that he knew where he stood, when everybody in the place knew he didn't, Billy never said anything that he didn't say three times. Rat-a-tat-tat, he used to go like a Gatling gun in this funny lass's voice of his. Long before the general strike, when I was working in his district one time I'd evidently done something he hadn't liked, although I'm buggered if I ever found out what it was. I was only a lad at the time so it couldn't have been very much. But whatever it was he never forgave me for it. A long time after, Bob Simpson had just set me on a job when Billy Cowell came by.

'What'sTurnbull doin'-doin'-doin?' he says. Bob told him he was giving me some overtime because one of his blokes were away. 'Get'im off-off-off!' He's unreliable-unreliable-unreliable!' And Bob had to put me off and give the job to somebody else.

Yet after this last lockout, the 1930 lockout, it was Billy Cowell who got me my green card. He never said anything to me but Harry Leas had been at the office when the undermanager said he would never have a Turnbull back in the pit. Billy Cowell had stood up to him in his own fashion. 'Gi' the lad a start, man. Giv'im-astart-giv'-imastart-giv'im-astart. Good lad isTom-goodladTom-goodladTom.'

He'd have known that if I hadn't got my job back our family would very likely have ended up in the Workhouse.

14

I'd been a coalminer for twelve years now and all the glory of working down a pit had gone. I was coughing like the rest of them, I was cursing like the rest of them, and like the rest of them all I cared about was how much went in my pay packet.

Although I was supposed to be getting 5s 10½d a day, by the time the 'off-takes' had been deducted it was a damn sight less. They'd offer you bonuses with one hand and then take them away in fines with the other. Never a month went by without they dreamed up some new way to rob you and I never saw a paynote, either my own or anybody else's, that didn't have fines marked against every single day.

A common trick was to call you back after your shift to work an extra three hours but then only pay you for two saying you'd taken too long to walk there and back. 'Walking to work' didn't mean walking to the pit from your house. 'Walking to work' meant the time it took you to get to the coalface or wherever it was you were working, from the bottom of the mine-shaft. It meant the time you were stumbling along, half-crouching, half-crawling over the stones and through the muck and water, often for miles, with the only light coming from the little lamp you were carrying. In other words, it meant your own time.

The simple truth of the matter was, rich as they were, the Coalowners resented paying us anything and it was a challenge for them to find ways of getting it back. It never occurred to them that we deserved a decent life with a wife and a home and a family, and that we should be entitled to proper medical attention if we fell ill or were badly injured or if our wives or children did. Nor that we had a right to provide for our old age. And the only kind of education they approved of was the kind of Church of England Sunday school stuff that taught you to 'respect your betters' and be content to wait till the next life for any rewards you might have earned in this one. Any more than that would have been filling our heads with 'all kinds of notions'.

The 'ascertainments system' was one of those schemes that seemed so reasonable at the airy-fairy stage when Cabinet Ministers and bishops and Tory newspapers were falling over themselves to say how generous and humane it was and how 'only fools and ingrates' could object to it. The argument they were making for this one was 'The miners will share in the bounty', as though that had ever been one of their priorities. With this plan there'd be no need for the Government to take over the coalmining industry as we wanted them to, because the Coalowners would be taking the miners on as partners so to speak. The way it would work was we would produce coal for one quarter of the year and then the Coalowners would sell it. Then after they'd deducted all their expenses from the income, the rest would be divided up and paid to us during the next quarter. The trouble was – and this was something the clevershites who wrote in the papers and were full of praise for never took into consideration – 'expenses' included the Coalowners' profits and the Coalowners pleased themselves what they would be. As soon as they put the scheme into operation, without even giving it a few months' grace, the greedy sods took so much out for themselves that we were worse off than ever.

They still wouldn't take my father back and unlike in the old days he couldn't just move to another pit, the List saw to that.

My father had always been a hard worker and for all his moaning and groaning he really liked working at the pit. He loved the company of miners, the crack and the argument, and he probably wouldn't have minded the strife if they'd paid him a half decent wage. But now he couldn't afford his one real pleasure in life, a couple of gills in the Stanhope. Like everybody else, if he had toothache he just had to find something to take his mind off it. If he was hungry he just had to go to bed that bit earlier. Yet Isabella Tanner never stopped yammering. To hear her you'd think it was his own fault he was out of work.

'If they won't let ye gan back, why divvent ye try somewhere else? I didn't get married so's I could end up in the flamin' Workhouse!'

At one time he would have clouted her. Now I think he was beginning to wonder about himself, wondering if he should have tried to leave the pit years ago and done something else. It was a lousy enough job as it was, without failing at it. If you go on strike and win, like winning any battle, you're a hero, at least in the eyes of your own. If you lose, you're nothing and you could end up a fool in everybody's eyes. It's not only the ones who win who think God's on their side, the ones who lose sometimes begin to think so as well. But it wasn't just the coalmines. Nobody could get any work. Skilled men couldn't get work in their own trade, let alone anywhere else.

The money I was getting wasn't enough to keep us. Some weeks we just scraped by. Others, because of fines or something else, I'd come back with next to nowt. More often than not I'd be working on an empty belly. We could only afford for me to take one sandwich, no margarine and usually no jam, to last an eight or ten hour shift. I often worked a whole week, morning to night, and sometimes right through the night as well if I could get a double shift, and at the end of it come away with a pay packet with less than fifteen shillings in it. But no matter how unfair it was, no matter if I was fuming inside, I couldn't afford to say a word. One word was all it took and you were finished. And if I were finished now, I'd have had it. We'd have all had it. Me working at Harton Colliery was the only thing that kept the lot of us out of the Workhouse, even though only just. And I was my father's only real hope of getting back. I was his main connection with the pit, with his workplace, with his marras and with his pride. With me up there every day on the spot, if any jobs came up I could maybe put in a word.

Whenever I came home at night, no matter how late it was, my father would always be waiting up. And he'd always have something hot for me, even if it was just a slice of bread and dripping and a few fried old and black potatoes. Some nights it would be the early hours of the morning when I got back and he'd be asleep in his chair. But he'd jump up as soon as he heard the latch and whatever it was he had waiting in the oven for me would be checked before he turned around, as though he had only sat down for a moment.

'Hello, son,' he'd say, wiping his hands on the sides of his trousers. He'd come over and pat me on the back. 'Get theesel' washed and I'll have this ready for ye by the time you're finished. The dish's already filled and there's the soap.'

I'd go and wash my face and hands and sit down at the table and he'd put my meal out.

'This'll do ye good. Eat up and enjoy theesel' and tell us all the news.'

He'd be watching me while I ate every bite and enjoying it almost as much as I was. I knew I was getting the best of whatever was in the house now. If ever there was a bit of bacon or an egg or anything, I'd get it and there'd be no argument. He came second, so he'd be ready if the call came. Isabella Tanner and the two lads would have gone to bed early. As the woman she'd have least of all.

'Len Smith was sayin' he heard tell Benny Brown got taken back. Have you seen him?'

'No… He might have, though. Tug Wilson did… Maybe things are easin' up a bit.'

Eating the meal and telling him any good news would never take very long and by the time I'd finished he'd have the bath off the back door and in front of the fire, filled with water already boiled in the kettle and the big wash-pan. Now I was back we were getting a small coal allowance again.

'Right, lad. In ye get… Now, what does that feel like, eh? Bend over and I'll scrub your back for ye.'

While I had my back to him and we couldn't see each others' faces, he'd maybe say 'So… Nowt yet then, eh?' in a kind of business-like manner as he was scrubbing away.

'Not yet, Dad. As soon as I hear, I'll tell ye.'

'Aye, I know ye will, son. I know.'

I kept telling him there was no need to stay up this late for me, that I was quite capable of getting my dinner myself. 'You're not ganna be in any fit shape for work when it comes if ye stay up every night... Whenever I get the chance for a double shift, I'm ganna be takin' it… Ye need your sleep.'

'What kind of a father do ye take me for? Lyin' in me bed when me own son's out workin' to keep us all? It's the least I can do!'

Every night when he asked the big question he'd always try to do it in a slightly different way, as though asking it in a different way might get a different answer. Sometimes he'd wait a while before he asked, other times he couldn't help asking as soon as I got in the door. There weren't too many ways I could answer. Depending on how I felt I'd usually say something I thought might bolster him up a bit. Other times I'd come back fed up and worn out and I'd be dreading him asking. Six times a week added up to more than three hundred times a year and there wasn't that many different ways of saying 'Sorry, Dad... Nowt.'

Now and then he'd manage a plucky comeback like 'Ah, shite on them! I wouldn't work for the buggers if they came to the door and went down on bended knee!' More often than not he wouldn't say anything, there'd just be this long-drawn-out sigh behind me as though there was an old woman in the room.

One thing gave him immense pleasure and satisfaction and that was an old wireless he had found on a scrap heap. He knew nothing at all about wirelesses or how they worked but he'd persuaded a pal of his by the name of Sid Nelson to pull his apart so they could see. The two of them spent hours and hours fixing this radio and my father would go to all the junk shops and sort through all the boxes of rubbish in one scrap yard after another, looking for old valves that might still have a bit of life in them and for other bits and pieces they needed that he couldn't make himself. It must have taken him two years to finally get it going and was he a proud man when he managed it! He had every neighbour in the street in and every one of his mates around to see his handiwork and 'have a bit listen'. He'd spend hours listening to it on the nights it went well and would then pass on the news and different facts he had learned to the rest of the street. It could be anything from the temperature inside Scott of the Antarctic's tent, to how tall Harry Lauder's father was. And late at night when he could get bits of Russian or French, he was glued to it. He'd sit in front of it with his chin in his hand and a concentrated expression on his face as though he was understanding every word. And when he got some music on, no matter what it was – whether it was piano music or jazz – and no matter how much crackling and fading away there was, he was made. My father thought the wireless was the greatest invention in the world.

Even my mother who'd been a very thrifty person, couldn't have kept two men, two boys and herself on what I was bringing in, so there was no way Isabella Tanner could have done it. And in the end she got my father to go back to the Guardians, though this time he didn't tell me he was going. As luck would have it the Outdoor Relieving Officer came one afternoon just after I'd got in from the pit. I was still getting washed when I heard a commotion at the door and my father's raised voice. I didn't bother myself because it didn't take very much to get him worked up these days. Then I heard Isabella Tanner yelling at my father and telling him not to be so pig-headed.

He must have suddenly realised I was in the house because I heard him say in a low voice, 'Is that wor Tommy? Why didn't ye tell me he was back? Quick! Get him out of it! Send him for a message or somethin'.'

'What message?'

'I don't know! Anythin', ye silly bitch! Just get him out the way!'

I went out the back and left them to it before she came in.

Half an hour later when I returned they still had company. My father was sitting at the table winding his thumbs with his eyes downcast. Even Isabella Tanner was silent, she was standing behind him. Sitting at the table opposite my father was this young drip and parked on the table beside him was a bowler hat and attache case. He was writing in a notebook with a fountain pen. He couldn't have been much older than I was.

'So, Mr Turnbull, can I report to my superiors that you will be carrying out these obligations?'

'Ye can tell them I'll think about it.'

'Think about this then, Mr Turnbull... Should you have failed to sell the items I have stipulated by the time I next call and if you cannot produce receipts of same, consideration of your case in this instance will proceed no further.'

After he'd gone I said 'Who the hell was that?'

'He was from the "you-know-who's", but it's not like it used to be. It's all changed now. It's a lot better than it was. It's the Public Assistance Committee that looks after these things now, not the Guardians any more. Those buggers are gone now...thank God.'

He stood up. 'We had to get him in, Tommy. We cannot gan on like this any longer. Your pay's not enough. But afore they'll give us owt, we've got to get shot of that chair. He said we only need three cos' there's the stool in the back... And the wireless.'

'What about the wireless?'

'That has to gan an' all.'

'What? It's just junk! I mean it just came from junk anyway.'

'We've also got to try and sell some of your mother's cushions.'

'The ones she spent hours and hours on when she was gettin' ready to have our Monica?'

'Aye.'

'What for?'

'Because they have the Means Test now and ye have to sell everythin' you don't need afore they'll give ye anythin'.'

'But why the cushions?'

'He said we've got too many.'

'We've only got four!'

'Aye, I know. But he says we divvent need that many. He said they might be worth somethin'.'

'They're worth somethin' to me!'

'Aye, I know. Me an' all... The trouble is...you're workin', son. That's the bugbear.'

Instead of being in a temper like I'd have expected him to be, he was speaking very quietly. I'd never seen him like this, it was as though all the life had been kicked out of him. I couldn't believe that that young twerp, that chinless wonder, that pimple in the arsehole of humanity with his little leather case had been able to do this to him.

'How d'ye mean?'

'Nowt, son. Except that as long as you're drawin' a wage we have to suffer because of it.'

'How's that?'

'They take your wage into consideration.'

'Do they now? Well, that's not much... What are ye ganna do about it, then? You're not expectin' me to give up me job, are ye?'

'God would strike me down dead if I even thought of such a thing! That's ne answer for anythin'.'

'What your father means is...the problem is...you're livin' in this house,' Isabella Tanner said.

'Shut your trap, woman!'

'D'ye want me to gan an' live somewhere else? Is that what yous want?'

'Is that what ye want to do, Tommy...when there's only you and me left of the family?'

'Course I don't. I just want to know what ye expect me to do, that's all.'

'This bloody Means Test is a wicked thing. It's makin' liars and frauds out of honest people... No, what I'll do is sell the stuff like he says. And then we'll see what he's got to say next time he comes round.'

'You're not ganna sell Mam's cushions, are ye?'

'Never! They'll gan next door for the time being. Mrs Gascoigne'll take care o' them.'

The newspapers said we were in the middle of a slump because of foreign competition and the 'Wall Street Crash', whatever that was supposed to be. In the first place, it seemed to me we'd been living in a 'slump' all our life. And in the second, what could stockbrokers jumping off skyscrapers in America have to do with the wages of a bloke down a coal mine in

County Durham? Why was it always the working people who had to suffer when somebody in some other part of the world messed things up? I'm bloody sure if some old wife jumped off the Tyne Bridge, stockbrokers in bloody New York wouldn't get the sack or have their wages halved. Yet here wages had gone down again, insurance benefits were being cut and on Tyneside more and more workers were being laid off in the pits, the shipyards, factories, every-bloody-where.

If these things really were like throwing a brick in a pond and the ripples spreading out, like the newspapers said they were, why didn't any of the ripples catch the rest of the population? No matter what happened they always seemed to be better off than ever. The same newspapers that brought the bad news and told us we'd have to be 'steadfast' and all that, were full of adverts for cars, fancy clothes, newfangled electrical things, places to go on holiday, gold spectacles, china teeth, and medicines that would make you live forever. Lovely semi-detached houses with bathrooms, indoor lavatories and gardens were being built in new estates all over the place. New dance halls and picture houses were being opened practically every week. And there were plenty of other activities and ways to spend your 'leisure' apart from dancing and going to the pictures. There were variety halls, boxing and all-in wrestling halls, speedway tracks, greyhound stadiums, football parks, cycling clubs, cricket grounds, painting classes, gardening clubs and practically anything else you could think of.

But they all cost money. Fine and dandy if you earned the average wage which was £5 but not if you were a coalminer. Not that I cared about dance halls and all that, all I wanted was a bike. But the kind I wanted, a racer with droop handlebars like they had in the cycling clubs, cost at least £7. With a father having to sell everything in the house to get money from the Guardians, I'd no more be racing around the country on a bike than I'd be poncing about on a dance-floor in a suit. It's just as well I hadn't got one or that would have gone as well.

In South Shields most babies had rickets, many of the kids had ringworm, and everybody knew somebody with TB. But state insurance only covered medical advice, not treatment. And even then it was only for the worker, not for his family. A miner across the street from us who'd been stood off for seven years for complaining about the weighman, had a wife and four bairns and all they had to live on was the thirty shillings a week he got off the Guardians.

It seemed like a sin to even think about a bike.

By 1932 more and newer kinds of cutting machines were being brought into the pit, each one bigger and faster than the one before. Although many of the old hand hewers had gone on to the pneumatic picks when they came in, they hadn't been very keen on them and they had no time at all for the big cutting machines. But the younger blokes like me were keen to have a go at anything new, the more modern they were the better we liked it. And at last I got sent to the face, the heart of the pit, the place where money could be made. When you were on datal or shift work it didn't matter how hard you worked, you never got any more. You only got less, for one reason or another. Now I was at the face, I'd be on piecework and they'd be paying me for breaking my back.

My first job at the face was 'gumming', which meant getting rid of the muck, and I did it with Geordie Gosling, Alfie Kinghorn and Billy Bell, my first real marras. After the coal had been cut, drilled and fired, somebody had to get rid of the stones and muck that came down with it before it went on to the conveyor belt or into the big tubs they were using. And when the caunchman ploated the stones out of the caunch with a long steel bar, we had to get rid of the muck that came out of that as well. Stonemen packed stones into the sides of the goaf and used them for gates and things that had to be built up, but we dealt with the muck. A 'gummer' was a muckman.

Sometimes we used shovels, sometimes we used our bare hands. When we'd got it into a pile, one of us shovelled it up and tossed it to somebody behind him and so on, until it got to the last man who shoved it in the goaf.

Of all the jobs I've ever done in the pit, this was the worst. No wonder they called it 'the murderers' shift'. It was heavy, it was dirty, it was monotonous and the roof was too low for you to work on your feet, even crouched. So all day and every day we shovelled on our knees for a penny farthing a yard, along a face that was 180 yards long. And when there was a pile with a lot of biggish stones in it you couldn't shovel from the bottom, you had to shovel off the top which is much harder. The end of the shovel strikes the stone head on and it's like an electric shock, it goes right through your teeth.

More often than not our legs were under water from the time we went in till the time we came out. Sometimes we got paid wet work, tuppence a shift, though not for the stuff we were kneeling in because that didn't count. To rate as 'wet' it had to be dripping on you from the roof and doing it nonstop. It was a very hot place as well but you got paid nothing for that because they thought heat should be counted as a luxury. So even though it was filthy you couldn't work with many clothes on. Underpants, boots and knee pads from Armstrong's the Saddlers in Green Street was the standard dress for gummers. Some fellers weren't even that formal and would wander about with nowt on but a layer of black dust and they'd work away like that all day and not give a damn.

There were things at the face I'd never experienced anywhere else, or at least nothing like to the same degree. Because we were cutting deeper and deeper into the wall, pockets of gas were being released all the time and it kept collecting under the roof because the ventilation was very poor this far in. And because it was the hottest place in the pit there were more flies than anywhere else and the stink from the you-know-what was worse. Then there was the noise of the cutting machine. Like with all machines it was worse for everybody else than for the one who was operating it and when you were kneeling down it was on the same level as your head. Hard steel blades slashing and screeching against stone and pneumatic drills hissing and hammering, meant there were no poetry recitations or singing in harmonies here.

Worst of all we were working in a permanent cloud of coal and stone dust. Cutting machines create far more dust than picks and it even bothered the Harton Coal Company, though for an entirely different reason. Stone and coal dust was getting into the coal we were sending up and we were told we'd be fined if we didn't keep it out. So we had to take a brush and sweep the face, the front of the coal judd and the floor, after we'd shovelled away the muck. We were told the floor had to be clean enough to eat our bait off, not that it would have made any difference to the bait. No matter how well that was wrapped up and no matter where you hid it, by the time you got it out it was always filthy. And by the time it went into your mouth it would be even worse. But your mouth was full of dust and muck anyway, so it wouldn't have made any difference. Keeping dust out of the bait wasn't important, it was keeping it out of the coal that mattered.

When we finished our shift another set of gummers would come on with their cutter and his gang and sometimes the gummers would toss their muck in our way if there was a long stretch to the goaf. You couldn't let them get away with it though, because it would slow you down having to shift their muck as well as your own. So when you came on you'd reckon what was theirs and chuck it back, and sometimes if you were really pushed you'd chuck on a bit more than that. Pitmen can be right awkward when they want, even with their own marras and these fellers were what we called our 'cross-marras'.

Every three months under the cavilling system we'd draw lots to see which district we'd be working in for the next three months and who with. This was so the same fellers weren't always working in the best places, because some places weren't only awful to work in, they might fetch very little into the bargain. Some had rich seams and the coal would be soft and easy to get but the dust would be hellish. Dandy Bank was like that and although you were sometimes allowed to swap cavils, nobody would swap you for that one. Other places might have a lot of very hard stone and less coal running through it than a pencil and you'd be damned lucky to get anybody to swap you for that either.

By the time I'd been at the face six months we were back on short time and getting only two or three days work a week. You just waited at home and if the buzzer went at five o'clock you knew you were working the next day. If it didn't, you knew you weren't. Then because fellers didn't know whether it had gone and they just hadn't heard it, they changed the system to once if you were on and three times if you weren't. I considered myself lucky to be getting even two or three days a week because half the pit was out of work. But going to work was like walking the gauntlet. Many of the fellers would be standing on their doorsteps and nearly all of them would say something to you, if only to show there was no hard feeling.

'All right there, Tommy?'

'Aye. Yoursel'?'

A few yards further on.

'Canny day, Tommy?'

'Aye, not bad.'

Out of the corner of your eye you'd see a curtain pulled back ever so slightly and you could feel a women's eyes on you as you walked along. If my father was out on the street he'd usually make sure I didn't have to pass him, but sometimes if he'd been up to the Colliery to see if there was anything for him and was coming back, it couldn't be avoided. I'd walk by and he'd be standing with his back to me talking to a group of fellers. They'd see me and tell him and sometimes he'd look up and nod. It was worse than anything that had ever happened to me down the pit.

A bit further on:

'Tommy.'

'Bob.'

'Give them hell for we up there, mind.'

'Divvent ye worry.'

At the corner of the street there'd be two or three or more.

'Can ye pass on a message for we, Tommy?'

'What's that?' I'd say without stopping or slowing down.

'Tell Roberts he's a little Welsh twat.'

'Right you are, Bill.'

I knew it was just that I was luckier than them this time and that if the boot had been on the other foot they'd have been doing the walking and I'd have been doing the standing watching. In which case I'd have been feeling the way they did and they'd be feeling the way I did. I might not be married but I still had a family to support. I wasn't doing anything wrong or doing them out of a job, not deliberately anyhow. But you had to keep telling yourself these things. I always made a point of walking up on my own because I think if I'd been in their shoes, I'd have felt worse seeing a whole gang going up talking and laughing the way you cannot help when there's a few of you together.

The thing was that in the back of my mind I could never forget that everybody knew crawlers got jobs, ones that used to doff their caps to the manager if they saw him in the street and wish him good day. And every time you saw them talking to one of the gaffers you'd wonder whether it was you they were dropping in. Ones like that never needed to worry about being kept on. But how do you prove you're not one of them if you're a hard worker and generally do as you're told? A man of thirty-eight might be standing with his hands in his pockets and his head bowed while his young son of sixteen and his old father of sixty stride past him on their way to work. And his only consolation would be that at least nobody would take him for a crawler.

Sometimes somebody would run down the street shouting 'There's been an accident at the pit! Five men injured!' And two dozen men would race each other to the Colliery to see if they could get the poor buggers' jobs. Or somebody might come back and say they've been given the sack and the words would hardly be out of their mouth before other men were putting their hats and coats on and slinking off. Everybody knew where they'd gone.

For the first time I really began to think about chucking it in. It was hardly worth it for the hours I was getting and nothing could make up for that half mile of faces all the way there and all the way back. It was the same with Norman Howard's allotment. After Norm had both his legs crushed and couldn't look after his allotment any more, I said I'd give him a hand. The Coal Company wouldn't give him anything because Norm had tripped and knocked his lamp out and they said it was a 'clear case of negligence'. He had three kids and a wife who was nearly blind. He could do nothing in the allotment himself, so to look after it properly I had to go down at least every other day to water the vegetables and do a bit of weeding. He was so grateful he said I could take whatever I wanted out of it. But I couldn't bring myself to take anything except the odd sprig of mint, no matter how many hours I'd put in. Nobody knew I was doing it for him and not for myself, because Norm was never there. So when they saw me carrying away a head of cabbage, a bag of potatoes and a few beans, they'd naturally think it was for me. Every time I went down somebody was always hanging about and it got to the stage that I'd wait till it was so dark I'd nearly have to feel my way around. I'd very quietly get the tools out of the bit of a shed because there were houses running right along the bottom of the allotments and the buggers could hear everything, and would just have got started gently hoeing, when a voice would come from over the fence, 'Your lettuces are comin' on canny there.' Or old Mrs Sinnott would come out of her house with some horse's manure she'd shovelled up from the lane that morning and saved for me. She'd totter all the way down her path with the shovel shaking and lumps dropping off the sides. Every now and then she'd stop and bend down to pick them up and then take ages to get back up and you'd hear her groaning with her rheumatism. 'Now don't go thinkin' I want somethin' for it, 'cos I don't. I'm only doin' it out of the goodness of me heart. So good luck with it.'

Sometimes I felt like shouting out 'Everybody for at least ten miles around, listen! These aren't my lettuces! Neither is the bloody rhubarb! None of the stuff in this allotment belongs to me!' Maybe I should have put a notice up.

Worst of all was having to take something back for Norm. No matter how well I wrapped it up they'd know what it was.

'This is the best time of all, isn't it? When the harvest comes in... Nobody can say ye don't deserve to enjoy it either...not after the back-breakin' labour you've put in. I was just sayin' the other day, "They can say what they like but I for one don't hope it chokes him. That feller's entitled to whatever he gets".'

I was even taking off my cap and making on I was straightening my hair in case they thought I was sneaking off with a few lettuce leaves under it. In the finish I told Norm he'd have to send one of the kids down whenever he wanted anything.

When people are hard up they don't always do what you might expect and they can be more generous with some things than others. They might be more ready to share an apple than a gill of beer for instance. Or a feller might break off from his mates and sneak away to have a few puffs of a dumper on his own, a dumper that had already been lit, puffed and nipped out three or four times already. What else would make a hard-working family go to bed early and get up late except that they were saving on meals. What else would make breaking an old saucer a sin or losing a shilling, a tragedy. When a man and his wife can come to blows over a small bottle of beer or a new hat pin, and a mother can scream at the top of her voice at her four-year-old daughter for upsetting half a cup of sour milk, people will do things they wouldn't normally do.

In many of the smaller mining villages there wasn't a kid left over fourteen because as soon as they reached that age they were taken away and trained to be footmen, chambermaids or serving girls. Kids from working-class areas made good servants because they were already used to hard work, they never forgot their place and they were far cheaper to keep than a good dog.

There was talk in Parliament about bringing in compulsory labour camps, the only example they were prepared to take from the new Russia. Apparently this was because 'decent people' were tired of seeing loungers and scroungers 'littering the streets'. A new word was invented for people who were locked out, laid off or sacked. The word was 'work-shy', and it was a clever word because it shifted the blame from the employers to the unemployed. Half-starved marchers who set out for London with a petition to Parliament were a good example. The PAC's were told to treat them as vagrants, the police told to treat them as a menace, and everybody else advised to give them short shrift.

If people stayed where they were when they were unemployed, they were workshy layabouts. If they walked on their badly shod feet, crawled or had even walked on their hands to another place to look for work, they were workshy vagrants. J.H. Thomas was now Minister of Employment so nothing could be expected from that department.

The good old times my father knew, or at least that he talked about, had all gone and he'd be the first to say so. His mother and father were dead long since and most of his brothers as well. His brother, Uncle Jim had gone after 1926 and we'd lost touch with him. His wife had passed on and he hadn't got much of a bargain when he'd tried to replace her. Two of his children were away and he might never see them again. He'd been kicked out of the pit because of his politics. But in any case his days as a hewer were probably over. Whenever factories were looking for workers they wanted nimble-fingered young women that would be content with a wage barely enough to keep them fed. They certainly didn't want middle-aged men with clubs for fingers who expected a wage big enough to support a family and a few gills of bass and half an ounce of shag into the bargain.

The hair on his head was now as grey as his tash. People used to say I was like him. I admit there wouldn't be much in it when it came to stubbornness and I probably took more after him than my mother when it came to looks and build. But there was one thing that would always separate us. And that was drink. Although he'd never been what you might call a 'bad man in drink' and had never hit my mother or bashed any of us, I could never forget the Sunday morning many years ago when he threw his dinner out the window. In my mind I can still see my mother on her hands and knees in the backyard picking up the bits of dinner mixed with pieces of dinner plate and glass. She loved him and yet he'd done a thing like that. I made up my mind that day that if that's what drink did to you, I'd never have anything to do with it. I signed the pledge because of it. Nobody asked me to and nobody knew I'd done it. But that was why.

Even though my father had been out of work for years and had no prospect of getting a start in the pit again, he wouldn't even consider moving anywhere else. Why should he leave a dole queue in South Shields to join one in Scotland or Nottingham or Wales? And why should he pull up his roots and go to live in a foreign country when he belonged here? This is where all his people were…his friends, his relatives, everything. If they were going to screw him for his principles here, they'd screw him just as hard anywhere else because he certainly wasn't going to change. He reckoned he'd paid dearly enough for his principles here in County Durham where they were formed and as far as he was concerned nobody had any greater right to live here than he did. He was no layabout and he certainly wasn't going to be classed as a vagrant.

Yet for all his stubbornness, and any pride he had left was bound up in it, he never kidded himself. It was one thing to walk into the Stanhope, or the lodge, or up to a crowd on the corner end and start spouting off and shaking your fist when you'd just come off a shift, when three-quarters of an hour ago you'd been hewing your heart out on your side in a pool of shitty water in a two-foot high coal seam. But it was a different matter altogether trying to talk pit when you hadn't seen the inside of one for seven years.

Although he liked nothing better than a drink in the Stanhope in good company, he wouldn't go in unless he had the price of at least one gill on him, except maybe for a quick look round. He might stand on the corner outside with his hands in his pockets looking the other way just in case somebody might bump into him, but he wouldn't go in off his own bat and just sit there with his tongue hanging out. Of course if he was already there collecting bets over a business gill, which he would be stretching out as far as was humanly possible, he wouldn't say no to a friendly offer from somebody. And a well-taken tip was usually rewarded with a wetting of the old whistle. But he wasn't a scrounger. He wanted a drink but he also wanted the hard grinding work that went with it.

Despite how I felt about drink I felt sorry for him because I knew how much he missed it and whenever I could I'd give him a few coppers. He got a bit from bookie-running and he'd sometimes pick up a few more here and there doing odd jobs. He'd go round the greengrocers in the market and buy their orange boxes for a halfpenny each and chop them into sticks. Then he'd tie them into little bundles with a bit of string or wire and go around from door to door selling them as firelighters for tuppence or threepence, depending on how full the bundles looked. What he made from his 'little ventures' as he called them, he tended to treat as pocket money. It wouldn't have made any real difference to the welfare of the family and it kept his spirits from flagging. He was having to deal with the Public Assistance Committee every week and he hated that more than anything he had ever had to do in the whole of his life. Going to work day after day in an area of a pit he knew to be dangerous had never bothered him and he would go off to it quite happily and never mention it. But two or three days before he had to go to the 'bloody Guardians' and he'd begin to get really worked up. He was a puffler who would stand up to any of them at the pit even though they gave him a hard time for it, and outside of it he would argue with anybody anywhere about almost anything. Yet the Guardians seemed to knock the life out of him. I think it was because they sapped all your pride before ever you went in.

15

I'd been in the pit fourteen years and was twice the age I was when I started, when at last I got my chance to cut coal. During that time I'd done every job in the pit and run round after this one and that, doing skilled work one day, unskilled the next, never turning my nose up at anything including three years' gumming in the hope that one day I'd be a cutter. I didn't want to be a deputy or an overman or anything like that because that would make me a bosses' man. This would do me, this was the job I'd always wanted. I was now going to be First Man on a cutting team, the modern day version of a hewer. In the pit this was the top job, this was the job that got you respect. And of course this was the job that brought in the money.

Here I was, right up against the face, as far in as it was possible to get, the farthermost limits of the pit. Nobody would be in front of me now. From now on I'd be like an explorer forging ahead day after day cutting his way through a rock-hard jungle. Nobody had ever been or even seen where we would soon be, where I was taking the whole pit to, because it had been sealed for a million years. The stuff we'd soon have in our hands would have been put there before man ever walked the earth. There were fossils of creatures that had lived and breathed before Adam and Eve, where we were now going. It gave you a very strange feeling. But no doubt that would soon wear off, the language around you would soon remind you which world you really belonged to. 'Howay, Tommy, ye dozy bugger! Chew the fucker up and let we get some money!'

The first cutter I was put on had to be operated on your hands and knees, the whole team worked the same way. The 'hogger', which was the air hose to the machine, had to be added to the farther and farther you went in, and you had to drag it over your shoulders, one man after another, with your lamp between your teeth. When you could stand up and straighten your back for a few minutes, the way you could at some time in most places in the pit, it made all the difference in the world. But if you were doubled up for eight hours at a stretch, it took weeks to get used to. Your spine had to change its shape, there was no other way for it.

The Cutter was in charge of the whole operation and all those working with him depended on him to get as much coal off the wall as fast as possible.

I'd cut a narrow band of coal along the whole length of the face which in this case was about sixty yards and the Second Man, Tommy Gibson, would rake it out. Then the driller, Georgie Coughlan, would drill holes three feet deep every yard or so from one end of the face to the other. He was followed by the firer, Frank Dixon who rammed powder into the hole, packed it with clay and fired it. Then the fillers, Alfie Kinghorn and Jackie Walker, loaded the coal as fast as they could into tubs. Also working away of course were the poor bloody gummers. Then came the timberers whose job was to support the new roof with the props that the drawers behind us had pulled out of what was now the goaf. This had to be done to relieve the pressure over where we were working. The roof could easily settle from six feet to three feet in a very short time but that was no reason for getting out. We just kept an eye on it. By that I mean an ear.

It was piece work but everybody depended on everybody else, not like the old days when a man hewed and put his own coal. So if one bloke was a bit slow there was always somebody right behind him ready to stick a boot up his arse. As a consequence you'd keep on cutting even though something was rattling loose rather than waste time getting it fixed. The timberer would use props that were rotten or split rather than going all the way out to get some more. And we would often ignore the roof when it was threatening, or carry on when there was gas about. Everything came down to money.

The amount of dust you copped when you were Cutter was far more than you got when you were a gummer. Kneeling down in a small space meant you couldn't help getting it in the face as it came off the machine. But you just had to keep your mouth shut and get on with it. If you didn't like it there were plenty waiting to take your place. Being concerned about your health not only cost you money, it cost everybody else as well. So if you were looking for a bit of sympathy or an excuse to go easy, this wasn't the place to get it. The attitude was you could bleat all you liked when you got home.

As First Man I was also responsible for the quality of the coal my team sent out, but it was a hopeless task. If we sent out one stone in a 10 cwt tub of pure coal, not only were we not paid for it but we were fined. If a tub wasn't full right to the brim, the same thing happened. Sometimes they decided they only wanted round coals and they wouldn't pay us if it was jagged or splintery. They wouldn't pay us if the coal was too small either, whether it was round or not – 'beans' they called it. Same with crushed coal – 'injured coal' they called that. Yet sometimes it was so dark you couldn't even see your own lamp because the light from it couldn't penetrate the dust. And if you were working in a district where ponies were used instead of an endless, the fillers would often have to squeeze it in their hand to make sure it wasn't pony turds they were chucking in, never mind stones or wrong-shaped coal.

The keekers and weighmen were the ones who rated the coal you sent out and they could be right sods. Even the checkweighman that we had elected through the lodge to check on the other feller was a right sod. You could send perfectly good tubs out-bye but there was nothing to stop them whipping a few coals off the top and putting a few stones in their place, or putting coals of the wrong size or kind in. Or they might swap the token you put on your tub with somebody else's. They had nothing better to do than scheme up ways of downgrading whatever was sent out.

Because nobody can decide what goes into your pay packet more than the weighman, there had been a checkweighman at every pit in the country since well into the last century, miners had insisted on it and it was now the law. We paid the bugger to check on the Coal Company's weighman and he was no better than the other bugger. He was as much a bosses' man as any of them. Fellers would say 'What we need is a check-checkweighman.' But you could go on like that till half the buggers in the pit were checkweighmen and you'd be paying the whole bloody lot. The buggers were all the same, just like politicians. You vote them in and once they're in, they do what the hell they like.

After I'd been Cutter for about six months we were put on the 'stunt system' which was supposed to be a bonus scheme. For every tub we filled over twenty, we were told we'd get an extra penny. Every tub over thirty, tuppence. And so on. So we flogged our guts out to fill as many tubs as we could. On a Monday we might fill twenty-two, Tuesday say twenty-seven, Wednesday we might manage thirty-one, Thursday twenty-six, Friday thirty-four. But then if there was a breakdown of some kind or a fall or some other trouble that had nothing at all to do with us, and we only managed to fill half a dozen tubs between next Monday and Wednesday, we'd be lucky to end up with our basic wage. This was because the bonus was calculated on the average and we'd never go a whole fortnight without something going wrong or being laid off for a couple of days for one thing or another. I've sometimes gone to the office on a Friday night and waited outside the manager's office for two hours to plead our case for the sake of threepence. I've knocked and knocked on his window, he's looked up, sneered and then just carried on with his papers. In the finish I've just come away. What else could you do? There was even a proper term for docking your pay, it was called 'rubbing out'.

Because Harton wasn't an exceptionally gassy pit and machines usually maim rather than kill, the greatest threat to life was from roof-falls. Any roof that wasn't properly supported would come down sooner or later. And every roof was moving all the time as pressure on it was added or subtracted from somewhere else. The pressure might come from up above or on the same level from some distance away. If the odd prop snapped you'd usually just replace it and count it as 'working weight'. The timber might 'sing' and the roof 'work' all day but we all knew the kind of sound that mattered and when it was time to get out. The trouble was you could only vouch for the roof that was directly above you, what was happening way back behind you was a different matter. And for the state of that, you're way out, you had to rely on somebody else.

Whenever there was a bad fall where somebody was trapped and maybe badly hurt, every man stood by to help. And although every colliery had its own rescue team nobody would wait until the rescue team got there before doing something. When anybody gets buried it's the blokes who are digging them out that are going hell for leather and getting all het up. The fellers yon side are the calm ones, they have to be. If you get excited you use too much oxygen.

You're not in this life very long before you have to get used to people dying of one thing or another or having awful accidents. And when somebody breaks his back or loses his legs down a pit people are upset about it. But when somebody gets killed the whole pit is affected by it.

It's regarded as a death in the family and there's always anger mixed in with the sorrow because every death is seen as unnecessary. There was the case of a lad of fourteen who was the eldest of five kids in a family where the father had been killed at the pit some years before and the mother had had an awful time trying to bring the five of them up on her own. At first they had just about got by. The miners had got up a £15 fund for her and the Coalowners were ordered to donate £5 after the inquest because he'd been killed by falling out of a faulty cage. But that didn't last for ever and the whole family were always in and out of the Workhouse. All of them looked forward to the day when the oldest lad could start work, bring something in and give them a bit of pride. That lad was killed the day he started and by the time they brought his crumpled little body out, not a man was left in the pit. Nobody knew the poor little mite yet hundreds of men lined up as they carried him across the yard. Old men, young men, big ones and small, soft and hard, all in filthy clothes, with hands and faces black with coal dust. Some had their heads bowed, some had their hands clasped. Some looked, some didn't. But there was hardly a single face that didn't have two white streaks running down it.

There were less deaths from gas explosions than there was at one time, because of the two-shaft law, better ventilation and safer lamps. Though not at some pits. At Harton, accidents causing serious injuries were far more common. Fingers, hands, arms, legs, feet and backs all copped it. Cutting machines, pneumatic drills, steel ropes, conveyor belts and heavy tubs don't go with darkness and cramped space, nor with weariness. Wages were so low that everybody worked every hour they could get, no matter how hard the work, no matter how dangerous the place. On top of that nobody had near enough to eat.

You never got to know the real facts but I think more than a few people did away with themselves, both men and women. You heard or read about 'accidents' that would make you think and I'm not just talking about pitfolk. If you were to believe the Socialists, fellers from universities who went around collecting facts and figures, a third of the country was living on the poverty line and another third was living beneath it. Even if people paid all their insurance contributions, what they got in dole wasn't enough to live on. It was £1 3s 3d a week for a married couple, 4s 2d more if they had two bairns. Then after six months, the Means Test. If they got through that they might get a total of 15s 3d.

If you were an ordinary human being, no great shakes but an honest and hard-working man or woman, nine times out of ten you'd be working under lousy conditions wherever you worked. And never would you be paid enough to live decently on. If you went to the Public Assistance, you were shamed. If you did neither, you starved. Some people just couldn't work, either because they were ill or because they were unfortunate in some other way. Neither the Government or the Church, Catholic or Protestant, seemed to care a damn. Odd individuals did from time to time, or said they did, but there weren't enough of them to make any difference. Yet every time you picked up a newspaper more and more luxuries were being advertised. Not for lords and ladies but for ordinary human beings. There must have been plenty of them able to afford things like that or they wouldn't have been advertised.

In June of 1933 a march was being planned that would leave from the centre of South Shields and make its way through Hebburn, Jarrow, Gateshead and Newcastle, calling on all unemployed people on Tyneside, no matter what their occupation, race, religion or anything else to join. Never a week went by without there was a march of one kind or another, some little, some big. Most just went from one end of the town to the other, others went all the way to London. The marchers weren't strikers, they were just ordinary people who were hungry, badly clothed and living in awful conditions, and sometimes they included women and children. Some of the marchers would be employed, most wouldn't. All of them would be undernourished, even by the Ministry of Health standards which changed every month, and all of them would have somebody in the family who was ill or had some disability. Every street had its cripples, humpbacks, epileptics, pigeon chests; its blind, harelips, clubfoots, mongols, albinos, buckteeths, cock-eyes, squint eyes and bad birthmarks; ones who talked queer, ones with stuff coming out of their noses or their ears, ones who had scabs or patches of hair missing; and ones who were a bit simple.

The marches had nothing to do with wages or with working conditions in coal mines, shipyards, factories or anywhere else. They were to get people out of their streets and on to the public highway to tell the whole world, especially their own Government, that they were unemployed. And that they were unemployed because there wasn't any work and they couldn't see any prospects of getting any. On Tyneside three-quarters of what everybody called the 'working class', had no jobs. They were neither workmen, working men or workers. So how could they be called members of the working class? The word 'work' had nothing to do with them, they were nothings. And maybe that's what they should have been called: the 'nothings class'.

Even though the days of strikes were long gone and the general strike just a bad memory, marches still weren't seen as pathetic demonstrations by poor human beings at the end of their tether. They were seen as armies of revolutionaries sweeping down to London to overthrow law and order. A dozen people gathered in a market place could be a 'breach of the peace', two dozen in a park, a 'riot'. Shopkeepers along the route would be warned to shutter their shops against 'expected looting', mothers to keep their children off the streets. The Government, and it didn't make a ha'p'orth of difference whether it was Liberal, Tory or Labour, were forever juggling with the 'poverty line'. Whenever they brought it down, the standard that is, they could bring the benefits down and still sleep easy in their beds at night. When people walked all the way to London to see their Prime Minister, sacrificing their dole because they were 'unavailable for work', to tell him they had no jobs and that they were hungry and their kids were sick, MacDonald had the gall to say 'Do people think they have the right to talk to me just because they walk to London?'

The Bishop of Durham, who got £140 a week plus expenses, and whose miners risked their necks in his pits every day for less than £2 a week – when they could get work that is – preached the old message that charity wasn't good for the soul. According to him 'in the long term it benefits only the giver, not the receiver'. Charity was 'a form of self-indulgence' and 'should be resisted at all costs'. Giving £1 16s a week to a miner with a wife and six kids, who'd been stood off ever since the general strike, 'wasn't helping' him or them. It was 'merely impoverishing the whole country' and 'impoverishing the recipients' characters' at the same time, the 'very people it was intended to help'. In other words it was better for a poor man to go to his grave early with a clean slate, than at the end of a normal life-span if that meant the Bishop and his congregation had to chip in.

Newspapers were full of statistics about the 'mental capacity' of the poor, who were called the 'residue of society', compared with that of the 'coloured races' who were considered to have about as much savvy as a well-trained dog. IQ levels were forever being discussed, though I never heard of any test for human kindness or decency being applied to anybody. If you'd asked most of them what decency meant, they'd have said it meant having all your clothes on. It depended on what paper you read how much you needed to eat of this or that every day to be healthy. Firms like Rowntrees and Tate & Lyle with a big stake in food, brought out high figures. They'd have you living on nothing but cocoa and syrup. The Medical Association, being 'more responsible', gave lower ones. Then came the Ministry of Health with the lowest figures of the lot. By any of these standards, none of the people who took part in the marches would have had enough to eat. They hadn't enough money.

I was at work when the marchers met in a field near Boldon but I knew my father had gone along, so as soon as I finished at the pit I went straight there. I felt I had to keep an eye on him these days. As I was walking along past the hedge before you got to the gate into the field, I could hear engines roaring in short bursts and a lot of yelling and screaming but I couldn't see what was going on because the hedge was too thick. I ran down to the gate and saw people scattering all over the place. There must have been a thousand or more running first one way and then another waving their arms and yelling their heads off. Driving into them were thirty or forty pollises on motor bikes. They were shouting and laughing every time they knocked somebody down with their bikes or whacked a skull with their truncheons.

'Boys in blue, one hundred! Layabouts, nil!' one of them shouted, and a cheer went up.

I looked all over for my father but it was hopeless in all this. Twice I was hit and I wasn't doing anything except walking around. But eventually the place cleared and the pollises rode off. I knew my father wouldn't have gone home until every last shout had died down and there was nothing left but a few scraps of paper. I was making a third check right around the edge of the field when I heard somebody laughing.

'Wha'cheor, Tommy lad!'

His nose was bleeding and the sleeve of his jacket was badly torn, otherwise he seemed all right.

'Where've ye been? I've been lookin' all over for ye.'

'I know ye have. I've been watchin' ye.'

'Why didn't ye tell me?'

'You know me, son. I'm a man of few words.'

He put his arm around my shoulder. 'Howay, let's gan back and see if there's owt for tea.'

Some people's houses you go into, the smell of the cooking puts you right off and you think if you had to live there you'd be throwing up all day. Isabella Tanner's meals weren't great but they weren't that bad. She did whatever she had to as far as the washing and the housework was concerned but no more than that and the place was never what you'd call homely. She didn't have it in her to make a house homely. Some women do, some don't. Maybe they're born that way, more likely it's the way they've been brought up. When Mam was alive, if ever there was a stink in the lavvy for example, even though it was after one of the neighbours had been in, Mam would never have said 'That's from them, it's up to them to do somethin' about it.' Mam would never have hung the washing in your way either. As far as Isabella Tanner was concerned, you had to get out the way. You either got your clothes dried or you had a comfortable seat. You couldn't have both. She was cussed like that.

Isabella Tanner either faffed on so much it got on your nerves or she was in one of her moods and you wouldn't get a word out of her. Not that I ever wanted anything from her. She was my father's choice, not mine. He might be able to make a wife out of another woman but that's not to say I had to try to make another mother out of her. He got on to her for this and that but she was really doing everything he had the right to expect. What she wasn't putting into the home I don't think she could put in.

What I'm talking about had nothing to do with not being well off, because we weren't that much better off when Mam was alive. It was in the way things were arranged, the way the curtains were drawn, the beds made, the table set. Mam would keep the dirty washing out of sight until she was ready to wash it. Isabella Tanner wouldn't, she'd let you see how much hard work you were making for her. Mam always made the house look as though we were more comfortably off than we really were and she'd put her hat and coat on and go and look for a few daisies or a bit of willow herb to brighten the place up even if it was raining. Isabella Tanner would never do that. Isabella Tanner always made you feel that this was the best she could do with the little you brought in and if you wanted any better you'd better bring in some more dosh. She never showed much love for any of us, not even for her own two. She never laid a hand on any of our family either, although she sometimes beat the living daylights out of Wilf. She was tough enough and she was no coward, I'll say that for her. One day Wilfred came home in a state because some kid at school had given him a right pasting.

'Who was it? Who tore your jacket?' She wasn't concerned that the poor kid had a bust lip and a thick ear.

'Mickey Wallace.'

'Mickey Wallace, eh? Right! Just wait till your father comes in.'

When my father came in she was waiting at the door…

'What? Let 'im stick up for himself, the little sap. I'm not gannin' to their house.' He came in and hung his cap up.

'I'll gan meself, then,' she said.

'Gan on then. Make a bloody fool of yourself.'

So off she went to the Wallaces'. She mistook Mrs Wallace's sister for Mrs Wallace herself and slapped her on the doorstep. Then she pushed her way into the house, grabbed one of the kids and clouted him. And when the father came down and tried to shove her out, she got stuck into him as well. She was full of herself when she came back.

16

Before we were very far into 1934 things began to change. Demand for coal was increasing at home and abroad. Durham coal was normally exported but more and more of it was now being used in Britain. Our old enemy Germany was building up its armed forces again and the British Government was beginning to get suspicious. Armaments factories like Armstrongs and Vickers were stepping things up, the shipyards were getting busy again and huge factories for the mass production of all kinds of things were opening up. All of them needed coal and they wouldn't be getting any from Germany for a long time. Working pits all over the country were being expanded and improved with up-to-date machinery and old and unsafe pits were being re-opened. Harton was opening up new seams and reworking old ones and hewers were needed in sections which had low or narrow seams that had never been mechanised, places like Second North for instance. All of this led to one thing, the most important thing of all in our house. Dad was taken back.

What a happy day that was for us. The truth of it was that none of us had ever thought we'd see the day. He was now fifty-eight and his hair was all white yet he was like a bairn on its first day at school. There was no talk of 'bloody pit this' or 'bloody pit that' now.

'I wonder if I'll still be able to find me way round. It's been eight years now, ye know. More than eight years. No, eight years in May… Anyway, it's been a bloody, bloody long time.'

'Maybe ye've got too soft,' I says to him. 'There's a new breed of men down there now. Tough and hard and –'

'What? Like you, ye mean? Divvent make me laugh! Jack Turnbull can still hold his own with anybody. Big or small, old or young.'

'This is the kind of men we've got down there now,' I said, curling my arm and making my bicep come right up.

'And where d'ye think ye got your muscles from? Wait till I get down there Monday. I'll show the whole bloody lot of ye. You're nowt but a bunch of pansies compared with what we were like in my and my father's day.'

He had rolled his own sleeve up and was looking at his own arm. He pulled it back down again fairly promptly. He saw me looking. 'Give it a week. That's all it'll take.'

To hell with the bloody Guardians, their Workhouse, and the Public Assistance Committees or whatever they chose to call themselves next. My father could now lift his head up where it belonged. The Stanhope Hotel was going to see a lot more of him from now on and people were going to be getting a lot more good advice than they'd been getting for many a while. Isabella Tanner was going to have to watch herself as well and not be so free with her tongue as she'd been getting lately. Real leather soles would be going on his boots from now on, bugger the hard cardboard. And first chance he got, he was going to get his allotment back. There were great prizes to be won for growing leeks nowadays, not silver cups that took up too much room and too much time polishing. They were giving useful prizes like clocks, irons and bed linen.

And then he was going to have a wireless, one that nobody but him was ever going to be allowed to fiddle around with or lose the bloody knobs off. It was going to be a brand new one, a His Master's Voice, the best you could get. Not one that crackled and sparked and kept fading away into some foreign language. They could keep his old one now. They could shove it up their arses, it was just about the right size. He didn't care about electric light, the gas mantle was ample enough. And he didn't care about fancy electric irons either, that's what Bella was there for, she'd been brought up on the old steam iron. She wouldn't know what to do with a whole lot of switches, she'd more than likely electrocute herself. But there was no substitute for an all-electric wireless, he knew that. So first he'd look into the matter of 'the electric' and then he'd see about the wireless. If the electric cost too much to put in, he'd get some damned good batteries.

When my father started back to work, which he did on the first shift of the first day, if he found it hard, and he must have done after all this time, he never complained. He was so glad to be back again, so full of it

'It's God I thank, and nobody else,' I heard him say to his old pal Walter Cairns when they were sitting by the fire on the Sunday night. 'Ye know what I'm ganna get, Wally? As soon as I save up the money I'm ganna get meself a wireless set. That's the only way ye get to know what's happenin'. Ye get the news, ye get all kinds of music, boxing commentaries, football results, variety hall, plays…everythin'. If it's worth hearin' about, ye'll hear it on the wireless. All kinds of things are gannin' on all the time on the airwaves. It's amazin', man. Right now in this room they're coming in through the window and out through the door. But you cannot pick them up without a wireless.'

'I think that's gannin' a bit far, Jack. Ye mean to say they're in my house, down the pit, in chapel and in the street? Everywhere? Like God? I only hope ye won't be too disappointed when ye get one, that's all I can say.'

'I know, man. I've had one!'

'That thing was ne bloody good! Who d'ye think you're kiddin'? I was in this house a dozen times or more when ye had it and I never heard it gan properly yet.'

'Aye, well ye won't now, because I had to get rid of it.'

'Anybody who made ye get rid of that was doin' ye a favour. It was a waste of good space, only nebody could tell ye that.'

'You just wait. When I get it, and I know the one I want exactly, you'll be the first to get an invitation to come round for a listen. Then ye'll be able to see for yourself... You're a proper bloody 'Doubting Thomas'!

'Aye, and some'd say that's the safest way to be in this world.'

'Christ! I thought I was an awkward bugger.'

'Tell me this then, Jack... If there're men in this country with the brains to invent things like that, why divvent they make the buggers Prime Ministers? The ones we get couldn't invent their way out of a paper bag.'

'Because those fellers wouldn't have anythin' to do with the likes of politicians… Would you, if ye had that many brains?'

When my father came home on the Monday night he was smiling but looked more tired than I'd ever seen him. He had his tea, which was fried tomatoes with a slice of fried bread, got into the bath in front of the fire and fell straight asleep, something I'd never ever seen him do. He'd asked me to scrub his back but I didn't want to wake him, so I did it with a flannel instead.

His hair was now snow white except at the edges where it had gone yellowish, the way his moustache had been for a long time. The whiskers on his cheeks were white, and only the tufts of hair in his ears had any black left. His shoulders were completely rounded, his chest was getting like a woman's and although he had very little fat there was no sign of muscle anywhere, only folds of skin. Eight years out of a hewer's life must be like eight out of a prize-fighter's. The skin over his body and upper arms was lily-white except for the many black bruises and red cuts. His old blue marks, the pitman's tattoo, were still there but all the others were fresh and there wasn't a square inch anywhere on his shoulders or back without some kind of injury to it.

By working every hour I could get and not spending a single penny on clothes or anything that wasn't absolutely necessary, I at last saved up enough money for a bike. I don't know how many times in the last ten years I'd started and had to give up but now nothing was going to stop me. If I got one and they tried to take it off me, I'd fight to the bloody death for it.

On the Saturday afternoon after the Friday pay packet that topped my savings up to £8, I went up to Newcastle with Billy Durkin and a few other pals to call on the best cycle shops in the North East of England. Billy had been a member of the Tyne Dock Cycling Club in South Shields for many years now and said it was the best club there was. I'd been with them a couple of times when I'd been able to borrow a bike but it wasn't the same. I wanted my own bike, I wanted to be a full-time member, I wanted to go everywhere they went. Nobody took you seriously if you were on somebody else's bike. You never got to know anybody that way. And you hadn't the faintest chance of getting a lass.

There were cycle shops in the Haymarket, right along Percy Street and all the way up Westgate Road and every one of them had all kinds of bikes in their windows and standing in racks in long rows on the pavements outside. There was some real beauties amongst them, smooth and sleek and fancy. The gears, saddles and brakes were all the latest design and they were finished in the most classy colours with silver and gold lines and squiggles. Black, dark green, dark red, dark blue, silver, even yellow for those that were colour-blind. I fancied blue but black was what I'd be going for, that's what most of the bikes in the club were.

As soon as you stepped inside the shop the smell of brand new bike just about knocked you out. Black, red and white rubber, bostic, dope, French chalk, leather saddlebags, lacquer and fine lubricating oil, it was like a beautiful meal. There were so many bikes hanging from the ceiling and so many rows of them gleaming in their racks on the floor, you could hardly get by.

The owner would give you a couple of minutes to drink it all in and then he'd come over in his blue overalls, wiping his hands on a rag and looking very serious. The smell coming off him would be fantastic. 'Wha'cheor, lads,' he'd say. 'Anythin' take your fancy yet? Which one of ye is it for? You, bonny lad? No? Ah, the handsome one! I might've known… Lookin' for somethin' light and fast with plenty class, are ye, son?' I'd just nod. You bet I am! 'Right, now we know what we're after, let's forget about the kids' stuff. Come over here, I've somethin' that'll suit ye right down to the ground. It's just in and it's really special. I don't sell bikes like this to just anybody. It wouldn't be fair on the bike.'

Oh God, this is where I've been wanting to come for so long! Keep talking, mister. The lads would be saying 'Tak it, Tommy. Afore somebody else does… If it was me, I'd go for that one definitely. I'd be ridin' out the shop on it by now.'

But I wouldn't be rushed. I'd waited years and years for this and I wasn't going to buy anything until I was certain in my own mind that it was exactly what I wanted. It was only going to happen the once.

After about three hours going back and forwards from one shop to the other the lads were getting fed up, even Billy who knew how important it was to get the right bike. But I still couldn't make my mind up.

'Howay man, Tommy,' Geordie Gosling says. 'It's only a bloody bike! Two bloody wheels and a bit in the middle, for Christ's sake. They're all good… Just take one and let's get back. I've got to get me pigeons in.'

'For God's sake, Tommy,' says Jackie, 'the bloody shops are all ganna be shut soon. I'd've bought that first one two hours ago and be back in Shields with it by now.'

'He's too bloody tight, that's the matter with him. He's hung on to his money so bloody long he's frightened to let go of it. He won't be satisfised unless he can gan back with more than he came with.'

'C'mon man, Tommy. Get your bloody money out. They're all good, anybody can see that.'

I wasn't going to be stuck with the wrong bike for the rest of my life just because these buggers wanted to get back to their pigeons or their lasses or whatnot. 'If yous want to gan home, gan. I'm not gettin' my money out till I see what I want.'

'Ye know what you are, Tommy? I'm sorry to have to say this, but you're a miserable, tight-arsed, little get… Why divvent ye just keep your money in your pocket and we'll all gan back home? Ye can gan to the bank with it on Monday. Those buggers'll be happy enough to look after it for ye. When you're an ould man ye can take it out again…if ye live that long. Ye'll be able to buy yoursel' a walkin' stick with a silver end.'

'Aye and if I'm around at the time, I'll shove it right up his arse, silver end first.'

I knew I could be a bit stubborn and a wee bit contrary but it was my money not theirs. I was the one who was going to have to ride it, look at it, take it here and take it there. And I was the one the lasses were going to be seeing sitting on it. I wanted something that was going to last forever. Buying this bike was going to be the most important financial decision I'd ever made. I was ready to buy one all right, in fact I'd made my mind up before I came out the house that I wasn't going to go back without one. But I wasn't going to tell them that.

We'd been around all the shops at least three times and the owners had stopped wiping their hands and getting up when they looked up and saw who it was again, before I decided on a 'Jack Adams'. Jack Adams used to be a racing cyclist and he made his own frames, everybody who knew about bikes knew about Jack Adams' frames. And in his shop he had this particular one, a lightweight racer, that was perfect. It had everything I wanted on it. We asked him to take it outside so we could have a better look. He looked at me as much as to say 'There's a limit to how many times I can lift all the other bikes out the way, bring a bike outside, stand around while you silly buggers gan on like a bunch of kids and still keep me hair on.' But he gave a long sigh and got on with it. This time there was no beaming smiles, no sales patter. He just fetched it out and said 'There you are.'

I carefully put my leg over the crossbar and grasped the handlebars.

'Ye'd better hang on to it if ye divvent want it wrecked, mister. He's never been on a bike in his life. Aaahaaa, aaahaaa, aaahaaa!' Sid Bell only had one lung and he made this bloody awful noise when he tried to laugh.

'Bugger off will ye, Sid! The rest of ye, an' all. Gan on. I'll catch yous up.'

I was back-peddling and changing the gears, they were as smooth as anything. The sun was shining on the silver wheel rims and glinting off the frame.

'Aye, mister,' I says. 'I think I'll take this one.'

'Hurraaaay! Yippeeeee! At bloody last! I thought we'd never see the day.'

'God, I don't believe it! He's actually ganna tak one! I thought he only went round cycle shops to annoy people.'

'Shut up, will yous! How much is it, mister?'

'Eight pounds, two shillings.'

'Eight pounds, two shillin's? But it says '£8' on the sign.'

'That's the lady's model, in the shop.'

'I've only got eight pound on me.' I was really disappointed and I thought it was a bit of a cheat. The way he had the price written on the card made it look as though the gent's was £8 as well.

'There's a nice one in the back for only seven guineas. Why don't you come and have a look at it?'

I just stood there. I knew what I wanted now. And it was this one. I was going to have to ask him to put it away for me and come back in a couple of weeks when I'd saved the other two shillings up.

'Gan on, Tommy,' said Billy. 'Have a look at it. At least ye'd be comin' back with some change in your pocket. We'll just have a wander up to the other place. They might have a better one for your money.'

I was really disappointed but I went inside. Mr Adams took me through into the back and showed me the 7gns. model but it was nothing like the one standing next to it which was exactly the same as the one outside.

'Na, I still prefer this one. It's the same as the one outside, isn't it?'

'The very same except the handlebars are a bit higher and so wide.'

As we walked outside he said 'You aren't from Newcastle, are ye?'

'No, we're from Shields.'

I went to have a look at the bike again. After a couple of minutes the lads came strolling up.

I was working the brakes with Jack Adams watching when Bob Brown said 'Look at that! There's a scratch under the crossbar. As soon as the rain touches that, it'll gan rusty.'

'What! Where?' asks Jack Adams, rushing up. 'Damn! How did that get there?'

'Ye'd be daft to buy it wi' that on it, Tommy. It looks to me as though somebody hasn't been too careful gettin' it in an' out.'

Mr Adams wasn't pleased at all but under the circumstances he said I could have it for eight pounds and I could paint over the scratch when I got back home. But I didn't want a brand new bike with a scratch on it. I'd rather wait a couple of weeks, even though I'd set my heart on going up to Tyne Dock tonight to see if I could join the cycling club and maybe go for my first proper run with them tomorrow.

'Tak it, man.'

'No, I'm sorry, mister but I cannot take it wi' that on. I've waited too long to do that.'

'Let's gan back to Shields, Tom. Fred Taylors'll still be open. If he hasn't got what ye want, he'll sharp be able to get it for ye. He's very obligin'. Ye'll get real value for your money at Fred's.'

'Look,' says Jack Adams, 'because you've come all this way and your heart is obviously set on this bike, I'm going to let you have it for eight pounds.'

'I divvent want it. It's –'

'Not this one. The one inside.'

'For eight pound? The exact same one as this? Without any scratches or owt?'

He nodded. I could hardly believe it! I went inside with him for the other one, and as he carried it out, I paved the way. I don't believe any bike had ever come out of that shop more slowly or with more care. I gave him the eight pounds, which during the course of the afternoon in my sweaty hand had become a hard greasy little wad. He opened it very carefully and then nodded. Unable to speak, I took my prize and carefully wheeled her off the pavement and lifted her over the gutter. The lads were all whistling and cheering. I got on the saddle, put my head down and after a shaky start when I nearly came off and the lads were all howling, I was away. I had come up on Billy's crossbar but I was going back in real style. There wasn't a better bike than this in the whole of England as far as I was concerned. It was faster, stronger and classier than any of them.

'I hope you buggers aren't ganna be holdin' me back,' I said. 'Cos I've got places to go and people to see.'

They all cheered again and people were turning and looking as we all wobbled off down Pilgrim Street on a motley of bikes with me in the lead.

As we were crossing the Tyne Bridge Bob says 'If it wasn't for us, ye'd've been comin' back the way ye came, with Billy's gear lever stuck up your arse.'

'How's that?'

'Who d'ye think put the two-bob scratch on the crossbar?'

'What!'

'Serves the bugger right. These cycle-dealers are as tight as a tadpole's arse, and that's watertight. They divvent come any tighter than that.'

I was hardly off that bike until it was time to go to Mass on Sunday morning. I was twenty-nine years old but just like a daft kid. When I'd gone round to Mr and Mrs West's, the club secretaries, my very first port of call, they told me the next meet was on the following Wednesday. And when I told them I'd be on shift then but that I'd gladly obey all the rules whatever they were, they said not to worry because they'd go ahead and put my name forward and they were sure the committee would let me join.

I spent the rest of the night cycling all over South Shields. Westoe, Harton, Chichester, Marsden, Horsley Hill, I paid them all a visit. Shields wasn't that big a town but I must have clocked up a hundred miles. I called on all my pals, rode past the houses of people who had bikes and those who hadn't, stopped for a while outside the Town Hall with my foot on the steps and my arms folded like William the Conqueror, went up and down Fowler Street and Ocean Road at least half a dozen times and back and forth along the sea front. Sometimes I sprinted as though I was in a race so people could say to themselves, 'Hey, look at him! He's like a bloody rocket!' Other times I just took it easy and free-wheeled so people could say 'Look at that! That's the way to travel.' I rode up to Mile End railway station and sat on my bike with one foot on the ground and my hands in my pockets, as much as to say 'What a lousy way to have to get from one place to another!' Until the guard came up and said 'D'ye want to bring that on the train, son?' Cheeky bugger! I got out of it then.

Ocean Road was packed with people going in and out of ice-cream parlours, tobacconist's, teashops, newsagents and sweetshops, and queuing up to go into the Odeon cinema. Young couples were walking arm in arm wandering about looking at whatever was going on and smiling at each other. The sun hadn't gone down yet and there was still a good shine coming off the chrome and young lads whistled with admiration when I went by. Every now and then I'd park my bike with the pedal on the pavement to keep it standing straight up and pretend I was going into a shop for something. Then I'd stand well back and watch. 'Look at that bike!' the fellers would say and they'd pull their girls over. 'That's what ye call a bike!' They'd get down on their honkers and take a look

at the gears and the chain wheel. 'I knew it! It's a Jack Adams. Only Jack Adams makes bikes like this… Smashin', isn't it? That's what I'm goin' to get one of these days.' 'When ye win the pools, ye mean!' the girl would say as she pulled him away. I'd wait till they were just about to go on their way and then I'd walk up, lift the bike up a few inches off the ground with a few fingers and then plonk it down as though I was bringing it back down to earth. 'See that! See how light it is?' the feller would say in amazement. Then without saying a word, no smile, not even a glance, I'd glide on to the saddle, reach down for the handlebars, and take off.
I never had another night like it, you can only do something like that once in your life and it was bloody wonderful.

The Belle Vue Cycling Club committee let me join their club as Mr and Mrs West said they would and although I wasn't able to get to the next few Wednesday or Saturday afternoon meets, I was able to get to the big one on Sunday which met after church. There were about forty or fifty members in the club and they were a really good lot. There were more lads than lasses and most of the lasses seemed to be already paired up but I hadn't joined just for that.

Straightaway I loved it. We would meet at the corner of Jacks Terrace up Boldon Lane and everybody would be raring to get off. I was always first there to make sure I didn't miss them but I usually hung back around the corner till there was quite a few gathered. Then I would quietly come up and tag on as though I'd been there all the time. Some of them, like Charley Jordison with his big cheery voice, would have something to say to everybody. Charley in particular would always try to get a laugh out of you.

'Hello, Tommy, lad! Been givin' that bike of yours another shine, have ye? If mine was as clean and shiny as yours, I wouldn't dare gan out on it, ha ha ha!'

It was a wonderful sight to see all the different bikes coming from all directions. Lads and lasses sometimes riding up on their own, sometimes coming in twos and threes, all smiling, all happy. If the weather was bad and the run had to be called off I'd have to make a real effort not to show my disappointment. They didn't ask for my opinion whether or not to call it off or take a chance on it, because they soon found out I'd go even if it was hoying it down. Rain, snow or hailstones, it wouldn't have made any difference to me. All week and every week I looked forward to the weekend the way I'd never looked forward to a weekend in my whole life.

Although it was called a cycling club and that's what it was, it was more of a social club than a sports club and the main purpose was to have a good time. Although some of them were dead keen and used to go in for races and marathons, most of the members just wanted to be able to get out of the town and away from their factories and offices or shops or wherever it was they worked, out into the country and into the fresh air. For those like me who sometimes worked a sixteen-hours stretch in a dark and bad atmosphere and then went home to the smells of bone-yards, piggeries, factory smoke and the stink of the Tyne, a place like Corbridge or Barnard Castle was like heaven on earth. I'd never realised that places like them still existed, that some people lived the whole of their lives in such places, people who'd never been further down into the ground than the dig of a garden spade.

As soon as you got out of the town past the last row of houses, you'd find yourselves right in the country, just as though you were sitting in the front row of the pictures and the curtains were being drawn back. The air would be cool and fresh and the smells of flowers, blossom and meadow grass, would be all around you. You'd pass by lovely houses and farms, different kinds of trees and bushes, streams with humpy-back bridges and all kinds of birds and animals. And all this without ever getting off your bike. On a bike you felt as though you were part of the countryside. I had bought myself a new cap, a diamond jumper and socks to match and I was just like the rest of them. My arms and face were brown and healthy and you could have taken me for somebody who belonged. And in no time I got to know the names of different places and how to pronounce them properly.

Every week as soon as I saw the first green field I'd be breathing in and out as deeply as I could. I'd be striving to get rid of all the dust and muck from every part of my insides and trying to fill myself with sufficient sweet air to last me until the next time. I knew it would be impossible to do but if the benefit only lasted till Monday afternoon it would be worth it. So as soon as we got out of the town I'd get started. I'd have my head down not paying attention to anybody or anything just concentrating on cleaning myself out and without realising it making a noise like a blacksmith's bellows. All of a sudden somebody would slap me on the back. 'Gan easy on the oxygen, Tommy. They'll be nowt else for anybody else the way you're carryin' on.' 'Oh... I didn't realise...' Everybody would laugh including me and I'd go back to normal breathing again. God, that air was beautiful. I could never get enough of it.

The great thing about bikes – one of the great things about bikes – was that we could go anywhere we wanted and come back any time we wanted without having to worry about train times or catching the last bus. It made you feel so free. You could put your bike down at a nice place and then go for a walk up a hill, or take your socks off and go for a paddle in a river and take as long as you liked. And when you came back there it was waiting for you like a faithful friend. Another thing about bikes was they cost next to nothing to run. A bit of oil and a regular wipe was all they needed.

Somebody might cycle past you when you are standing on the corner of a street and you might think you could nearly run faster. But see where they are in half an hour and they'll have covered that ground with very little effort. You could never walk to a place like Hexham or Alnwick from South Shields and back in a day unless you were a world champion walker. And there's no way you could talk and sing and laugh at the same time. On a bike you could do it all and never give it a thought.

We'd usually set off in two's and if you didn't have a partner you'd ride along with a pal. But it didn't matter who you were with because all the time there were jokes going backwards and forwards up the line. Everybody was part of it and nobody was ever left out. They wouldn't let you. Like as not you'd find yourself with somebody else on the way back, maybe somebody who was supposed to belong to this one or that one and they were having a bit of a tiff. There was very little traffic on the roads so most of the time we had them to ourselves and we could afford to have a bit carry-on, although club rules said you weren't supposed to.

Most of the bikes were the black all-weather Hercules, Raleighs or Royal Enfields but some of the lads had made their own from bits and pieces. There were a few tandems, though they were mainly ridden by married couples. You couldn't afford to have a tandem if you weren't married because if your lass packed you in, you'd had it. You'd have about as much chance of getting a feller to sit on the back of your tandem and be content to peddle away behind, as getting him to run with it on his back.

Sometimes we had treasure-hunts or mystery runs, paper-chases if it wasn't too windy. It paid you to stay at the front during a treasure hunt because as soon as some of them came across a clue, they'd read it and if they didn't pocket it they'd certainly chuck it as far away as they could. Even the ones who were laying the trail would sometimes get the clues out of order and scatter them all over the place, so you wouldn't know whether you were coming or going. Particularly if any of them were pitmen.

At Whit we went to Mitford which was a lovely quiet spot on the River Wansbeck near Morpeth and we camped in a field for the whole weekend. The lads collected wood and made a fire and the lasses fried chips and bacon and boiled kettles for the tea over it. It was sunny all weekend and the lads just went around in vests and the girls in blouses. We had running races and mixed relays, long jump, high jump and hop-skip-and-a-jump competitions. We played rounders, water polo and hot rice. The lads looked for birds' eggs and rabbits and the lasses picked wild flowers and water cress. We played them at quoits and if they won we had to buy them a Mars Bar. If we won they had to buy us a packet of Woodbines. Both prizes cost the same – tuppence. After tea we went for walks, played charades, lotto, cards and dominoes, and then sang songs until nearly midnight. I'd never known anything like it. It was wonderful. That was the only word to describe it. I never realised life could be so much fun as this. All the time I was half expecting somebody to tell us to get out of the field, stop playing and tell me I had to get rid of the bike. It was freedom and I couldn't quite believe it.

At August Bank Holiday we camped at Cook's Green near Fatfield. Charlie Jordison's father had a haulage business and Charlie was on the dole, so a few days before, he and his father had taken down all the gear which included the ladies' lockers and the food as well as the bell tents and primus stoves. What a time we had there! There were stacks of things to do. We got rowing boats out on the river and the lads were boarding each other's to try and knock each other into the water. It was great! We had what we called a 'Daft Sports' weekend with a 'Daftman' and 'Daftwoman' as overall winners. The events were things like twenty-a-side rounders, jelly-and-spoon races, stilt races, hopeless obstacle courses, blindfold sack races and football matches with all-in wrestling allowed.

Whenever we went for day runs we'd take sandwiches and foldy kettles with us and have a picnic in a nice shady spot. There was one particular couple in the club, a bit older than the rest of us, who seemed to know every nice spot in the county as well as the name of every village and every little church and monument, even in the most out-of-the-way places. Just as there was always somebody who knew the names of the different trees and wildflowers and butterflies, which birds laid only white eggs and which stones would be most likely to have crayfish under them.

And there was always somebody who seemed to know every verse of every song that had ever been written. One feller was particularly good at ghost stories and last thing at night he would have the girls shrieking as he told his tales around the campfire. Several in the club were good at first-aid which was a good thing because somebody was always cutting themselves on a tin can or spraining an ankle jumping off a tree.

They came from all walks of life and some had very different views to us pitfolk. Sometimes you'd find yourself in a group of maybe five or six and they'd be talking about all kinds of things, things I'd never talked about or heard talked about, things to do with art and travel and the different ways different people lived. All my life I'd seen everything from a pitman's point of view and I'd always thought all decent people would see things in exactly the same way. I now found that wasn't necessarily the case. They sometimes did but by no means always. I never said much myself because I preferred to listen to other people chewing the rag, especially when they seemed to know what they were talking about. One of the things I learned that had never occurred to me before, was that the world wasn't just divided up between those on the coalowners' side, and those on the coalminers'. There are people who know and care about what goes on in coalmining, there are those who know and don't care, and there are the great majority who haven't the faintest idea.

Every summer South Shields had a carnival. Not to celebrate anything in particular but just for the fun of it. And all the local clubs and associations took part no matter what they were. Each one had its own banner and you had to march along in Pierrot suits or something just as daft, playing kazoos and banging drums. You didn't need any musical talent for that, so everybody joined in. It was the first time I'd ever taken part in anything like this and for me it was a great day, another wonderful experience. Right through Shields we went. Tyne Dock, Chichester, the Market, Ocean Road and ending up at the fairground near the beach. What a change from the kind of marching I'd been used to. This time, instead of people shouting and yelling at you and calling you names, they laughed and cheered as you went by. They liked you for bringing a bit of pleasure into their lives. Even the pollises grinned at you. Here I was marching down the road looking like an idiot blowing through a comb covered with a bit of tissue paper and people were patting me on the back and little girls were running after me and tugging at my trouser legs.

When the winter came and we couldn't go for runs so often, the club organised what it called 'surprise parties'. These were usually at either the Smithwhites' or the Colemans' because their houses were bigger than anybody else's. The Smithwhites had three lasses in the club, Allie, Evelyn and Nan and their house was always the most popular because from the mother down they were all smashing cooks. Mrs Smithwhite's family had their own bakery business, Jacksons' the Bakers, and you could see why. Apart from whatever pastries and tarts her three daughters made, Mrs Smithwhite would usually lay on something special like a tin of salmon to make sandwiches with. And the other lasses in the club would bring fancy cakes, buns, scones or whatever they had tried their hand at in their own homes. Tea, sugar and milk would be provided out of the club funds. By the time everybody had brought all their stuff and it was all set out on the table, it was like a feast. It was a good job the lads weren't expected to bring anything because if I'd brought anything cooked in our house, they'd probably have kicked me out the club. I'd never tasted cooking like we got at the Smithwhites'. You get into the habit of eating food because you have to and thinking nothing of it. You look at it, you see it as nourishment and you eat it. And that's all there is to it. If you're hungry enough you'll eat anything. Our house was bad enough since Isabella Tanner took over but some of my pals' houses, like Willy Gibson's! All I can say is you'd have to fill a pan with catshit and bring it to the boil to make it smell like that. God knows what it tasted like. And the lot of them would be eating it day in, day out, all their lives and chatting away and never turning a hair.

After we'd all set to and there were only a few crumbs left on the Smithwhites' table, we'd carry all the furniture out into the yard except for the good stuff which went into the passage and the piano and crackets which stayed where they were. Then the singing and dancing and all kinds of mad games would start. We never played ludo or anything, only noisy games that everybody could join in, like musical chairs, charades and forfeits. Some of the lasses were always wanting to play kissy games but Mr Smithwhite would have none of that in his house, not with his three daughters playing.

Jack Robinson, who was courting Evelyn Smithwhite, would fetch his ukulele banjo and somebody else would bring a concertina or accordion and there'd be at least two or three mouth organs. None of them were what you'd call great musicians although a couple of them might have thought they were but all of them could knock out a tune. And the first one to come out with a tune you could recognise, you joined in with. If any of them hit a few wrong notes you'd drown them out with the singing and pretend you hadn't noticed. I say 'we' but I don't mean me. I was the sort who was quite happy watching other people singing and dancing and making fools of themselves. If they'd had to rely on me to organise the games and get things going, they'd have cried themselves to sleep first. Not that I was a killjoy or anything like that, I just wasn't what you'd call a born entertainer. I couldn't dance without kicking ankles either. Mine, theirs and anybody else's that were handy. And I had such a terrible singing voice the headmaster at school used to give me the cane for it. He thought I was deliberately doing it and while he was whacking me he'd be telling everybody it was a grievous sin to sing hymns that way. I once told him I couldn't sing any other way and he gave me another thrashing for telling fibs. He said none of God's children could ever sing that bad. If he'd heard my father he'd have known where I got it from. My father once said to me, 'Tommy, if ye ever have to sing for your supper, you're ganna die of starvation, son. There's ne two ways about it.' He could talk! If there was one worse singer in the whole world than me, it would have to be him. But still he was right. So whenever there was singing going on and I saw somebody looking at me, I'd just move my lips. Not a sound would come out but it would usually satisfy them. I found there was no way you could tell whether somebody in a group was actually singing or not if they were moving their lips, unless you went right up to them and practically shoved your ear into their mouth. You have to do something though because you always get somebody at a party who isn't happy unless they think everybody else is doing what they want them to do, they'll even stand up and wave their hands as though they were conducting a choir. They're never any good themselves. If they were, they wouldn't want to hear you. At least I don't kid myself, I know a good voice when I hear it and I know how to clap my hands. Anyway I was dead shy, I always have been.

Christmas was the only time I ever saw any drink at the parties. And even then it was only one bottle of port between about forty, so it couldn't have worked out at much more than a teaspoonful each. Yet the parties would sometimes go on till nearly morning. The only time there'd ever been any singing or dancing at our house was at my father's wedding, and nobody had been celebrating it but him.

17

Everybody said colliery managers were swines and some said overmen and deputies were little better. Once a bloke took any kind of gaffer's job no matter how low down, he might have kidded himself that he was still one of the men, but he never kidded anybody else. He'd crossed over to the other side and he was now in the Coalowners' pocket and he'd never again be trusted. The managers had big houses in their own grounds with tennis courts and fish ponds. Overmen wouldn't have that but they weren't very far off, they were certainly more like managers' houses than miners'.

All of them, even the managers, had started off as ordinary miners. They had studied in their own time and got their Deputy's Ticket which meant they knew how to do every job down the pit.

The overmen were responsible for production and the deputies were responsible for safety, and between them they organised the day-to-day work in each district. And if there was a bad roof, flooding, a release of gas, a machine breakdown or any serious trouble between the men, they were the ones who had to sort it out. If they couldn't and the manager had to be brought in, like as not they'd get a bollocking as well. The cavilling, when lots were drawn to see which district the face-workers would be working in for the next three months, would be organized by the overmen and they were the ones who decided how much the various jobs were worth. They'd decide whether or not you should get an extra penny for having to kneel in dirty water all day or be docked because you hadn't done your job properly. Some of them were closer to the men they came from than others were. Some of them dressed and talked the same way you did, others would put on airs and graces and forget that one time they were nothing. And you'd have to be a fool to trust any of those. Some might egg you on to speak your mind about one thing or another as though you were just talking among mates, and then afterwards it would go straight back. There were different overmen for different shifts, like with the other gaffers that worked down the pit. But no matter what they were like as individuals, every one of them knew they had one job and that was to get as much coal up and out of the pit as possible, as quickly as possible and as cheaply as possible.

The first manager I worked for, a man called Bobby Hahan, would spoil you for managers. Anybody thinking they were all going to be like this feller were in for a big surprise and I was one of them. Everybody just called him 'Bobby', I called him 'Mister' because I was just a lad. There was no bowler hat or suit or anything like that, the way it was with other managers, he just wore a cap like the men. And if he wanted a chow of tobacco and hadn't any himself, he'd walk up to anybody he thought might have one and say 'Gis a chow, Jack,' no matter what the feller's name was. Likewise they could walk up to him and say 'Can ye gis a chow, Bobby? I haven't a speck.' And if he had, he would. Whenever he had anything to say to you, maybe to tell you off for doing something wrong or messing about, he'd always come straight out with it. He wouldn't start by asking you a lot of sarcastic questions and trying to make a fool of you in front of everybody. His father had medals made for the Harton miners who had fought in the War and paid for them out of his own pocket. Most of the others wouldn't have pissed on them if they'd been on fire.

With the Coalowners, the managers and the doctors, it was a constant battle. Bobby Hahan was the single exception. Some were right bastards, others were proper shits. But they were all hardhearted. Like with Dr Marks you couldn't appeal to their better side because they didn't have one. Coalowners, and that certainly included the holy Bishop of Durham and the doctors and others that served them, thought that however bad the conditions in their pits were, we could put up with them because we were born to it. No matter how dark and filthy or uncomfortable and dangerous, that's all we were fit for as far as they were concerned. And the fact that enough of us survived to mine their coal for them was proof they were paying us sufficient. The letters they wrote to the papers and the things they said in Parliament showed they thought we were no better than animals. Not that they'd ever treat their retriever dogs, their hunter horses or their screeching peacocks the way they treated us. Yet the same ones were forever spouting about 'decency and humanity', 'justice and honour' and 'civilised and Christian virtues'.

More than anybody else the managers and undermanagers did the Coalowners' dirty work for them. Without somebody else to run their collieries and supervise their pits there wouldn't have been any coal industry, because no Coalowner would have done it. Managers not only knew what every job at the colliery involved, they'd get in the same dangerous cage the miners went in and go down into the pit. Some of them stayed down all day.

A few of the managers were madder and more contrary than any miner and Mr Gardener was one of them. He was a county type and used to come to the pit in a rugby strip complete with shorts and boots. God only knows why, he certainly wasn't going to get a game down there. He would come down where he could be seen, stroll around for a bit and then pretend he was going off. But instead of going he'd hide around the corner and listen to the fellers calling him worse than muck for maybe ten minutes. When he could take no more he'd suddenly leap out and start yelling at them. They say people who listen at keyholes never hear any good of themselves. Gardner was living proof of it.

Mr Parrington was one who ended up in court for painting a race-horse. As if he didn't have enough money already, he had to buy himself a champion racehorse and then camouflage it with white paint to make it look like an outsider. 'Tried' to camouflage it, I should say, because unfortunately for him it rained cats and dogs the day of the race and the horse kept changing colour as it went round the track. It came in last but even so somebody still lodged a complaint. He was had up and it cost him his job so I doubt if he did much painting after that. He hadn't been that bad a bloke as managers went.

Mr Robinson wasn't just a stickler for time, he was a bloody nutter with a watch. If you were on shiftwork, which meant you were paid by the shift, and he saw you packing up a few minutes before your time, he'd run after you shouting 'Come back, ye bloody rabbits! You're away too sharp! I want your names so I can dock all your pay!' You'd all scatter in the dark and he'd chase you all over the pit. He wasn't too bad, he was just crackers.

Scrotty looked a bit like Robinson but he was a different kettle of fish altogether. He was a cracker as well but a real swine with it. Scrotty had a thing about pinching and according to him there was more coal carried away on miners' bikes than by the Harton Coal Company railway. One night the silly sod stopped everybody in the pit from going home for a full hour while he searched every single man, just because he'd put his watch down and couldn't remember where. Another time he bashed a young lad on the head for five minutes non-stop and then picked up a prop and laid into him with that. He'd have killed him if they hadn't taken it off him. He was screaming at him at the top of his voice for not wearing a cap, and raving on about what would happen if he had an accident and hit his head and then tried to blame the Coal Company. Scrotty died quite young but I never knew anybody who shed any tears over him.

But Mr Roberts... he was special... Every other manager including even Scrotty you could at least have a laugh at behind their backs. You might dislike them but you weren't afraid of them. But there was nothing funny about this feller. I've never in my life known a man more hated than he was...not even Churchill.

Roberts knew everything there was to know about mines and mine machinery. And because he'd spent a long time in the South African mines he knew how to handle slaves, which is all men who worked in mines ever were, as far as he was concerned. There were plenty of good engineers on Tyneside and in other places a lot closer than South Africa, so he certainly wasn't picked for that reason. He was picked to fix Durham miners, not German machines. Durham had the reputation for having the stroppiest miners in the country and the Harton Coal Company must have thought Roberts would be just the man to put them in their place. Maybe they wanted to make an example of us, maybe they thought he would be able to break our spirits. Whatever their reason for bringing him all that way, nobody could have been blamed for thinking that no matter how stroppy we were, the Harton Coal Company had managed very well on their own.

Roberts was an ugly little man with a horrible scar down his cheek. Now I know you shouldn't hold a man's looks against him and normally I never would. But in this feller's case you just couldn't help it. He looked exactly like what he was, a snake. He never looked anybody in the eyes but he always knew who was coming or who had just gone by and he could tell who was working in a hole even though it was pitch dark. He was as clever as he was nasty, and that's praise indeed for his mental abilities. In a matter of a few weeks he'd learned the name of every man in the pit from top to bottom and very shortly after, he'd found out what each man's strengths and weaknesses were. He could tell you by your footsteps, your voice or your mark on a piece of paper. And when he knew you, he knew how far he could go with you.

He was always there before every shift started and if you were one minute late getting there even though you might have run for miles in the rain, he'd put his arm out and say 'Right! Every man behind my arm, get out of here.' You'd then have to go home and keep coming back every day at the beginning of every shift, where he'd be waiting for you, to see if you could get started again. Once you were out, he had you exactly where he wanted you. If he thought you were too tough, you stayed out. If he thought you could take a fair bit of bullying or that you would take it because of your circumstances, you had a good chance of getting back. He thought every man worked better if he had a taste of punishment every now and again, he even said so.

Roberts liked going down the pit. He wasn't one for sitting amongst a lot of papers in his office all day and he didn't wait for complaints to be brought to him by overmen or the like, the way some would. Nor did he deal with pufflers or spokesmen of any kind. If there was any trouble he'd jump in the cage, go down into the pit to whatever flat or district it was in and head straight for the one who was complaining. It wouldn't matter whether it was because of a dangerous machine or an argument between one of the men and one of the gaffers, he would handle everything the same way. He would use the foulest, most insulting language and try to make everybody who was listening feel stupid and useless whether they were involved or not.

To Roberts, managing a colliery meant managing the miners. And that meant having everybody afraid of him. You could be working away talking and laughing with your mates and then all of a sudden the whole place would go quiet. You'd turn around and there he was, standing there watching every move you made, listening to every word you said.

He would sack a man on the spot, whether he was down the pit, in the yard, the heap or anywhere else, just because he didn't like the look of him. Maybe he'd seen what he thought was a look of defiance in the man's eyes or had noticed his fist beginning to clench. In the case of hard men and there was a good few of those in the pit, he'd know better than to say anything to them in a lonely place with only their mates as witnesses. What he would do with those, was go to the lamp cabin and take their lamp and tokens away after they'd finished their shift and gone home. When they came to work next day they'd know they were laid off. There was no doubt that it was his intention to get rid of all the hard men and have only crawlers left, but he'd break a bloke like that if he could, rather than sack him. This would make him feel big and it would serve as a lesson to the rest of the men.

Because he made it his business to know the character of every man, he'd have a fair idea of his chances of breaking any particular one. He'd know how many kids the man had and if any of them were sick or disabled. He'd know if they lived in a Colliery house, if they were very religious, if they owed money or if they had some impediment or family thing they were touchy about. And he would use any or all of it. 'One of these days I'm going to crucify you,' would be one of his favourite sayings. And if he used it on you, you knew you'd have to watch yourself, because he meant it.

Paddy Cain was one of the brightest fellers in the pit and he was studying for his Deputy's Ticket at Sunderland Tech. He worked night-shift so he could go to college a couple of times a week. Roberts disliked clever men even more than hard men and he detested Paddy. His way of dealing with fellers like Paddy who he knew the other men respected, was to stroll up when they were working with a bunch of their mates and put them down in some way. You could tell he'd carefully thought out whatever he was going to say beforehand so he'd be ready for any answer the man might give. This was the one time you ever saw him smile – when he thought he'd got the better of somebody. And the more deputies, overmen and anybody else present, the better he liked it. And if ever he came across one he thought definitely had the edge on him, he'd get rid of him damned quick. There were some clever fellers at Harton and he went through them like a cat goes through pigeons.

Paddy had a cool temper, he knew exactly what Roberts was up to and he never let himself get riled up. At least once a week Roberts would come up and say something to him and Paddy would just smile and never say anything out of line. One day Paddy and me were working with a gang of fellers laying a track when Roberts appeared as usual out of nowhere. Paddy must have guessed Roberts was there, because one by one, the dozen or more fellers had stopped talking. Never mind, Paddy just goes on working and keeping his head down. He knew Roberts hated anybody looking him straight in the eye, to him that was pure insolence. Paddy didn't want any trouble although he knew Roberts would have come specially for him, so he kept shovelling away and whistling quietly to himself.

'Doing quite well at college, I hear, Cain?' Roberts says.

'Not too bad, sir,' says Paddy not looking up but just carrying on with what he's doing.

'Especially good at arithmetic, I believe... Is that right?'

'Not bad, sir.'

'Right... Come here.'

Paddy stands up and turns around.

'Let's see...' says Roberts making out he was thinking what to say, when everybody knew he already knew exactly what that was. He pointed to one of the tubs we were using to carry the gear for the track. 'How many shovelfuls of coal would it take to fill that tub?'

Quick as you like Paddy says 'One, sir...if your shovel's big enough.'

You could tell by the way Roberts's jaw dropped that that was one answer he hadn't come prepared for. Before he came down he'd have known exactly how many shovelfuls it would have taken, how many average-sized lumps of coal it would have taken, the diameter of the barrel, its cubic capacity and everything else. But he hadn't allowed for a big shovel... All the men were grinning including Paddy who couldn't help himself but nobody said a word. Roberts stood there staring at Paddy for a good three or four minutes and you could see he was fit to bust. Then he walked off. Twenty minutes later the foreoverman came up and told Paddy he had to report to the Office at five o'clock. When he got there Roberts was waiting for him.

'From now on I'm stopping the nightshift and putting you on days, laddie. They've taught you enough at college already. You don't need to go any more... One other thing... If I ever get as much as one word of lip out of you, you're finished. Understand? Finished at every pit in every coalfield in the country. You're a smart-arse and there's no room for smart-arses in my pit.'

There was no way anybody could win with the man. He picked ones out that would take whatever he had to give, either because they weren't very bright or because they couldn't afford to lose their job and say terrible things to them. When they didn't answer him back he'd say even worse. He mocked people who weren't as smart as he was, he despised those he thought were weaker and he got rid of any he thought were better than him in any way. You could never say anything that would persuade him to your way of thinking no matter how right you were. Nobody had any influence over him except the Devil. He was also a bad man where women were concerned. He had some blokes' wives and they let him just so they could keep their jobs. Once it had happened they found there was no going back; they might have kept their jobs but they had lost their wives and their self respect.

There was one feller he never stopped tormenting just because the feller was a pacifist. This particular time he was heaping insult after insult on him to try and get him riled up but the feller just took it all and didn't say a word. In the finish Roberts picked up the feller's lamp and split his head open with it. The feller was very badly injured and off work for a long time and we thought we had Roberts for sure. Not even Roberts could get away with this, not in front of all the witnesses that had been present because the feller was a hospital case. But when he came out of hospital and the Union came to take his statement, he took back everything he had said. The next thing was he was back at work and promoted. Sometimes otherwise good men will do things when they're up against it and then they're never able to live it down. Men like Roberts buy their souls. If there's a place lower than Hell, that's where Griff Roberts will be right now.

Some of the overmen and deputies were a pain in the backside but some of them were canny blokes. If a lad was cheeky or did something wrong, they'd usually just tell the lad's father to clip his lug or do it themselves, rather than report him to the Office. And with the men they would genuinely try to sort things out. As far as deputies were concerned, because they were in charge of safety down the pit and most of them were prepared to risk their own lives to save the men's, they were generally seen more as friends than enemies. That's not to say there wasn't some right sods amongst them from time to time. But no deputy had much influence and none of them had anywhere near the power the manager had, nor did the overman. The manager controlled the whole pit, the whole colliery. He answered to nobody but the Coalowners.

I had never been one for the girls and I'd never been out on my own with one until I joined the Tyne Dock Cycling Club. Now that I was in the club I'd sort of see them home if nobody else would and I once went to the flicks with Frances Coleman, though that was mainly because somebody else had let her down.

The one lass in the world I really liked was Alice, the eldest of the three Smithwhite sisters – 'Allie' everybody called her. She was good looking and had fair wavy hair. Probably it was because I had such a thick, black, dead-straight thatch myself that I liked girls with her kind of hair. Allie never wanted for boyfriends and was very sure of herself. Whatever was going on she would always be in the middle of it with her strong lilting voice telling everybody what to do. All the Smithwhite women had lovely voices, though the rest of them weren't quite as boisterous with theirs. My mate Billy Durkin was Allie's boyfriend so I didn't let anybody know I fancied her. In any case I wouldn't have dared say anything to Allie because she was so outspoken and I was so shy. She could have possed me, mangled me and hung me up to dry if she'd wanted to. Being stuck for words was never a problem with Allie.

At one time she never used to smile because she'd had a hole in one of her front teeth, although I didn't know it then. Her mother had been left a bit of money by Allie's Grandma Jackson, Mrs Smithwhite's own mother and she'd decided to share it out amongst her family. Jack, Allie, Evelyn, Bob, Nan, George and Ruby were all to get an equal share. At the time Allie was dying for a bike and Mrs Smithwhite knew it so she said 'Allie, you can either have a bike or you can have the hole in your tooth patched. Take your pick.' Allie was maid-of-all-work at home, being the eldest daughter, so she couldn't earn any money of her own. Although she wanted the bike so she could join a cycling club, she felt there was no point joining a club if she was going to have to keep her mouth shut all the time. But she was pretty sure there was enough money in the kitty for both so she plumped for the bike and joined the club. Then she promptly came in crying her eyes out because everybody in the club was supposed to be laughing at the hole in her tooth. Mrs Smithwhite couldn't bear to see her so upset, especially if this was going to happen every time she went out on her bike, so she paid for her to have her tooth done as well.

I'd been in the club about six months when Billy Durkin had a birthday and Allie had apparently sent him this nice tie she'd been saving up for quite a while for. But the birthday came and went and Billy never said anything about it and when Allie asked him he said he'd never received it.

Charlie Jordison and Joe Armstrong were both in the club at the time and the two of them were as thick as thieves. Joe's father had a paper shop in Stanhope Road and people used to say that even though Joe's eyes were so bad he would mix the Daily Mail up with the Daily Worker, he never made a mistake where money was concerned and he could see the twinkle in the eye of the wren on a farthing from a hundred yards. They had an African parrot with a pile as big as an Egyptian pyramid under its perch that everybody used to say had been there just about as long and if the parrot didn't manage to nip you on your way in to the shop, it would swear blue murder at you on your way out. Anyway Joe, what with his queer eyesight, his broken nose and hare lip and Charlie with his big red bloated face looking a bit like a porker, were never able to get a lass of their own. They'd been at the Crown Picture Hall this night and seen Billy Durkin with Frances Coleman and that Billy was wearing a new tie. They knew it must have been the tie Allie sent because when Allie had something to say, she wouldn't wait for the place to clear before she said it and she'd brought the matter up with Billy at the club in front of everybody.

'You mean to tell me you never got it? Even though I sent our Evelyn round to post it through your letter box?'

'No tie came through our door, Allie. I would've remembered it if it had.'

'Not a red and black one with little grey paisley thingamebobs? With yellow centres?'

'Are ye sure Evelyn posted it through the right door?'

'Course she did! And if she can be bothered to go all the way to your house and put it through your letterbox, after I've gone to all the bother of wrapping it up, it's a bit much that you can't be bothered to pick it up, put it on, and say thanks! If you didn't like the colour and you'd had the gumption to tell me, I could've changed it for another one!'

'Allie, I don't know what to say... It sounds like a smashin' tie. As soon as I get back home I'll see if anybody's put it somewhere and not told me.'

'Why like, do a lot of ties come through your door? So many that people have to shovel them up and put them away so they can get by? Is that what you're trying to tell me?'

'Honest, Allie. Ye've got me all wrong.'

Whether the two ugly-looking buggers were trying to get in with Allie or whether they were just jealous of Billy who seemed to have all the luck, I don't know. But I do know they couldn't wait to tell Allie everything and that included Billy sitting with his arm around Frances while wearing Allie's tie. That was the end of Billy as far as Allie was concerned and what she said to him after Joe and Charlie had given her the bad news, couldn't be repeated. Maybe it was to pay Billy back or Frances or both of them, that she turned to me. Maybe she thought picking up with me would be an even bigger insult than if she'd taken up with Joe or Charlie. Whatever the reason I was probably the only one to come out of the whole thing completely satisfied. I'd waited so long for somebody like Allie to come into my life, there was no way I was going to mess things up. If she got Evelyn or anybody to shove a tie, a pair of socks or anything through our door, I'd sharp pick it up.

I think Allie and I suited each other. We were both as blunt as pick handles and we both loved a good laugh. Allie would laugh at anything anybody said or did that was daft. Somebody with a lot of airs and graces getting cut down to size was the kind of thing that particularly made me laugh, things like that could never happen too often. She had a hell of a temper but she'd soon get over it. I was slower to get annoyed and slower to forgive but I was careful not to get annoyed with her.

I'd a lot to be grateful for where the Tyne Dock Cycling Club was concerned and I got on so well they even made me captain, the only position of authority I've ever held. I didn't want to take it but Allie made me. 'Go on,' she said. 'They want you more than anybody else or they wouldn't have picked you. It won't be for ever you know.' So I did and I was glad I did. Although I couldn't go to every meet, because I took every shift I could get at the pit, I never missed a one when I had the chance and neither did Allie. I knew it meant her going off with them on her own sometimes but I had other plans going on in my mind and I wanted every penny I could get.

So far there had been no objections raised about me in the Smithwhite household, none that had come to my notice anyway and everything seemed to be going along hunky-dory. Mr Smithwhite, Allie's father, was a good plumber and he was as well respected for his honesty and workmanship as he was for his family. We knew that because ever since we came to Shields we'd only lived up the street and around the corner from them. And I'm sure they had as much respect for us as we had for them. If ever my father passed Mr Smithwhite in the street he'd always greet him and when my mother was alive she'd have done the same with Mrs Smithwhite. But the real test of what you think of somebody is how you feel about them marrying your daughter. Then you don't need to strive for reasons to explain why they aren't as good as you are, they just roll off the end of your tongue. And that's what happened with John

Smithwhite. Everything was fine as long as I was just a friend, one of the club members. But as soon as he saw Allie and me were getting serious he felt he had to put a stop to it.

I don't think the fact that we were pitfolk bothered him. At least he never said it did, although I wasn't so sure about some of the women in the house. The main thing was that I was a Catholic and apparently he hated Catholics. Like a lot of tradesmen Mr Smithwhite belonged to the masonic and they used to have a few drinks and then get all het up about Catholics. Why they did I hadn't the faintest idea. They were a bit like the Ku Klux Clan except that instead of dabbing you with tar and setting you alight, they stopped you from marrying their daughters.

One night he must have heard Allie and me saying goodnight on the front step and out he came in a hell of a temper. I was never to see her again, I was never to come near the house again and he wasn't going to have any daughter of his 'turned into a skivvy to a Catholic pitman with a couple of dozen kids'.

There were seven survived in his family and only three in ours. And he knew it so I don't know how he could come out with something like that. And everybody knew Allie was a maid-of-all-work in their house so he could hardly tell me I'd make a skivvy of her. But there was no arguing with him. He'd come out to say his piece and then bugger off back in and that's what he did. He hadn't come out to let me say mine. Luckily for me if Allie was any less stubborn than I was, it was only by a very short hair. And although I couldn't go to the house any more, not even for the club parties, we still met. Several times I brought some of my free coal allowance in a wheelbarrow for her mother – something you could get sacked for – as a kind of peace offering. But Mrs Smithwhite wouldn't take it and I'd have to wheel it all the way back again. All it did was cause trouble at both ends.

'Where ye gannin' wi' that?' Isabella Tanner would say when she saw me all dressed up and going off with the barrow.

'Never you mind,' I'd tell her. 'It's my coal. I worked for it and I'll do what I like with it.'

Then when I got to the Smithwhites' I'd be standing in the back lane just waiting for the word to fill their coalhouse up and Mrs Smithwhite, who wouldn't even come out to have a look at it, would say to Allie, 'We don't burn dirty pit coal on our fire.' Allie would come out and tell me and I'd say something like, 'Where does she think hers comes from? Off the trees in the West Park?'

I think Mrs Smithwhite was probably only trying to find excuses to back Mr Smithwhite up because she'd always been very kind to me before the business with him on the step. The whole thing seemed daft to me. Allie wasn't allowed to bring me to her house because Catholics were 'no damned good' and I wouldn't fetch her to our house because Isabella Tanner didn't think Protestants were any damned better. And I certainly wasn't going to risk having her being unpleasant to Allie. My father had been born a Protestant and my mother was born a Catholic and they had been quite content and there was no bother out of either of their families, none that I ever knew of anyway. And I could never say the Turnbulls were any better than the Kellys, not for any reason. Or the other way about. It didn't make any sense to me at all.

Allie and me made up our minds we wouldn't be stopped unless we wanted to, in which case we would be stopping without any help from anybody else and we still saw each other at the club and other places as well. When I came back from the pit I'd look in the shops on Stanhope Road to see if she was doing any messages. And if I had no luck there, I'd hang about at the bottom of her lane to see if she came out to beat the carpets.

In case I wouldn't see her at either place, I'd have a little letter ready to give to Evelyn or Nan with a few simple words put into a sort of poem. A lot of pitmen think they're great poets and somebody would always be spouting away in the dark. If any of it took my fancy I'd write it down first chance I got and use it on Allie. 'Eeeh, you're quite the poet, Tommy Turnbull. Did you know that? I'm not kidding. You are. You should go in for one of those competitions, "Bard of the North", I think they're called. You never know, you might win a prize.'

'Aht, it's nowt much,' I'd say trying to sound modest. And I'd probably score a few extra points for that.

I never put the letters in an envelope, I just used to fold them up until they were the size of a postage stamp. Like a fool, I thought it would make it more private. I trusted Evelyn and Nan, the two of them had gentle open faces and they would nod very seriously and promise to keep it a secret. 'Oh, yes, Tommy,' they would say. 'Oh, no, Tommy. You can trust us, Tommy. We'll give it straight to Allie.'

Aye, and butter wouldn't melt in my mouth, Tommy. It wasn't until a long time afterwards I found out that none of them had ever been given straight to Allie. She'd got them eventually but not until the two of them had read every line in every one of them and split their sides laughing.

Evelyn Smithwhite was courting Jack Robinson, who was a clerk to the Public Assistance Committee of all people, and taking him home for tea every Sunday. Mr Smithwhite was quite happy about him. He was a clever feller, he had a good job and his mother had a little grocery business. Jack and Evelyn had met at the club just like Allie and me had and Jack was a Catholic just like me. Allie knew Jack was a Catholic and told Evelyn it wasn't fair that she, a younger daughter, could bring Jack to the house any time she liked, when I was never welcome at all. Evelyn agreed and so the two of them got together.

Evelyn waited for the right moment which was after Mr Smithwhite had come back from the Stanhope, had his Sunday dinner and was settling himself down for a little nap in his rocky chair before taking the dog to the park to watch the bowls. Then she took his slippers off the dog and fetched them herself and when he was smiling at her with his eyes half shut, she came straight out and told him Jack Robinson was a Catholic. She was fairly certain he wouldn't stop Jack from coming to the house seeing as she was his favourite. All he did was pull a face.

'It's still all right for him to come to tea though, isn't it, Dad?'

'I suppose so… He's already comin', isn't he?'

'You can't stop Jack Robinson from coming,' says Mrs Smithwhite. 'He's a very decent lad and he's been coming to this house –'

'I've just said so, haven't I?' Mr Smithwhite says. Then he closed his eyes and settled himself down again. Allie then changed places with Evelyn.

'If Evelyn can bring Jack Robinson, can I bring Tommy Turnbull?' Allie then asks. 'Because I love Tommy just as much as our Evelyn loves Jack. What's good for one daughter should be good for another. I'm older than Evelyn and –'

'All right, all right! Stop yammering.' He put his hand to his bald head and scratched it and yawned without opening his eyes.

'Does that mean "yes"?'

'I suppose so, I suppose so. If that's what you really want. Anythin' for a bit of peace.'

18

Allie and me were married at St Peter and Paul's, Tyne Dock, on Easter Monday, 1935 and Evelyn and Nan were Allie's bridesmaids. Isabella Tanner said she wouldn't be going to the wedding and had told my father he shouldn't be going either even though we were being married in a Catholic church. My father said 'Bella, ye can please your bloody sel', like ye always do. If ye want to gan, gan. If ye divvent, stop away. But I'm the lad's father and I'd be gannin' even if he was marryin' somebody as bloody awkward as you.'

In the taxi on the way to the church Mr Smithwhite had told Allie she still had time to change her mind. She only needed to say the word and he would stop the taxi and they could all go back home. But once they got to the aisle, he wouldn't be made a fool of. 'So make up your mind now or not at all.' 'It's already made up,' says Allie. 'And I won't change it here, there or anywhere else.'

When we came out of the church the club were there with their bikes above their heads, making an arch for Allie and me to walk under. I hadn't wanted any fuss but Allie had gone ahead all the same. There was nothing Allie liked better than a 'big do'. 'You only get married once,' she kept saying. She had arranged for a man from the Shields Gazette to come with his camera and for Evelyn and Nan to practically drown us in confetti. All the relatives from Jilbert were there and any of my marras that weren't working. Ones that had just come off shift and hadn't time to go home and get changed just stood back a bit. All the Smithwhite relations were there of course, as well as the neighbours on both sides. And most important of all my father was there with our Monica who'd come all the way from Southend. Because it was my wedding day, I was off until ten o'clock the next morning so we had plenty of time to enjoy ourselves.

Friends and relatives were very kind to us and most of them had gone out and bought wedding presents, even though none of them were well off and some of them would have been a lot worse off than Allie and me. All the womenfolk had been able to make something useful and some of them had done some really fancy designs and patterns on things like rugs, blankets, pillow cases and tea cosies. Tea cosies were things nobody was ever short of and if you had too many, the kids could always wear them for hats in the winter. Only wise heads had put hands in pockets because nothing we got would be wasted. My father now had another allotment and out of his leek prizes came a clock, half a tea set and six mousetraps, so some good had come from the many nights the whole house had been stunk out from him boiling his secret concoctions on the kitchen stove. 'Leek soup' in our house meant soup to feed the leeks with.

As soon as Allie and me had got engaged we'd picked out the furniture we wanted at the Downtown Furnishing Company and started paying for it at five shillings a week. The owner had stayed open until eight o'clock one Saturday night to wait for me coming off shift. Who wouldn't? – he knew he was on to a good thing when he found out we were getting married. By the time I got there, Allie, Evelyn and Nan between them had ordered just about everything in the shop. 'This is what I'm going to sit on when I come to visit you,' sort of thing. No wonder he was all smiles and rubbing his hands when I walked in. 'Good evening, Mr Turnbull. How are you, sir? Pleased to see you again.' 'Again'? I'd never been in the place in my life until tonight. Allie had, but not me. And as for 'sir', the only time anybody ever called a pitman 'sir' was when they thought they were going to get some money off him.

When Allie showed me all the stuff she'd picked out I says 'What are we ganna do with all this? We're not ganna be livin' in Buckin'am Palace, ye know. Not on my wage.'

'You men haven't the faintest idea of what it takes to furnish a home,' she says. Both Evelyn and Nan were nodding away like a couple of nuns.

'I've an idea that lot's ganna cost a bob or two, for a start.'

'A girl only gets married once in her life,' says Nan.

I was thinking 'Just as well, at this rate.'

'Anyway,' says Nan,' I wouldn't marry a man who was as mean as sin.'

'Tommy's not mean. He's just very careful,' says Allie.

'Very, very careful, if you ask me,' Nan says.

'Come on, we don't want an argument over it,' says Evelyn. 'You and me'll go outside, Nan, and leave the two young lovers to it. Let them talk it over amongst themselves.

'Young lovers'! I wish these women wouldn't talk so flamin' daft. If the fellers at the pit knew I was putting up with all this, they'd think I was a proper bloody sap.

As they were going out Nan calls out to Allie, 'Make sure you get that little vanity table, Allie. And the blanket chest!'

Eventually the two of them went out. Now I only had Allie to deal with.

'Now, look here, Tom,' she starts. 'A girl only...blah, blah, blah, blah, blah. And what you men don't realise is...blah, blah, blah, blah, blah.'

I knew if we didn't get it here we'd end up at some other place just like it, it wouldn't be any cheaper there and she wouldn't be settling for any less. To give her her due, when I asked her to marry me, she told me straight out she wouldn't start her married life with any second-hand stuff and that if I couldn't provide her with what she wanted she'd find somebody who could. Looking at Allie with her chin out and her arms folded was looking at somebody whose mind was already made up.

'How much, then? For everythin'?'

'It's all oak, you know. My mother always says –'

'How much, Allie?'

'It's the latest fashion and everybody –'

'How much?'

'Twenty-five and we can pay for it so much a week.'

'Twenty-five what? Twenty-five bob? Twenty-five bob's a lot for a few sticks of furniture.'

'No, you silly fool! Pounds! Twenty-five pounds.'

'T-w-e-n-t-y-f-i v-e-P-U-N-D!!'

'It's a real bargain. Anybody can see that. Mr Lewis said he's being generous because we're getting married.'

'He would! He's hardly ganna be tellin' us he was robbin' the shirts off wor backs.'

'Ahh, Tom. Come on, now. It would make me very happy. It's only five shillings a week.'

'Aye, five shillings a week for the rest of our lives... What if I get stood off at the pit or there's another long strike?'

'If, if, if... We cannot live our life like that or we'll never have anything.'

So I slowly signed the agreement and out of the corner of my eye I could see the smile on Allie's face getting bigger and bigger.

'I told you not to give in to him,' I heard Nan say when Allie went out and told them.

The day before the wedding, I'd hired a threepenny barrow and me and Allie's brother Jack had pushed it all the way up Stanhope Road to our flat in Owen Street. Although it was piled to the skies and Jack was so well tanked up we'd zigzagged from one side of the road to the other, everything was still in one piece when we got to the front door. Jack Smithwhite was another feller who could never pass the Stanhope Hotel, there were quite a few of them in Shields. I had to keep reminding him that Allie would go crackers if we scratched anything and that she'd go for him as well as me. Jack was a bit of a lazy bugger, he was nothing like his father and I don't think he had much regard for things. We hadn't gone more than a few yards up Whitehall Street, not even as far as Stanhope Road before I realised I'd made a bad choice asking him. It was just that he'd been available, he was more often out of work than in. I think he thought I was going to pay him for it, when the truth is I was in two minds whether to tell him to bugger off back to the Stanhope.

But now we were there I could breathe again and I was beginning to think Jack wasn't such a bad assistant after all. He could be a sulky bugger when he liked, especially when the drink was beginning to wear off, but if he'd had a skinful he'd laugh at anything. All we had to do was lug it up to the stop of the stairs into the room 'and Bobs-ya-runcle' according to Jack.

Before we started up the two flights of stairs I went up to have a look... Window there, we'd have to be careful of... Landing here, where we could stop for a rest... That bit of banister, we'd have to watch for... Fine... So up we went, with me at the bottom guiding the tipsy Jack who was stepping one very slow step up and then one very quick one back down. It was a wise decision me being at the bottom, I hadn't realised how weak he was. They should shove him down the pit for a couple of months, that would soon harden him up. It seemed to me that he was hanging on to the far end of whatever it was we were carrying, rather than lifting, so I was having to shove it and him up the stairs. As soon as he opened his mouth to complain, I was shouting 'Heeeeeave!' and ramming it into his belly so he was completely winded. At least that way he'd cushion it against hitting the wall.

'We'll have to get somebody else to give we a hand, Tommy. I'm not used to this kind of – Oooooffffffughhhh!' he groaned as I shoved it right at him and kept ramming it in with every step I took up.

When I got to the top he was flat on the floor and his nose was bleeding a bit.

'What d'ye say there, Jack? I couldn't quite catch it.'

'It'll be a long time afore I do somethin' like this again, I can tell ye… I'm gettin' too old for this kind of lark.'

I didn't know his exact age but he couldn't have been more than thirty or thirty-one.

Eventually we got everything up and last but not least the dressing table which turned out to be a real bugger. I'd thought the job was more or less finished when we'd got to the front door but in fact it was only beginning then. Getting the stuff up these bloody stairs was ten times harder than getting it up Stanhope Road. The dressing table was so awkward even with all the drawers out, because of its shape. I made up my mind that if ever I had to do this again I'd borrow a screwdriver and take the mirror off first. At every turn we'd had to twist it first this way and then that. But rather than skin his knuckles like I was willing to do, Jack would puff and pant and moan and swear at the dressing table, the stairs, the walls, me, anything but himself.

'Right… Let's have a tab,' I said. So we sat ourselves down and I got the Woodbines out.

'That's a canny drop,' I says as I lit up… I'd hardly got the words out of my mouth when the bloody dressing table took off and down it went, a damned sight faster than it came up, all the way to the front door and out onto the street. Not once did it get snagged on any of the dozen corners, skirting boards, stairs and banisters that had got in the way when we had been bringing the bugger up. It hadn't paused even on the landing. If you'd been standing by you'd have thought somebody was driving it.

'Hell!'

'Doesn't look like it wants to be up here,' says Jack.

After we'd finished our smokes and brought the dresser back up I found some sticky brown tape in one of the drawers and taped the back of the mirror up. And when it was done there were only a couple of thin pieces in the middle missing. 'Hey! Me bloody nose's bleedin'!' Jack yelps when he takes a look in the mirror.

When we got back he wasted no time telling Allie what had happened and no doubt that it was my fault. Funnily enough there was no big fuss, nothing like what I'd expected. Instead she and her mother had sat up half the night bubbling to themselves about all the bad luck we were going to have.

Cracked mirror or not Allie and me knew we were very lucky to have our own place. We had two whole rooms to ourselves. The front door was shared with Mrs Winter and the back door with Mrs Porter and there was never any bother out of either of them. The tap and the lavatory were in the yard so we kept an enamel bucket on the landing for water, and a jerry somebody had got us for a wedding present under the bed. My marra Jackie Brown did the painting and decorating and we put two of Bobby Smithwhite's pictures up on the wall. Bobby had done them with pastels at school. One of them was a babbling brook going under a bridge and the other one was a ruined castle. He'd framed them with glass and passe-partout and that was his wedding present to us. Those were the first pictures that had ever been on the walls of any house I'd ever lived in and I quite liked them.

We soon settled into the ways of man and wife. Allie had her ideas of what a good wife should be and I had my ideas about what a good husband should be and we both did our best to make each other happy. Allie was nearly as good a cook as her mother already and every day we had a hot tasty meal. What a change from Isabella Tanner. Ten years of that woman's meals and you could sit down to anything and be grateful for it. Not that I ever said that to Allie in case she'd taken it the wrong way. From what I hear Isabella Tanner would have made a perfect army cook, some place where they put you up against a wall and shoot you if you complain.

On a Sunday we had Yorkshire pudding with mint and gravy, that always came on its own first, the way it was always done in the Smithwhite household. Then we had lamb or rabbit, sometimes beef, with peas and sprouts or runner beans and cabbage. Salt, pepper and vinegar and a bottle of sauce was always on the table. I liked heavy brown sauce with everything, Allie liked light red tomato, so we treated ourselves to both and made it last and it didn't cost us any more in the long run. On a Monday we'd have a fry-up of Sunday's left-overs followed by a slice of Allie's gorgeous slycake. Tuesday we'd have potpie, then tapioca pudding. Wednesday, leek pudding and roly-poly. Thursday, mince, peas and mashed potato followed by new baked bread. Friday, a pennorth each of fish and chips fresh from the shop, followed by suet pudding and treacle. Saturday, pork with peas pudding or saveloys with pickled onions and any cake that was left. When we were eating our meals we'd always sit by the window together and watch the world go by. No matter what shift I was on Allie would always wait to have her dinner with me. I never asked her to do that, she just decided that's what she wanted.

From now on I had scones with margarine and jam sandwiches beautifully sliced to take to the pit for my bait. No more cock-eyed dry crusts, sometimes with a lick of jam, sometimes without.

No wife could have looked after any man better than Allie did me but she was by no means a slave. She'd done everything she was told to do when she lived at home because she had no choice. But once she got her own home that was the end of that. A father was one thing, a husband was a different matter altogether. And because I was easy going she'd have had me doing everything her way if she could have got away with it. She said my habits were too 'pitmatic', like the time I cut my bread on the table instead of the plate and sliced through her damask cloth. Some of my ways she changed and some she didn't. But I'd always listen to her and if I thought it was fair I'd do whatever she asked me to do. If I thought it was just because it was the Smithwhite way of doing things and for no other reason, I still might, but more often I wouldn't.

One thing she did straightaway was toss out all my long-johns and get me vests and underpants instead. She reckoned they were much easier to wash. The washing she definitely found hard because she'd never been used to anything like pit washing. A plumber might get some lead marks on his overalls, a bit of rusty water on his shirt and a bit of muck from getting under sinks but that was nothing compared with what a pitman brought back. Every day his cap, vest, shirt, socks, pants, everything he has on, get soaked with sweat and water that's little better than what runs in a sewer. And everything sticks to it. Coal dust, stone dust, grease and oil from the machinery and whatever he picks up from the floor. It gets on his clothes, underneath his clothes and right into the fabric itself. Soaking won't bring it out. The clothes which are always of heavy material – they wouldn't last if they weren't – have to be dadded, boiled, possed, boiled again, scrubbed, rinsed two or three times, put through the mangle a couple of times, carried out in a heavy basket and then pegged out on the line. And if it rains they might be in an out several times before they go onto the clotheshorse and then get ironed. This takes a lot out of everything. Underclothes, outer clothes, and woman. And if that woman isn't very strong, as my Mam wasn't, or if she's carrying a bairn and maybe nursing another, it's hard. Sometimes in the winter for weeks and weeks on end everything has to be dried in the house and you can hardly see the fire for wet clothes and the whole place is dripping wet. And when at last the clothes are dry or as dry as they're going to get before they have to be put on again, she'll have to get out a needle and thread and patch up what she's scrubbed away.

Women of Allie's generation were better off than my mother's and grandmother's because we now had pit baths and this saved tramping the coal dust and muck into the house and it did away with the need for the tin bath every night. Though it didn't make the washing any easier.

It had taken Harton a long time to get the baths in and even then we had to pay for them ourselves. We had been paying threepence a week out of our wages for ages but by God it was worth it. To be able to get under a hot shower after a ten- or twelve-hour shift when you could get one and see all the muck being washed down the plug-hole, was a great thing. With the tin bath you had to steep in it for a while and then get somebody to pour kettles or pans of water over you to wash off the scum. And the floor always got wet no matter how careful you were as though there wasn't enough damp in the place already. And there was no privacy at all.

The trouble with the pit baths was that although you fetched a lot less dust and muck into the house, you brought in a hell of a lot more fleas. Because with the baths came the lockers. Although most blokes took their clothes home at least once a week for washing, some blokes hardly ever did and others never at all. And in no time the stink from the lockers was something shocking. It was from those dirty sods that the rest of us got 'The Itch' and there was no way we could avoid taking that back home. Their lockers were breeding cages for fleas, lice, ticks and every other kind of vermin. Their hides must have been made of leather because I honestly don't think they ever noticed what must have been crawling all over them. The fleas could have been having a football match with the lice in the middle of their back and the dirty buggers wouldn't have been any the wiser.

But no amount of hints or insults would make the slightest difference to them, they were thick-skinned in more ways than one. You could wait until one of them came in and then say aloud to somebody, 'Pooaarrhh! What the hell's that?' Like as not the dirty bugger would turn around and say something like, 'One of you two dirty buggers must've let off. Nebody strike a match or the whole bloody place'll gan up, ha, ha, ha!'

You might be more blunt and say to somebody, 'Pooaarrhh! Smells like a rat's crawled up somebody's arse and died.' The feller you were talking to might sniff the air and say 'More like a bloody horse, if ye ask me. And at least a month ago, at that.' The one you were talking about might carry on getting changed, not even bothering to look up, and then have the gall to say 'It's you man, Tornbull. Ye were born with ya face too close to ya own arse!'

In the finish you couldn't take any more and somebody would have to report it. They'd tell the attendant, 'Number so-and-so's stinkin' the bloody place out. Ye'd better do somethin' soon or there's ganna be trouble'. Then he'd send somebody along to spray their lockers with disinfectant. There'd be no messing about with those fellers. They'd just rive open the locker door, turn on the hose pipe with one end in a bucket of ammonia and drench the whole bloody lot from top to bottom, clothes and all. When the bloke came and found all his stuff drenched, he'd more than likely only gripe about his baccy being soggy or his racing paper ruined.

They say you find things out about people when you have to sleep in the same barrack room or tent with them that you'd never expect and aren't likely to find out otherwise. If it's true it must be no less true for 'ablutions' as they were called. Some blokes who would never sing a note down the pit would sing their heart out when they got under a shower. Others would fight and throw water at each other just like kids. They'd put their hands around the corner and change the water in your shower either to scalding hot or freezing cold. And others would go daft at the sight of another man's tackle. There were those that were in and out in a flash as though it was sulphuric acid instead of water coming out of the tap and there were those who'd have stayed in all night if they'd got the chance.

Although I worked with blokes every day who never wore a stitch, I didn't do it myself. Not for religious reasons or anything, I just didn't like the idea. People thought we were low enough as it was. But apart from that I always had the feeling I was somehow protected if I had something on. Not that a piece of cloth would be much use if the roof came down or you got hit with a hook and chain. Some people think wearing a little silver medal with a saint's head on it will stop a train from crashing. Me, I just like keeping my pants on. Baths are different of course I know that. Ones who would never dream of strutting about the pit with nowt on might have no qualms at all when they got to the baths and they'd stand about like Greek statues as though they half expected you to toss them a coin or something. This was the type of feller who would take himself very seriously and never mess about and he'd usually be a singer, at least he thought he was a singer. Generally he would get in and there'd be a lot of gushing and splashing until he had the water just right. Then he would fancy he was Peter Dawson and get into a few songs like 'In an English Country Garden' or 'On The Road To Mandalay', sung very loud. After a while the singing would die away and the water would gurgle to a stop and there'd be dead silence. This would be when he was having a good look at himself to see if he had anything anywhere that he wasn't too happy about like a lump in his neck or a few grey hairs around his thingy. When he was quite satisfied that he was still perfect, the body beautiful would take over and he'd start breathing very deeply, holding his breath and flexing his muscles. These types of fellers were buggers to get out. They'd completely forget they were supposed to be going home and that's why they were in there. Then you'd hear the jungle call and you knew they'd had enough for today and that Tarzan would be stepping out shortly.

Although there were no rules and regulations about how you were to go about it, the usual thing was to wash your feet last, so whenever you saw a feller washing his feet under the curtain thing you'd stand outside. He'd then see your dirty feet standing and would oblige by hurrying himself up and usually he'd come out to get dried. But there were some awkward buggers that stayed in just because they knew you were waiting outside. It wasn't because they were concerned about getting themselves clean because some of them would be in for half an hour or more and come out very little cleaner than when they went in. Some stayed in because they were proper gobshites. The water would loosen their tongues and they'd be arguing the toss over the top with anybody no matter how far away they were, until there was nobody left to bother with them. There were a few who'd never scrub their backs because of a superstition about water on the back weakening the spine, but a lot fewer than people think.

After we got the baths in you didn't need to feel ashamed about walking the streets dirty any more and you could go back and forwards to work as clean as anybody else. Long gone were the days when I'd be proud to go home black from head to foot and covered in muck, the novelty of that soon wore off. But we were still easy to recognise. Nobody but a pitman carried his own water bottle to work. For most people if they wanted it, drinking water was never very far away. But the miner had to bring his own and because he could lose half a stone in weight in a single shift at the face, he had to bring plenty. Apart from his bottle there was the way he walked. It was a very solid walk from somebody who spends more of his life in the grip of gravity than most other people in the street and he showed more interest in the sky when he could bear to look up. And it was a very tired walk. When you got close up, after the baths came in that is, he'd be unmistakable. What might have looked like cheap old tattoos a few yards away were his blue marks, ancient pit scars. Coal has stayed well preserved underground for millions of years, it easily lasts in a man's skin for his short lifetime.

When the housework was done, it wasn't Allie's idea of a good time to sit and stare at the four walls. She loved going out and wanted us to have a bit of fun while we could. She hadn't been able to get out that often when she lived at home and she knew when a couple of bairns came along it would be harder still. The thing was a pitman's job was much different to the steady regular day work of a plumber and I had to take every extra shift and every hour I could get no matter when it was. Allie appreciated that, she knew whenever I had a night off I'd always go for a walk with her and that if she wanted to go and visit her sisters or her friends while I was working, that was fine by me. In fact I was glad if she did her family visiting on her own because I wasn't keen on all the socialising stuff. I'm grand at a party when there's plenty going on and you can just sit back in a corner and enjoy everything. But when you have to sit and talk about this and that and a whole lot of other tripe, with one or two people hanging on to your every word, I'm happier out of it altogether.

For me Saturday was always the special day. I'd usually be home by half past twelve and in the afternoon I'd go to watch Sunderland with a few of my pals. Allie loved dancing and she would usually go to the Saturday afternoon sessions with Lily, Jack Smithwhite's wife. Jack preferred the Stanhope to the Palais and the only sport he went in for was having a bet on the horses. Sunderland had a great team, as good as Newcastle United any day, and they were a great crowd of supporters.

Saturday night was our night of the week. No matter what the weather was like or whatever else we'd done or hadn't done in the afternoon, we always went to the Pictures after tea on a Saturday night.

There were any one of half a dozen picture houses we could go to, either by walking or by bus and Allie would have found out everything that was on and where. One week we'd go to see something she liked such as a musical with Jeanette MacDonald and Nelson Eddy or a sloppy romance with some pansy like Rudolph Valentino. And the next we'd go to see something I liked such as a Roy Rogers cowboy or a William Powell detective. We both liked a good murder whoever was in it.

No matter how hard things had been during the week – maybe you'd had to go to work in the rain and slush every day and there'd been nowt but trouble when you got there – come Saturday night you could put it all behind you. You'd stand in the queue for three-quarters of an hour and the doorman would only be letting a few in at a time and you'd think you mightn't get in and everybody would be saying what a miserable bugger he was. And then it was your turn and you were in.

Nobody really minded standing in a queue, it was all part of it. If there wasn't a queue outside a good picture house you could be pretty sure there was nowt but tripe on, just like with shops. If women saw a queue anywhere they'd join on from sheer force of habit and then they'd ask somebody in front of them what they were queuing for. When you were standing in the queue outside the pictures there'd always be a couple of disabled old soldiers playing an accordion or singing for a few coppers. A few of them were a nuisance but some of their antics were really funny.

When we got in, while I was getting the tickets Allie would be buying the sweets and popping into the ladies. If she was a while I might pop into the gents to save going in the interval and then we'd meet up in the foyer and be pleased to see each other again. Then we'd take our coats off, go through the doors and we were in.

Immediately you were hit by the thrill of hundreds of people all watching the same thing. You'd come into their world and you had to respect it, and as the usherette was shining her torch to show you where to sit, you were looking at the screen and getting into it and maybe laughing or whatever the case may be before you even got there. As you went along the row everybody would stand up and their seats would clash back except for a couple of moaners, but you'd just shove your behind in their faces and say sorry and let them get on with it.

When you sat down it was lovely and comfy and a warm glow would come over you. As soon as we had settled ourselves in Allie would squeeze my hand and we'd sit back ready to really enjoy ourselves. In a few moments we were going to be in snowy Alaska, sunny Brazil, busy New York or somewhere just as exciting. Sometimes we'd have got there in the middle of the picture but that didn't matter because when it finished we'd just stay on and watch the beginning up to where we came in. That way you'd have seen the whole show and understood bits you hadn't quite understood before and sometimes it was more interesting that way. You'd see those who thought they could never be together because of cruel fathers or wars or whatever, and could hardly believe what you already knew, that it would all turn out in the end and the hero and heroine would get married and probably inherit a load of dosh. And you'd see the bad'uns who didn't deserve to get away with what they were doing, not knowing what we did, which was that they were all going to get the chop before the picture was over.

If you got there at the start of the show the posher places would have a feller playing an organ that came up in front of the stage from down below. He'd play a few lively tunes until the place filled up and everybody got settled and then the curtains would part and he and his organ would disappear and nobody even noticed.

There was usually a little documentary about how a potter makes a jug or about the wonderful work missionaries were supposed to be doing for black babies in Africa, something that was intended to make you feel safe and proud to be British. What I liked was the newsreel because you could see what the people you'd been reading or hearing so much about looked like. The King and Queen, Churchill, Chamberlain and the rest of them. They always looked smaller and older than you'd imagined. Take away their top hats and gowns and they'd look no different from anybody else.

Whenever the big picture was in colour a cheer would go up from any kids that were there, and the women would go 'Ooohh!' as they snuggled themselves into their seats and squeezed their men's arms. They knew the dresses would all be in colour and you knew they'd be satisfied even if the picture was a load of tripe.

If it was a musical or a singing cowboy and it was a rough place, the audience would join in the chorus and sing their heads off along with the picture. Anything went at the Imperial or the Crown at Tyne Dock. It didn't cost you much to get in but you'd pay for it when you got inside. When you were a kid you never noticed the sweaty smell or the greasy hard seats and the fleas never bothered you till you got back home. It was a different matter now though. But sometimes you'd have no choice, either because they hadn't had any cheaper seats left at the posher places or because you'd already seen it.

If it was an 'A' picture at a place that was on the ropy side, as many as half a dozen kids at a time would come up and ask you to take them in. 'Take us in, will ye, mister? I've got me own money. Look.' They'd hold a scruffy little paw out with a few sweaty coppers in it. 'Just two of yous, then,' you'd say. 'He's me brother,' a tiny little one would yell out, running up with his scruffy face and pointing at one of the two you'd agreed to take in. 'All right, all right,' you'd say, annoyed for letting yourself be blackmailed into taking any of the little beggars in. 'Now there's no ice-creams or sweets or nowt... Do yous hear?'

'Oh no, mister. None o' we like ice-cream. Do we, lads?'

'Na, ne sweets neither. We all hate sweets 'cos tha bad for ya teeth.'

They knew when you were a mile off whether you were going into the pictures or not and they'd come racing up and practically knock you over. Some couples would say 'Sorry, sonna, we're not going in,' and the woman would give them such a sweet smile. The same ones would then walk on looking straight ahead as though they were going somewhere else and then suddenly make a dash for the stairs and up to the paybox. They knew they were safe there because none of the little beggers would get past the commissionaire, and they'd look back over their shoulder smiling and congratulating each other as though they'd escaped from a gang of armed robbers instead of three or four snotty-nosed kids with the behinds hanging out of their pants.

By the time you got to the paybox with your 'family' by your side and were counting your money out on the little counter, there'd be a couple more with faces that would tear your heart out. Ones you remembered you'd told to scat before you agreed to take this lot in, the lot that were now hanging on to you for grim death. The cashier would say you hadn't given her enough for 'two and three halves', and you'd know one of them had gypped you. You couldn't hold an inquest into which one, so you'd pay the extra and they'd hang on to you till you'd got them inside the door. 'Right! Now beat it, the lot of ye,' you'd say. Most would take off the minute they were in and you wouldn't see them again. But every now and then you'd get one little'un who should have been in bed hours ago, following behind as you were following the girl with the torch. 'I want to go to the netty.' 'Get lost!' you'd be whispering to him as you were walking up the side and pulling his hand off your jacket. 'We aren't your mother and father.'

Some of them were real pains and you had to be careful they didn't see where you went or they'd backtrack, especially if they'd seen you getting any sweets on the way in. I've seen Allie and me bent almost double all the way to the back and then down the centre aisle just to keep out of the light. And when we've finally got a seat after creeping round and round as though we'd sneaked in for nowt, Allie's said 'No more, Tom. I'm not going through that again. If you want to bring half the kids in Shields in with you, you can come on your own and I'll go with our Lil.'

Unless it was a top-class place like the Odeon, you'd sometimes find you'd been stuck beside an old tramp who'd got in through the toilet window and was snoring his head off. Again if it wasn't the Odeon you might get some silly bugger who would argue with something somebody had said on the screen or would keep making daft remarks that you couldn't help laughing at even though you were bloody annoyed. Then some right grumpy sod would be telling you to shut up because you were laughing. Somebody else would then stick their neb in and shout at them to shut up. Then those two would have an argument. Then the chucker-out, an ex-pug who looked as though he'd lost every one of his fights, would come down the aisle flashing a torch the size of a Goblin vacuum cleaner. He'd shine it in people's faces and tell ones that had never said a word to be quiet or he'd hoy them out. In no time hardly anybody would be watching the picture, they'd all be turning around and putting in their own two penn'orth.

Because of the commotion the manager would come down with the usherette by his side and then you'd have three of them blocking the view. 'Get out of the light, the lot of yous!' people would be shouting. Though if it was a 'manager job' the picture would more than likely have been stopped and the lights put on.

'Right! Which one is it, Albert? Those two? Right. You two, out.'

'It was him along there.'

'You! Out!'

'I'm gannin' nowhere! I've never said a word since I came in.'

'Out! And no argument!'

'Get out yoursel'! I've paid for me seat and I'm stayin' in it till I've seen the end of the picture.'

'Somebody fetch the manager, will they?'

'He's here! That's him.'

'Fat lot of use he is!'

'Shut up, the lot of ye! If I have to come down here once more, I'm chuckin' this whole row out.'

Sometimes the chucker-out would grab somebody with the manager helping by holding on to his waist and pulling from behind with the usherette hanging on to him. Whoever it was being pulled might have a couple of mates behind him and a tug-of-war would soon be under way. Eventually the manager would give up and go away leaving the chucker-out standing like a sentry at the end of the row. A few minutes later the lights would go off and the picture would start again after a bit of a splutter. Ten minutes later a big bobby would come quietly down the aisle, the chucker-out would point, the bobby would curl his finger and somebody, sometimes two or three, would get up and leave. There was always some entertainment at the pictures no matter what was on.

19

Something happened to Jackie Shaw when he was driving one of the big Star-and-Locker cutters and I got his place. His cross-marras on the other two shifts, Jack Telford and Jack Brown were now my cross-marras.

The Star-and-Locker was a monster. You got on this thing and drove it like a huge bloody tractor. It had forty-six pick heads and worked like a giant corkscrew, churning out coal and everything else as it ate into the solid wall. The face moved back so fast we were all the time having to keep adding to the conveyor belt and bringing it farther and farther in. After a while Jack Telford went to be a deputy, so Jackie Brown and me took the extra hours and worked the seam between us. We each had to work twelve hours a day to do it but it suited both of us and Jackie was a great bloke to have as a cross marra. I was now earning more than I'd ever done and although my father wasn't in the front rank any more, he was doing all right. Men who were skilled with the pick were still needed to remove coal that the firer or the cutter had left behind, and in places that were either too small or too awkward for machines.

There had always been dust down the pit – coal, stone and muck dust – even out-bye. But on a machined face it was far worse than it had ever been anywhere and there was nothing you could do except keep breathing it in and swallowing it. The hand cutters I'd been using were nothing compared with this. It got in your eyes, up your nose, in your hair, in your lungs and in every nook and cranny in your body. If you were cutting with the wind you got the dust blast. If you were cutting against it your Second Man got it. Whichever way the area was ventilated, somebody got it. Sometimes you'd be doubled up over the conveyor for nearly quarter of an hour at a time trying to bring enough muck up out of your lungs to clear a space for the air. And then you'd have to cough so hard to clear your windpipe to let the air past that you'd nearly bring your insides up. When you got a good face like Dandy 20 that teemed the coal off, the dust would be so thick you'd have to keep stopping the machine and staggering off into the goaf where all the shit was, because it was the only place you could get any air. And with a face nearly two hundred yards long like in Howler 5, you might as well not bother to bring your lamp because it was so bad you practically had to feel your way about.

But as always when you were First Man you could never stop for more than a few minutes at a time because the other blokes would be on to you all the time to get back. Every minute you spent coughing meant something off everybody's pay packet. They were having to put up with dust and muck just as much as you were with a cutter as big as this one, so if you didn't damned well like it you could damned well get down off the seat and give it to somebody else.

Sometimes you'd try not to breathe at all for a spell or to breathe less. But after a while your chest would practically burst and you wouldn't be able to help taking in a great big gulp. Then you'd be back where you started, only worse. Some fellers tried sticking bits of rag up their nose to see if that would keep the muck back but they got clogged up in no time. It didn't matter what you used, cotton wool, lint, muslin, five minutes was all it lasted. I don't know what they were doing with the ventilation because some places would be like an oven one minute and like a hurricane the next.

If a machine broke down so badly you couldn't fix it yourself and had to send for the mechanic, the rest of them would moan like hell and give you looks as much as to say 'What the hell've ye done now?' as though you'd buggered the bloody thing on purpose. And when the mechanic came they would always try to get him to say it was your fault so they could moan a bit more. When you were tearing at the wall like a maniac there were no complaints, and that was the only time. If they heard something at the back end of the machine that sounded as though the whole thing was ready to blow up, there wouldn't be a peep out of them. There was never any 'Ye better slow down, Tommy. I think it might be overheatin'.' More likely it would be 'Divvent fash yoursel'. These things are meant to gan flat out. The hotter they get, the better they gan. Get on with it, man!'

If the mechanic couldn't mend it there and then, there was hell on. Because if it had to be taken away you could count yourself very lucky to get work somewhere else and even if you did, your pay packet would be a lot smaller.

So when the mechanic came and you'd already lost valuable time, you'd be telling him it was only something small and pleading with him to be quick about it. None of you would give him a minute's peace and if you thought he was making too much of a job of it you'd curse him.

'These blighters are very, very tricky.'

'What are?'

'These collars... Out the road and let's see what I'm doin'! Ve-ry, ve-ry tricky.'

'Cut the slaver and get it fixed, will ye!'

'Just as I thought...ju-st as I thought.'

'What's what ye thought?'

'The collar's split. These things are always going. It's because –'

'Well I hope ye brought a new one with ye?'

'No, I didn't'

'Why the hell not...if the fuckin' things are always packin' in?'

'Because I'm just a fuckin' mechanic! Not a fuckin' spare-parts factory!'

'Ah come on now, George. Divvent be like that.'

'The whole thing's ganna have to come out. The crankshaft looks as if it's banjaxed as well.'

By this time he'd probably had enough and was beginning to walk off in a huff.

'I'll send the lads down for it.'

'Ye know what you need, George?' somebody would shout after him.

'What's that?' he would say without turning round.

'A red hot poker up your arse. Hot end out!'

'Thank you, Robert. I'll remember that.'

If the cutter was really buggered it might take a week or more to fix it. And if it had to come out altogether it could take a month. During that time you'd have to take shiftwork, datalwork, anything you could get anywhere in the pit and be glad of it. Otherwise you were back on the corner of the street.

Allie and me were now living in Vine Street just behind Tyne Dock Station and not far from my father's place in Lemon Street or her mother's in Whitehall Street. It was a bigger and better place than Owen Street and we'd got it because Allie was expecting our first bairn. Nowadays whenever she wasn't doing the housework she was making little hats, coats, socks, gloves, anything that could be made with a ball of wool and a couple of knitting needles. She loved doing it, she was good at it and she was really happy. And so was I. Relations and friends were forever giving us bits and pieces they'd had for their own bairns that they didn't think they were going to need any more. 'If I do, I'll ask for a lend of it back,' they'd say, laughing. Most people took good care of their things and cots and prams would last for years and go back and forwards and round and round. Expecting always seemed to be a bit of a joke to some people, especially sisters for some reason. Grown women they consider themselves to be, yet they can still roll their eyes and giggle like school-girls. Mrs Smithwhite seemed pleased with the news but Mr Smithwhite didn't seem too chuffed.

On top of all the gear and stuff we had all the advice anybody could ever need. Mothers-in-law, aunts, great aunts and sisters-in-law, particularly those who'd never had any kids of their own, were all standing by to deal with any emergency. Even I learned how you had to deal with baby wind and how not to mistake it for laughing. Or smiling, was it? On the one hand we were told we had to let it cry and not keep picking it up every time it whinged or it would get spoiled; on the other that no baby cries for nothing. We were getting all shades of opinion. I'd always thought there was nothing to it, I'd no idea so many things could go wrong. Everybody knew Chinese women had theirs in the paddy fields where they were working. They just wrapped them up, put them on their back and carried on weeding. But I only mentioned it the once.

Allie and me were perfectly content as man and wife, at least I was anyway and I'm pretty sure she was. If Allie didn't say there was something wrong you could be pretty sure nothing was. We hardly went out these days except for our Saturday night out to the pictures but we didn't need to. We were busy making a home, a real comfy little home ready for our own little family. We still kept up with some of the friends from the club but we had stopped going for runs with them when we found the way Allie was. Quite a few of them had married each other and gone their own way. I used the bike for work and I still loved being on it but Allie had put hers away for the time being. In any case I was working double shifts, weekends, every hour I could get. Everything went straight into the house.

I had a job, we had a canny place to live, and most important of all we had each other. There was nothing more we could ask for really apart from a little one of our own. We were both hoping for a boy though as long as it was properly formed and healthy it wouldn't matter what it was.

On the night of the 2nd of June, 1936 I was dog-tired after a shift that had been nothing but trouble. The cutting machine had broken down time and time again and I'd done everything I could to get it going. I'd been right under it with my head in the filthy oily water, pulling this and tapping that, not knowing what I was doing but trying to do something. The ventilation had been bad even though they knew there was a lot of gas in the flat and all of us had headaches and numb hands and feet and had to keep going into the goaf to spew up every half hour. At least when the cutter was going, it stirred the air up and spread the gas out. On top of that I'd had a pain in my guts that hadn't let up for three days. That was probably something I picked up from the wet. In this particular section it had been foul right from the start and when you're splashing about in it in the dark, kneeling in it and shovelling in it or lying in it to get under the cutter, you cannot help some of it getting in your mouth. Even though you try your best not to swallow it, sometimes you cannot help it.

In the finish we'd had to send for the mechanic. Things were very tight as far as getting temporary jobs was concerned so the situation was that if I couldn't cut coal I wouldn't get a sosser. And the men who worked with me wouldn't get a sosser either. It didn't matter a damn whether it was my fault or not. And if the cutting machine was still jiggered at the end of our shift, neither would Jackie Brown and his team. Jackie and me always did everything we could to make sure we handed over the machine in good order to the other when he came on shift. It was a pain in the neck having to spend maybe eight of your twelve hours trying to get the bloody machine to go, with the mechanic at it as well and everybody now kicking the wall instead of the machine. But it was a really bad day when you had to pass the trouble on to your marra.

Eventually we'd got it fixed and it was going when Jackie and his team came in. We'd been at it all day and I hadn't cut enough coal to fill a bloody bucket. But by that time I was glad just to get out of it. I wasn't caring about the money and the other lads were the same. We had heaved and hauled that massive machine by hand so the mechanic could get at it without it having to be taken away, for hours. And that was after all we'd done when we were trying to fix it ourselves. 'Another day like that and they'll be layin' me out,' Alfie said. 'I'm not kiddin', Tommy. I'm completely shagged.'

Because the baby was due any day, as soon as I finished at the pit I'd pedal home as fast as I could. Tonight even my bloody bike was buggered. Both tyres were flat and the pump gone. Some idiot's idea of a joke, no doubt. I was knacked enough as it was without having to run home with my bike on my back. But that's what I did.

As soon as I turned the corner at the top of Vine Street I saw a group of neighbours in their pinnies with their arms folded standing outside the front door and I knew it had happened at last. All the carry-on at the pit went right out of my head as I ran down the street with a grin on my face so big and stupid I could feel it, dumped the bike outside the door, pushed my way through into the house and raced up the stairs two at a time. Allie was lying in bed as white as the sheet. As soon as she saw me she started to cry. 'Oh, Tom! Oh, Tom...' I looked around. The cot was in its usual place but it was still empty. Then the midwife came up and whispered that the baby had been born dead. It was perfect she said, only it was too big. It was over a stone in weight and had been too much for Allie. That night I made a little coffin out of a box I got from the corner shop, tucked it under my arm and me and Mr Smithwhite went up to the cemetery with it. We buried it in a place they had for things like that, there was no service or anything. We did what we had to do, I said the 'Our Father' my way and he said it his and we came away.

I don't know what had happened exactly, nobody told me much. Everybody had just looked grim and I suppose they were leaving it to my own imagination. I never asked Allie about it and she never said anything but she took it pretty badly. In the weeks that followed the weight just poured off her. She was pale and weak and on top of that all her lovely hair dropped out. Two months after the birth that wasn't really a birth, she was completely bald. What with that and being so thin and haggard she looked more like an old man than a young woman. When I took her for a walk in the park in a wheelchair I borrowed from the lodge, she'd wear this great big hat with a tight woollen cap underneath that came up to her ears at the sides and right down to her eyebrows at the front, so that not one inch of her scalp and very little of her face could be seen. She was so poorly for so long I wondered if something had taken hold of her, and I wasn't the only one.

By now, at Harton as well as the rest of the Durham pits, things were getting tight again. The threat of war seemed to have gone, the shipyards were getting slack and huge stocks of coal had collected. The modern pits in the Midlands and Scotland were producing the kind of coal that was wanted for the home market and they were producing it more efficiently than anybody else. The result of all this was that more and more Harton men were being laid off every day and those that weren't, were getting fewer and fewer hours.

My father was one of the first to go just like always. I was no more a bosses' man than he was but my way was to get on with the job and keep my mouth shut. It was one thing to speak the truth when you were asked for your opinion or to come out on strike when the union told you to. It was another thing altogether to harp on non-stop. All that did was get you a bad name. Some blokes would argue with anybody and everybody no matter which side they were on. They'd even defy their own union and run it down and go their own way and then turn around and complain when the same union didn't get them what they wanted. My father wasn't that bad. But as far as the Harton Coal Company was concerned he didn't need to say anything at all. There was nothing he could say, he'd already said enough.

There had been some trouble which had ended in a strike for several days over whether deputies should be taken on to the management side entirely. The Coalowners were in favour of it because it meant they'd have more control over us. We were against it because deputies were responsible for safety down the pit. More than a hundred men had died in Durham pits in the past year. Added to that was a steep rise in serious injuries, most of them caused by all the machinery we now had to deal with. We didn't want deputies cutting any more corners than were being cut already.

My father would still criticise and try to get me to do things his way even when he'd been laid off. It was almost as though he was in the right because he was laid off and I was in the wrong because I wasn't. When I joined the Union it was because there were more good men in it than out of it, and that was still the case. So as long as I was in it, I'd stick by it. My father was as good a union man as anybody but he'd criticise it and he'd criticise the lodge the same way he'd criticise anybody or anything else he thought deserved it. I never had anything against blunt or quick-tempered men because you knew where you stood with them. Without them there never would have been a union. But it's no good everybody talking at once, it never is, it gets you nowhere. I was happy to let the Union do my talking for me, they could do it better than I could. And they could do it better than my father, even though he wouldn't admit it.

We were now back to the situation where I was in work but my father, my uncles and many of my best pals, weren't. Yet if I chucked my job in, one of them would have taken it. They'd have had no choice. Not that that would have solved many of their problems because very soon I was down to less than two days a week. Allie and me were now very hard up. She wasn't able to take in washing or anything because she still wasn't right yet and any jobs going for women, whether in the factory or in the home, were all physical jobs with very long hours. Pit washing for one was enough for someone like Allie who'd never been brought up to that kind of work. I think the pit washing had been too much for my mother. God knows how Grandma Turnbull managed. Not just among pit folk but wherever you looked, even the bonniest lasses quickly turned into grey-haired, hard-faced, middle-aged women.

Because Allie hadn't been well I hadn't wanted to get on to her but for a while now I'd been getting concerned about the number of commercial travellers that kept coming to the door. If they were coming when I was in, it was a safe bet they were coming when I was out, especially when they knew they'd get short shrift from me. They were all over these days and they were becoming real pests. The only way was to be very firm with them and say no every time, because when one of them saw another getting his foot in the door he'd work twice as hard to get his own in. And once they had a hold over you they wouldn't be satisfied till they had you in hock up to your neck. They always started off with things that cost just a few coppers a week, a kind of a Christmas club that had nowt at all to do with Christmas. Then they'd have you buying luxuries like electric irons and Hoovers and all kinds of things you had no need of. And before you knew it, you'd have chalked up a debt so big you couldn't pay. Then they'd come and take it all back off you and you'd end up losing your self-respect as well as your money.

New things kept appearing in the house nearly every week. A new fangled hot water bottle that would never leak, an unbreakable tea-set, a towel that would always stay fluffy, shirts that didn't need to be ironed, it just went on and on. In the finish, poorly or not, I had to have it out with her.

'Allie,' I says, 'Where's all this stuff comin' from? I hope you're not gettin' us into debt.'

'Don't start making a fuss here just because things aren't goin' right at the pit, Tommy. I'm not in the mood for it... They're just a few little bits and pieces I've been getting to brighten the place up a bit and try and make life a bit easier. I don't go spending all the housekeepin' on myself like some I could mention.'

'But I'm only workin' two days a week! And things are gettin' worse, not better.'

'I know how hard you have to work and I'm making sacrifices all the time... But there's a limit.'

'I'm not complainin' about havin' to work hard. I'm complainin' about not gettin' the chance of it.'

'You men have no idea how hard it is trying to make ends meet.'

'Makin' ends meet is what I'm talkin' about!'

She began to cry. I didn't want to upset her any more than she was already so I let the matter drop. Maybe she'd be more careful now and I'd keep a bit more of a watch. I'd heard how women sometimes do silly things when they lose a baby and that going on a spending spree was one of them.

About a month later I was coming down the lane from work when I saw these blokes carrying furniture out of the house. I rushed up.

'What the hell's gannin' on?'

'What's it got to do with you?' one of them says.

'That's our furniture!'

'Not any more it isn't.'

'I'm tellin' ye it's mine! I paid for it!'

'Oh no ye didn't, sonny boy. That's why we're takin' it back.'

'What d'ye think we're ganna sit on if ye take away all wor chairs?'

'Yous can sit on your fat behinds as far as I'm concerned.'

I grabbed hold of the legs of the armchair I always sat on when I came home from work, which they were now hoisting up into the van.

'Bust this and you're ganna be payin' for it,' one of them says.

I pulled and they pulled and the stuffing began to come out of the seat. I let go, it was pointless wrecking it. They just laughed and flung it in the back of the van and clashed the door shut.

I was still standing there when Allie came out.

'Oh Tommy, what have I done! Are you all right, pet? They've taken just about everything. Our lovely settee and armchairs, the carpets... I got behind with the payments and I was robbin' Peter to pay Paul. I know it was a stupid thing to do and I wish God would strike me down dead for it.'

She was standing there with her head in her yellow hands, bald patches showing through her hair, weeping bitterly.

I put my arm around her. 'Divvent tempt him, lass. Ye know ye divvent mean it.'

'Everybody in the street'll know by now.'

'So what? We've committed no crime.'

'Their curtains have been going back and forth all afternoon.'

'If they've nowt better to do than look out their windows at other people's misfortunes, they can count themselves lucky is all I can say... Howay, let's gan in. We've still got a roof over wor heads, haven't we? They didn't tak that an' all, did they?'

She smiled. 'You're a good man for taking it so well, Tom.'

'I don't know about "takin' it well" but there's nowt much we can do now except get on with it.'

When you lived among pitfolk they'd no more get pleasure out of seeing somebody in trouble than they would if it was themselves. We'd lived with bailiffs, repossessions and evictions ever since coalmining began. There was no shame in standing up to your employer and getting punished for it. It was heartbreaking and it was unfair but there was no shame in it. And if you were evicted for it or evicted because you were ill or had been badly disabled and could no longer work, there was no shame in that either. I don't think any decent working people would look at it any differently. Allie had stepped over the line a bit but she hadn't been dishonest. It was the other buggers that were, they were the ones who took advantage and they were the ones who came out on top.

I was coming home from the pit late one night when the flashlight on my bike went out, at least it went down to just a brown glow. The battery had been shot for a long while and I'd been heating it up in the oven every day before going to work to get a bit more life out of it. That worked fine for going out in the dark from home and it would just about last me till I got to the pit. But coming back in the dark was a different matter. One of my pals, Pete Lawson, was going around the scrap yards collecting dumped batteries. When he got home he would empty the sack out on the kitchen table and he and his wife would sort them all out. They'd test every one with a bit of wire and a bulb. Ones that had no life at all in them were put to one side to have the lead stripped off. The others they would do up by scraping off the corrosion, hammering the dents out best they could and giving them a clean up with a bit of emery cloth. Then they'd sell them two for a penny. Pete had said he would save me a couple of good ones and I'd been meaning to go around.

A pollis stopped me. I told him the battery had just gone and that I was going to get a new one as soon as I got paid. It made not the slightest difference to him and I ended up in court and was fined ten shillings. I had to beg for time to pay, ten shillings was a small fortune to me and Allie now. I was told I could pay in instalments of a shilling a week but the judge made it plain that if I didn't keep them up I'd go to jail.

Hard though it was, we managed. We were eating swedes instead of potatoes, kale instead of cabbage, fish instead of meat, and a lot less of it. Allie was putting patches in clothes that should have gone to the ragman and we were selling most of our coal allowance, keeping only the barest amount for our own needs. We went for walks instead of to the pictures and I'd given up going to the match. We stopped the paper and made do with what the groceries were wrapped in. To hear some people you'd think they'd die if they didn't get their newspaper every day. That wasn't the way it was with us. We'd been getting the Daily Express because Allie liked it, it wouldn't have been my choice but it didn't matter now. We still found out everything that happened even if we were a day or two behind. If anything big had happened like Sunderland winning the League or the world coming to an end, we wouldn't have needed the Daily Express to tell us.

When Allie found out she was expecting again it was partly good news and partly bad news. As Catholics we had no choice in the matter. Through thick and thin we'd kept up the threepence a week for Shepherd and Raffle's doctors' club, so this should cover us for anything that might happen this time although we prayed nothing would. Allie was gradually pulling herself together again and her hair was starting to grow back, the colour was coming back into her cheeks and she was beginning to smile again. As far as she was concerned it was good news.

All of a sudden we were all back at work full time, my father as well. Nobody seemed to know why and certainly nobody was hanging back to ask. As always there was no shortage of rumours, this time centring around the new German leader Adolf Hitler who it seems was building up a huge army and getting ready for action. Whatever the reason there was certainly plenty of work at the pit, more than there'd been for ten years. And that's what mattered. Hitler could do what the hell he liked as far as I was concerned. For the first time ever, miners were allowed a week's holiday.

War broke out the day Allie and me went on ours but it didn't make the slightest difference. Neither of us had ever been away for more than the occasional weekend with the cycling club and that had been four or five years since. We'd been planning this holiday for weeks and weeks and had made up our minds that nothing was going to stop us. If Hitler came over, he'd have to wait till we got back. Blackpool was the place, and Bill and Lilly Bell and Stan and Bessie Harrison who we were going with.

Allie and me went with Stan and Bessie on the train and Bill and Lilly went on their motor-bike and sidecar. We had written away to an address in the Daily Express – which Allie had insisted on getting again as soon as things began to look up – to hire a family tent for a week on a campsite near Blackpool. Because it was the cheapest site on their books, it was five miles out of town and that was where Billy's motor-bike came in. It was all worked out in advance. Every day Billy would take Lily into town, drop her off to book the deck-chairs and order the hot water and then come back for Stan and Bessie. In the meantime me and Allie would be walking in the same direction. After he'd taken them, back he'd come for Allie and me, me on the pillion and Allie in the sidecar. The next day the order would be switched around so Allie and me went next and Bessie and Stan after that. It was a right carry-on and we all had a great time, just like in the old days when we were all in the club together.

Blackpool was a smashing place. There were huge amusement arcades and dodgem cars, coconut shies and air-rifles for the men, fortune-telling and roll-a-penny for the women. Candy-floss machines, huge toffee apples on big sticks and fish-and-chip shops as good as any in Shields. Brass bands played during the day and dance bands at night. They certainly weren't kidding when they said they had plenty of lights. There were hundreds of them, they must have cost a fortune in electricity. The fairground was far bigger than Shields's and nearly as big as the hoppins at Newcastle. The air-raid sirens went a few times but we couldn't have cared less, we were too busy enjoying ourselves.

It seemed no time at all before Allie's time came, though she said it had been a long haul for her waiting and worrying and scared stiff anything would go wrong again. She'd got herself a book called 'Home Care' from a second-hand shop and she must have read it from cover to cover at least three times. She'd listened to all kinds of advice from all sorts of people, some good, some of it tripe I thought. She'd done all the things she'd been told she should do and none of the things she was supposed not to. She'd get out of bed slowly and go up or down the stairs one at a time, pretending she had a basket of eggs on her head or something just as daft. She ate enough but not too much, wore clothes that weren't too tight and avoided putting bath salts in the bath water. She tried not to listen to blood-curdling tales about the birth itself but sometimes I'd come back from the pit and see by the look on her face that somebody had been scaring the living daylights out of her. Some women are never happier than when they're reeling off list after list of diseases, deaths and disasters. To listen to them you'd think nothing ever went right with any birth. At Mass the priest would sometimes mention the 'miracle of birth' and you'd certainly believe it if you listened to some of Allie's pals.

Allie started her labour on the last Sunday in January but after a short while it stopped. And that's the way it went all day. On, off. Off, on. In the finish she said 'I think you'd better go and fetch Dr Hodgson.'

I says 'Are ye sure? Are ye positive?'

'Yes, yes! Go on, will ye! I can feel it comin'… Quick!'

So I ran up to Dr Hodgson's house. But when I got there he wasn't in, only his stand-in was there and he looked as though he was still wet behind the ears himself.

'Dr Hodgson's away,' he says. 'You'd better tell her to hang on till he gets back.'

'When's that ganna be?'

'He should be back on Tuesday.'

'Tuesday! Ye must be kiddin'? How's she supposed to do that?'

He just shrugged.

'Ye mean I'm supposed to tell her to just switch off for a couple of days? Till it suits Dr Hodgson? What about you, then? Aren't you any good? I don't care who comes, as long as he knows what he's doin'.'

'If it's an emergency I –'

'On second thoughts, don't bother. If you're not too sure of yourself and I can see by your face that you're not, I'm not either. I'll tell her to hang on if she can. If she cannot we'll get somebody else.'

When I got back Allie was hanging out the washing.

'He's not comin' yet, is he?' she says. 'Good.'

'Bloody good job an' all by the looks of things,' I says. 'If he was, you'd look pretty damned silly.'

How she managed it or whether it had been a false alarm or what I don't know but hang on she did. And on the Tuesday I went up to Hodgson's to see what the score was.

'Hang on till after my evening surgery,' he says. 'I'll have more time to examine her properly then.'

'If she hangs on much longer, it'll be late for school,' I says.

'What will?'

'The bairn.'

He obviously didn't think it was very funny but neither did I really. I was getting fed up with all this palaver because I knew it was upsetting Allie. Had she been given the wrong date, was there something the matter or what? She was probably going to have a hard enough time of it as it was. Tears were never very far away these days and the slightest thing would fetch them on. That wasn't like Allie, normally she never cried for nothing. Her way was to lose her temper.

On the Friday the baby was born, but its cord had got tangled between its toes and it had 'strangulated' itself, so Dr Hodgson said. Later on he said Allie would never be able to give birth to boys and that it should have been delivered by a Caesarean operation in a hospital. Whether it should or it shouldn't, it was too bloody late now. Allie cried night after night and there was no consoling her. Over and over she kept saying God was punishing her for something…that maybe he was angry because she'd changed her religion…maybe he was teaching her a lesson for losing the furniture…or maybe sometime she'd taken his name in vain without realising.

One night Evelyn and Jack Robinson who were married now came with their second baby Johnny. They already had one boy Joe and there had been no trouble with either of them. Not thinking, Evelyn plonked it on Allie's knee the way women do with their sisters and Allie nearly went hysterical. Afterwards when they'd gone not knowing what they'd done wrong, Allie realised this sort of thing wasn't doing her any good and that there were still other babies to be had. Most women lost one or two, either as babies or before they were ten years old. It had happened to her own mother. I would try to find the right words to say like, 'You cannot miss what ye've never had,' or 'It's better to lose them before ye've had a chance to love them,' but I always seemed to put my foot in it. Marras would say to me, 'Time's the only real healer, Tommy. Give her time, she'll get over it.' They were right, though 'time' can sometimes take quite a while.

A few months after the upset over Evelyn's baby a friend of Allie's had twins and it had taken a lot out of her. Allie had offered to give her a hand with bathing the twins and things like that until the friend got herself put right and I said we might as well give them the bits and pieces we'd got in for our own that we hadn't used yet. In any case it might be better if we started afresh and got new ones next time. Allie thought it was a good idea and that new things might bring us better luck so she collected everything up into a parcel and I went over with her to carry it. I wasn't interested in listening to a lot of blathering on about babies' bottles and stuff but I didn't want Allie humping anything too heavy. As soon as we got inside the door Allie's face immediately dropped. She was shaking and could hardly speak. She'd already seen the twins a couple of times and I thought she was getting over the fact that some people are lucky enough to have perfect babies first time and without any bother.

'What's the matter, Allie?' I says.

'Here, sit yourself down,' says Irene. 'I'll make a nice cuppa tea. That'll soon make you feel better.'

Off she went, came back with the tea and we'd barely got the cups to our lips when damn me if Irene doesn't burst into tears. So she sits down now and Allie starts comforting her. After about five minutes when she'd pulled herself together a bit she tells us she's crying because she has two babies, a boy and a girl, and she doesn't know how she's going to manage. Her husband only worked on the buses and... Bugger me, if Allie doesn't start up again. One's bubbling because she's got two and the other because she hasn't got any. It was obvious that neither of them was much comfort to the other, and I was sitting there in between the two of them about as much use as a lump of putty, so I said we'd better come away till another time.

As soon as we got outside Allie says 'Don't you know who that furniture belongs to? That settee and those two chairs?'

'Them I expect,' I says.

'That shows how much you care! They're ours, the ones they took back.'

'Well, even if they were, they're not ours now. Ye can hardly blame Irene. They were ganna gan to somebody. They might as well gan to her as anybody else.'

What more can you say? I was a bit choked myself I suppose, but we had other ones now and were quite content with them. You cannot hang on to everything just because you got it on your wedding day.

20

Chamberlain had been tough enough when it came to standing up to his own people, at least those that were so poor they had had to get down on their knees and beg to the Workhouse Guardians, as my father had to do. Not so tough however when it came to Hitler and the well fed and fully employed Germans. He stayed just long enough to get us into the War and then he was gone. By May, 1940 Churchill was in charge.

Churchill wouldn't surrender to anybody. He fancied himself being to us what Hitler was to the Germans or Roosevelt to the Americans. Many people might have sat by their wirelesses night after night waiting for a few golden phrases from him for them to hang on to. But not pitmen. We didn't think the sun shone out of his fat behind and we didn't need him to keep our spirits up. We knew that his real enemy was the working class. Whether it was the working class of Nazi Germany, the working class of Communist Russia or the working class of his own country, it made no difference to him. Nor whether they were miners, factory workers, sappers or anything else.

The Government knew that in the modern age coal was essential to winning a war, so men were no longer being sacked for next to nothing in the pits. At first, as long as they did their work, that was all that mattered, and hewers and hard men who'd been told they would never again be needed when times had favoured the Coalowner, were now being brought back. These fellers were tough and fought for their rights but they weren't political men. They'd argue about the weight of a tub of coal but they were neither fascists nor communists.

But after a while, so many men who preferred the army to the pit and wanted to fight were being brought back against their will, that Churchill thought he might have a problem with them. So strikes were banned, 'negligence' became criminal and anybody who complained about lousy working conditions or wages was made to feel like a traitor just because there was a war on. Holidays, which had only just come in after more than two hundred years, went out again. It was fine and dandy for manufacturers of ammunitions and supplies to take breathers, along with the Coalowners, and it was all right for them to make fortunes all over again and demand whatever they liked from the Government all over again. But woe betide any of their workers who demanded a decent place to work in and a decent wage to go with it, let alone holidays. It was nothing less than sinful for people like us to ask for anything at such times as these.

Absentee Boards were set up at the Colliery and they fined you every time you were a few minutes late. You now had to 'report for work'. You were made to work in districts that had been abandoned because they were too dangerous. You had to go into places so low and filthy you wouldn't have put a dog in them. Now they decided who was fit and who wasn't, not lodge or colliery doctors. And the rapid increase in serious accidents and deaths that followed was as much due to their efforts, as to the Coalowners for refusing to spend any money on safety. Other workers didn't have to put up with this and unskilled women working in munitions factories earned more than we did.

Miners were now insisting on their right to be allowed to join up even though the country's need for coal was now enormous. Churchill could rant and rave and threaten till he was blue in the face but they would neither be bullied or persuaded. As long as it was Churchill making the appeal they wouldn't listen. Eventually he realised this and put Ernest Bevin, a Labour man and not even an MP, in charge of the mines.

Bevin immediately stopped miners going into the Forces. He brought back old miners who'd been on the scrap heap for years and took back ones that were still around after the blacklisting of 1921 and 1926 – those who'd been told they'd never again see the inside of a British coal mine. Even then there weren't enough, so he started a scheme whereby men who were being called up had a choice of going into the pits instead. But those that tried it soon changed their minds. So he brought in his 'Bevin Boy' scheme, where lads of eighteen who were eligible for call-up would have to go down the pit instead of into the Forces if their name began with a certain letter. They were billeted in two's on ordinary householders, often young women no older than they were, whose husbands were overseas fighting in the War.

These lads hated the pit. They had no background of it and they didn't understand the pitman's humour or his way of doing things. They were afraid of the dark, terrified of the machines and petrified of being cooped up miles underground. They would do the least amount of work possible and not do it properly in the hope of being brought out and sent into the Army. Other young lads who had heard what the pits were like, started volunteering for the Forces when they were seventeen rather than waiting until they were eighteen and risking losing in the lottery for who went down the pit. Ones still in the pit were now volunteering for the Front, the parachute regiment, anything. As far as they were concerned nothing could be worse than the pit. They said pits were terrible inhuman places and they couldn't see how anybody could survive in them. Some of these lads might have made good soldiers but they made lousy miners. To us they were a danger. Down a mine where everybody has to depend on everybody else they were nothing but a nuisance.

As the War went on and coal became even more vital, Bevin realised the answer to increasing production was to treat miners like human beings, rather than stuffing office boys and painters-and-decorators' apprentices down a mine shaft and expecting them to double output. So wages were increased, safety helmets were brought in, working conditions improved and promises given regarding public ownership after the War if Labour got back into power. It's a sad fact that it had to take a world war for a coalminer in Britain to get a decent wage but that's what happened. Pits weren't any safer and there were more accidents every day because of so many men working such long hours, but at least we were managing to get out of the gates with money in our pocket. And I was now getting four pounds a week.

As far as doing our bit for the fighting went, we had to join either the Home Guard or do fire-watching during air raids. Nearly all the ones who volunteered for the Home Guard had either been in the Army and were brought back by Bevin or were old soldiers from the First World War. They got to have their own rifle and uniform and march around as though they were somebody important. As far as the rest of us were concerned, army officers were going to be no better than colliery managers, so we were happy to do fire-watching.

If Hitler had got as far as South Shields and the Home Guard were all like Dickie Leonard, he'd have flattened the place. Rumours of an invasion had got so bad that Dickie wouldn't go anywhere without his rifle, he even had it propped up by the side of his bed. How nobody within five miles of the pit – or whatever the range of an army rifle is – was shot, was nothing short of a miracle.

Nobody would have given a damn if it had just been a matter of him humping it around and making an ass of himself but more often than not he had a bullet up the spout. He would load it to show off, prance about and have a lot off and then go away and forget to take the bullet out. We naturally expected they were just blanks they'd given him but one day he was clarting about doing his rifle drill at the Office and the bloody thing went off. The bullet went straight through the ceiling and right between the legs of McEwan, the chief clerk, who was sitting at his desk in the room up above and just about shat himself. When he came down the stairs he was ready to tear Dickie apart with his bare hands. A bullet in the arse from a fool like Leonard wasn't McEwan's idea of dying for your country.

'You imbecile! You reckless, useless heap of shite!'

'Sorry, sir... I forgot it was loaded,' says Dickie.

'I'm going to have a word with somebody about you, Leonard. You're not fit to be in charge of a lethal weapon. I wouldn't give a bloody pea-shooter to a lunatic like you!'

As if he hadn't done enough already Dickie says to him, 'I'd appreciate it if ye'd call me "Sergeant Leonard" when I've got me uniform on. It's for morale and I'm entitled.'

'Morale? Morale! You wouldn't know what the fuckin' word means! What about my fuckin' morale! Now get away from here and take that fuckin' thing with you! If I ever see it in this building again, I'll shove it so far up your back end it'll go through your fuckin' skull!

One night I was coming on shift when I heard this voice shout 'Halt'. I knew it was Dickie so I paid no attention and just carried on.

'Halt or I'll shoot!' he yells.

This time I stopped.

'Get your hands up!'

'Divvent be so bloody daft.'

'What's your name?'

'You know fine well who it is. Ye've known me for twenty bloody years...more's the pity.'

'What's your name?'

'Adolf Hitler. Who d'ye think?'

'Right!' The silly sod then said I had to accompany him to the Deputy's Office for identification. There I was with my hands up walking along with him behind shouting 'Right, left! Right, left!' so everybody could hear.

'Shut up, ye stupid sod!' I says to him as we were going along. 'You're makin' idiots of the two of we.'

'Silence! You're my prisoner!'

I couldn't tell whether he was kidding or not, he really might have a couple of screws loose for all I knew. But he had the rifle, ten to one there was a bullet ready to come out of it and from this distance it would make a hell of a mess. So I thought I'd better play along, rather a live idiot than a proud corpse. When we got to the Office he stood there in the light pointing the gun straight at my head and shouted 'I require someone to come out and identify this man who has been found trespassing on Government property.'

I knew for sure now that I'd done the right thing, he was obviously completely off his rocker. The deputy was old Quigley who could hardly walk because he'd lost a foot in a pit explosion many years before, he'd only been brought back because of the War. You could hear him coming down the stairs. Thump...scrape, thump...scrape, thump...scrape... When he got halfway down and saw the two of us standing there, me with my hands up in the air and Dickie with the rifle, he says 'You stupid bloody tit, Leonard! Do you mean to tell me you've brought me all the way down here to ask if Tommy Turnbull's a bloody Jerry? If the buggers at the Front are anything like you, we might as well all surrender and be done with it. Now take your rifle and bugger off! Go on, Tommy. Pay no attention to the bloody fool. Something'll definitely have to be done about him. This sort of thing has to stop.'

They did eventually get him moved but it wasn't easy. They couldn't move him to another pit and have him create havoc there so they had to make a case that his behaviour was a threat to coal production. The next thing we heard he'd been made a cook in the Territorials and put inside for making soup in an old petrol can. He wasn't a wicked feller but he was better locked up.

Dickie had tried in his own way to do things by the book but was genuinely stupid. Andy Curran on the other hand could have passed exams that most fellers wouldn't have had a hope at, yet in his own way he was a far bigger looper than Dickie. Dickie had always expected an invasion by sea, and when he wasn't arresting somebody who worked at the Colliery or a neighbour who lived a few doors up the street, he could usually be seen staring into the east.

When Andy Curran took over, he was convinced the invasion would be by air and that one dark night hundreds of thousands of Germans were going to drop out of the sky, though not the way you saw them doing it on the pictures. 'Clever buggers, the Jerries. They're not like the stupid buggers over here.' According to Andy, when they came, it wouldn't be a case of long bodies with two arms stretched upwards hanging on to a parachute, slowly drifting down in a searchlight and just asking to be picked off by ack-ack guns. 'When these fellers come they'll be inside metal locker things and every one'll have its own Morse code equipment so they can link up with one another. So ye can't afford to wait till they open the door and jump out. Ye'll be dead before that.'

He'd got permission to stand on the platform of the pulley wheel at the head, the highest place in the colliery. And most nights when you came off shift, you'd see his silhouette up there on one knee, rifle pointing upwards as he searched the sky for his metal lockers.

One night Bill Blyton and Paddy Cain decided to have a bit fun with him when they came off shift. It was a dark dirty night and Andy was having no joy up aheight so he was only too happy to come down to investigate when Bill whistled up and told him he'd heard a strange noise coming from one of the sheds. Andy put a bullet in the breech and was down in a jiffy. The two of them then went off, dashing from building to building one at a time and waving each other on, just like they did on the pictures, Bill making damned sure that Andy was always in front. Paddy meanwhile was inside an old lamp cabin and tapping on the corrugated iron with a bit of wire.

'Listen to that!' says Bill. 'Morse code, isn't it?'

Andy listened. 'Aye it is but it's making ne sense.'

By this time Andy had got himself worked up into an excitable state and Bill was getting concerned they'd taken things a bit far. He knew that Andy was a dead shot and he was worried in case anything happened to Paddy. 'Put your gun down a minute,' says Bill. 'I've somethin' to tell ye.'

'Shsh!' whispers Andy. 'There's somethin' movin' over there.'

'Where?' says Bill. 'I cannot see anythin'. Put your bloody gun down a minute, will ye?'

'Get down! I can see the bastard!'

Quick as anything Andy aims and fires and something big and heavy flops to the ground about fifty yards away.

'My God!' Bill almost sobs.

There'd been no 'Halt, who goes there?' or anything, the way it would have been with Dickie Leonard. He had just put a bullet in it whatever it was and it had dropped like a brick.

'Jesus Christ! What the hell was that?' shouts Paddy, rushing out of the cabin.

Bill quickly grabbed the rifle from Andy who had gone into a kind of trance. 'Paddy, come here! Quick! Andy's just shot somethin'! Pull yourself together, Andy. We've got to go and see what the hell ye shot.'

The three of them went over slowly circling around. Paddy was first to go up to it.

'Bull's-bloody-eye, Andy,' he says stepping back. 'It's a pit pony…and it's one of ours. You'd better find a parachute before tomorrow or you're in shit up to your bloody eyeballs. You'd've been better off shootin' one of us.'

Solly Macklin used to go round checking that people had their blinds drawn during the blackout. If you so much as struck a match to light your tab when he was around, he'd blow it straight out. He was only five feet tall and as is often the case with little blokes the bit of authority went to his head.

Kieron Doyle lived in one of the Colliery houses at Whiteleas. He had eight kids and he was digging a huge hole in the garden to make a bomb shelter for them all. You were supposed to make it about six feet deep, cover it with a sheet of corrugated iron and then heap it over with earth. These shelters which the Government told you how to make were just like little hidey holes. As far as protection from bombs was concerned, from things that could bring down cathedrals and shatter dams, you might as well have covered yourself with the Daily Telegraph. So Kieron had made up his mind that his kids were going to have a shelter to beat all shelters and by the time it was half done, it already looked more like a mine shaft than a hole for an Anderson shelter.

Seeing as it was Colliery property, Solly, who came from Belfast and didn't like Kieron who came from Dublin one bit, was never off his back. Every night he'd go around.

'I can see a light on in there! Put it out!'

'Fuck off, will ye, Solly,' Kieron would shout from inside the house. 'There's eight kids to put to bed in here. We've got to have some light to see what we're doin'.'

'Do you want the wardens round?'

'Course I bloody don't!'

'Put that light out then!'

'Which bloody light?'

'The one that's coming from the crack under the door.'

'Christ almighty! The planes are supposed to be up in the air.'

'They can still take readings.'

'Don't be so fuckin' daft!'

'This is Colliery property and if you don't put that light out immediately it will be my duty to fetch the wardens. And fetch the wardens, I will!'

'You bastard, Macklin! You fuckin' bastard!'

Kieron always put the light out in the end but he was sick of it. One night when the rain was absolutely stotting down he put a little midgy lamp on the far side of the hole he was digging for his shelter, took away the covers, put all the lights on in the house and then sat back and waited.

The rotten weather would have Solly shittier than ever, and the lights would attract him like a moth to a Lenten candle. Kieron had been waiting less than twenty minutes when he heard Solly shouting outside. Immediately he and his missus and all the kids struck up singing, leaving Solly shouting himself hoarse outside. When Solly could take no more he belted on the door.

'Yes?' calls Kieron in this sweet voice.

'It's Solly Macklin!'

'Yes, Solly, old chap? What can I do for you?' Behind him all the kids were laughing their heads off.

'I don't know what's going on in there but every light in the house must be on. Don't you know there's a war on?'

'Sorry, Solly,' says Kieron. 'I clean forgot about it. Thanks for the reminder.'

Kieron then puts every light in the house out and they all go dead quiet. A couple of minutes later there's another knock on the door.

'Open the bloody door!' shouts Solly. 'There's something at the bottom of the garden!'

'Not on your life, whoever ye are!'

Kieron's missus and the kids were laughing behind him and Solly must've been able to hear them.

'What do you mean, "whoever I am?" I told you! It's me, Solly Macklin!'

'How do we know you're not a Jerry in disguise?'

'There's a light down there, in your garden. There… I'm not kidding!'

'I cannot see owt. Maybe ye'd better investigate, had ye? That is, if you're who ye say ye are.'

A few minutes later there's a big splash followed by a hell of a lot of shouting and yelling, and Kieron and his wife and kids nearly laughed themselves sick.

There can be few times when there are more rumours flying about than during a war. One of the reasons for it I think is because the most unlikely things can happen, both in the battles themselves and here at home. And some of the queerest are to do with bombs. Many times you heard it said that the Luftwaffe wouldn't bomb collieries because most of the machinery in them was German and they wouldn't willingly destroy anything they'd made themselves. Considering how coal was such an important thing in war, I found this hard to believe. I don't think it was for the want of trying, I think they just missed them. Most pits were out of the way rather than in cities or along rivers where the factories usually were. And from the sky the ramshackle heapsteads of collieries must have looked more like farm buildings than the kind of huge long sheds you get with engineering factories and the likes. If a bomb was dropped near a colliery you could say it was a bad shot because it missed the colliery, or you could say it was a bad shot because it missed somewhere else. Only the buggers who had dropped it knew where it was supposed to go, on the ground you were only guessing.

Whenever there was an air raid the cage wasn't allowed to go up or down, so if you were already down the pit you had to stay there. Some nights we waited as long as four or five hours to come up after a twelve-hour shift. The pit might have been one of the safest places you could be when bombs were dropping but everybody wanted to get home to make sure their wife and bairns were all right. So if you were down and had finished your shift you sometimes had to play hell to come up because the blokes operating the cage could be right awkward buggers when they were in the mood.

One night we were coming away from our stall at the end of the shift when somebody came to tell us a bomb had come down the shaft. With the noise the cutting machines make, a bomb could have dropped right behind you and you wouldn't have heard it.

'What d'ye expect us to do about it?' I says.

'Avoid it.'

'We'll do that all right... Where is it?'

'In front of the cage.'

'How did it get there?'

'I don't bloody know. They can bounce and roll and do all sorts of things.'

'Is somebody comin' to shift it?'

'I suppose so.'

'Well I hope they're sendin' the Army and not some bugger from the Home Guard!'

We met up with some other fellers at the kist and were told to wait there until the backoverman and deputy had a proper look at the situation. We waited quarter of an hour, then half an hour, and then an hour.

'To hell wi' this,' says Alfie Cowan. 'I'm not stayin' here all bloody night. Our kid's home on leave and he's only got forty-eight hours.'

And off he went.

'There's nowt we can do till they come for us,' says Ken Davidson. 'Somethin' must be up or they'd have come for us by now.'

'They've probably forgot about we, more like it.'

'I'm gettin' fed up an' all,' I says. 'I'm ganna see what's up.'

We had walked about halfway to the shaft when Alfie comes running back.

'Hold it, lads!' he shouts. 'The bloody thing's just lyin' there! It's bloody huge!'

'Is it tickin' or what?'

'It's just lyin' there waitin' to gan off!'

Instead of going the other way, which might have made a lot more sense, we all hurried to the shaft as fast as we could to see the bomb for ourselves. When we got there, there was a ring of fellers standing around it. Frankie Bingham the electrician was saying to the backoverman, 'Well Ned, you're in charge. What ye ganna do? What does it say in your little book of rules about defusin' bombs?'

'Bugger all,' says Ned. 'When these rules were drawn up bombs hadn't been invented.'

'Shows ye how bloody out of date they are.'

'This is a job for the Army, not the Colliery.'

'How're the buggers ganna get down if the cage cannot gan up?' says Frank.

'Why not pour some watter over it?' Gillie Wilson says.

'Divvent be so bloody daft!'

'Where's the deputy?'

'Nebody knows.'

Everything was quiet, we were all staring at it. If it had gone off we'd have all gone with it.

Somebody farted.

'Hush, man! Any vibration could set it off!'

'Look at Alfie!' Gillie said, pointing. 'He thought it was the bomb gettin' ready to gan off! He nearly shat hesel'!'

Everybody was laughing.

'Get a grip of yourselves, ye stupid buggers,' said Ned. 'I'm tryin' to think. You're like a bunch of bloody kids, the lot of ye.'

Two others farted and everybody except Ned laughed. Mind it was pretty nervous laughter.

Ned was looking very worried, the rims of his eyes were always red and sore-looking. Outside the pit you'd never have taken him for a pitman, more a Methodist preacher which is what he was in his spare time. Right now I'd have been happier with Bob Gibb, the foreoverman, no matter how bad a bugger he was. Ned wasn't the sort of bloke for an occasion like this.

The bomb was like some great big iron egg ready to hatch. God knows what its innards were like. Maybe it was just an empty shell, one that had got missed on the conveyor and that's why it hadn't gone off.

'Why can't we just leave it where it is and get out?'

'The cage might set if off, the bloody racket that thing makes,'

'If the Army cannot come down because we cannot get up, what the hell are we doin' just standin' here like vestal virgins waitin' for the sacrifice?'

'What about the other shaft?'

'The fuckin' cage is out of order. Its been like that for at least a week. By rights we shouldn't even be down here.'

'It could maybe be started in an emergency,' said Ned.

'No it bloody cannot, Ned. You know that as well as I do,' said Frankie, 'so don't go makin' a liar of yoursel'. They're still supposed to be workin' on it... But I'll bet there's ne fucker workin' on it right now.'

Frank was a massive bloke, solid as a rock and made for the pit. Only Oxley Brush was stronger than Frank and Oxley was the sort of bloke who could toss an iron girder over a conveyor belt. Frank and Ned made an odd pair yet they always seemed to end up together. If Ned had a technical problem he couldn't deal with, he'd always turn to Frank before he turned to anybody else. Frank was rough as guts but he was very clever. He was a good bloke but he had no home life at all. His wife was always messing about, she drank whatever money they had and never looked after him or the kids properly. Ned's wife would often do his washing and put his bait up with Ned's when Frank's wife was having one of her fits. It was Ned and his wife who kept Frank from beating the living daylights out of her.

Our shift had finished over two hours ago and it was freezing cold standing at the bottom of the shaft.

'How did the bloody thing get here in the first place is what I want to know,' somebody said.

'I couldn't give a rat's arse how it got here. All I want to know is how are we ganna get the bugger out the bloody way so we can gan home.'

'Yous do realise that if this thing gans up we could all be out of jobs for the rest of wor lives?'

'Jesus, will ye listen to him? If this thing gans up, that'll be the least of wor problems, mate.'

Frank was down on his knees looking under it. 'It must've bounced half a dozen times to get right along here. There's no other way it could've come this far.'

'So what?'

'So it must have a hide even thicker than yours.'

'What about it?'

'So it's probably capable of takin' a fair amount of knockin' about.'

'Divvent kid yoursel', Frankie! It's probably taken all the knockin' about it's ganna take gettin' here!

Nobody said anything for a few minutes and everything was quiet, all the machinery was stopped.

'I'm ganna take it up,' says Ned. 'It's the only way. When I get to the top I'll get somebody to gis a hand to shift it and do whatever needs to be done with it. Then yous can all come up.'

There was dead silence as Ned spoke. 'But I'm ganna need somebody to gis a hand with it into the cage. The rest of yous had better get back in-bye. Wait there for half an hour, then come back. If it's ganna gan off it'll have gone off by then and ye'll hear the bugger. If everybody gets in the cage together we could all be blown to smithereens.'

There must have been a dozen voices said 'I'll give ye a hand, Ned.' But Frank put his arm out. 'Me and Ned's ganna take it up. The rest of yous, beat it... Gan on... I want to get to me bed sometime the night.'

Alfie and I came back to say everybody had gone and to give a hand lifting the bomb. There was no way even Frank could have lifted it with only Ned on the other end. Very carefully the four of us lifted it up and carried it into the cage. It wasn't as heavy as I thought it might be but I was shaking. We put it down ever so gently on the cage floor.

'Whoops,' says Frank, in a whisper. 'Me bloody finger's jammed underneath.'

I looked at him. 'You're kiddin', aren't ye?'

But he wasn't. He was trying to pull it out himself.

'Ease it up a bit, lads,' said Ned… 'Right… That's it.'

Frankie took his boots off and positioned himself so the bomb was perched between his two huge dirty bare feet resting against his insteps. He took a hold of the bar, sat on the bomb and told us to get out.

'You as well, Ned… Gan on! Out! I divvent need anybody else now.'

Ned was standing in the corner with his red eyes, black face and white creases. 'Gan on, lads,' he said in a very tired voice. 'Out you get.'

Alfie and I got out.

'It's only a little'un but it's very comfortable,' Frankie said with a big grin on his face.

'Good luck!' we said, and off we went leaving them to it.

Half an hour later we were all out and the Army had sent a squad to deal with the bomb. When I came on shift the next day it had gone.

A thing is either a tragedy or it isn't. In my opinion there's no such thing as a 'near tragedy', the way papers put it. Tragedies become legends. 'Near things' are soon just jokes and their heroes are no better than clowns. When a hundred men are instantly killed in a pit explosion, the whole world calls it a tragedy and a disaster. When one man is mangled to death every day of the year, it isn't even noticed.

On New Year's Eve, 1942 I went to my father's to first-foot the house. He'd had a canny drop to drink and was in a merry and chatty mood. He got on about the old days with his brothers and Grandma Turnbull when he was just a lad, about Witton Gilbert and the collieries at Bearpark and Esh Winning, about all the old faces and places. And then he went on to my mother and our John and Monica and began to get a bit sentimental.

I'd listened to him a good while so I said I'd better be getting back because I'd left Allie on her own. I didn't like leaving her too long, not now that she was expecting again.

'She'll be all right. Allie's a tough one,' he says. 'Any case she's always behind time, isn't she?'

'Maybe but I'm gannin' now. So happy New Year and we'll see ye tomorrow. Why don't ye come to our place for a change?'

Spending the day with Isabella Tanner running the show wasn't my idea of a good way to start the new year and it probably wasn't his either.

'Aye, all right then. We might come for wor dinner after Mass.' He knew what a great cook Allie was.

When I got home Allie was sitting by the door with her hat and coat on and her bags packed.

'Happy New Year, Allie,' I says. 'Off on holiday are ye?'

'I've started,' she says in this weak voice. 'I've been waiting ages for you.'

'Started? This time of night? On New Year's Eve? It's half past one, man! There'll be nobody there. You're not due for another fortnight yet. They'll think we're bloody crackers if we gan up there now.'

I thought she'd probably been sitting on her own and got herself worked up the way she sometimes used to, so I tried to pacify her and get her to go to bed. But she'd have none of it and insisted I take her up to the hospital. So I took her and she was right. And she had it without any difficulty at all, at least none that I was aware of. It was a little girl and she was perfect. We were both over the moon. As soon as I got back home I got down on my knees and thanked God. Anne we called her and she wasn't a spot of bother.

What a change in Allie now she had a bairn! She was in great shape and fitter than ever. All her hair was back, a bit darker but still nice; she'd put all her weight back on and she never stopped singing.

Wartime for a coalminer wasn't that different to any other time except that we had all the work we wanted and it wasn't a constant battle with the Coalowners. We had the same gaffers we always had and the same filthy muck and dust. The work was more dangerous because the pressures were greater, but we were better off and that was the most important thing. As far as getting killed goes, whether you got killed in the pit or on the battlefield made very little difference to us. They'll tell you there's glory in being killed in war. Whether there is or there isn't, there's certainly none in being killed down a pit. The only real difference is, if you work in the pit you're likely to see more of your family.

I heard Wilf had joined the Army and Bernard was in the Navy but I've no idea what happened to them. Whether our John was called up in Australia or not I don't know either. Allie's brother Bob went in the RAF, George became a dispatch rider in the Royal Engineers and Nan went in the NAAFI. Jack Robinson joined the Royal Army Service Corps straight after Dunkirk where his brother Joe had been killed, even though it should never have been allowed because he only had one eye. And there were many more, relations and friends, just like there'd been in the First World War. There were so many, you couldn't just sit and worry about them all, you just had to get on with it.

By the time the War ended pitmen's wages were higher than they'd ever been and with all the rebuilding everybody was talking about, coal was supposedly going to be more important than ever. At last we were in a strong position. Before the situation changed again we needed a law to guarantee a national minimum wage, a law to make sure all pits were made as safe as possible and a law that would allow coalminers to get involved in politics if they wanted to, just like anybody else. Doctors had a right to and did, lawyers did, and practically every employer in the country did. And most important of all we needed a law that would prevent us from being sacked for no good reason. And not liking somebody's face, wasn't a good reason.

Peter Lee had once been the greatest leader Durham pitmen ever had, but because he'd said something at a meeting after the 1926 strike about how 'not a penny off the pay, not a minute on the day' was not quite the way he saw it, he was booed out of the grounds. It was a small thing and maybe there was a misunderstanding but pitmen are funny people and he was never forgiven. Now two other local men had come along, Jim Kelly and Sam Watson.

Kelly and Watson had done more than anybody to form the new National Union of Mineworkers out of the old Miners Federation of Great Britain and miners everywhere respected them. Kelly was chairman of the Durham Miners Association and Watson was secretary. Kelly had the same style as Arthur Cook and was a dreamer like Cook. Watson was tough like Arthur Henderson but with a better mind and he could hold his own with anybody. No politician could make him look a fool. The trouble was Kelly and Watson didn't like each other and even though they behaved like brothers when they were up on the platform, off it they were more like Cain and Abel. They both had big followings and Kelly realised that sooner or later the Union would be split because of it. For the sake of the miners Kelly gave way and Sam Watson became our champion. Some said it was the best choice, others didn't.

Two months after the War there was a General Election. Churchill had convinced a lot of people that he, more than any general, any army, navy or air-force, any ammunition factory, any number of Catholic Masses or Protestant prayers, Lancashire banjo-players or singing mill girls, had won the War. And he had convinced himself that to show their gratitude the people of Britain would make him their Prime Minister for ever. Because Chamberlain had thrown his hand in as soon as the War started, Churchill had got himself head of the Coalition even though he had never been elected Prime Minister by anybody. And during the War because there were no elections, nobody else was given the chance to see if they could have done things any better. But if he thought that the miners and the rest of the working class had forgotten what kind of a man the peace-time Churchill was, he was very much mistaken.

Whatever Churchill thought the civilians of Britain owed him, when the soldiers, sailors and airmen returned home, they didn't feel they owed him anything. And as soon as the electioneering began and he started all over again with his crush-the-worker stuff, he was talking himself out of Downing Street and off the face of the map. If he thought that people who had given so much were now going to take off their uniforms and go back into their slums, back to unemployment, the PAC's and Means Tests, he couldn't have been more mistaken. Everybody remembered what had happened to those who had returned from the First World War to a land that was supposed to be fit for heroes. And when he ranted on about Clement Attlee's promised Welfare State with its greater employment, its free medical and dental services, its better education, and its nationalisation of coal, electricity, gas, steel, transport and even the Bank of England, he not only put paid to his own chances, he put paid to those of his whole damned party.

'Let Churchill Finish The Job!' was the slogan the Tories used and they couldn't have picked a worse one.

Finish what job? Finish off the miners? Finish off the unemployed? Finish off the poor and sick? Finish off the whole working class?

A new Labour Party romped in under Clement Attlee with such a majority they wouldn't need to rely on Liberals or anybody for support this time. Jack Lawson, an ex-pitman from Chester-le-Street, thrashed Viscount Lambton the heir to the Earl of Durham. There wasn't a single MP in the County of Durham that wasn't Labour. Never had there been a Labour Party like the one we had now. Ramsay MacDonald was dead and buried, Churchill was being treated for depression and everything was going to change. The old ways were gone and hard times for ordinary people were over. The Labour Party, the socialists, could do anything they wanted.

21

It was 1946, a beautiful Saturday in July, and the Durham Gala was back again. There could never have been a better mood for a gala than this one. We were celebrating the end of the Second World War and the beginning of a new age for pitmen and all working men and women, at least in Britain.

Most of us called the gala the 'Big Meeting'. 'Durham Gala' sounded a bit too posh. We didn't want anybody thinking it was like the 'Oxford Rowing Regatta' or the 'Badminton Horse Trials' or anything. Anyway 'Big Meeting' was a better description because it was the one time in the year when you got together to have a good time with all your relatives, friends and neighbours, some you wouldn't have seen for a year or more. There'd be ones who'd stayed behind when you had moved, and those who'd moved on themselves. And back they'd come from as far away as Scotland and Wales. Men back from the War and only recently demobbed would be there with their medals and scars, some of them blind or with arms or legs missing. But everybody who could walk or be carried would get there one way or another because this was the pitman's pilgrimage. This was the place to settle old scores with Labour politicians, because they wouldn't dare not be here. This was where they'd be told what a bunch of bloody old windbags they were, no matter how well they'd done.

Allie, me and the bairn were dressed in our best clothes with big rosettes pinned to our chests and little flags and balloons in our hands when we followed our band down Boldon Lane at half past seven in the morning past all the people standing waving in their doorways. The lodge had given every miner half a crown and a train ticket to Durham City and when we got to Tyne Dock Station men from every pit in Shields were piling onto the special train with their families. Everybody was happy and laughing and full of cheer. The bairns had been given a huge toffee apple in one hand and a rasper if they were little, or a kazoo if they were bigger, in the other. When the toffee apples came out of their mouths, the raspers or the kazoos went in. When the raspers or kazoos came out, in went the apples.

Anne was all done up with long white stockings and a satin frock for when her uncles and aunts saw her and even though her dark brown hair was dead straight like mine, Allie had managed to get a bit of a kink in it. As soon as she saw all the other kids getting on the train she insisted on getting on by herself. So while I had the bags with the picnic and stuff in my hand Allie was lifting her feet one at a time to make sure she didn't slip. I could see what was going to happen but a few people had got in front of me and I didn't want to shout in case Allie got a fright and the bairn fell. As Anne was getting on she was clagging up the back of the hair of the kid in front with her toffee apple and it was running straight down the back of this kid's neck. The kid turned round and began to twist but its father was pulling it on the train and shouting to somebody inside. At the same time Anne was getting her own hair done from the kid behind her. The father of the one in front suddenly yanked his bairn on and away it went with our Anne's toffee apple stuck to the back of its head.

'Ah, she's lost her apple,' Allie said when we got on board, not having seen any of what had happened.

'Good riddance an' all,' I says.

'Shame on ye, Tom.'

Five minutes later she was standing with another apple that was half-eaten and looking as if it had been kicking around the platform for a couple of days.

'Ugh! Give me that here!' Allie says. 'Come here so I can have a good look at you.'

Any minute now she was going to see the back of the bairn's hair.

'I'm just gannin' for a tab,' I says and I went out along the passage. I'd see if any of my pals were around.

By the time the train got under way, wherever you looked there were little cream blouses and little white shirts covered with long strings of sticky brown slaver. Ones that had been fighting were in an unbelievable mess and every few minutes a mother would come fleeing past chasing her kids from one end of the train to the other to try and get them cleaned up before we got to Durham. Whichever way you went, up or down the train, you could hear smacks and yells and the areated voices of mothers arguing the toss with one another about who had done what to who, and how their own bairns had never done anything wrong in the whole of their lives. But by the time we got to Durham people were singing and the kids had been pretty much tidied up, at least as good as they were ever going to be. The menfolk had had a smoke and agreed that the world was going to be a better place to live in, and the women had all plonked themselves down to take the weight off their ankles and agreed that rationing couldn't end soon enough, while at the same guarding their Tizer and Sarsparilla from kids who never had their hands out of the carrier bags. 'Mam, can I have a ginger snap, then. She's had one... Mam, Mam, Mam, Mam! Nobody ever listens to me. It's not fair!'

'Will ye shut your face!'

There'd be a loud smack as a meaty hand landed on a little ear and took in a cheek and half the side of its head at the same time. After a couple of seconds, as though it took that long for it to register or for it to decide what to do, there'd be a loud bawl. But they soon got over it.

At last we pulled into Durham station and the whole train emptied out on to the platform except for only one passenger that I could see. He was a workman in dungarees smelling of lead. He was half asleep and looked really glad of the peace as he snuggled himself in a corner with a contented smile on his face.

It was like D-Day in Durham City. There were flags strung up across the street, greetings and good wishes in the shops, bands playing, people marching, shouting, laughing, horns hooting, drums banging and whistles blowing. Crowds from different lodges and collieries were arriving every minute on trains and buses and shouts and yells would go up as people saw their friends and relatives. The streets had been closed to traffic since eight o'clock and every shopkeeper along the route the procession would take had boarded his windows up. Not because of any violence or anything like that but simply because the streets were so narrow and the crowd so huge.

You didn't need to drink any liquor to feel drunk, just being there was enough. The procession was bigger, longer and more colourful than I'd ever seen it and it went right through the city, down the Main Street, over the little bridge, up the Silver, round all the narrow bends, past the Cathedral, past the Shire Hall and up to the racecourse. Every lodge had its own banner and all the men and their families would cheer when their own came past with its band swinging its drumsticks and blowing its trumpets and the bandsmen looking so smart and proud. At the end of the procession a huge crowd was following and once you were in it there was no way of getting out of it. I got in with a gang from Harton and shouted to Allie that I'd see her and the bairn up at the racecourse.

Once the procession was over people began to spread out and sit down with their friends and you could breathe at last. 'Gan to Durrim for ya rights' is what people used to say and now was the time for the big talkers to get up. Politicians, pitmen's leaders and anybody else who had anything to say, got up and said it. This year we had Clem Attlee who was Prime Minister, Nye Bevan who was Minister of Health and Hugh Dalton who was Chancellor of the Exchequer. Bigwigs they thought.

'We put yous there and only we can keep ye there! And what's more important...and divvent any of ye forget it...we can put yous back out just as easy!' My father was shouting the same warning to everybody who got up onto the platform no matter who it was. A vicar who got up to bless everybody got the same treatment.

The speeches were no more than claptrap really, everybody knew that. What they did in their Houses of Parliament down in London was what really mattered, not what they said at a hooley up here in Durham. But they were all part of the fun and if they hadn't been there, there'd have been hell on.

After the speeches and a picnic on the grass there were stacks of things going on in the way of amusements. The Cathedral was holding a service with three pit bands taking part. There were rowing races on the River Wear and every pit and gambling game you could think of had a school going on somewhere along its banks. The pubs had a licence to stay open all day and apart from cool drinks you could get games of cards, dominoes, darts and all kinds of board games from ludo to tiddlywinks. The only way you could get into any of them was if you got your money out first and put it on the table where everybody could see it. Even then you'd have to wait a long time to get into the big games where half-crowns were changing hands. I was playing crown-and-anchor in one place and somebody shouted 'There's the bloody Bishop gannin' past the window!' I looked up and when I looked down again all my money had gone. The Cathedral was practically the only place in Durham you couldn't have got a game of three-card-brag. I'm talking about inside. There were plenty games going on the grass and under the trees, outside. As far as all the gambling was concerned a hint must have been dropped to the pollises to turn a blind eye for the day, it was probably always the case on gala day – especially this one. So if like me you were daft enough to lose your dosh you could expect no sympathy at all from that quarter.

The bands marched back about three o'clock in the afternoon and you could go down and see them off if you wanted to. Pit bands only had wind instruments but they could play anything from Beethoven to Paddy Reilly. Anything the BBC orchestra could play, these fellers could play and they wouldn't have you nodding off after five minutes either. The rules for bands were strict in some ways but not in others. For instance nowadays you didn't have to be a pitman to play in a colliery band. Jack Macintosh played for us and he was a chemist from Sunderland. He was a cornet-player and it was a toss-up between him and Arthur Laycock who was the best. Eventually he went to work for the BBC and became 'Director of Music' or something. Dickie Carr was another great cornet-player. Dickie had been on the wireless when he was only twelve. His father had been a famous cornet-player as well and his mother had been a concert pianist. Black Dykes was always after him but he wouldn't leave Harton. He could have gone a long way if he hadn't spoiled himself with drink.

If a band cheated and tried to bring in a professional or somebody from outside the area, they were nearly always found out and disqualified. Rivalry was so keen that when bands were doing their Sunday morning practices spies would be sent from other lodges to see what they were playing, how they were playing it and most important of all if there were any new faces amongst them.

Although the bands went all over the country to play at rallies and all sorts of things for the Union and for the Labour Party, whenever anybody was killed at the pit their band always had to play them to the cemetery if that's what the family wanted. It wouldn't have mattered if they were playing in a concert in LandsEnd or a competition in John O'Groats. When they got the call, back they came.

Ever since my father had brought us to Shields we had always ended Gala Day at Bearpark with his relations. We were all looking forward to it, Allie as well, and this time we'd be taking our little daughter with us. He'd been getting impatient since about half-past three but Allie and I were enjoying a bit of a stretch out in the sun and letting Anne have a play on the grass with the other kids.

'What time is it there, Tommy? I think me watch must be slow.'

'Twenty to four.'

'We'd best be gettin' ready to gan soon.'

'There's plenty time yet, Dad.'

'We can't go too soon, Dad,' says Allie. 'They'll still be in the middle of cooking and everything.'

'Aye I know. But we don't want to be late either.'

We got on the bus at five o'clock and all the way there he was moaning about the Durham beer, like he did every year. Everybody on the bus must have been sick of him, particularly if any of them were Durham people.

'If it wasn't that I was dyin' of thirst back there, wild horses couldn't've made me sup it. But I regret it now I can tell ye. The bloody brewers draw it straight out of the Wear an' do nowt except put it in a bloody bottle...stick a bloody label on it...and call it "beor". Then all they have to do is wait for some poor thirsty oul' fool like me to come along.'

I don't know how bad the beer was, though it couldn't have been very good because I've known him take his own and carry it around with him all day until it was ready to explode. But it must have been obvious to everybody on the bus that he'd done more than just wet his lips with it.

When we got to Bearpark the front door of every house was open, and judging from all the shrieking and laughing coming out, every one was full of people. They'd be making every guest feel welcome and making them forget all their troubles so that when the time came for them to go home they'd be sending them away with heavy bellies and light hearts.

There were so many at Aunty Bella's that the men were standing out in the front street with their cups and mugs and jam jars in their hands and a huge jug of beer on a cracket beside them.

'Somebody pour me a sup o' that, quick, afore I drop!' my father shouted to them while we were still halfway up the street.

'How's it gannin', Jack, ye oul' bugger?'

Somebody in the doorway shouted 'It's wor Jack with young Tommy and his missus! And the bairn!'

The front doors of pit houses were always wide open if the weather was fine. Even when they were closed to keep the rain out they were 'pulled to' rather than what you'd call 'shut'. Everybody from the postman to the rent man just walked in. So if anybody ever knocked on the door you knew it was trouble. And whenever somebody got off the bus at the cross or off the train at the station, there'd always be somebody to let you know. 'Bellaaaahh! Thou'd better put the kettle on! Looks like your Eddie comin'!' This was the Jilbert telephone.

As we walked down the street people we hadn't seen all year were calling out to ask how we were, to tell us our bairn was bonny and to say we were all looking well.

'Thou are ganna have trouble wi' that one afore she gets much older,' they said as we walked up the path. 'What do thou think, John?'

'I wish I was forty years younger and I'd be after her meself. She's a little smasher... Maureen is it they call her, Tommy?'

'Anne.'

'Oh aye. "Anne" after your dear mother I'll warrant. Well she'd add grace to any name, that one. She's as pretty as a picture.'

'How, Jack!'

'How again, Sid.'

'Wha'cheor, Tommy!'

'Hello there, Mr Fenwick.'

'That's a fine lookin' bairn you've got there. She cannot be one of thine though Tommy, is she?'

'Aye.'

'Thou wouldn't think so, would thou, Bob?'

'Not with a father that looks like that and a grandfather that looks even worse, thou wouldn't, ha ha ha!'

'Only kiddin, Tommy. Only kiddin', son... Here, gis your hand. Good to see ye.'

Inside, even though the house was packed with people talking with their mouths full and sandwiches or buns in their hands, and people coming in all the time for more supplies to take out, you couldn't see any of the table for the amount of food on it. There were plates piled high with pease pudding, saveloys and sandwiches. There were jars of pickled onions, pickled cabbage and pickled beetroot. There was ham-and-egg pie with the steam still coming off it, apple tart and rhubarb tart. There was fresh lettuce, radishes, tomato slices and cucumber. There were Yorkshire pastries, chocolate cake and coconut macaroons. There were tea towels and skimpy cloths covering stuff just out and smelling gorgeous and still the oven was going. Most of the men were drinking beer, most of the women were drinking tea. 'Lovely cuppa tea, that was, Bella. Just put me right... There isn't a teeny drop more in that pot is there? Just to top it up a bit? Thanks, love.'

Afterwards when nobody could eat any more and some of the older ones were beginning to fall asleep, the men went outside and the women cleared away and washed up. Soon there was the clang of horseshoes hitting a metal spike and loud cheers and groans, while inside the cards were being dealt for newmarket to be followed by knockout whist. When the women lost, they'd just laugh. But outside when the men lost the whole street knew about it. 'Look at that! What a bloody fluke!'

Long after it had become too dark to see properly and grown men had fallen out over the toss of an old horseshoe, everybody headed inside and the musical instruments came out. For about five minutes, accordions, concertinas, mouth organs and fiddles were taken up, squeezed, blown, and fiddled about with. Apologies were made for out-of-tune instruments and rusty musicians and the audience had to say 'Gan on, man, thou art a great player!' And then all of a sudden the whole place was jumping with music. There were jigs and reels for drunken fools to crash into women's laps and get a laugh. There was accompaniment for Allie to sing 'Goodnight Irene' and a couple of other love songs and get great applause afterwards. They really appreciated somebody from outside taking their turn like everybody else and getting up and doing their stuff. There were gentle Irish and Northumbrian airs where you could hear every note and see the tears collecting in the eyes. And in between times there were sobering recitations about the 'Disaster of '59' and funny ones about 'Pete the Putter' and 'Harry the Hewer'.

At the end of it all, those who could walk home walked and those who'd missed their buses or trains slept on the floor. Those who'd brought up everything they'd eaten twice over into the midden were vowing never again to touch a drop and their womenfolk were rolling their eyes.

Once a year was enough. Nobody could take two Durham galas in one year.

22

On the stroke of midnight on the 31st of December, 1946 a flag was hoisted high at Harton Colliery which said 'This Pit Belongs to the People!'

This wasn't just any New Year's Day, this was the beginning of a new era. This was the day our fathers, grandfathers, uncles, brothers, cousins and friends had been waiting all their lives for. The plans to make Britain a welfare state had been worked out by the socialist thinkers many years ago, all it had needed was the right people in Parliament. And they were there now all right. Three hundred and ninety-three of them. If they couldn't do it, nobody could.

Apart from nationalising the coal industry and all of the other things they said they'd nationalise, Attlee's Labour Government brought in the National Health Service, the National Assistance Board and the National Insurance Fund. People who couldn't afford to go to the doctor's before, no matter how serious their illness, could now go for anything and it would cost them nothing. People who couldn't see properly could get their eyes tested for nothing. If they had cataracts they could now have them fixed. If they needed glasses they would be given them. Because of malnutrition and because people hadn't been able to afford to go to the dentist except to have a tooth extracted that they or their family hadn't been able to pull out, most people had a mouth full of rotten teeth. Now not only could they get teeth filled, if they wanted they could get the whole lot out and get dentures instead. And it was all free.

Teeth were nothing but a nuisance and an eyesore as far as most people were concerned. Now there'd be no more pain, no more drilling, no more brushing. You just got the lot out, top and bottom and got two perfect rows of false teeth. You took them out when you went to bed and dropped them in a glass of water. Next morning when you woke up there they were, clean and smiling at you. I hung on to my old ones but Allie lost no time getting rid of hers. 'You don't know how long this's going to last. I'm getting mine done now while I have the chance.' She came back looking like a film star and never stopped giving toothy smiles to everybody. They all did. People who had never smiled before, either because they were ashamed of their teeth or because they never had anything to smile about, were smiling all over the place. People began to like dentists and doctors. The National Health Scheme was one of the greatest things any Government ever did. A haircut was about the only thing you couldn't get on it.

One more great thing the Labour Government did: they put an end to the payments we had been making to the Guardians for over twenty-one years by cancelling out all debts.

At the Durham Gala we had been told that a National Coal Board was going to be set up to run the newly nationalised mines. What we hadn't been told was that all the managers, undermanagers, overmen, deputies, keekers and weighmen put there by the Coalowners, were being kept on. Even the Chairman of the National Coal Board was to be Lord Hyndley of the Harton Coal Company. Although the state was buying the mines from the Coalowners, the Coalowners were still running the show. The same sods that had always made such a bad job of running the coal industry and had always been hated by the millions of pitmen who worked in it, were still there, still in charge. Whether this was a shady deal being done, whether it was yet another example of a Labour Government being faint-hearted when the moment of truth came or whether it was just plain bloody stupidity, we didn't know. But we certainly didn't like it. Surely the Government didn't think it was going to make that lot vote Labour? Because if they were that green they wouldn't be running this country very long.

It was soon obvious that the real difference Nationalisation was going to make to coalmining was that the state would now be paying for everything. Paying for more efficient machinery, for more safety measures and to have pits brought more up to date. Most important of all the state would be paying the wages. And this included paying whatever the 'directors' demanded for their 'expert management skills', their big cars and their fancy expenses. Added to that, the state would have to find the markets, suffer any losses and pay any subsidies.

If the sods who had owned the mines all these years had known Nationalisation was going to be like this, they'd have been pushing for it as long and as hard as we had.

During the First World War, bit by bit the Coalowners had craftily scrapped all of their old machinery and got the Liberal-Tory Government to put new stuff in under the emergency arrangements, because they knew they'd be getting the mines back as soon as the War was over. But during the Second World War when the Coalowners thought they might very well lose the mines after it, they wouldn't replace a thing. If the Government wanted to replace something, all very well. But not those swines. They stopped replacing even the cheapest and most basic items. Rusty bolts and rotten props stayed in place until they snapped. Nothing either down the pit or at the heapstead was maintained properly. There was gas, there was flooding, there was insufficient light even though the big pits had long been electrified and there was unnecessary amounts of filth and rubbish. Yet as soon as the Labour Government was elected, and the greedy sods knew for certain that their mines would be taken over, they quickly removed everything that was any good in the way of machinery and equipment, including what Bevin had installed during the War and sold it for as much as they could get. Even the hard seats in the waiting area at the top and bottom of the shaft that we'd put in and paid for ourselves were taken away and sold. They didn't even leave so much as a hammer to knock a nail in with. If that wasn't burgling the way it is with any common thief, I don't know what the word means. And still they were kept on as employees.

By the time the state took over the pits were in a shocking state. More men were working in them than ever before yet they were less productive and more dangerous than they had been for many years. Although the Coalowners were being paid salaries by the National Coal Board, and weren't having to pay a single penny out of their own pockets to keep them going, the pits weren't just taken over and given to the nation like in some kind of Robin Hood story. They had to be bought. And they were bought at the prices the Coalowners decided, prices so high it would take the nation twenty years to pay.

Although the Labour movement had been preaching public ownership for fifty years, when it got the opportunity it didn't know what to do with it. It was like a hot bun straight out the oven. You're dying to eat it but it's too hot too hold so you're tossing it from one hand to the other, terrified in case you drop it and knowing that as it's getting cooler, it's also going stale. Attlee had given six months' notice to everybody in the coal industry and then nationalised it as he said he would. It was now up to the workers to do something through their unions, to really make a go of it, not just think 'Great, it's ours! Now we can do what the hell we like with it.'

But we were too ignorant. Organising a nationwide industry from the inside, doing it from the bottom up, calls for a lot more than being handy with a pick and shovel. You need to know about graphs and statistics, finances, home and foreign markets, the very latest mining methods. For that you need education and we were very poorly educated people. Those like Paddy Cain who'd done the best they could for themselves had had to turn down extra shifts to go to college and do their homework. They'd had to be fit enough to find the energy for it and they'd had to be single men. If you were a married man with a sick wife and little mouths to feed you couldn't have turned down shift-money for years just so you could read your books. And if for one reason or another you failed your exams first time around, you'd have to study harder and make even more sacrifices to make sure you didn't fail the next time.

And if you'd made the time and had the opportunity to study while you were working in the pit, you'd have studied for your Deputy's ticket because that would have got you more money. There were such things as Workers Education Association classes but the main thing they taught was how to toe the line. They taught you things to keep your mind off politics, not on them. Nobody who went to night classes at a Mechanics' Institute ever got to be Chancellor of the Exchequer no matter how bright he was. In any case re-organising an industry as big as coalmining, the mess it was in, would have taken the best of minds with the best education more like six years than six months.

What we needed was to be able to put our trust in men who were clever, tough and honest. But men like that have always been hard to find. Plenty have one of the qualities, some have two. But very few have all three. And you need a number of such men because if you only have one or two they'll be voted out the door, down the stairs and onto the street. Men like Alf Robens and Manny Shinwell came along from time to time but like Ramsay MacDonald, they were really only interested in themselves. Sam Watson wasn't turning out to be altogether a saint either.

Even without any great shakes amongst us and even though the old lot were still there, big improvements still happened in the first twelve months. Wages increased and national agreements came in. This meant you wouldn't get any more for working in a dangerous pit where the coal was hard to get but you wouldn't get any less either. Safety inspectors were appointed and the system of checking the coal sent out was much better. Gloves were supplied for certain jobs and pithead baths were improved. Helmets that had a light on the front powered by a battery that could be recharged every night were given to every man, although he had to pay half. The idea that certain diseases could be caused by working in a coal mine was being looked into. Arbitration boards were set up to deal with grievances. Scholarships were being offered to young fellers with a good head on their shoulders. The NUM was becoming solid and powerful and the Government had to listen to it and treat it with respect. Quite a few ex-miners were getting into Parliament, though they only referred to themselves as 'pitmen' when it suited. Rehabilitation centres were being built for disabled miners who could no longer work down the pit. Pension schemes were brought in. And even though we had the same faces in the same places they couldn't ride us quite the way they used to.

Things were better than I ever dreamed they could be. I was now making good money as a Cutter and Allie and me now had two lovely girls. Christine was born in March 1948 and both Anne and her were big, fat and healthy.

Isabella Tanner was a good bit younger than my father and unlike him she never smoked and if she drank it could really only have been very little, so everybody assumed she would outlast him. One day she said she was feeling poorly and insisted my father fetch the doctor. Nobody got the doctor in my father's house unless somebody was practically dying. Any doctors that we had ever had to deal with had been hard-faced, sarcastic men who were never able to do anything when you really needed it and if you were a miner they treated you and your family like dirt. So my father wouldn't have gone for a doctor unless he thought she really needed it.

When this particular one came he gave Isabella Tanner a quick examination, closed his bag and said there was nothing the matter with her.

Isabella Tanner never gave a damn what she said to anybody. 'I wouldn't have sent for ye if there was nothin' wrong,' she says to him. 'If ye don't know what's wrong, why can't ye be honest enough to say so. Instead of standin' there tellin' me there's nothin' the matter when I'm tellin' ye there is!'

'It'd be a damned fine thing if I had time enough to waste on the likes of you,' he then said to her.

'You cheeky bugger!' she says. 'Now you've come through my door, so ye know where it is. Now get out of it and don't ever come back!'

Whether out of cussedness or what, God knows, but she died that night. My father woke up in the morning and there she was lying beside him quiet at last. It was the 2nd of May, 1950 and she was fifty-eight years old. Wilf and Bernard had left home a long time ago so there was now only my father left. After the funeral when my father and me came to have a clearout, the place was like a treasure trove. Inside an old trunk was a pair of tea towels with the price tag still on that had never dried a cup in their life, a nice fluffy eiderdown still inside the cellophane wrapper, a set of embroidered pillowcases, wool blankets, and umpteen other things that had never been used and had never been seen.

'I don't know whether this stuff was her own and she thought we weren't good enough for it or whether she was plannin' to leave and set up house somewhere else,' my father said. There was money in every old jug you laid hands on.

'What d'ye make of it? Was she preparin' for another war d'ye think?'

'Even she cannot answer that now, so it's no use askin' me. But I'll say this... Afore ye gan an' get yoursel' married again, ye want to sell it and get it all spent. Whoever's it was, it's yours now. I'd enjoy meself if I was you while ye still have the chance.'

He did as well because when I buried him a year later there wasn't a penny left.

He'd been drinking in the Stanhope and taken a bit of a turn. He'd sat quiet for a while and then told his pals he wasn't feeling too grand and was going on home. Up he got and out he went without saying anything more. That had been about half-past one in the afternoon and he just came away on his own. After he'd left his pals knew there must have been something wrong because he never left the Stanhope without being asked at least a dozen times. He must have only been back in the house quarter of an hour before he died, because a neighbour had heard him going in and had called in shortly after. He must have sat down at the table with his arms folded in front of him and then just slid forward

– and that was it. If he'd wanted to make one last speech there was nobody to listen to it. It was the 18th of September, 1951. When I went up, his body looked like a very old man's.

The last couple of years he'd been getting too old for anything and they'd got rid of him from the pit for the last time. The fires in him had burnt out long since and what was left had been more ash than ember. He was no longer a coalminer and if he couldn't be a coalminer he wouldn't want to be anything. Since Isabella Tanner died he'd lived on his own which was what he wanted. It meant he could please himself where he went, what he spent and when he came back. But the real centre of his life had been the pit and his family and now he had neither. The Stanhope was really only a watering hole. Anybody who spent all their time there was already finished and he was too honest with himself not to have known that.

So that his family would have enough to live on – and they never for a single day had any more than that, and many a time they had a lot less – he had done heavy manual labour, all of it underground. He had worked in conditions far worse than I'd ever known and he'd done it for more than sixty years.

When he was lucky enough to be in work he'd willingly spend twelve hours under the ground, nearly a mile down and several miles in, along a tunnel no higher than would allow a 3ft tub to get by. With an eighteen-inch pick he'd had to buy with his own money and had to pay the Colliery to have sharpened every day, he would lie on his side in filth that rats had ran out of. Even the Colliery didn't call it 'water', it was just known as 'wet'. All day in a space often less than two feet high he had hacked away at the coal, being careful to do it in such a way that the pieces coming off would be large because he didn't get paid for small stuff. When he'd cut away so much that the two-foot high roof was sagging and he could feel it beginning to press on his shoulders, he'd lever himself out, get some sprags – little wooden props – and hammer them in with the side of his pick. When he reckoned it was holding sufficiently he'd start shovelling the coal into a tub. When it was full to the brim he'd push it maybe thirty yards to the hauler for the putter to take out-bye. Then he'd get back in and start all over again.

If he was working in a place where the seam was wide enough to be fired he might have a filler working with him. He would undercut it first and somebody else would do the firing. Scattering before the firing down, was the only chance he got to stretch his legs. The minute the shots were fired he'd be straight back with the place still reeking of powder and the air choking with dust. As soon as the loose coals had been cleared enough for him to get in, down he'd go on his side and away he'd go again, chip, chip, chip at the coal. If he had an audience he'd be giving an up-to-date commentary on the gaffers, the Coalowners, the Government and the general state of the world. Every now and then he'd laugh at his own joke and have a spit. 'I wouldn't give ye tuppence for the whole damned lot!'

This was the job he had to fight to keep all his life and these were the kind of conditions he would seek. He'd let himself be tempted away from a safer pit or district because working in dangerous places with weak roofs, gas and filth, would bring in extra tuppences or threepences. If he complained because the people he worked for wanted to increase their profits by cutting his wage, they sacked him. And if he complained because they wanted to increase their profits by increasing his hours but not his wage, they sacked him. After he and his family had starved and gone without until they could take no more and he had suffered the mocking insults of the world, such as that he was 'dirty' and 'lazy' and 'greedy', that he was 'totally selfish', and finally that he was a 'traitor', he would either have to beg for a loan from the Workhouse Guardians or crawl back to the Colliery and beg for his job back.

It wasn't the darkness and filth, the heat and exhaustion or the fear and pain that got to him. That was the lot of any pitman. It was the hypocrisy and greed and the injustice and humiliation. But it never stopped him. He argued, shouted, cursed, threatened and cheered all his life. He was as much a fighter as any fairground pug, never a champion but always fighting. Nationalisation came too late for him and he only lasted a few months after being finished at the pit at the age of seventy-two years.

'May you enjoy a long and happy retirement,' they'd said to him.

For about twenty years I'd had dermatitis on my hands and arms caused by the cheap unrefined oil they used down the pit. It had started with the skin going dry and cracking, the way old leather does when it's left outside, and I couldn't grab any handle or anything without leaving lumps of thick hard skin on it. Sometimes my hands would be like lumps of raw liver for weeks until the skin grew back. And when it did it would gradually thicken and harden again and I'd be back where I started.

When the skin was on, my hands looked as though they were covered with elephant skin and felt like it but at least they didn't hurt so much. When it was off, especially just after it had come off and was still wet and sticky, blowing on them with warm breath was like blasting them with a blow torch. Allie had made me all kinds of gloves at one time or another but when the skin was on, it came off with the gloves when I took them off, and when it was off I couldn't bear having them on.

When it first started I went to see the skin specialist at the Infirmary but he was useless. His ointment might have worked if I hadn't had to work with the lousy oil all the time but it was all over the cutting machines. As soon as I touched anything the ointment came off and the oil went on. 'You aren't giving the ointment a chance. Try taking a few weeks off and then we'll see.'

Some of these fellers seemed to think you could do what you liked if you worked at a colliery. You wouldn't get a prescription like that from a colliery doctor. As far as he was concerned, if the specialist couldn't do anything, nobody could. And neither of them wanted to get involved in anything where they might have to write or sign something that meant anything in the pit could be to blame in any way.

Over the years I'd go back to the Infirmary every now and again to see if they'd got anybody better or any new treatment and I'd be sent to see this one in Shields, that one in Sunderland, another one at Newcastle. Then back to Shields and around and around until I got fed up and decided to leave it alone for a spell and see if it would eventually clear up by itself. All in all I'd seen umpteen different doctors, and a good few must have been promoted and gone off somewhere else because younger ones would keep taking their place. They'd done nowt for me so I can only assume they were promoted on the basis of the years they'd put in rather than on the people they'd put right.

One day Billy Bell says to me, 'Tommy, why divvent ye gan up to Newcastle and see Dirty Dick? He cannot be any worse than the buggers you're gannin' to... Some folks swear by him.'

Over a year had passed since I'd seen the last skin specialist and my hands were still no better so I thought I'd give this Dirty Dick feller a try. I'd heard about him before; everybody had, but I'd never thought of going to him myself. Allie wasn't too happy about it but the next chance I got I took the train up to Newcastle, I couldn't use the bike any more because I couldn't hold the handlebars without leaving my own handlegrips behind.

Dirty Dick was a quack chemist with a little shop off Blackett Street in the middle of the town. I don't know what his proper name was even to this day but if he isn't in jail by now I'd be surprised if somebody hasn't done him in. Anyway this particular Saturday afternoon I went up to Newcastle and found this little alley at the back of Blackett St where I'd been directed. I'd been told that women inhabited the street at night and I could well believe it but there didn't seem to be any of them when I was there, just some of the funny folks you always see in places like these.

Halfway along I came to this queer little shop with all kinds of bottles and jars of medicines and herbs, powders and contraptions, you name it, in the window. This had to be the place. There were pills to pep you up, pills to put you to sleep. Lotions to make your hair grow and lotions to stop it going grey. Powders to make you go to the toilet and ones to stop you going. Ointments for warts, creams for spots and salves for every kind of ache and pain. Hanging up were weird gadgets to straighten your back or to get rid of unwanted fat and others to stop you getting pregnant. Rows and rows of false teeth of all sizes that you could go in and try. Same with specs, hearing aids and jockstraps. They seemed to have something for everything. 'Surely they'll have something for as simple a thing as dermatitis,' I thought to myself.

I'd been told that Dick was an ordinary chemist and only did the quacking as a side line. The chemist and the handywoman had always been the poor people's 'doctors'; the chemist would cost you more than the handywoman but not nearly as much as the doctor. You'd go into his shop and have a word with the woman behind the counter. She'd then toddle off into the tiny passageway between the little shelves packed with bottles and jars where the chemist spent all his time, and the two of them would be talking in low voices and you would see him peeping at you through the bottles and her nodding towards you. He would then come out in his little white coat and come over and breathe on you with his lozenge breath, he nearly always seemed to be sucking something. He never took you anywhere except into a corner where you whispered and he talked loud enough for everybody to hear what he was saying and be very impressed. Everything was done and dusted right there standing up with all your clothes on. You told him what was wrong with you and he gave you something for it. He didn't bother about any diagnosis or anything. He was full of his own importance but he was nothing like a doctor, never bullying or sarcastic, and many people preferred him.

But it was obvious that this place was no ordinary chemist's, not by a long chalk. For a while I stood outside reading about the miracles this feller was supposed to have worked and reading some of the grateful letters from people all over the world that he'd practically brought back from the dead. If even half of it was true I was going to be going back to Shields a happy man. As I was going through the door I realised I didn't know what to call him, there was nothing in the window that told you what his name was and I could hardly walk in and ask for 'Dirty Dick'. His real name might not even be 'Dick' let alone anything else. And I didn't know for sure that this was the right place, though from the looks of things it must have been. I hadn't a clue what to say but I had to say something so I went up to this girl at the counter and said 'Is, er...Dick in?'

'Who?' she asks in this loud voice.

'Dick.'

'Dick?'

'I'm not sure but I think it's somethin' "Dick".'

I didn't know whether she was having me on or whether I really had come to the right place.

'Look,' I says, 'I've come all the way from South Shields to get somethin' for my hands. Is there anybody here who can give me anythin'.'

I showed her.

'My God!' she says.

I whispered 'I've been told there's a feller round here called 'Dirty Dick' who might be able to help me.'

She told me to wait and then went into the back. After a while this feller in a white coat came out. He didn't say he was Dirty Dick and he didn't say he wasn't, he just asked for a look at my hands.

'Mmmmnn... Pit oil, you say, eh? Just a minute.'

He went away and came back about twenty minutes later with a bottle of brown stuff and a jar of pink ointment with a strange but not altogether unpleasant smell to it.

'Take a spoonful of this every night,' he says handing me the bottle, 'and rub this cream over your hands,' he says handing over the jar. 'It'll take a fortnight to bring the corruption out but once it's out, it'll clear up in a few days and you won't believe they're the same hands.'

I took the stuff, paid him his money and came away determined to give it a try. It had cost enough so I drank every drop of the medicine as he told me to and rubbed in every last bit of the cream.

He was right about two things. Something came out all right and if they hadn't been on the end of my arms, I wouldn't have recognised my own hands… Or my feet for that matter and my feet had been all right before. They were covered with weeping ulcers. In some places on my hands, which were the worst, they were so deep they went right down to the bone. Just so I could work Allie had to make these cotton wool pads that I tied around my hands. She got me a pair of boots that were two sizes too big and I did the same with my feet.

I hardly need say I didn't go back to Dirty Dick or whatever his name was and I didn't recommend him to anybody else. I couldn't go back to the hospital doctors either for a while because not only were my hands worse than before but my feet were bad as well, although they weren't quite as bad as they were at first. In the finish I had to go and see if they could do something because the pain from the grit in the dust and the vibration from the cutters was so bad. And when I was coming home at night and Allie and me were having to wash the muck out off the ulcers because they were always festering, it was even worse.

At first I didn't say anything to them at the hospital about Dirty Dick because the way I looked at it was either they could cure it or they couldn't, knowing about him wouldn't make any difference. It would only make me look a fool. Anyway they'd had their chance. I'd gone to those buggers long before I ever heard the name 'Dirty Dick' and they hadn't been any good either. That's why I went to him. And I knew that once I mentioned his name the Coal Board would blame everything entirely on his poison and my stupidity. That would put paid to any argument about their cheap oil having anything to do with it. By now I was sick of the sight of skin doctors and they must have been just as sick of me. Skin doctors are a funny lot and I don't think they're any good as doctors at all. I think they probably get low marks in their exams and that's how they get to be dermatologists, because skin problems aren't a life or death matter.

Every time it was the same old tripe. 'How old are you? Where do you work? What's your wife's name? How many children have you?'

I'd say 'I'm sick of tellin' ye all that. What d'ye do with what ye write down? Hoy it away as soon as I gan out the room?'

Sometimes they'd say they wanted me to come back the next day to let a new batch of students see my hands. Talk about the blind leading the blind! Either that or somebody wanted to take some coloured snaps… They seemed to think nobody's time was worth anything but their own. And then when I did come back I'd have to listen to a bunch of spoiled brats showing off and asking if I'd ever had such and such a disease with a name as long as Ocean Road. 'Tell me what it means and I'll tell ye if I've ever had it,' I'd say.

Then they'd turn away to themselves with a look on their faces as much as to say 'We've got a right bloody clot here!'

Apart from the time it took to get there and back and the time I spent with the doctors, God only knows how much time I spent sitting in waiting rooms, standing in corridors and lying in cubicles. In the end I said 'Look, I cannot keep on comin' up here. You might get paid to see me but I don't get paid to see you. If there's anythin' ye can do apart from proddin' and pokin' and askin' the same bloody questions over and over again, do it. But if there isn't, say so and we won't waste any more of each other's time.'

'There's one thing that might work but I can't make any promises,' this one says with a smile on his face. 'We could take some skin from your buttock and graft it onto your hands. But we'd only be able to do one hand at a time.'

I still hadn't told them about my feet and I wasn't intending to either. If they made a good job of my hands, then maybe I would. As it was, my feet were very slowly getting better on their own.

'It would require a number of operations over the space of perhaps two years… How do you feel about that?'

'Let's get on with it. It cannot be any worse than what I have to put up with already.'

'Right,' he says. And a couple of days later I was in. And when they'd finished it looked grand.

A month later I had to go back to have it checked.

'Well, how is it?' says the one that had done the operation.

'Champion,' I says. 'I'm obliged to ye. When can ye do the other one?'

'I'm sorry,' he says after he'd taken a look at it, 'but I'm afraid we're going to have to do it over again. We apparently didn't cut deep enough.'

'How's that?'

'Do you see that?' He was pointing to a part that was a bit blackish. 'It hasn't taken properly.'

He must have seen me put my hand down to my behind because he says 'It was deep enough there. It's your hand I'm talking about. We'll have to scoop much deeper.'

'Ye mean ye have to make the holes even bigger before ye fill them in? Is that what ye did last time?'

He smiled. 'You're a coalminer, aren't you? I'm sure you've experienced a lot worse than that.'

'That's as maybe but I'm not made of stone. What bothers me about the scooping part is, if you make the holes bigger, then don't manage to cure it, I'm ganna be worse off than I was before.'

'There's an element of risk in any operation. We aren't God, you know.'

'Ye divvent need to tell me. But I think some of your pals ought to be told.'

So they did it over again and then half a dozen more just like it over the next couple of years. None of them lasted and slowly but surely every last bit withered and came off. They then sent me to a new bloke who was using X-rays or some kind of rays. They were no bloody good either but at least you didn't feel them and they weren't robbing Peter to pay Paul.

One day I was really fed up with it all. Some of the ones I was seeing now wouldn't have been born when I first started coming.

'Do none of ye know what this is?' I asked this young feller who was taking down the notes.

'Don't you know?'

'No, I don't. That's why I'm askin'.'

Without looking up from his writing he says 'You can never be completely cured. You've got skin cancer caused by chronic arsenic poisoning. Maybe this will teach you to stay away from quacks.'

At some time I'd told them about Dirty Dick when they were asking about all the different treatments I'd tried. And they'd asked me a lot of questions about him. What his medicine tasted like? What colour was it? What was his ointment like? Was it gritty or was it smooth? Did it have any smell? And they had done a whole lot of blood tests. But nobody had ever said a word about arsenic or cancer to me. My colliery medical report had it down as a 'psychosomatic psoriatic condition aggravated by improper treatment by an unqualified person or persons'.

The winter after Nationalisation was so severe that bread and potatoes had to be rationed but the demand for coal was enormous and that was good for us. Attlee had asked for the support of all workers by not striking or demanding higher wages for a few years so that he could stabilise the prices of everything and end rationing. And we had done what he asked. He had promised he would gradually do away with all piece-work and that one day there'd be a minimum wage of £19 per week for face-workers throughout the whole coal industry. At this time every union in the country was stronger and more solid than it had ever been and the prospects for all of us looked very good. Attlee respected the unions and he had to because we'd put him where he was.

Everybody abuses power when they get too much of it and I think that happened with some of the unions. Because working people had been under the heel for so long and now they weren't, they couldn't help shaking their fist in nearly everybody's face at the slightest excuse. Some of the so-called 'workshop practices' that started coming into the pit, such as where everybody would down tools and sit in darkness rather than fix a tiny panel bulb on a cutter just because it was an electrician's job, did nobody any good. It was being awkward for awkward's sake. And the newspapers only had to get hold of something like that or show one strike to be unreasonable, for everybody to start saying that all strikes were unreasonable and that so were we.

The smoke hadn't cleared after the Second World War before Churchill had begun telling everybody that Russia who had been our ally was now our enemy and that communists in Britain were trying to overthrow the Government...the exact same thing he'd said after the First World War. And he made up a ridiculous lie about an 'iron curtain' that was supposed to have come down to separate us from Russia and China and the rest of the communist countries. Yet everybody believed it. The Americans who had only come into both world wars when they were half over, were now supposed to be our closest ally, especially seeing as they had the Atom Bomb and we now took our lead from them. Whatever and whoever the Americans disliked, we were to dislike. And if they decided to wipe out every communist in the world, no matter where or how many, we were supposed to go along with it.

Clement Attlee was a Labour Prime Minister and supposed to be a socialist and he was head of a very strong Labour government with ex-members of all the big unions in it yet he went along with all of it. And because of it, people in many jobs had to sign papers to say neither they or any members of their family had ever had anything to do with the Communist Party. One of the problems for the National Union of

Mineworkers, the NUM, was that people mixed it up with the NUWM which was the National Unemployed Workers' Movement which had always had connections with the Communist Party. We had to try to break the association with the name to show that we weren't communists, even though we had great sympathy with their movement and didn't really have any quarrel with communists either.

To its shame the Attlee Government said strikes in Britain were being lead by communists and they brought in fines and imprisonment to punish strikers. The attitude of the Tories had always been that if you weren't against Communism – which meant if you weren't prepared to go and kill them all wherever in the world they were – you must be a communist yourself. Now a Labour government was saying virtually the same thing. I've never been a communist and never wanted to be but I've known some damned good men who were, men I'd have trusted my life with.

Communists were only socialists when all was said and done. The Tories weren't and never pretended to be. The Liberals weren't and never wanted to be. And many in the Labour Party weren't, not when it came down to it. But just as the rest of the country had been brainwashed into thinking miners and workers were well-nigh all communists, the miners and workers were letting themselves be brainwashed by the same people into thinking that Communism was some kind of evil, rather than a kind of socialism.

Even under a Labour Government there were still explosions and any amount of other disasters down the pits and they were badly in need of modernising. And at the same time as we had Poles and other foreigners working in Durham pits they were talking about closing them because the demand for coal was less. The real reason was they were importing so much of it and they didn't want to spend any more money on their own pits. Once the Coalowners had been paid off, they were quite happy, there was no need for a coal industry. Burnhope Colliery was closed as early as 1949. It was Attlee who should have finished what he started, never mind Churchill.

Although the situation was far from perfect, it had never been any better as far as the miner was concerned. Some of the awful things that my father, me, and any pitman that had ever lived had once had to put up with were gone and we could only hope they were gone forever. By the time I was fifty, I and Harton the pit I worked in, had come through

Liberal, Tory, Labour and Coalition governments, two world wars, two long lockouts, strikes, privately owned and publicly-owned periods of employment and changes in mining from hand-held picks and ponies to gigantic machines and conveyor belts. And these were just the big things.

As far as my home life was concerned I'd come from what was really just a tiny hovel owned by a colliery that could have put us out at a moment's notice for the least bit thing, to a council house that I could live in no matter where I worked. I could walk to work and come back from it in clean clothes like anybody else. I had a lovely healthy wife with perfect teeth which if she decided she didn't like she could change for others and it wouldn't cost her a penny. I had two lovely healthy daughters who were born in hospitals and had received the best of medical care ever since. Every day of their lives they had good food to eat, they were well dressed and had shoes that fit. They went to good schools and had all their school books provided. They always got presents on their birthday and at Christmas and sometimes at other times as well. Their home was nicely decorated and had comfortable furniture with carpets and proper tablecloths, an inside upstairs lavatory, a wireless, a record-player and a washer. They went with both their parents for day-trips on the train on Sundays in the summer and to Butlin's Holiday Camp at least once every two years. There was little else I could ask for. I only wish my mother and father could have had some of it.

But I never let myself be kidded that any of it came because of the generosity of any government or the humanity of any of its politicians. Nor that it came from any Church, Catholic, Protestant or any other. Nor that it come from the efforts of any one man. I knew, and would never forget, that it came because of the strength of the trade unions… ours and others. And nothing else. And I never for a moment doubted that without the unions we'd all be back where we started and in less time than it would take to bake a cake.

Recently my chest had been giving me quite a bit of bother. I'd been driving a cutting machine eight hours a day for twenty years and by now I must have had a load of coal dust inside me. All the time they were bringing in bigger and faster machines, each one making more dust and more noise than the last. From the moment you switched the cutter on you were working in thick clouds of coal dust, shale dust, clay and whatever other shite got in the way of the huge blades. Some of it was as thick as grains of sand, other stuff was like a fine powder that never settled even when the machine was off, as though somebody was shaking out bags of cement.

The masks they gave you were worse than useless. They clogged up in no time and then you wouldn't be able to breathe at all. In any case it was too hot and claggy to have anything fastened over your face for more than a few minutes. No matter what you did or what you put on, the dust always got underneath and irritated your skin, more so under the mask. As for the goggles, you'd have needed windscreen wipers going nonstop to see through them. Most of the time you couldn't even see the wall in front of you.

The fillers had to judge where the conveyor belt was from the direction of the noise because they couldn't see it unless they were practically touching it. And with the noise of the cutter engine and the cutter itself going at the same time, even that was a job. So if only half the stuff they shovelled at the conveyor landed on it and the rest went yon side of it, they'd have to keep going around and shovelling that up. But the visibility was exactly the same on the other side so the same thing would happen there. So they might have to shovel up, lift, and hoy two shovelfuls, to get one shovelful to stay on. And you couldn't have one man on one side and one on t'other or they'd be hoying stuff into each other's faces.

But the dust didn't just hang in the air or float downwards. Because of the movement of the conveyor belt, the ventilation currents and the turbulence caused by the cutter blades, it was like being in a tornado. Dust was sucked up from the conveyor belt, the floor and the coalface and swirled all over the place. It never got a chance to land or stay down. And you could easily lose your bearings and your sense of balance if you didn't watch yourself. Your mouth felt as though it had sand in it and you had to put your finger in and bring out a load of dust from between your lips and gums, top and bottom, and from under your tongue, and fling it on the floor. Then you had to shove your finger up your nose to get that out. You had to leave your eyes. There was no woman with the corner of a hanky moistened with her own spittle telling you to come by the window and she'd gently wipe a speck out for you, down here. You just had to get used to working with grit in your eyes.

To breathe you had to suck in everything that was in the air. Dust, oil fumes, filth, gas and whatever else had been down there for a million years: it all went in.

The first cough was the one to put off for as long as you could, because once you started you wouldn't be able to stop. It was the same at home in bed for me now, because I was coughing as much out of the pit as in it. As the irritation built up in my lungs and throat like a volcano that was getting ready to erupt and I couldn't hold back any more, I'd try to wheeze my way out of it. When the coughing started the violence of it would give me a headache and sore throat and it frequently made me vomit. At times I coughed so hard I had to put my hands over my eyes because they felt as though they were being forced out of their sockets. My tongue and throat would feel as though they were turning inside out and my lungs were coming up.

Allie would say 'Tom! For goodness sake!' as though I was doing it for the sake of it. 'I know,' she'd say when I couldn't speak and was just making a sign with my hand, 'but you cannot be doing yourself any good, coughing like that.'

I knew it must be a pain in the neck lying next to somebody who went on and on coughing but I couldn't help myself. I'd lie there fighting it as long as I could and then when I finally gave in, it was worse than ever.

Because of the efforts of the Union to come out with the truth – nobody else had even tried – I now knew that forty years down a coal mine doesn't just give you a 'bit of a cough' or 'a touch of bronchitis' like we'd always been palmed off with. Pitmen were now seeking compensation in court for chronic illnesses caused by the pit, especially lung diseases. Two hundred pounds wouldn't make the disease go away but it was better than nothing if you were going to be unemployed for the rest of your life...a remainder that would probably be short but almost certainly not sweet.

Everybody was coming to realise that pneumoconiosis was the main disease caused by working in a pit but it was a bloody hard battle for anybody trying to go down that road. The medical profession might recognise it as a pit disease but the Coal Board, the Government in other words, wouldn't. Whatever you had, if it wasn't recognised by them you'd had it as far as compensation was concerned. Fellers who'd smoked a few tabs in the times when they'd been able to afford them, all of them outside of the pit, were being told that that was the cause of their problem. As though anybody could compare the thin bit of smoke from a Woodbine or a home-rolled, five minutes here, five minutes there, with the filth you breathed down the pit all day and every day. You were never allowed to smoke down a pit. If they'd searched you and found a lighter or matches or anything, you'd have been sacked on the spot and nobody would have had the slightest sympathy for you. There's no such thing as a 'chain-smoking miner'. He wouldn't have had the opportunity, let alone the means.

A bloke disabled or diseased by the pit could spend so long fighting in the courts he'd be dead before they reached a verdict. They could give you a medical certificate to say you were no longer fit for work when it had taken quarter of an hour for you to get up off your seat and struggle through the door. But getting them to say it was probably due to working in one of Her Majesty's coal mines was a different matter altogether. No pitman I ever knew went around all day worrying if he had this disease or that and I didn't either. It was just that sometimes when you'd coughed so much you'd nearly choked, you couldn't help wondering how much more of it your body could stand.

At my age, I was still only in my fifties, I couldn't afford to give up the pit. I couldn't have got a job anywhere else and I didn't give a thought to one. I could probably have got work out-bye that wasn't as bad as the face but I'd waited too long to be First Man to give it up now and the drop in pay would have been too much. Allie and me now had a nice house in Oak Avenue that we were renting off the housing association in Cleadon, with all the various bits and pieces that go to make a home comfortable. Anne and Christine were still at school, growing out of clothes, wanting records and bikes and the things teenagers want these days and eating more and more every day. Allie had her own interests like her whist-drives and bingo, I had my garden and we all looked forward to our Butlin's holiday every year or so. It's amazing how yesterday's luxuries soon become today's necessities. So dust or no dust I wasn't going to take away from my family the few comforts that make life so much more pleasant.

Every day when I came home after my shift there was always a lovely cooked meal ready and I'd sit at the table and enjoy it in peace. When I'd finished I'd have a sit in my armchair with a cup of tea and have a read of the paper for a bit. Then I'd work in the garden until dark. Tomatoes and chrysanthemums were my speciality but I grew all sorts of vegetables and flowers. When it was time to come in and I'd tidied everything away, I'd come up to the house and stand on the steps at the top of the garden. I could fold my arms and feel like a Roman emperor, the way the garden sloped down so steeply. I'd have myself a cigarette, watch a flock of pigeons having a last fly around and maybe have a word with a neighbour if he was out fixing his bike or something. When I went in I might fill in the pools and have a listen to 'Ray's a Laugh' if it was on, or 'Take It From Here'.

This was what I'd been working for all my life and I wouldn't let anything bring an end to it now. I now had the same kind of warm family life I'd known when I was little and my mother had been alive, the kind of life that had disappeared completely after she died. All pitfolk are very homely people and their families are more important to them than anything on earth. I loved my wife and my two daughters. They meant everything to me.

The pit itself meant nothing, nothing but hard work and constant strife. I had long since given up whistling my way there and laughing my way back. I was there for the pay packet and for nothing else. My marras meant the same to me and so did the Union but the Labour Party was a hell of a disappointment. They were full of principles and promises that they themselves never measured up to. The majority of them in either their politics or their private lives were no different to the Tories. Any that were, like Anthony Wedgewood Benn or Willie Hamilton, got shoved out. Even Union men when they'd reached the position where they could have done some real good, hadn't the character to resist privilege when it was offered to them. They would be the first to complain about Ramsay MacDonald yet they behaved in exactly the same way. One after another they knelt down and accepted knighthoods and peerages and disappeared into the House of Lords and you never heard from them again. They tried to say they'd have more influence there and that they would carry on the fight. But they kidded nobody but themselves.

23

Just as the Star-and-Lockers had put the old hewers out of a job, the power-loaders now did the same to the Star-and-Locker men like me. By 1965 most of the moneymaking jobs down a pit were being done by machines. And the machines were getting bigger and more complicated all the time. You practically had to be a mechanic to cut coal now. The hewers, putters and horsekeepers, the fellers I grew up with, weren't even wanted as wastemen. They were waste themselves now.

I couldn't work with the power-loading machines because my chest was so bad I couldn't breathe properly any more. So I was brought outbye to do datal work with other fellers who had once gone at it hammer and tong from the minute they came on to the minute they came off but were also now beyond it. Unless you were young and fit and raring to go you weren't allowed anywhere near the face. I was still only sixty but the pit has a habit of making men older than they are and I was definitely one of the old'uns as far as the new young faceworkers were concerned. I was now doing the 'wasters' shift', I'd become one of the group even the young lads down a pit had always treated as a joke. We did the sweeping up, looking after the roadways and jobs like that...and we were paid the going rate for it. Nobody who is young can imagine a lame spluttering old fool ever having been anything else. You couldn't say 'Hey, hing on a bit, son...' Long before you got to 'When I was your age,' they'd be gone and you'd only be left with the sound of their laughing.

Then really big changes came. Not just to our pit but to the whole industry. Coal itself was in the dock. People who didn't work in pits or didn't get any of their income from coal wanted to live in smokeless zones. They wanted to be nice and warm and have unending supplies of hot water in their homes, but they didn't want all the faff-on and mess of lighting fires with paper twists and bits of sticks and yesterday's cinders and with shovels balanced on the fire grate to hold up the Sunday Sun for a bleezer. They didn't want to have to keep shouting 'I hope somebody's watchin' that fire!' and then have to race in to grab the bleezer before it singed the hearth rug and sent flakes of soot all over the room. Most of all they wanted the air outside to be perfectly clean. Not because their washing was hanging out on the line, because they didn't do that sort of thing any more but because they wanted their children to breathe fresh air and they wanted to breathe it themselves.

One month it was oil, the next it was nuclear power. Then it was oil again. Then they were talking about extracting what they called 'natural gas'. And not only from the ground but from under the sea. Gas from under the sea and oil from under the sea. They wanted any damned thing but coal. In fact in many mining areas, even in Northumberland and Durham, you couldn't burn coal in your own fireplace without breaking the law.

Because hundreds of men had been taking hundreds of tons of coal out of Harton day after day for over a hundred years, it was nearly worked out. Westoe, what used to be called St Hilda's before the name stunk, was opening up now and the two pits were being joined together. This way they could use each other's roadways and shafts and share the washery which was a huge thing for sorting and grading the coal. And they were going to call it a 'super pit'. Some politician must have dreamed that up. No miner I've ever known would call any pit a 'super' pit.

Now that my own days as a miner were numbered, silly though it seems to say after all I've said, I realised Harton Colliery meant a lot to me. Not the Colliery but the coal mine itself, the Pit. I'd never worked a single day of my life anywhere else or for anybody else and most of my daylight hours since I was a lad had been spent in it. You could dump me anywhere in Harton pit without my lamp or any kind of light and I'd be able to find my way out even now.

Poor health or a disability is something you have to learn to ignore when you work down a pit. You get on with your job and hope that if it doesn't get any better, at least it won't stop you. A pit disease is something different. It's something that comes on very slowly and has a way of saving itself up until you're getting ready to retire. It'll hit you when you're putting up a little set of shelves in the corner of the sitting room or painting the ceiling in the spare room, little jobs that have been waiting for years. Suddenly you find you can't raise your arms above your head without getting breathless and you're too fagged out to climb the stairs for a lie down.

Some lads have been killed the first day they went down a pit and many others haven't lasted much longer. When I started the going rate was for one in fifty to be killed and for one in two to have a serious accident or get a fatal disease before they retired. But when you're young you just laugh things like that off, you think nothing could kill you. And I have to say I've been one of the lucky ones as far as pit accidents are concerned. I've never had my back broken, never lost an arm or a leg, a hand or a foot or an eye. And my father, who'd worked in the pit even longer than I had, was the same. He lived long enough to retire, though only just.

I'd had the kind of things all miners get, from septic cuts to bad guts, backaches and bronchitis, and 'eye stygmus' due to the dark. Plus a few things like the skin trouble which had spread up my arms and to other parts now. And I'd had my share of hernias. Sometimes I'd only be out of hospital a week after having one patched up and then I'd cough out another bugger. Then I'd have to wait another six months to get that patched up. Once it even happened in hospital but because there was a waiting list they sent me out and told to me to come back when it had got a bit worse. A couple of days in the pit soon fettled that.

Blokes used to say the hospitals were in league with the colliery doctors. I don't know whether that was true or not but they were certainly scared of anything that might be a compensation case. If you were in a bad way, they'd more than likely say it was your own fault even though you hadn't asked them for their opinion. What they were telling you was you hadn't a cat's chance in hell of getting anything. If it was an accident it was almost impossible to prove it was the Colliery's fault and not carelessness on your part. Clever fellers they might have been, but no matter how much they knew about operations or diseases, they'd know no more about all the various things that had gone into how an accident had happened down a pit, than the man in the moon. Yet their opinion was often what decided the matter. And if they could see that whatever was wrong with you couldn't have been your fault, they'd make out it wasn't all that bad.

So if you ever got anything, it would never be very much. Neither the old Coalowners or the Coal Board would ever think of it as conscience money. They'd call it an 'act of good faith', which meant they thought of it as an act of charity on their part. And if ever the doctors said you were all right and you said you weren't and you either stayed off or didn't do your job properly, you'd be had up for malingering. Colliery doctors have always been like army doctors … hard as nails. A colliery doctor couldn't care less whether you felt all right or not. All he cared about was getting you to your feet and into the cage. His job was to save the Colliery money, not to practice medicine. All he had to know was how to tie a nylon stocking round a fan belt.

Many years ago, not long after I first went down the pit, I was sent to work in a really stinking place and the muck I had to kneel in gave me a bet knee. One day it swelled up so much, I couldn't go to work. My father, who was laid off at the time, went for Dr Marks to bring his lance. Marks told him the leg had nothing to do with the pit and that we must have TB in the family. My father was so angry and insulted by it that he grabbed hold of him, shoved him all the way down the stairs and ran him right out into the front street. Marks never forgot it and neither did my father. Neither of us ever went to him after that unless we were forced to. The likes of Marks were no better than the sods that owned the mines. No wonder they used to say the colliery doctors had shares in them.

Long after that, when I was a grown man and working as a Cutter, a 'hogger', which was a very powerful air hose, flew off and dislocated my knee. None of the fellers I was working with could manage to get it back so they carried me all the way out from the face along miles of bumpy ground into the cage and up to bank. And was I glad when we got there! Then they got somebody to wheel me over to Marks's place in the wheelbarrow and that journey wasn't much better. Marks took one look at it, grabbed it, and twisted it back. 'Right!' he said. 'Back to work.'

He mustn't have got it right back into its proper place because every now and then for months after it would keep coming out, especially when I was going up or down the stairs and then I'd have to drag myself back to him.

'Bugger this,' I said to Allie one day. 'I'm not gannin' to Marks any more. We'll gan to the Infirmary'.

The two of us then spent an hour getting my knee sufficiently into place and tied up with bandages for me to go up to the Infirmary. All the way there we were very careful stepping off pavements and getting on and off buses. But by the time we got there the knee had gone back in again. When we went in this doctor says 'You'll have to show me how it is when it's out'.

'How am I supposed to do that?' I says. 'It's back in now. Me and wor lass spent half the mornin' tryin' to get it in so we could come up here. And somethin' must've happened on the way to make it go in itself. You're not expectin' me to knock it out again, are ye?'

He took this little rubber hammer and started tapping it. First at one side and then at the other, each time a bit harder.

'Carry on like that an' ye'll knock it out yoursel',' I says just kidding.

'You do it, then!' he shouts. 'You damned pitmen are all the same!'

'Like hell, I will!'

Five minutes later we were going down the steps of the main entrance and I was so mad I slipped and my knee shot out.

'Howay, lass!' I says. 'Back in! Quick!' With one arm around Allie's shoulder, the two of us went hopping back up the steps, in the door and straight down the corridor as if we were in a three-legged race. We were laughing our heads off. I had to wait more than an hour to get back in to see him but in the end I did.

'There you are,' I says. 'Satisfied now?'

He put me on a table and he and a student pulled and rived at it this way and that till I thought I was going to yell out with the pain. They were like a couple of furniture removers. Even Marks would have done a better job. Finally it went in and they patted each other on the back.

'Whew! I'm all out of breath,' the one in charge says straightening his tie and tidying himself up. 'Right, Mr Turnbull. Come back in six weeks and I'll operate.'

One afternoon, during the time between seeing him and going in for the operation, I got my fingers caught between the steel rope and the rollers on the tubs and lost the end of a finger. They bandaged it up at the first aid hut and then sent me to the hospital to have it amputated at the joint. It wasn't serious enough to spare a 'driver' for the 'wheel-barrow ambulance' so I walked to the hospital myself. First aid at the Colliery came out of a tin box. The horsekeepers provided better first aid for their horses.

Because it had happened early on in the shift Allie wouldn't be expecting me back for a good while yet. So to save worrying her because she was just getting over having Christine, and because I thought I'd be finished at the hospital and back home by the end of the shift, I didn't bother to send word. As it turned it out I wasn't as quick as I'd thought. And in the meantime some silly bugger had found the end of the finger down the pit, wrapped it up in a bit of bait paper and kept it in his pocket till the end of the shift. Then he'd gone round to Oak Avenue and showed it to Allie who nearly had a fit. Some people bury things like that but when I came home it went straight in the bin.

When they sent for me at the hospital I went in and they did the operation on my knee. It was right as rain for a couple of months, then it started coming out again at the least excuse. In the end I just got used to it. I learned which way to climb stairs and which way not. Now I can whack it in with one blow of my fist. It's just a knack like anything else.

In 1968 the Coal Board thought it was time I was given the boot, so along with the other 'wasters' at Harton I was made redundant. I'd have preferred to have been told I was 'retired', though it was the same difference. As far as the money was concerned, I'd only be ten bob worse off sitting on my backside looking out the window watching the ships go by, than doing what I was doing in the pit. I'd been on permanent night shift for a long time now. It was the only way I'd been able to hang on and I was sick of it. So if the end had finally come, it had come and that was that. I'd never shed any tears before and I wasn't going to start shedding any now.

The lasses were both married by this time and Allie and me had moved to a little house in Marsden. You could smell the salt and seaweed in the air and from the kitchen window I could see right out to sea. If I took my time I could walk down to the beach. 'See ye tomorrow, lass,' I'd say to Allie. 'If there's a fair wind, that is. If not, I'll try to get back for the weekend.'

In winter there sometimes wouldn't be another soul and I'd have the whole beach to myself.

I was never one for lying in so I'd always get up early in the morning, go out for some fresh air and then come back and make breakfast for Allie and me. I didn't have sufficient puff to look after a big garden any more so I had a lawn put in. By now my hands were mostly dry but the skin was so hard you couldn't make a dent in it and it was covered with little lumps. If somebody came to the house, especially an inspector from the Department of Health and Social Security or some twerp like that, I'd always shake his hand when he went out. What a bloody shock he'd get! His face would be a real treat. I think he thought he must have grabbed one of those 'horny-backed toads', or whatever they're called, from South America. He would look at his own hand and then look at mine and you could see what was going through his mind. 'Please God, don't let me get leprosy!'

As soon as he'd gone Allie and me would laugh ourselves silly. 'Did ye see the look on the stupid bugger's face! Look at him gannin' down the path. He's still lookin' at his bloody hand!'

For years I'd been cockling up black froth with red flecks in it and hadn't paid it any heed. But in recent months it had got very thick, almost like jam and I had a hell of a job getting it up. I cut down on the cigarettes as Allie had been on to me to do for ages, I tried this cough mixture and that and Allie rubbed Vick's on my chest and back. But nothing seemed to make any difference and I was out of puff all the time. Even going to the lavatory used all my breath up. Allie said I should go and have it seen to and I said I would if it hadn't got any better by the time we came back from Butlin's. We'd already booked for Clacton and paid our money.

By the time we came back from holiday it was worse. I had an appointment to see Dr Evans the skin specialist shortly after, so I mentioned it to him. He sent me straight up to the chest clinic to see Mr Bannister the surgeon. There was no messing about with this bloke. He put me on a treadmill machine, took some X-rays, poked about and did some other tests and then said 'You've got a growth on your lung, Mr Turnbull. No more tests are necessary. We'll operate tomorrow.'

That was the fastest medical service I'd ever had and I wasn't sure I wanted it but he didn't give you any time to think. 'Oh aye,' I says. 'And will that be a Shotley Bridge or a Seaham Hall job?' All miners knew about those places.

'Shotley. Fill this form in and give it to the Sister.'

That same night I was in. Allie took my clothes away and said she'd bring in my bits and pieces when she came back the next day, after the operation.

They must have had a contract with British Paints to buy up all the cream and green camouflage paint left over after the War because it was so thick on the walls, doors and windows, it looked like it had been put on with a trowel. It might have made you feel safe during an air raid but it was about as cheerful as a mortuary. They obviously didn't expect anybody in here to live long enough for it to bother them.

First thing next morning they took me away into this room, put me on a table and without so much as a 'by your leave', shoved a huge metal tube with a microscope at one end straight down my windpipe. They all had masks on but I could recognise Bannister by his eyebrows. There was no anaesthetic or anything.

Of all the things that had ever been done to me in hospitals this was the worst. It was as though they were getting right inside of me. At the top end Bannister and one of the others were looking down into my lungs – at least I presumed that's what they were doing – and they were talking among themselves in medical language, the way they do. I could see right up into their faces but they weren't looking at me, only my insides. I was sure something was going to burst if they carried on shoving it down and twisting it around but I couldn't stop them. I couldn't do anything. I couldn't say anything. I couldn't move. I could hardly breathe. They must have had some idea what it would feel like to have somebody doing this to you. Though if they did, they weren't bothered in the slightest. Bannister said something and the other two chuckled. As I lay there I thought, 'This afternoon that bloke is going to be in there himself'.

When they were finished looking they turned away and talked among themselves and they weren't in a hurry at all. Then they turned back and started hauling the thing out of my throat. It felt as though my lungs were being dragged up with it. I felt sick, I felt weak and I was scared. I thought if this was just the start, if this was just the preliminaries, God knows what's coming next.

Somebody stuck a needle in my arm.

The next thing I remember was a nurse, she couldn't have been any older than our Christine, saying 'Wakey, wakey, Mr Turnbull. It's all over now.' She was pushing something up my back end. 'It's to help your breathing.'

I was stiff, my chest was bandaged and I was bloody sore but I just had to force the words out. 'It must've been some operation if I'm ganna be breathin' through there from now on.'

After a while Bannister came in with his little gang. He gave me a bit of an examination and asked a couple of questions, then he started talking to the other doctors or students or whatever they were. I didn't understand what they were saying because they were using so many long-winded words and they were still talking about me while they were wandering off towards the next bed. He was a real hard case, that feller. He probably had to be because most of the people in this place would be going out in a box. He had a bloody nerve asking me how long I'd been smoking when he smoked like a bloody chimney himself.

There was something I had to say to 'Dr' Bannister or 'Mr' Bannister, or whatever he called himself, and I was going to say it before he left this ward. The nurse had explained they study so they can call themselves 'Dr', then they study even harder so they can call themselves 'Mr' again. I'm entitled to 'Mr' and I haven't passed an exam in my whole life.

I waited until he'd gone all the way down to the bottom and was on his way back up the other side and I never took my eyes off him. I'd a job to attract his attention because he certainly didn't look as though he wanted to be interrupted but I managed it and he came over.

'Yes, Mr Turnbull?'

'I realise you're the doctor here and I know ye've a job to do. And I'm sure ye do it to the best of your ability. I hear ye tellin' these people here what to do and because they work for ye they've no choice but to do it. But I don't work for ye. So don't think ye can do whatever ye like with me because ye cannot.'

'You must realise you're a very sick man, and – '

'I don't care how sick I am, neither you nor anybody else is ganna shove that bloody tube thing or anything like it down my throat again. If I'm so bad I need things like that to keep me gannin', leave me be and let me gan in peace.'

One of the young fellers started to say something but Bannister put his hand up and stopped him. He never said a word, he just looked at me with a bit of a smile, shrugged his shoulders and off they went. One of the nurses that had been listening came over as soon as they left the ward. She put her little hand on mine and I couldn't even feel it because of my skin but I could see the tears in her eyes.

'Don't worry,' I says. 'I'm well used to the likes of him... Is there a tennis court near here?'

'There's one in the park.'

'Put wor names down and I'll give ye a game as soon as I get out.'

It must have been awful for young lasses working in such a place. Maybe it was their punishment block or something or where they sent the ones that failed their exams. It just didn't seem right putting young girls in a place like this, they were different to the doctors.

I could now feel death like I'd never felt it before. Down the pit you never stop to think about it. Here you had all day and night. People were being wheeled in, eyes shut, mouths wide open, as though they were dead already. Maybe they hadn't been checked since they left home, a rough ride in an ambulance was all most of them would need to finish them off. All through the night, lights went on and off and curtains were being pulled around different beds.

On the Sunday night I went through what they called a 'crisis' and I fought like hell to stay alive. Every breath was a battle and without the oxygen machine I'd have gone. There were several of us all gasping for it and the nurses were wheeling it first to one, letting him have a shot of it and then wheeling it over to another. We were sharing an oxygen mask to stay alive, like kids sharing an ice-cream cornet.

Although I'd always been a fairly good Catholic and always gone to Mass every week and Confession at least every Easter, I'd never had what you might call a conversation worth having with any priest. Even young ones wet behind the ears talked to you as though you were a naughty little boy with no brains even though you might be a grandfather. Yet of all places there was one in a bed on this ward you could really talk to. He was an old one, the best I ever met and a different kettle of fish altogether from the first one I ever knew.

The night after my crisis he came and sat down by my bed and talked, not only like a priest and a scholar but also as a man. Why I listened to him was because he was in there himself fighting as hard as anybody else to stay alive. And when he told me he'd been one of the ones fighting for his share of the oxygen bottle the night before, we both had a good laugh. Whether he was just kidding or not, I don't know but he certainly struck the right chord with me. He talked about death in such a beautiful way…about the tide of life gradually ebbing away and the little waves of hope and strength that come and go as the tide goes farther and farther out…and then at last the deserted shore with not a soul left behind… He talked about the end of hardship and strife and the end of all pain and suffering…of seeing God and our mothers and fathers in Heaven and of long dead little brothers and sisters and dear friends. Listening to him I thought I was already there. We said a prayer together and I fell asleep. When I woke up I was a bit disappointed, to tell the truth. It was back to clashing pans, old men groaning and farting and the innocent little nurses doing their best and rushed off their feet.

Later on the priest came over.

'Be thankful,' he said.

I got out a week later.

24

I still had most of one lung at least for the time being and I was thankful for that. I had left the old priest behind and I can only hope he was able to give as much comfort to himself as he had to me. Now I'm grateful every time I open my eyes in the morning and realise God has decided to give me another day and I don't waste any of it lying in bed. I get up and do something even if it's nothing more than looking out the window. I can always make sure there aren't any shipwrecks or any swimmers in difficulties and even though I couldn't exactly run down and dive in, at least Allie could run to a phone box. Nothing gets by the little pair of binoculars the lasses got me when we moved here.

As long as I have my wife and my family and enough pension to live on, I'm content. If it's a fine day and I'm not feeling too bad I'll go for a walk along the street or maybe down to the beach. And if it's not I can shut the door and come back in. I can always find something to occupy myself with. And if I couldn't, Allie certainly could. I like music, especially old dance music and I can put on one of my tapes in the cassette player and listen to it while I'm fixing the buckle on Allie's handbag or reading the paper. We still get the Daily Express and it's no better than it ever was but it doesn't look as though I'm ever going to break Allie of the habit. We have a television now and after tea I'll watch a comedy show if there's one on. I like The Two Ronnies, Morecambe and Wise and Frankie Howard. And I never miss Come Dancing if I can help it.

I still get the Coal News to keep up to date with things and I meet my old mates when I go to collect my pension and we talk pit. Freddie Moralees and Tim Defty are still around and we still argue about what went wrong and what went right and whether Arthur Scargill is better for these times than Arthur Cook would have been. What bothers me today is that miners seem to be a bit too self-satisfied and inclined to forget that everything they have was got for them by the Union. And that what the Union got came out of a hundred years of hardship suffered by millions of men, all of them pitmen just like they are. And that without a single strong union, they're nothing. If they say 'Now we've got what we want, we don't need the Union any more,' they'll be making the biggest mistake of their lives. The first chance they get, the capitalists will take it all back. And then pitman and worker will have to start all over again.

For every Anthony Wedgewood Benn the capitalists lose, there are a million others they don't. When he came out of the Aristocracy, a whole pile from our side nearly knocked him over in the rush to get in, many of them the sons and daughters of working-class parents; first into the Tory Party, next into the knighthoods.

When I think how many trade-union and Labour men we've put up over the years that have gone into the House of Lords where they're no use to anybody and make very poor ornaments, it's enough to make you weep. The very place they cursed about when they drank in working-men's clubs and later on again when they were begging for your vote, now becomes irresistible to them. When you see what was once a baldy working man now wearing a curly white wig instead of a flat cap, carrying a sash and sword instead of an adjustable spanner and walking slowly in a fur-lined gown as though he were the King of Diamonds, a man who would look better kneeling under a sink in a pair of greasy overalls, it's bloody ridiculous. A bloke who used to pinch your sandwiches down the pit might now be taking lessons on how to curtsy to the Queen. Fools like that kid nobody. Least of all the lot they've gone to join.

There's never been more than a handful of real socialist politicians in the whole history of the Labour Party. Most of the seats have been occupied by men no different from those on any of the other benches. I've never heard of any man in any party ever being elected on the basis of his character. Wealth yes, pals yes, brains maybe. But never ever on the strength of his character. The same goes for lawyers, doctors and clergymen.

I believe in treating a man with respect if he's earned it. But to me, calling any human being and I don't care who he or she is, 'Your Serene Highness' or 'Your Worship' or anything like that, is a load of utter shite. If the Queen or any of the rest of them came along the road outside our house I wouldn't step out the door and wave to her. Not because I've anything personal against her but because I'm not interested in her or her family. I've a family of my own. She has a perfect right to come up here and see who she likes and then she can get on her way again but she'd be wasting her time if she came all the way expecting to see me. I owe her nothing. Neither she or any member of her family has ever done anything for me. Out of a wage that was barely enough to live on I've always had to pay towards her and her family's upkeep and I've never had any choice in the matter. Millions of people in this country have lived in terrible poverty and she and her whole family have known about it, yet every single one of them has gladly gone on living in the lap of luxury and never once dipped in their own pocket or raised a finger to help. Not for one crippled man, not for one mad widow, not for one sick bairn.

They say wisdom comes with age. So does senility. I'm seventy so I'm not too sure where that leaves me. I might say I had the one, my two daughters might very well say I had the other. Hardly a month goes by without I'm at one of my old marras' funerals. I don't say much. I think just being there in the background out of the family's road is all you can do. I get some comfort from seeing them lowered into the ground and knowing they'll never have to move from that spot and that nobody in this life will ever be able to ill-use them any more. And I know that before very long I'll have seen my last one without knowing it. No pitman grieves about going into a grave. He knows very well what it's like down there. And I cannot grumble about my life because I got what I always wanted which was to be a coalminer. It wasn't because I thought the pit was going to be a beautiful place and it wasn't because I thought it would make me rich. It was because I thought there were no better men on earth than the ones that would be working in it and I wanted to spend my life amongst them. And I wasn't disappointed. I found they were men who didn't need to preach about 'manliness', 'honour' or 'humanity'. They lived these things without ever stopping to think about it.

When I'm walking in Shields and look up and realise a street I'm about to go down is named after a local Coalowner – as many of them are – out of puff though I might be, I'll avoid it and go down another if I can. I know it won't change the world and the man himself might be dead long since. But if putting his name up means anything, then so should refusing to respect it. Maybe one day they'll start naming them after pitmen. What could be better than to walk down a street called 'Paddy Cain St', if that's not just the wishful thinking of an old fool?

Epilogue

Tommy Turnbull died of pneumonia, so the death certificate said, on the 5th of April, 1982 . He was seventy-six years old.

My name is Joe Robinson and I am his nephew. It was to me that he told his story, though I had to prise it out of him. My father, Jack Robinson who married Evelyn Smithwhite, Allie's sister, was of all things clerk to the Workhouse Guardians when they first got to know each other through the Tyne Dock Cycling Club. After that, as a Relieving Officer, my father was responsible to the Public Assistance Committee that carried out the means tests which were such a hateful part of life for the unemployed in the 1930s. My father never humiliated or ill-treated anybody but the association was enough for Uncle Tom. They were always genuinely friendly towards each other, although because my father moved to Newcastle with his job within a year of their meeting, they never saw each other except at family events once or twice a year.

Uncle Tommy was the only pitman, the only miner of any kind in our family, and he was more different from the rest of us than the differences of all the other relatives put together. I am sure that nobody except Aunty Allie really understood him. At weddings and even at the New Year's Eve parties which Aunty Allie used to hold at their home in Cleadon, he was shy and taciturn with adults and would always sit by a window or in a corner out of the way, with his cigarette. If the 'do' was at their house, he would already have secreted himself before any of the guests arrived and he wouldn't get up to greet anybody. There were never any strangers so nobody needed to work out for themselves that he was the host. At somebody else's he would gradually worm his way into the position on the extreme periphery by the kind of devices he would have used as a child, several pews back, to inch his way into the confessional by the side route.

At their house Allie did all the pouring of drinks and passing of food. Tommy looked after the rolling and smoking of his cigarettes – never trading with anybody else. If any of the grown-ups apart from Aunty Allie spoke to him, he would answer if it could be answered with a 'yes' or a 'no'. If it required any more he would twist his head and make a kind of off-hand sound that was impossible for anybody to follow up. In anyone's home but his own, he would never remove his cap. Even his muffler would only come off if he and Allie were there for a 'big do', like a wedding that could last many hours. The cap and muffler were the most reliable indication that he was not on what he considered to be his own territory and that he could well be as it were, 'just passing through'.

If you were just a kid, he was absolutely impossible to deal with. None of us could understand why Uncle Tom Turnbull – we called him 'the Uncle Tom with his cap on' because we had another whose surname was 'Talbot' – always wore a cap indoors. My brother Johnny and I had been brought up to believe that even women, who had many privileges as far as head coverings were concerned, especially if they were Catholic, should always eventually take theirs off even though it was sometimes a lengthy and delicate job with all the lethal hatpins that had to be withdrawn and sheathed one by one. And we had been told it was the height of bad manners for any man to wear any kind of hat indoors except for a paper one on Christmas Day, you could tell there was no way Uncle Tom would have been seen dead in one of those. So we just used to stand and stare.

Everybody knew he had a thatch of short thick indestructible hair because whenever he scratched his scalp his cap would slip askew until he had finished, after which it immediately went back to its proper place. He gave the lie to people who used to say excessive wearing of a hat or too much underwater swimming made you go bald. He was so unlike bald Uncle Jack Smithwhite who in his vanity wore his cap everywhere especially in his own house, yet never in anybody else's, even though he wasn't famous for his other manners. If it wasn't the cap, it certainly wouldn't have been the water because neither of them were the ten-lengths-under-water-before-breakfast type. So there was no discernible reason for the perverse wearing of Uncle Tom's cap indoors. If you asked a grown-up why, you would be told not to be cheeky. The only thirst to be taken seriously at those gatherings had nothing at all to do with knowledge. Maybe Uncle Tom had no more faith in the plaster ceilings of council houses than he had in the roofs of Harton Pit. Whatever the reason, nobody, not even Allie – the only person who could ever get him to do anything and even then only if he was considering doing it in any case – would ever have suggested he remove his cap. Despite the cap, everybody liked him, nobody understood him and everybody left him alone.

It was a mistake, if you were just kids, to let yourselves be buffeted by grown-ups' big behinds or moving chairs into Uncle Tom territory. Because although he would never move himself, not even to come to the table to eat, he would be waiting, ever vigilant, like a spider in the shadows.

'What do yous two think you're doin' here?' he would ask in a low voice that nobody else could hear. You now knew you were ensnared and wouldn't be able to get away until some grown-up, usually Aunty Allie, saw your predicament and rescued you. A large part of Aunty Allie's social duties would be to safeguard innocent young children if she and Uncle Tom were invited anywhere.

Johnny, my younger brother by a year, and I would just stand there, red-faced, heads hung, never for a moment forgetting the rules, 'Speak only when you are spoken to and watch what you say', and even more importantly, the cardinal rule that 'Little boys should be seen and not heard'.

Now that he had engaged your attention, there was no way you could blend back into the general hubbub. He would now develop the game, his rules, his way.

'If I'd known yous two were ganna be here, I wouldn't've come.'

'Why?'

'Cos I wouldn't.'

What could you say to that? But he hadn't finished by any means.

'A pollis was at wor door the other day, an' he was lookin' for yous two.'

'What for?'

There was a gleam in his eye now we were hooked.

'Why should I tell you? I might only get into trouble meself.'

'We won't tell you told.'

'How do I know that? What proof have I got?'

'Because, because...'

'"Because because" is ne answer. If ye've got proof, get it out. Put it in me hand where I can see it.'

One look at that hand, which he would quickly withdraw when he saw it himself, would drop any jaw. Then Aunty Allie would come over.

'Ah, Tom. Leave the bairns alone. They don't know where they are with you.'

'It's not my fault. The two of them's been tryin' to scrounge a tab off me. I'm ganna tell their father next time he comes over here.'

All the years I knew him and of all the many times I encountered him, I never got a straight answer, never got the edge on any verbal exchange, not even when by virtue of my years I was no longer bound by the Fourth Commandment. During the Second World War when our own Mam was away having our Michael, which was a long and complicated business, Johnny and I were sent to 'stay with Aunty Allie for a while'. We knew exactly what that meant and we cried about it. But it was during those few weeks we spent in Aunty Allie's and Uncle Tom's home with its strong flavour of the pit that both Johnny and I developed a deep affection for Uncle Tom that has lasted ever since.

A couple of months after our being foisted on the Turnbull household, back home in Newcastle several pairs of Bevin Boys were foisted one after another upon our own, but those memories were by no means as sweet.

After I had grown up, a claim which Uncle Tom would always dispute, and I had written two biographies, I approached him about writing his. To my astonishment, he agreed. One of the unspoken conditions was that I suffered without complaint his referring to me as a 'Young Tory', something I wasn't and never have been. If he thought it true, I am certain he would never have let me see into his life in a way I am sure he had allowed no other. Not, I am sure, because I had been tested in his crucible of unflagging tantalisation for thirty years and not been found wanting. But because he was beginning to fear that people were forgetting things they had no right to forget and not bothering to learn things they had no right to remain in ignorance about.

Britain's power, wealth and authority was built on the coal that pitmen like my Uncle Tom extracted from its mines. The fact that these things have long since been squandered had nothing to do with the pitmen. They, by dint of courage, hard work and hardship, only gave Britain the wherewithal. Others, by virtue of incompetence, greed and complacency, have lost it. Now everyone knows that no matter how deep how many miners go down how many mines, no amount of coal could restore Britain's power and influence. And maybe that is just as well. However, it also means that a great tribe of people, now decimated, degraded and dispersed, will vanish and this country will be forever as impoverished by this loss as have the Americas by the loss of their Apaches and their Incas.

This matters.

Glossary

areated	annoyed
bairn	child
bait	carried lunch
bank	surface, out of pit
bass	strong beer
bet	infected
blackdamp	stythe (carbon dioxide)
bogey	flat cart with four small wheels used mainly by children
bubbling	crying and whingeing
cage	lift down into mine
canny	(1) decent gentle sort of person; (2) doing well; (3) quite
caunch	stone above a roadway
cavilling	drawing lots to decide workplace
choppy	concentrated horsefeed: hay, straw, oats, beans etc.
chow	tobacco chew
chummin	empty coal tub
clagging	making sticky
clarting	messing
dadding	slapping garments against a wall to shake out dust
cracket	oblong stool
CWS	Co-operative Wholesale Society
dataller	one who is paid by the day
divvent	don't
dook	duck down
dosh	money
drag	draw on a cigarette

dumper	cigarette that has been put out
ettled	arranged
ex-pug	retired pugilist or boxer
faff-on	fuss
fash	bother
footer	football
foreshift	first shift
gammy leg	unsound leg
gan	go, going
ganna	going to
gannin'	going
geet	great
get	(1) get going; (2) contemptible person
get on about	talk about
gis	give it to me
gns	guineas (1 guinea = 21 shillings)
gob	mouth
gypped	cheated
hadaway	begone
handywoman	unqualified woman who did nursing, 'laying out' etc.
ha'p'orth	halfpence worth (next to nothing)
have a lot off	have much to say for oneself
heap	heapstead, buildings at bank
het	heated
hing	hang
honkers	heels
howay	come on
howk	hawk up
hoy	throw
in-bye	in towards the coalface
jowl	to test with an iron bar
judd	the cut part of the coal seam ready for blasting
keeker	overseer on coal screens
kist	(1) deputy's box; (2) meeting place down pit
loss	lose

lowse	(1) end of shift; (2) uncouple, leave off
lugs	ears
marra	very close workmate
mast	infuse, as in tea-making
midden	earth closet
netty	toilet
nowt	nothing
onsetter	man in charge of cage down the pit
oppo	opposite number, mate
out-bye	towards the shaft
overman	foreman
owt	ought, anything
palony	huge sausage
ploat	poke out stones etc., with long steel bar
poke	handkerchief for wrapping bait
pollis	policeman
poss	agitate with a stick, as in hand washing
put	to fill and convey coal in tubs
rocky chair	rocking chair
shuggy boat	fairground swing
skelp	clout on scalp
slaver	saliva
sonna	sonny boy
sosser	sou, small coin
stot	bounce hard
tab	cigarette
tash	moustache
tassel	boy's penis
tother	the other
twist on	whinge
welted	thrashed with a belt
wha'cheor	what cheer? (how are you?)
wife	woman
windy pom	pneumatic drill
wor	our
young'un	young one